STATS™ Canadian Players Encyclopedia

Neil Munro & STATS, Inc.

STATS
PUBLISHING

Published by STATS Publishing

A division of Sports Team Analysis & Tracking Systems, Inc.

Dr. Richard Cramer, Chairman • John Dewan, President

**This book is dedicated to Duke Snider, a Hall of Famer
who not only played for the Montreal Royals,
but spent years as an Expos broadcaster.
He was my first baseball hero.
— Neil Munro**

Cover photo by Jed Jacobsohn

First Edition: March, 1996

ISBN 1-884064-29-9

Acknowledgments

Ever since the first appearance of *The Baseball Encyclopedia* in 1969, I have wanted to see a detailed publication listing all the statistics compiled by all of the Canadians who played major league baseball. As it turns out, the compilation of such a record was almost as time-consuming and demanding as the work of the original encyclopedia itself must have been. Most of the research in compiling this statistical and biographical record was carried out by myself over the last 10 years, but several individuals played an important role in assisting with this publication.

John Dewan and Don Zminda at STATS, Inc. freely contributed their advice on this project as well as their assistance in setting up the computer systems used for developing the batting, pitching and fielding charts for the presentation of the statistical data. Don also acted as editor for the manuscript. The most common batting, pitching and fielding categories, as well as the basic player information, come from the files compiled by STATS, Inc.

The work of William Humber and Jim Shearon provided invaluable insight into the history of baseball in Canada, as well as on the background lore of many of the Canadian-born players. I highly recommend their books to any readers seeking a more in-depth treatment of these subjects.

Bill Deane provided a great deal of assistance and encouragement for this project, not only during his years as head of the research department at the National Baseball Library, but also in helping to compile pitching data for baseball's first 40 years. Much of this involved a boxscore by boxscore search through old newspaper game accounts.

Pete Palmer, co-editor of *Total Baseball*, was especially helpful in uncovering some of the batting, pitching and fielding data from the nineteenth and early twentieth century that was otherwise unavailable, even at the National Baseball Library in Cooperstown. In particular, Pete provided the data for many statistical categories such as hit by pitch, wild pitches, balks and passed balls that do not appear in other encyclopedias or even in the early baseball guides.

In addition to John Dewan and Don Zminda, a number of other people at STATS, Inc. assisted in the completion of this book. Scott McDevitt and Rob Neyer worked on formatting, typesetting and editing the material, while Drew Faust and Ron Freer are responsible for making the cover look as good as it does.

While the work in compiling the statistical information presented in these pages was largely my own effort, however, the many baseball encyclopedias and guides which have been published over the years have proven to be an invaluable source of information for checking the accuracy of the data presented here. While the statistical data given here will differ in some respects from the "official" record of major league baseball, I believe that it is the most accurate available to date. Nonetheless, the endless task of checking baseball's statistical record for accuracy is bound to uncover some mistakes in the numbers presented here. The author would appreciate hearing from readers about any errors which they have noticed or uncovered.

— Neil Munro

Table of Contents

Foreword

by William Humber

Think of Canadian sport and the first thing that comes to mind is hockey, but only baseball has remained popular through two centuries of the country's development. There is far more to this story than simply the ill-fated Montreal Expos or the recent success of the Toronto Blue Jays.

The 19th century was distinguished in Canada by a kind of friendly anti-Americanism on the one hand and almost slavish respect for things British on the other. Yet given a choice between baseball and cricket, two leading symbols of those countries, the American game won hands down.

By 1905 Samuel Moffett's report on the Americanization of Canada warned that "the native game of lacrosse is not able to hold its own against the southern intruder." He was further vexed that Canadian papers had lengthier reports on National and American League baseball games than the proceedings of the British Parliament.

The simple reason for this was the significant role that Canadians played in baseball's evolution. We now know that the Abner Doubleday creation story is a lie, a fabrication, a whole suit formed cut of a fabric with no more substance than a junk bondsman's stock portfolio.

Now this is not to imply that Canadians have an equal claim to baseball parenthood. Part of the challenge is to think in somewhat different terms than national identity. Regionalism is the key to an understanding of baseball's development throughout North America. It emerged out of local experiments like the Massachusetts game, the Philadelphia game, the New York game, and something called the Canadian game. Each of them looked like baseball, but by 1865 the New York game was moving quicker than Union troops to solidify its primacy.

The Canadian game was an eleven-aside affair played in southwestern Ontario. There are ambiguous references to ball games in Toronto as early as 1803. The first newspaper reference to a bat and ball game appears in Nova Scotia in 1841, and rounders type games were played in British Columbia in the late 1840s. There is as well a famous account of an 1838 game in Beachville, Ontario, whose authenticity lies in the surrounding details of spectators, incidents, and players rather than its author's remembrance some 50 years later of distances between bases.

What is significant about all these accounts, however, is that they have no connection to each other, nor is there anything particularly Canadian about them other than the fact that they happened in Canada. But of equal note is the lack of anything particularly American about early records of baseball in the United States. The Americanization of baseball's identity is a Spalding-come-lately phenomenon. Nothing has or ever will change this identification, not even a Canadian making the Hall of Fame, a Canadian team winning several championships, or a Canadian-born player leading his team to the World Series (okay, that hasn't happened yet, but Larry Walker's fans suspect it may not be far off).

Alongside the game's significant heritage in Canada is the contribution of Canadians to the game's official record. Over the past 15 years this field has received considerable attention thanks to Colin Howell's work in the Maritimes, Donald Guay and Merritt Clifton in Quebec, Dave Shury and Brenda Zeman on the prairies, Geoff LaCasse and Pat Adachi in British Columbia, and in Ontario, among others, Jim Shearon, Nancy Bouchier, Bob Barney and Brian Kendall. Add to this team Neil Munro who has the figures and stats to back up his research.

Writing a country's baseball history can be a tangled affair. How for instance do we define a countryman? Is it based on residence, birthplace, citizenship, or self identification? If Jimmy Archer thought of himself as a Canadian even though he was born in Ireland, is that good enough to qualify him? Since Reno Bertoia and Kevin Reimer's fathers had Canadian citizenship at the time their sons were born outside Canada, does this not in fact make the future ballplayers dual citizens? Kirk McCaskill has a Canadian location on his birth certificate, and this makes him a Canadian whether he wants to be thought of as one or not. After all, his father was a professional hockey player. Sounds Canadian to me.

Most assuredly, Bert Blyleven and Orel Hershiser are not Canadians even though both spent at least part of their youth in Canada, and Hershiser even played some hockey. But what of Jeff Heath and George Selkirk, who, though born in Canada, left at a young age and learned all their significant skills in the United States? Should their achievements be in a separate category from those of Tip O'Neill or Terry Puhl?

That's the fun of the topic. Readers will see that Neil Munro has his own take on these questions. He introduces us to the lives of Canada's best players and in the minutest of statistical detail reveals accomplishment and failure. Each of these facts is a germ in the art of rendering men's lives significant. Baseball is ultimately a complete circle, though we are still uncovering its perimeter. The parts contribute to the whole and sometimes they can be as meaningful as Dick Fowler's no-hitter or as apparently insignificant as Mel Kerr's one major league appearance as a pinch runner.

William Humber is the author of five baseball books, including Diamonds of the North: A Concise History of Baseball in Canada *(Oxford University Press, 1995).*

Introduction: Baseball in Canada

The Early Years

While baseball is the "national pastime" in the USA, it has also been a very important sporting activity in Canada for more than one hundred and fifty years. Legend has it that baseball was "invented" by Abner Doubleday in 1839, in Cooperstown, a small village in New York state. This myth was developed more to satisfy political and economic needs rather than historical fact. Baseball was never really invented, but rather evolved over a very long period of time, from a game played by boys, to one played by men, to a professional sport. Unfortunately, it continues to evolve as a business interest to this day. From its predecessor games of cricket, rounders and town ball, baseball developed with many local variations, including some in the different geographic regions of Canada. Baseball served the needs of the population of two growing countries. Amateur baseball clubs sprang up to provide people with social and athletic diversions from the demands of work. Resplendent in the fresh air and the great outdoors, yet not so demanding of skill or effort as cricket, baseball was as popular in the cities as it was in the rural communities.

The initial charm and appeal of the sport, its novelty, relaxed pace, and escape from work in the offices, factories, and farms for the young men who played it, would eventually be replaced with a drive to win and hone one's skills. In turn this would lead to various types of payments for the best players and finally to organized professionalism. More than one hundred years ago, people began to lament that money and greed had corrupted the game and ruined its purity forever.

From the mid-1850s, Henry Chadwick, the "Father of Baseball," championed the game endlessly, hoping to establish for baseball in America the same esteem that cricket held in Britain. He made the New York game the most popular version of the sport. While extolling its virtues, Chadwick helped to define and refine the rules and scorekeeping system of baseball. He made lasting contributions to its statistical compilation and record keeping. His printed box score would do for baseball what stock-market quotes and bond prices did for the world of business. In addition, the recording of strikeouts, hits, and runs would forever secure the deeds of baseball heroes in history. Even today, we can recount the accomplishments of baseball stars long since passed away by simply scanning through their lines of batting and pitching statistics preserved in record books.

After the American Civil War, the game spread throughout the country, carried by returning soldiers and prisoners of war. The press proclaimed baseball to be "The National Game" in America. In 1871, the first true professional baseball league was formed, the National Association. Today, most baseball historians do not consider the National Association to be a "major league" despite the fact that the game's best players played a regular schedule with a resulting champion at the end of each season. The league lasted only five years as it was beset by problems. Franchises would come and go in midseason. The ballgames themselves were plagued by gambling, drinking and some players fixing their outcome. A team was likely to just skip a road trip near the end of the schedule if it feared losing money on that trip. Ultimately, the National Association was replaced by the National League of Professional Base Ball Clubs in 1876, and that league continues as the National League to this day. While the first few seasons of play for the NL were almost as troublesome for owners and players as were those of the National Association, the league would eventually stabilize and be recognized as the true beginning of major league baseball.

During this same period, baseball was evolving in different forms in Canada. While teams playing baseball in southwestern Ontario accepted Chadwick's version of the rules in 1860, many variations of the game were enjoyed much earlier in Canada, certainly before 1839 when Doubleday "invented" the game. Regional bat and ball games often featured more than nine players, and used different methods for recording outs and concluding innings and games. The most noteworthy early game was played on June 4, 1838, in Beechville, Ontario. That contest was described in great detail by Adam Ford, a young witness to the game, in a letter to the *Sporting Life* nearly 50 years later. Ford recited the names of 21 of the players who participated in that 1838 game. As well, he explained the playing rules used and even the construction of the ball. On June 4, 1988, those 21 players from that game were posthumously inducted as honorary members of Canada's Baseball Hall of Fame, along with five other Canadians who would make major league reputations many years after 1838. The baseball game played in Ontario, before the adoption of the New York rules, had featured five bases and 11 players on each side. A team had to retire all 11 opposing batters to conclude an inning. Fittingly, it was known as the Canadian Game.

There are also references to different versions of bat and ball games in many other provinces of Canada before the adoption of the New York Game in Ontario in the 1860's. Some of these were much closer to cricket or rounders, reflecting the British influence in Canada, but others were imported from south of the border by American immigrants. Even today, Canada is characterized as much by north-south connections as it is by east-west ties. Typically, ball teams in the Maritimes would play the Massachusetts Game against New England teams, teams from Quebec would play against New York clubs, and teams in British Columbia would play a west coast variation of baseball against teams from Washington state. However, the New York Game soon spread from Ontario to all regions of Canada. This version of the game was extremely popular in Montreal by 1865. Manitoba had a three-team professional league by the 1880's, and baseball even reached the Yukon early in the twentieth century.

Despite the fact that baseball's major leagues were very slow to move north to Canadian cities, several Ontario communities had franchises in American-based professional minor leagues by the 1870's. Many Canadians also made it to the major league level as players, not only in the National League, but also in the American Association and the Union Association, by the 1880's. Indeed, two players, Mike Brannock and Tom Smith, both from Guelph, Ontario, had played in the ill-fated National Association during its five year run a decade earlier. Brannock played three games for the Chicago entry in the National Association in its very first season in 1871, collecting one hit in 14 times at bat. Several Canadian players played for teams of the International Association, which billed itself as a rival to the NL during the late 1870's, but the first Canadian to appear in a major league game was Bill Phillips, from Saint John, New Brunswick. Phillips played first base for Cleveland in its debut year in the NL in 1879. Phillips was held hitless in his, and Cleveland's, first big league game on May 1st. Phillips did hammer out three hits, the first ever recorded by a Canadian, in his second game, on May 2, 1879. He registered those hits off none other than John Montgomery Ward, a legendary baseball figure and future Hall of Famer. Phillips played in all but one of Cleveland's 82 scheduled games in 1879, batting .271. He did not have any home runs that year, but he would become the first Canadian to hit a home run in the 1880 season. Not only had baseball come to Canada, but a Canadian had arrived in baseball.

The Minor Leagues

Many baseball purists believe that the minor leagues capture the true spirit of the national pastime today. Certainly their players seem to exude an unbridled enthusiasm for the sport, before they are infected by the commercialism of the majors. Many Canadian cities and towns have played host for minor league franchises. Toronto and Montreal have fielded some of the most successful minor league clubs in baseball history. Altogether, at least 75 Canadian communities, covering all 10 provinces, have fielded minor league teams since 1880. Most of these were cities and towns playing in American-based minor leagues that operated in the northern states. In 1913, no less than 24 Canadian communities had minor league teams, a number not equaled before or since. Many of these teams played in either the Canadian League or the Western Canada League. Some hockey stars, Canada's version of Deion Sanders or Bo Jackson, spent their summers in the lower minor leagues to keep in shape in their offseason. Toe Blake, Doug Harvey, and Rocket Richard were among these. Harvey in particular was an outstanding hitter with the Ottawa Nationals of the Border League, and a member of three pennant-winning clubs there.

Today, four Canadian cities have Triple-A teams: the Ottawa Lynx of the International League, and the Edmonton Trappers, Calgary Cannons and Vancouver Canadians of the Pacific Coast League. As well, Lethbridge, Medicine Hat, St. Catherines and Welland currently host teams at the lower minor league levels. In addition, Winnipeg and Thunder Bay have teams in the Northern League, while Regina and Saskatoon play in the North Central League, both independent leagues.

The minors use a wide variety of league, division, and playoff formats to determine championship teams each year, probably to ensure that a large number of cities are able to claim bragging rights for winning something. Accordingly, a number of Canadian cities have won their share of league or division titles, first or second-half pennants, and playoffs. However, a few have won some important championships at the highest minor league levels during the last century. Probably the most successful Canadian minor league franchise has been the Toronto Maple Leafs of the International League. The Leafs won pennants or playoffs no less than 15 times, and won the Junior World Series four times (including once in the Eastern League, which the International League was formerly called). The Montreal Royals won the International League pennant or playoff 11 times, and the Junior World Series three times. As well, both the Toronto and Montreal Triple-A franchises boasted many outstanding players who would go on to become stars at the major league level.

One of the most memorable Junior World Series title-holders was the 1946 Montreal Royals. That was the team which Branch Rickey selected for Jackie Robinson to break baseball's colour bar before he moved up to

Brooklyn. Montreal was a natural choice for the debut of baseball's first acknowledged black performer of the 20th century. The large French majority in the city offered some sympathy for the plight of blacks in America, because they also felt a measure of discrimination by English-speaking Canadians. As well, Jackie and his wife Rachel could feel secure at home while living in a French-speaking neighbourhood while they were away from the ballpark. It was probably not even known at the time, but the last recognized black player in professional baseball before the colour line had been instituted was Hippo Galloway, who played for Woodstock, Ontario, in 1899. In 1946, Robinson led the International League in batting (.349), runs (113) and stolen bases (40), while leading the Royals to the pennant and playoff championships, and finally the Junior World Series title. Robinson was so popular in Quebec that the fans wanted the Montreal Alouettes (of the Canadian Football League) to sign him to play that fall. Robinson's Montreal Royals drew record crowds wherever they played. It is significant that one of the racial insults thrown out against Jackie was "Go back to Canada, black boy!" That 1946 Royals club featured a number of players who would also soon move up to the major league playing fields. Dixie Howell, Earl Naylor, Al Campanis, Spider Jorgensen, George Shuba, Steve Nagy, and Jack Banta were included among those.

Two years later, the Montreal Royals came back again to win the International League Pennant and Junior World Series. That 1948 club showcased future Hall of Famers Duke Snider and Roy Campanella, as well as soon-to-be major league stars Don Newcombe, Sam Jethroe and Bobby Morgan. Future TV star Chuck Connors also played for the 1948 Montreal team. When the Dodgers moved west to L.A., the handwriting was on the wall for the Montreal club, even though it was still fielding excellent teams. By 1959, the Dodgers were sending their top prospects to Spokane of the Pacific Coast League, and the following year was the last for the Montreal Royals. But it would take less than a decade for baseball to return, as Montreal would unveil the National League Expos in 1969.

Toronto was the sight of Babe Ruth's first home run as a professional baseball player. He hit it while playing as a pitcher with Providence in his rookie minor league season in 1914. The stadium for Toronto's entry in the International League at the time was called Hanlan's Point ballpark. Out of all the Toronto Maple Leafs teams that brought home championships, two of its most memorable were two of the last. The Maple Leafs won the International League playoffs for Toronto in both 1965 and 1966. A Triple-A farm club for the Boston Red Sox, Toronto was the final training ground for a number of players that would go on to star with the Bosox. Manager Dick Williams, along with Reggie Smith, Joe Foy, Russ Gibson and Gary

Waslewski, would later play for the American League miracle pennant winners who would rise from ninth to first in 1967. The Toronto Maple Leafs were the most successful minor league franchise of the 1950's, at least from a financial and attendance standpoint. They were owned by Jack Kent Cooke, an entrepreneur who would go on to similar sporting ownership success in the NFL and NHL. Cooke was frustrated by not being able to obtain a major league baseball team, and after he sold the club, Toronto's days in the minor leagues were also numbered. As with Montreal, Toronto would wait one decade, until 1977, for the Blue Jays of the American League to bring major league baseball north of the border into Ontario.

The Triple-A teams in Ottawa and Vancouver, in particular, have had great success in recent years, both in terms of attendance and glory on the diamond. Ottawa, which currently serves as the top farm club for the Montreal Expos, broke the International League attendance record in its first season of play in 1993, when they drew nearly 664,000 spectators. In 1995, the Ottawa Lynx won the Governors' Cup, awarded to the International League playoff championship team. Vancouver won six half-pennant titles (the Pacific Coast League uses a spilt-season format) in the decade from 1985 to 1994. Vancouver fans have longed to join Montreal and Toronto with a team in the major leagues for years now. No doubt it would be a very successful franchise in either league, but it would be a great addition for the American League with natural rivalries with Toronto and Seattle. So far, it has not received much interest as an expansion possibility from either major league.

The Major Leagues

Big league baseball finally came to Canada in 1969, when the National League welcomed Montreal into its fold. Then, the asking price for an expansion team was $10 million. Today, that figure would probably not even get an interview for a city hoping for an expansion franchise, but in 1969 many thought the price exorbitant. Toronto didn't even bother to apply at the time. This probably explains Montreal's successful bid when many other American cities seemed to hold the inside track. Montreal had just show-cased a most successful centennial celebration with Expo '67. This international exposure would also help the city secure the 1976 Olympic Games, and provide the present-day home for the Expos in Olympic Stadium (actually Stade Olympique). It is also believed that the Los Angeles Dodgers played a significant part behind the scenes in helping Montreal win an expansion franchise. Of course, Montreal had been an outstanding Triple-A farm club for the Dodgers when they played in Brooklyn. Major league baseball had finally taken the plunge and expanded beyond the borders of the United States. The NFL has yet to make a similar move, while the NBA waited more than 25 years to expand northward.

Montreal drafted mostly experienced players—albeit experienced castoffs that nobody else really wanted—to stock its new team. Their number-one selection in the expansion draft was Manny Mota. Their second pick was Mack Jones, who would hit the first major league home run on Canadian soil. Jones instantly became a Canadian hero when he got off to a great start in 1969. Other Expos provided occasional heroics during that first season. Bill Stoneman, a castoff from the Cubs, pitched a no-hitter for Montreal on April 17th, in only the ninth game ever played by the Expos. The real star of the early years was Rusty Staub, nicknamed "Le Grande Orange" for his red hair by the Expo faithful. The Expos obtained Rusty in a trade for four players and $100,000. Staub slammed 29 homers and batted .302 in Montreal's inaugural season. He followed that by belting 30 home runs in 1970, and he then hit .311 with 97 RBI in 1971. Staub was a Montreal fan favourite because he learned to speak French and lived in Montreal during the offseason. Nevertheless, he was traded to the New York Mets for Ken Singleton after his fine 1971 campaign. Singleton would have one good year for Montreal in 1973, before himself being dealt away to Baltimore in 1975. Some other notable accomplishments by the Expos in their first few seasons included a second no-hitter by Stoneman, Mike Marshall's league-leading 31 saves and record 92 games pitched in 1973, and Ron Hunt's all-time record of being hit by 50 pitches in 1971.

By the end of their first decade, the Expos showed the makings of a very good ball club. Their outfield of Andre Dawson, Warren Cromartie and Ellis Valentine was thought to be the best in baseball, while other stars like Gary Carter, Steve Rogers, Larry Parrish and Tim Wallach earned the Expos the tag, "Team of The Eighties." Some trades also brought a few other exciting players to Montreal for brief flashes of greatness. Ron LeFlore swiped 97 bases for the 1980 club, and Al Oliver won the 1982 batting crown (.331) while leading the league in hits (204), RBI (109) and doubles (43). The team was in the pennant race every year, but always seemed to fall just a little short. The 1981 club was the second-half winner in a split-season format made necessary by a player strike which caused the cancellation of one-third of the regular season. Montreal defeated the first-half winner Philadelphia Phillies in a division playoff, but lost the deciding game of the NLCS to the Dodgers on a two-out, ninth-inning home run by Rick Monday. This is the only time that the Expos have reached postseason play. Unfortunately, in 1994 when they were en route to perhaps their greatest season, their pennant hopes were dashed by yet another player strike.

Montreal's farm system has produced some very fine players. Andre Dawson, Gary Carter and Tim Raines could all wind up in the Baseball Hall of Fame some day. Dawson was considered by many as the best all-around player in the game, at least until his damaged knees slowed him. Gary Carter has probably been the best catcher in baseball since Johnny Bench. Montreal also developed Larry Walker, the British Columbia native, who already holds several offensive records for Canadians and threatens to grab many more before he retires. Walker will probably finish up as the best non-pitcher to come out of Canada. On a sad note, however, the realities of the economics of the game today threaten to make it difficult for the Expos to compete with the wealthier teams in the future. Montreal is in danger of losing its franchise to greener pastures because of low attendance, the differential in the value of the Canadian dollar, and the relative lack of finances of the present owners. Still, Montreal has fielded an exciting team in virtually every season, and some of the greatest players of the last half-century have displayed their skills for Montreal fans in the 27-season history history of the Expos.

Toronto almost gained a National League franchise in 1976, when a deal to purchase and move the San Francisco Giants fell through at the last moment. Toronto did obtain an American League expansion franchise in 1977, and Seattle gained a team that same year. Toronto took the opposite approach to Montreal in drafting players for its first few years. They went for young players whose futures lay ahead rather than behind them. Their first pick in the expansion draft was Bob Bailor, a player with only 14 major league games under his belt at the time. While the fans endured a rather dismal team those first few seasons, the Blue Jays were patiently developing future stars through their farm system, a number of good trades, and inspired draft choices. The Toronto organization built up a dedicated and competent network of scouts and minor league officials, and today stands as a model for future expansion teams. The Blue Jays won the AL Eastern Division Championship in 1985, just their ninth year of existence. Featuring the best outfield in the majors with George Bell, Jesse Barfield and Lloyd Moseby, a steady flow of slick infielders like Tony Fernandez and Damaso Garcia, and a fine pitching staff led by Dave Stieb, the Blue Jays were the real "Team of The Eighties." Jesse Barfield, and later Fred McGriff, would win home run crowns for Toronto. The team also captured the AL East Division Championship in both 1989 and 1991, and lost the 1987 and 1990 titles in the last week of each season. In many ways, the 1985 club held the most hope for Blue Jays fans. George Bell was the AL's Most Valuable Player, belting 47 homers along with a league-leading 134 RBI. The team won a Canadian-record 99 games during the season, and at one point led the ALCS three games to one over the Kansas City Royals. However, Toronto dropped the last three games of the series, with the last two heartbreaking losses coming at home.

In 1989 the Blue Jays moved into the Skydome with its retractable roof, and they were the envy of baseball. Toronto broke baseball's single-season attendance record for three straight years, and in 1991 became the first team ever to draw more than four million fans. It seemed as though any crowd less than 50,000 was a poor turnout. General manager Pat Gillick, who ironically had earned the nickname "Stand Pat" for shunning most trades while building up the team through careful player development in the early years of the Jays, pulled off one of the most significant trades in history just before the 1991 season. Gillick sent slugging first baseman Fred McGriff and Gold Glove shortstop Tony Fernandez to San Diego, in exchange for outfielder Joe Carter and second baseman Roberto Alomar. Following another playoff loss in 1991, Gillick put the final pieces together when he acquired free agents Dave Winfield and Jack Morris. In each of his last years at the helm in Toronto, fans would anticipate Gillick's adding one more All-Star to the Blue Jays just before the trading deadline. His moves paid dividends when Toronto not only won the 1992 playoff against Oakland, but went on to defeat a gifted Atlanta Braves club in the World Series, four games to two. Toronto used seven pitchers in winning the final game 4-3, scoring two runs in the 11th inning. The Blue Jays had taken baseball's World Championship outside the United States for the first time. It would not be the last.

The 1993 club had some changes, most notably Paul Molitor replacing Dave Winfield as the DH, but the result was the same. That season, first baseman John Olerud flirted with a .400 batting average into August, and finished as Toronto's first batting champion with a .363 average. Olerud also banged out 200 base hits, 107 RBI, and led the AL with 54 doubles. Gillick had been spurred to trade McGriff because Olerud had been waiting in the wings. Molitor and Alomar finished behind Olerud in the batting race to give the Blue Jays a 1-2-3 sweep in that category. The Blue Jays won the 1993 ALCS over the Chicago White Sox in six games, and capped off the year by beating the Philadelphia Phillies to win the World Series. They won it by taking the final game in thrilling fashion on a game-ending home run by Joe Carter. That home run ranks with those hit by Bobby Thomson in the 1951 NL playoffs and Bill Mazeroski in the 1960 World Series as the most dramatic in baseball history. This time, the Jays had a Canadian on their roster, as Rob Butler, a reserve outfielder, managed one hit in two pinch-hit appearances in the 1993 World Series. Butler was born in East York (in Toronto) seven years before the Blue Jays' first appearance in the major leagues.

Toronto was still the defending World Series champion to start the 1995 season as the 1994 player strike forced the cancellation of the series that year. However, several key players seemed to grow old together in 1995, the pitching faltered badly, and the Jays were never in contention. This time the Blue Jays would have to unload high-priced stars and lose players to free agency as they began a rebuilding process. Indeed, Pat Gillick, the architect of the two World Series winners, would himself depart from Toronto, taking over as general manager of the Baltimore Orioles late in 1995. However, no major league team has generated the excitement that the Blue Jays have during the last decade.

The Players

First there is a need to define exactly what we mean by a Canadian here. As well, we have to clarify which leagues are considered to be major leagues.

For the purposes of this book, we will count only those players who were born in Canada as being Canadians. This may sometimes go against the feelings of the ballplayers themselves. Kirk McCaskill thinks of himself as an American, even though he was born in Kapuskasing, Ontario. Kirk's father was a hockey player, and traveled throughout his career. Kirk lived in Kapuskasing for just two years and then moved to Nashville, Tennessee. Kirk grew up in the United States, and in fact, when he was drafted by the Winnipeg Jets of the NHL, the *Official National Hockey League Guide* inexplicably listed his birthplace as Paradise Valley, Arizona. On the other hand, Kevin Reimer was born in Macon, Georgia, and is not listed as a Canadian here. Kevin's father Gerry was a Canadian citizen playing minor league baseball in Macon when Kevin was born. But Kevin grew up in the Okanagan valley in British Columbia, where he excelled at baseball as well as hockey and golf. Just to add a little more international flavour to his career, Kevin turned down a pay cut from the Milwaukee Brewers to play professional baseball in Japan in 1994.

In defining the major leagues, we will follow the accepted guidelines used by all of the baseball encyclopedias today. Obviously, the National and American Leagues are major leagues. The NL has operated from 1876 through 1995, while the AL has been considered a major league since 1901 (although some have pushed unsuccessfully for its 1900 season to be accorded major league status, as well). In addition, the American Association from 1882 through 1891, the Union Association for 1884, the Players League for 1890, and the Federal League for 1914 and 1915 will be included as major leagues. These are rather arbitrary choices, but they do follow the existing practice. The Union Association was certainly not as strong as many minor leagues have been. The Players League, on the other hand, featured far more of the best players in its one year of existence than did the National League or American Association that year.

Using these definitions, there have been 179 Canadians who played at the major league level between 1876 and 1995. Even this number is somewhat doubtful, because the birthplace of several 19th-century players remains something of a mystery. In the roster of players given here, you will see that several are missing some important biographical information details. Ten of the 179 players have only "Canada" listed for their birthplace. For some of these players, and for a few others currently believed to have born in the USA, their country of birth is just a guess at this time. As biographical research continues, we are sure to find a few more Canadians who played in the majors, and we may also find that some "Canadians" were actually born in America or Europe. For now, we will tabulate the records for these 179 players. Just as several of these Canadians moved to the United States at an early age, there are five additional players who were born elsewhere, but were raised in Canada. Indeed, two of these five, Jimmy Archer (born in Ireland) and Reno Bertoia (Italy), are members of the Canadian Baseball Hall of Fame. The other three players are Hank Biasatti (Italy), Sheldon Burnside (USA) and the aforementioned Kevin Reimer. Their playing records will be included here, but will not be counted in the lists of Canadian record-holders.

The 179 Canadians were thought to represent all 10 provinces, but Jim McKeever, once credited to Newfoundland, was actually born in New Brunswick, according to the latest research. The provincial breakdown of these 179 is as follows:

Province	# Players
British Columbia	9
Alberta	5
Saskatchewan	7
Manitoba	3
Ontario	98
Quebec	20
New Brunswick	15
Nova Scotia	10
Prince Edward Island	2

As mentioned earlier, 10 players are identified only as being born in Canada.

Several Canadians have played with one of Canada's two major league clubs. Since 1977, a total of 35 Canadians have performed in the big leagues, and seven of these were with the Toronto Blue Jays. Toronto has recently acquired Paul Quantrill of Port Hope, Ontario, so their number will increase to at least eight in 1996. Not to be outdone by the Blue Jays, the Expos acquired Rheal Cormier from the Red Sox early in 1996, so their number of Canadians will also increase by at least one next season. Montreal's record of showcasing Canadians is better yet. Of the 41 Canadians who have reached the major league level since 1969, 11 played with the Expos. One player, Denis Boucher, has played with both Canadian big league clubs. Denis also combined with fellow Canadian Joe Siddall to form only the second Canadian battery in major league history. This took place on Labour Day, September 6, 1993. The first Canadian pitcher/catcher combination appeared back in 1883 when Tip O'Neill pitched to John Humphries. While O'Neill began his career as a pitcher, he would later gain fame as a slugging outfielder. The first Canadian to play with the Expos was relief pitcher Claude Raymond, who joined the team midway through 1969. Raymond was born in St. Jean, Quebec, so his appearance in Montreal was especially sweet. The first Canadian to play for the Blue Jays was infielder Dave McKay, in 1977. Many Canadian fans were disappointed that Toronto did not pick up future Hall of Famer Ferguson Jenkins, when he was available near the end of his pitching career.

Many of the Canadian players were in the big leagues for very brief stays. Seventeen of the 179 played in just one major league game. Fifty-three others appeared in only one season at the big league level. At the other end of the scale, 17 Canadians have enjoyed major league careers of 10 years or more; nine of these played in more than 1,000 games. Jenkins' 19 seasons in the majors is the most for any Canadian.

While Canadians have played at every position around the diamond, with possibly only first base being underrepresented, the number who have appeared at the different positions has changed significantly over time. Half of the Canadians were pitchers, although this was not the primary position for many of these players. Canadian pitchers were particularly well represented in the 19th century, and also during the last 50 years. The 1960s and 1970s witnessed the appearance of several top-flight Canadian relief pitchers. While Canada contributed many fine catchers from 1900 to 1920, very few Canadians have played the position since 1921. Most of the best infielders from Canada played in the 19th century, while outfielders have appeared with regularity in almost every decade since 1880.

Four Canadians went on to manage ball clubs at the major league level after their playing days were over. Actually, Arthur Irwin served as a playing manager for four years. Three of these four—Irwin, along with Bill Watkins and George Gibson—won more than 400 games as managers. The fourth, Fred Lake, won 163 games in parts of three different seasons. At the age of 43, Lake inserted himself into three games as a pinch hitter while managing the National League's Boston club. Both Irwin and Watkins managed pennant winners, Irwin with Boston of the AA in 1891 and Watkins with Detroit's powerful NL entry in 1887. In addition to these four major league managers, many Canadian-born players also managed teams at the minor league level when their playing days were over. Included among these were Frank O'Rourke, George Gibson, George Selkirk, Tip O'Neill and Pete Ward, to name just a few.

Between 1884 and 1890, there was a "World Series" between the National League and American Association pennant winners, so Watkins' championship club went up against the American Association-winning St. Louis team in 1887. The biggest star for that St. Louis club was none other than Tip O'Neill, perhaps the greatest Canadian batter of all time. O'Neill was coming off a year in which he batted .435. (It was officially listed as .492 in contemporary sources, because they counted walks as hits in 1887.) Watkins' Detroit Wolverines, as they were called then, defeated O'Neill and his St. Louis Browns, 10 games to 5. They scheduled this 15-game series to be played in 10 different cities, and even though Detroit had clinched the title by winning eight of the first 11 games, they still played out the last four games. Can you imagine the major leagues returning to this format today?

George Gibson was at the helm of the Pittsburgh Pirates in all but one of his seven years as manager. He brought them second-place finishes three times—1921, 1932 and 1933—but never quite made it to the World Series. However, "Moon" Gibson did play for a World Series Champion with Pittsburgh in 1909. The complete managerial records for all these men are listed at the end of the player register in this book.

A total of 10 Canadians have played in the modern World Series since it began in 1903. Of these 10, George Selkirk certainly made the biggest impact. He played in no less than six Fall Classics between 1936 and 1942, collecting 18 hits in 68 at-bats. George was also the only Canadian to hit a home run in the modern World Series, smashing two against the Giants in 1936. Ron Taylor pitched in two different World Series, appearing with the 1964 St. Louis Cardinals as well as the 1969 Miracle Mets. Other pitchers participating in the World Series were Johnny Rutherford (1952 Brooklyn Dodgers), John Hiller (1968 Detroit Tigers), and Reggie Cleveland (1975

Boston Red Sox). These were also three of the most memorable fall classics in baseball history. The remaining Canadian World Series participants were Bill O'Neill (outfielder with the Chicago White Sox in 1906), George Gibson (catcher with the 1909 Pittsburgh Pirates), Jack Graney (pinch hitter with the 1920 Cleveland Indians), Larry McLean (catcher with the 1913 New York Giants) and, as mentioned earlier, Rob Butler (1993 Toronto Blue Jays). When the next Canadian pitcher collects a World Series victory, he will be the first, because none of the Canadian hurlers appearing in the World Series has won a game yet.

Three Canadians played in the fall championship format used in the 19th century: Tip O'Neill (four times with St. Louis of the American Association), Arthur Irwin (the first Canadian in the World Series, playing with the NL Providence Grays in 1884), and Fred Lake (catching one game with Boston in 1897, when the first two teams in the National League staged a playoff series for the Temple Cup). Jimmy Archer, born in Dublin but raised in Canada, played in two World Series; for the 1907 Tigers and for the 1910 Cubs. Archer is also a member of the Canadian Baseball Hall of Fame, being inducted in 1990.

Canadians have two major obstacles to overcome to reach the big leagues at all. The first is obvious—the climate. Canadian summers are just too short to provide many youngsters with the necessary playing time to develop as major league baseball players. That might explain why so many Canadians make it as pitchers. If you can throw a baseball 90 miles per hour, you will get a long look by major league scouts, even if your other skills may need a lot of polishing. However, the skills needed by a player at the other positions are so demanding that only the most talented athlete can pick them up with relatively little playing experience. The second hindrance for would-be Canadian big leaguers is the lack of opportunity at the amateur, high school and university levels. One reason for the relative paucity of amateur baseball organizations in Canada is the weather, of course. Still, much of the limited resources of schools and communities have been channeled into hockey in Canada. This is changing slowly over time, in part because of the efforts of the Blue Jays and Expos in developing future Canadian major leaguers. But many of the "Canadians" listed in the register here moved to the United States at an early age, and learned to play baseball south of the border.

Still, as the statistics which follow will attest, many Canadians have fashioned impressive records in major league baseball over the years, and one Canadian, Ferguson Jenkins, was accorded baseball's highest honour when he was inducted into the Baseball Hall of Fame in Cooperstown in 1991.

Canada's Best

Of the 179 Canadians to play major league baseball, some were stars, some held on for a few seasons and some just made it up for a cup of coffee. I have selected 25 players out of these 179, to provide a little more information than just their bare statistical records. I will outline their background, career highlights, and some of their disappointments as well. These 25 will undoubtedly include most of Canada's best players. Many are names that you will recognize, while some you might not. Following a brief biographical account of these players, I will select my own all-star team from these Canadians. Here are their 25 stories. . .

Ted Bowsfield   1958-1964

Edward (Ted) Bowsfield was born in Vernon, British Columbia, in 1935. He grew up and learned to pitch in Penticton, where he played semi-pro ball at the tender age of 14. Though he dreamed of one day pitching for the Yankees, he was drafted by the Boston Red Sox. In 1955, Boston sent him to pitch for San Jose (which was Class-C ball at the time), and Bowsfield responded with a 9-7 record and struck out more than one batter per inning. His explosive fastball led some to predict that the lefthander would be the next Lefty Grove. He pitched four seasons in the minor leagues, getting by with not much more than his great fastball, then joined the Red Sox near the end of the 1958 season. In his very first game in the big leagues, he got to watch Jim Bunning toss a no-hitter for the Detroit Tigers. Bowsfield entered the game in the ninth inning and got the last three outs for Boston. The highlight of his first season was beating the New York Yankees three times in a row. His victims were Bob Turley (twice) and Bobby Shantz. Turley lost only seven games in 1958, as he won the Cy Young Award and led the Yankees to a World Series victory. Bowsfield finish 1958 with a 4-2 record and a 3.82 ERA in 16 games.

By the end of 1958, Bowsfield had developed a sore arm, probably because of poor pitching mechanics. His minor league instructors had been reluctant to tamper with his motion because of that blazing fastball. In 1959 he tried to pitch despite the pain in his shoulder, but he was hit hard by opposing batters and sent back down after pitching only nine innings. He came back in 1960 but was traded to Cleveland partway through the year. His combined record for both clubs was only 4-6 that year. Bowsfield might have been finished as a major league pitcher then, but he was picked up by the newly-formed Los Angeles Angels. He posted two winning seasons with the Angels, despite their expansion status. He was 11-8 in 1961 and 9-8 in 1962. In 1961 he pitched 157 innings and posted a 3.73 ERA while striking out 88 batters; all personal bests for him. He was the only Angel starter to turn in a winning record in 1961, their first season.

By this time his fastball was gone, so he got by with a good curveball, a change of pace, and a screwball. Bowsfield was sent to Kansas City for the 1963 season in a rather bizarre move involving Bo Belinsky. Belinsky was to be traded to the A's from Los Angeles, but some Kansas City writers found out about the deal and printed the story before Bo knew of it. The commissioner's office voided the deal because the press knew of the trade before the player had been informed. So Bowsfield was sent to the A's in place of Belinsky. (One wonders how Belinsky, a bigger star in Hollywood's night life than he was on the mound, would have fared in Kansas City.) Bowsfield lasted two more years with the A's, pitching mostly in relief. He almost had a no-hitter in 1963, giving up only two base hits in the ninth inning of a game against the Twins. In another game against his old Boston club, he set down 27 straight batters after giving up a leadoff double to Felix Mantilla.

After those last two years in Kansas City, the pain in his pitching arm forced Bowsfield to give it up. He had won 37 games and lost 39, while pitching 663 innings over his 215 big-league games. Bowsfield had a brief fling with the Vancouver Mounties of the Pacific Coast League before calling it quits for good. When his career was over, he spent many years as the stadium manager for first the Angels, and later the Seattle Mariners. He was elected to the Canadian Baseball Hall of Fame in 1988.

Jay "Nig" Clarke   1905-1911, 1919-1920

Jay Clarke was born in Amherstburg, Ontario, in 1882, the descendant of United Empire Loyalists. As a boy, he attended Assumption College in Windsor, a Catholic high school and one of the first Canadian schools to feature a baseball program. At least six Canadians who played major league ball participated in the Assumption baseball program: Reno Bertoia and Hank Biasatti (both from Italy), Pete Craig, Joe Siddall (a catcher for the Expos in 1995), John Upham and Jay Clarke. Typical of the insensitive nicknames given at the time, Jay was called "Nig" because of his dark skin colour. The name stuck with him throughout his big league career. After playing baseball at Assumption College, Clarke went into the minor leagues as a catcher at the turn of the century. On June 15, 1902, while playing with Corsicana, a team in the Texas League, he reportedly cranked out eight home runs in one game against Texarkana. This feat is thought to be a minor league record for one game. The final score was a resounding 51-3 for Corsicana.

Clarke made it to the major leagues with the Cleveland Indians in 1905. Surprisingly, he was immediately traded to Detroit after playing just five games with the Indians, and then, just as quickly, was sent back to Cleveland after getting into only three contests with the Tigers. He settled in with Cleveland and was their regular or backup catcher through the 1911 season. His best year was 1907, when he batted .269 while playing in 120 games. Clarke had earned a regular spot for the 1907 season by pounding the ball at a .358 clip in 57 games during 1906. He hit .274 in 1909 but his batting marks fell off notably after that. Clarke, like many catchers to this day, was more noted for his fielding work than for his batting prowess. He was considered one of the best defensive catchers in the American League between 1901 and 1911. Along with George Gibson and Jimmy Archer in particular, Clarke was one of a number of top-line major league catchers from Canada that played during the period from 1900 to 1920.

Clarke had a long interruption in his major league career from 1911 to 1919. After being sent back to the minors in 1912, he would later serve in France with the "Devil Dog" contingent of the U.S. Marines during World War I. He returned to play with the Philadelphia Phillies in the National League in 1919, batting .242 in 26 games, and then finished up by playing three games with Pittsburgh in 1920. Altogether, Clarke appeared in 506 major league games, 462 of those as a catcher. His career batting average was .254, and he hit six home runs in that dead-ball era. Clarke worked in a Ford auto plant in River Rouge, Michigan, after his playing days were over, and he died there in June, 1949. He is a member of the Canadian Baseball Hall of Fame.

Reggie Cleveland   1969-1981

Reggie Cleveland is the second winningest pitcher to come from Canada. Needless to say, he is a long way behind the number-one man, Ferguson Jenkins. Cleveland and Jenkins were actually teammates on the Boston Red Sox during 1976 and 1977, and again with Texas in 1978. Reggie was born in Swift Current, Saskatchewan, in 1948. However, his family moved frequently, so Reggie got to pitch sandlot baseball in many different towns and cities in both Alberta and Saskatchewan. Like a number of great athletes in other sports, Cleveland was playing against grown men by the time he was in his mid-teens.

Sam Shapiro, a friend of then-Cardinals manager Red Schoendienst, alerted the St. Louis organization about Cleveland, and they signed Reggie to a professional contract when he was 18. After four years in the minors, he got his first call to the big leagues at the end of the 1969 season. Cleveland started one game and gave up four runs in four innings, but was not involved in the decision. After being sent back to Tulsa of the American Association in 1970, he again was called up to St. Louis, and this time was 0-4 with a 7.62 ERA in 26 innings. By 1971, Cleveland was in the majors to stay. After losing his first two starts that year, he won his first major league game on April 26th against Juan Marichal, a future Hall of Famer. Cleveland finished 1971 with a record of 12 wins and 12 losses in 34 starts. He pitched 222 innings and struck out 148 batters while walking just 53. As a result of all that, Cleveland was named the Rookie Pitcher of the Year by *The Sporting News*. In 1971, the three other starting pitchers in the Cardinal rotation were Steve Carlton, Bob Gibson and Jerry Reuss. Those three would eventually combine for 800 major league victories!

In 1972, Cleveland pushed his win total up to 14, although he also lost 15 games. He struck out a career-high 153 batters. In one hot stretch, he won seven games in a row, including shutouts against Juan Marichal and Tom Seaver. In 1973 Reggie had perhaps his best year, winning 14 while losing 10, and posting an ERA of just 3.01. One of his wins came against Fergie Jenkins in Wrigley Field. Despite having pitched three straight good seasons, Cleveland was traded to the Boston Red Sox in December. In those three campaigns in St. Louis, Reggie had started 99 games with no relief appearances, but in 1974 Boston manager Darrell Johnson used him 14 times in relief and 27 times as a starter. His record that year was 12 wins and 14 losses.

In 1975, Cleveland was a member of a strong five-man rotation which took the Bosox to the World Series. The rotation of Rick Wise, Luis Tiant, Bill "Spaceman" Lee, Roger Moret and Cleveland won a total of 82 games. Reggie was 13-9 in 31 games. In the ALCS, Cleveland became the first Canadian pitcher to start a league playoff game (the playoff format had only been in use since 1969). He left with the game tied 3-3 after five innings, but the Red Sox would go to win on their way to a sweep of the Oakland A's. In Game 5 of the World Series, he lost his only start, 6-2 to the powerful Cincinnati Reds. Cleveland also pitched two scoreless innings in relief. This was one of the most exciting World Series ever played, as Boston came back to win Game 6, 7-6 in 12 innings on Carlton Fisk's famous home run just inside the foul pole. However, Boston lost a Game 7 heartbreaker and the Reds were World Champs.

In 1976, the Red Sox added Ferguson Jenkins to their starting rotation, giving them the two winningest Canadian pitchers on their staff at one time. Cleveland won 10 games in 1976 (with a 3.07 ERA) and 11 games in 1977, his last year as a starting pitcher. Reggie had now won 10 or more games for seven consecutive years. After pitching just one game for Boston in 1978, Cleveland was dealt to Texas, joining Jenkins, who had gone there at the end of 1977. Reggie was used exclusively in relief in 1978, pitching in 54 games and saving a dozen of them. Cleveland was then sold to Milwaukee for the 1979 season, but he slipped badly, winning only one game in six decisions. He came back in 1980 to post an 11-9 record, even starting in 13 of his 45 games pitched that season. Cleveland's last year in the majors was with Milwaukee in strike-shortened 1981. He was 2-3 in 35 relief appearances when he left the team near the end of the year.

In his career, Cleveland pitched in 428 games, 203 as a starter and 225 in relief. He won 105 games and lost 106 while working in over 1,800 innings. He also had 25 saves, and 930 strikeouts against only 543 walks. His wins, losses and innings pitched rank second among all Canadian pitchers. His strikeouts are fourth behind Jenkins, Hiller, and McCaskill. He is third in career shutouts with 12. He returned to Canada after that 1981 season and now makes his home in Calgary, selling cars. He is also a member of the Canadian Baseball Hall of Fame, and certainly one of the best pitchers ever to make the journey down from north of the border.

Bob Emslie   1883-1885

Bob Emslie was born in Guelph, Ontario, in 1859. Ferguson Jenkins holds just about every career pitching record set by a Canadian, but Bob Emslie owns most of the single-season marks. He set those standards in 1884 with the Baltimore Orioles of the American Association. While Emslie's pitching career was as bright as a shooting star, it was also just as brief, as he lasted only three seasons in the big leagues.

In 1877, two Ontario baseball clubs joined the American-based International Association. Although this league billed itself as a rival to the newly formed National League, it really tried to compete on a different basis. The failed National Association (1871 to 1875) was unable to resolve the competing interests between the players, who would jump to another team whenever they saw a chance to make more money, and management, who were interested only in revenues and standings. The National League, which formed in 1876, was clearly set up to represent the interests of the team owners. Players would not be allowed to break contracts, and the teams would conform to a rigid schedule of games that did not allow for exhibitions with clubs outside their league structure. The International Association, on the other hand, was geared more to the needs of medium-sized communities which wanted to have the flexibility to play against any other baseball organization when a buck could be made from it. Thus two Canadian cities, London and Guelph, joined this league in 1877, and in fact the London Tecumsehs won the league "championship" by beating a club from Pittsburgh in the season finale in October. London even turned down a chance to join the National League for the following season, because of the restrictions they would have had to endure in giving up their lucrative exhibition games against other Canadian independent ball clubs. Otherwise, they might have been the first major league team north of the border, beating the Expos by some 90 years.

Bob Emslie pitched for another London team, the Atlantics, that played exhibition games against the International Association's London and Guelph entries. He learned to pitch in Ontario in the late 1870s before moving on to the minor leagues in the USA. At the time, some Ontario baseball clubs could probably be considered to be the equal of the best professional baseball teams playing south of the border, outside of those performing in the National League. While the details of his minor league record are pretty sketchy, Emslie did play for the Harriston Brown Stockings in the early 1880's. He made his major league debut with the Baltimore Orioles of the American Association on July 25th, 1883. While John Doyle, from Nova Scotia, was the first Canadian to pitch in the majors (he pitched three games for St. Louis in 1882), and Tip O'Neill, better known for his batting, was the first to register a big-league win, Emslie did pitch the first shutout by a Canadian. He did this on September 13, 1883, when he tossed a three-hitter at Cincinnati.

With Baltimore in 1883, Emslie posted a 9-13 record. Still, that was not a bad effort for a last-place team that would win only 28 games all year. He started 23 of the 24 games he pitched, completed 21 of those, and fashioned a 3.17 ERA in 201.1 innings. The next year, 1884, Emslie helped his Baltimore team move up to sixth place (in a twelve-team league) as he ran up the best single-season pitching record ever enjoyed by a Canadian. Emslie started and completed all 50 games he pitched, while posting a 32-17 record. He worked 455.1 innings, tossed four shutouts, and struck out 264 batters while walking only 88. He also gave up 419 hits and 241 runs. None of those figures was really very unusual for that period, however. In fact, Emslie ranked only seventh in victories in the American Association, eighth in innings pitched, and ninth in complete games in 1884. Three times he went up against Billy Mountjoy, from nearby London, Ontario, winning once but losing twice. (Mountjoy, incidentally, won 19 games for the Cincinnati Reds in 1884. The Reds had been a charter member in the National League in 1876, but after missing the 1881 season they joined the newly formed AA in 1882 and won its very first pennant. But the Reds had dropped to fifth place by 1884.)

After a poor start in 1885 (Emslie had just 3 wins and 10 losses after his first 13 starts), the Orioles sent Bob to the Philadelphia American Association club. However he lost his first four starts there, and returned to the minor leagues. In his three-year stint in the majors, Emslie's record was 44 wins and 44 losses in 91 games. Still, his 85 complete games ranks third among all Canadian pitchers, and his 3.19 ERA is the fourth-lowest mark. After his pitching days were over, Emslie returned to the AA as an umpire in 1890. The next year he transferred to the NL, where he served as an umpire for 34 years, from 1891 to 1924. While working a semi-pro game, Bob spotted another Canadian, Jack Graney, pitching for St. Thomas. Although he recommended him as a pitcher to the Chicago Cubs, Graney would later enjoy a long career as an American League outfielder. Emslie died in St. Thomas in 1943. He was elected to the Canadian Baseball Hall of Fame in 1986.

Russ Ford   1909-1915

Russell Ford was born in Brandon, Manitoba, in 1883, and was the younger brother of Gene Ford, who pitched briefly for the Detroit Tigers in 1905. The Ford brothers are one of a pair of Canadian siblings to make it to the majors. The only other brother combination was Arthur and John Irwin, who played in the 19th century. (The Erautt brothers almost became the third pair of Canadian brothers in the majors. Joe was born in Vibank, Saskatchewan, but brother Eddie was born in Portland, Oregon.) Russ Ford is best known for "inventing" the emery ball. While pitching in the minor leagues, he accidentally discovered that by scuffing a ball slightly, he could make it break very sharply as it approached the plate. Like many pitchers of that time, Ford had used the spitball earlier in the minor leagues, so opposing batters and sportswriters alike assumed that his remarkable breaking ball was simply a wet one. This was a legal pitch at the time, and several of his contemporaries used it to carve out Hall of Fame careers. Ford did not reveal that his fast-breaking curve was due to his scuffing the ball with emery paper until many years later.

Russell's older brother, Gene, was born in Milton, Nova Scotia, in 1881. The Fords were part of the Canadian migration west, and lived in Manitoba two years later when Russ was born. His family moved to the United States when Russell was nine years old. According to Ford, he learned his baseball fundamentals while attending school in Minneapolis. His first minor league team was Cedar Rapids, for whom he pitched in 1905 and 1906. After winning 22 games there in 1906, he moved on to pitch for the Atlanta Crackers of the Southern League.

While pitching for Atlanta in 1908, Ford discovered his emery pitch. When warming up before a game, Ford sailed a pitch over his catcher's head and into a wooden pillar. When he used this scuffed ball for his next few pitches, both he and his catcher, Ed Sweeney, were amazed at the way it broke off suddenly, just before it crossed the plate. Ford tried to duplicate the scuff mark on other balls with broken glass and sharp stones, but eventually found that he could use a small piece of emery board to get the desired effect. He first wrapped a piece of emery paper over his ring, and cut a small hole in his glove to scuff up the ball, so that opponents would not notice it. Later he sewed a piece of emery board right into his glove between the fingers. In 1910, with his "secret pitch," Ford compiled one of the best rookie records any pitcher has ever had. He had been drafted by the New York Highlanders (soon to be renamed "Yankees"), and pitched in one game near the end of 1909. Ed Sweeney had already joined the Highlanders late in 1908, and the pair would work together there for the next four years.

In 1910, Ford was almost unhittable. He won 26 games while losing only six, as he completed 29 of his 33 starts. He even saved three games in relief. His ERA was 1.65 and he struck out 209 batters while walking only 70. Even better was his ratio of hits allowed to innings pitched. Russ yielded just 194 hits in 299.2 innings, fewer than six hits per nine innings. He also pitched eight shutouts, still a record for a rookie pitcher. (This record was tied by Reb Russell with the White Sox in 1913, and later by Fernando Valenzuela with the Dodgers in 1981.) Ford followed that year by winning 22 games against only 11 losses in 1911. This time his strikeouts were down to 158, but he still gave up only 251 hits in 281.1 innings as he posted a 2.27 ERA. The New York club, which finished second in the American League in 1910, slipped to sixth in 1911 and finally to last place by 1912, losing over 100 games. Ford's record reflected this plunge, as he was just 13-21 in 1912. He still managed to complete 30 of his 35 starts that year. In 1913, he was 12-18 as the Highlanders finished in seventh place. That year, Ford also lost a no-hitter on a ninth-inning infield hit.

When New York wanted him to take a pay cut for 1914, Ford jumped to the newly-formed Federal League, where he signed to pitch for Buffalo. (He actually signed a four-year contract, but the Federal League would fold after only two years.) Ford used his emery pitch to post a 21-6 record in 1914, and his 1.82 ERA was second best in the loop. In 1915, his last major league season, he slipped to a 5-9 record. Ford had developed a sore arm in 1913 and his strikeouts declined sharply after that. Furthermore, his secret emery ball was no longer a secret. Others had learned of the pitch, possibly from Ed Sweeney. Now every fading ballplayer, from sore-armed pitchers to infielders who could not hit the curveball, took a shot at reviving a lost career by throwing the emery pitch. By 1916, the pitch was banned from baseball. Ford tried to revive his own pitching career with Denver of the Western League in 1916 and Toledo of the American Association in 1917, but that was it for him as a pitcher.

He worked at a variety of different jobs after his baseball career was over, moving frequently. Ford died in 1960, in Rockingham, North Carolina. While he probably did not really think of himself as a Canadian, Ford still fashioned a most impressive pitching record and is near the top of the list of Canadians in most categories. His 99 big-league victories now ranks fourth, just behind Kirk McCaskill's 101 wins. His 2.59 career ERA is easily the best, as is his winning percentage (.582, based on 99 wins and 71 losses). He ranks second in shutouts, with 15, and second in complete games, with 126. Ford is another deserving member of the Canadian Baseball Hall of Fame.

Dick Fowler   1941-1942, 1945-1952

Dick Fowler is the only Canadian to throw a no-hitter in the major leagues. He pitched it against the St. Louis Browns on September 9, 1945. Ironically, it was his only win that season. Fowler had just returned from serving with the Canadian Army during World War II, and the game was his first major league start since 1942. In his no-hitter, he walked four batters and struck out six, and only five balls were hit out of the infield. Yet the outcome of the game itself was in doubt as Browns pitcher John Miller also did not allow a run by Fowler's Athletics through eight innings. However, when Irvin Hall drove in Hal Peck with the winning run in the bottom of the ninth, Dick Fowler wound up with Canada's only no-hit pitching gem.

Fowler was born in Toronto in 1921. He began his minor league pitching career in Cornwall, Ontario, and then quickly moved on to Batavia and then Oneonta in the Canadian-American League. Fowler was 16-10 with

Oneonta in 1940, at the age of 19. He got a tryout with the Toronto Maple Leafs in the last week of the 1940 season because their schedule went longer than Oneonta's. In 1941, Fowler had a 10-10 record with Toronto (which finished in last place in the International League that year), and then was called up to pitch for Connie Mack's Philadelphia A's in September. Dick went from one tailender to another, as the A's finished in last place in each of his first two years there. Fowler was 1-2 in 4 games in 1941 as a 20-year-old rookie, then went 6-11 in 31 games in 1942. He was used primarily in relief but also as a spot starter those years. After finishing up with a 1-2 record in seven games at the end of 1945 (his no-hitter being his one victory), Fowler then became a regular in Philadelphia's starting rotation for the next four years. One other pitcher for the A's during those four seasons was Phil Marchildon, also from Ontario, while yet another Ontario hurler, Bob Hooper, joined Mack's club for 1950.

The Athletics were a pretty bad club during most of Fowler's early years. In 1946 the team finished last again, this time losing 105 games. Dick posted a record of only 9-16, but his ERA was a fine 3.28. In 1947, he lowered it to 2.81, third best in the American League. This time he was 12-11, and he completed 16 of his 31 starts. For whatever reason, the period from 1947 to 1951 in the AL featured the highest ratio of walks to innings pitched in league history. In each of those years, the total number of walks exceeded the number of strikeouts posted, usually by a wide margin. When you read over the pitching records for Fowler and Marchildon, as well as for some of the greatest pitchers of the game—like Bob Feller, Bob Lemon and Hal Newhouser—you should bear this fact in mind when wondering why those hurlers displayed such poor control. So even though Fowler walked 76 while striking out 50 in 1948, and gave up 115 free passes while fanning only 43 in 1949, he still was one of the top pitchers in the AL during those years. He won 15 games both years, posting fine records of 15-8 in 1948 and 15-11 in 1949. Fowler pitched over 200 innings every year from 1946 to 1949, while completing at least half of his starts in each of those seasons.

Fowler missed much of the 1950 season with bursitis in his pitching arm, and although he came back somewhat in 1951, he never had a winning season again. Dick was just 1-5 in 11 games in 1950, and 5-11 in 22 starts in 1951. In 1952, his 10th and final year in the majors, Fowler finished at 1-2 in 18 games, mostly in relief. His ERA was over 5.00 in each of those last three years. In 1953, still only 32 years old, Fowler returned to the minors. Dick pitched for Charleston in 1953 and 1954, but that team was last in the American Association both years. It seemed that Fowler was forever destined to toil for last-place ball clubs. He never got a call back to the majors, even though he pitched pretty well both seasons.

Fowler, considered by all who met him to be one of the game's great gentlemen, suffered a number of tragedies in the last years of his life. His son Tom suffered from cancer from an early age, and the Fowlers had a difficult time paying the medical bills. Dick himself suffered from epileptic seizures, probably brought on by stress. Fowler contracted liver and kidney disease and died in Oneonta in 1972, at the age of 51. He had made his home there (near Cooperstown) since 1941. His wife, Joyce Howard, was from Oneonta, and he worked there after his baseball career was over.

Dick Fowler won 66 games and lost 79 in his 10-year career with the Philadelphia Athletics. He pitched in 221 games and completed 75 of his 170 starts. His ERA was 4.11 in just over 1300 innings of work. He is also a member of the Canadian Baseball Hall of Fame, elected in 1985.

George "Moon" Gibson   1905-1918

While Larry Walker has been the only Canadian to win a Gold Glove Award for his fielding prowess, George Gibson certain would have picked up a few of them for his trophy case, had the award been instituted back in 1900. Gibson was considered to be one of the greatest catchers and field generals of his day. George was born in London, Ontario, in 1880. Perhaps the best baseball in all of Canada was played in that region during the 1870's and 1880's. George learned his baseball fundamentals there by playing semi-pro ball for several years before he moved on to the Eastern League in 1903 (it would be renamed the International League a decade later). Gibson played with Buffalo and then Montreal of the Eastern League, and in 1905 he was batting .290 for Montreal when his contract was purchased by the Pittsburgh Pirates. Although he hit just .178 against National League pitching in both 1905 and 1906, he replaced the veteran Heinie Peitz as the team's regular catcher midway through his second year in Pittsburgh.

Gibson's batting marks appear anemic at first glance, but this was the era of the dead ball. George hit as well as most catchers of that period, displaying some power and a little speed to go with a careful batting eye. But like most other catchers, Gibson was not kept in the game for his batting. He was considered a fine handler of pitchers, and was especially good at developing young hurlers. He also had a strong throwing arm, and is one of the few catchers to record over 200 assists in a season, registering 203 in 1910. Gibson led NL receivers in games caught each year between 1907 and 1910. In 1909, he became the first player ever to catch 150 games in one season. This remains a rare feat today, with a 162-game schedule, but during 1909 (with its 154-game schedule) before the days of improved equipment and medical treatments, it was truly a phenomenal accomplishment. Gibson led NL catchers in fielding average in three different seasons. George did bat over .250 five times, peaking at .280 in 1913, and .285 in 1914. In 1909, the year the Pirates became World Champions, Gibson batted .265, with career bests in RBI (52), hits (135), doubles (25), triples (9), sacrifice hits (15), and stolen bases (9). After the 1916 season, when his batting average slipped to .202, he was picked up on waivers by the New York Giants, because John McGraw (one of the most astute figures in baseball history) wanted him to work with the Giants' young pitchers.

After two years in New York, Gibson played briefly with Sacramento in the Pacific Coast League. In 1920 George returned to Pittsburgh, this time as field manager. Gibson brought the team home fourth in 1920 and lifted them to second place in 1921, only four games behind McGraw's New York Giants, who would wind up winning four pennants in a row, beginning in 1921. Gibson's Pirates faltered badly in 1922, and George left in midseason with the team below .500. After serving as a coach with the Washington Senators in 1923, Gibson was back to the NL, first as a coach and then as manager of the Chicago Cubs, in 1925. Gibson replaced Rabbit Maranville as Cubs manager near the end of that season, but Chicago was already a last-place team by then. George was then out of the major leagues until 1932, when he returned to manage the Pirates. Once again his Pirates placed second, both in 1932 and 1933, but George was let go for good when Pittsburgh started slowly in 1934. Of the four Canadians to manage in the major leagues, Gibson had the best winning percentage (.546), based on 413 games won and 344 lost. Gibson eventually returned home to London, Ontario, where he died in 1967 at the age of 86. He was the last Canadian to manage a big-league ball club, and he was elected to the Canadian Baseball Hall of Fame in 1987.

George Gibson is best remembered for his role in the 1909 World Series. This was to be baseball's showcase, featuring the two best players in the game, Ty Cobb for Detroit and Honus Wagner for Pittsburgh. In the end, Wagner outclassed Cobb in every respect. Honus batted .333, stole six bases and drove home six runs while Cobb could manage only a .231 batting average and two steals. Detroit had many fine baserunners and had led the American League with 280 stolen bases that season, but Gibson put a stop to that in the Fall Classic. Pittsburgh stole 18 bases, but the Tigers swiped only six, and Gibson gunned down five Bengal runners trying. Actually, Gibson outhit Cobb himself in the series, batting .240, and he even stole two bases.

For whatever reason, Canada produced many fine catchers during the first two decades of this century. Jimmy Archer, Nig Clarke, Larry McLean, and Frank Owens were all outstanding receivers, but George Gibson was the best of the bunch and maybe the best in all of baseball at the time.

Jack Graney   1908, 1910-1922

Jack Graney was born in St. Thomas, Ontario, in 1886. He played semi-pro ball there and was discovered by another former Canadian ballplayer, Bob Emslie. Graney was a pitcher at the time, and he was given a tryout with the Chicago Cubs in 1907. However, the Cubs released him to Rochester, and after a few games there he moved on to pitch for Wilkes-Barre in the New York State League. His contract was then purchased by Cleveland, and he was invited to their spring training camp for 1908. His major league pitching career lasted only two games, however, because he was hit on the hand by a batted ball and literally knocked off the mound. Graney was sent to Portland of the Pacific Coast League, where he compiled a 12-13 record as a pitcher in 1908. Jack started to spend some time in the outfield with Portland, and in 1909 he played 98 games in the outfield while still pitching in 39 games. In 1910, he was again called up to Cleveland, this time to stay there as an outfielder. Graney would remain with the Indians until 1922, making an appearance in the 1920 World Series as a pinch hitter with the Tribe.

Graney was a leadoff batter and a good defensive outfielder, playing mostly in left field. While he did not hit for power or a high batting average, Graney was on base frequently via the walk. He led the American League in bases on balls twice, with 94 in 1917 and 105 in 1919. In his rookie year (1910), Graney batted .236 in 116 games. In 1911, he improved to .269 and played in 146 games, scoring 84 runs as a leadoff hitter. His average was usually near his career mark of .250, while he played as a regular outfielder from 1910 to 1919, baseball's dead ball era. His best year was probably 1916, when his 41 doubles tied for the American League lead with teammate and future Hall of Famer Tris Speaker. Graney finished second to Ty Cobb in the AL in runs scored, 106 to 113, and also placed second to Burt Shotton (of the St. Louis Browns) in walks, 102 to 111. In 1916, Graney hit a career-high 14 triples and even led his team in home runs, with five. He was a good baserunner, and would steal 20 or more bases three times in his career.

Graney's best batting marks came in 1920 and 1921, when he was no longer a regular. He hit .296 and .299 during those two campaigns. By 1922, Graney had slipped below .200 and was used mostly as a pinch hitter. He left

Cleveland in midseason to take a job as manager of Des Moines, Iowa, the Indians' farm team in the Western League. In his 14-year stint with Cleveland, Graney played in 1402 games. He made 1178 hits in 4705 at bats, and collected 219 doubles and 79 triples. He also drew 712 bases on balls and stole 148 bases. Graney established many career records for Canadian-born players, but most have since been eclipsed by Jeff Heath and Terry Puhl. After his days as a minor league manager were over, Jack operated an automobile dealership and then worked in the investment business. Graney suffered large financial losses during the 1929 stock-market crash, and was struggling as a used-car salesman when he got a call from a Cleveland radio station to try out for a job broadcasting Indians games. Graney passed the audition, and thus became the first former athlete to move into the broadcast booth. Graney remained as the Indians' play-by-play announcer for 23 years. He died in Louisiana, Missouri, at the age of 91 in 1978.

Because he was a leadoff batter for most of his career, Graney achieved a number of major league firsts. He was the first major leaguer to bat against Babe Ruth (who broke in as a pitcher in 1914). Graney singled to left. Jack was also the first ballplayer to come to the plate with a number on his uniform. In 1916, the Indians experimented with having their players wear a number on their uniform sleeve. The number corresponded to their position numbers as they appear in a scorecard. Today, the Cleveland branch of the Society for American Baseball Research (SABR) remembers Jack Graney by naming their chapter after him. Here at home, the *Jack Graney Award* is given to a broadcaster or writer each year in recognition of outstanding media contribution to Canadian baseball.

Jeff Heath   1936-1949

Jeff Heath was born in Fort William, Ontario (now part of Thunder Bay) in 1915. His parents were British citizens, as was Jeff until he had difficulty re-entering the United States after an exhibition baseball tour of Japan in 1935. Jeff became a U.S. citizen shortly after that incident. When he was only one year old, his parents moved to Victoria, British Columbia, and then on to Seattle, Washington, three years later. Heath learned to play ball in a Seattle high school and was chosen the best amateur baseball player in the Pacific Northwest when he was selected for that tour of Japan. Unlike many of the other players described thus far, Heath never had many ties to this country. But though he never thought of himself as a Canadian, he did occasionally express pride in the fact that he was born in Canada. Nevertheless, he may have been the best hitter of any Canadian-born baseball player.

His minor league career began with Zanesville of the Mid-Atlantic League in 1936, where he smashed 28 home runs while batting a resounding .383. The next year in Milwaukee of the American Association, he continued his torrid batting, pounding the ball at a .367 clip. Heath received a brief callup to the majors with the Cleveland Indians in both 1936 and 1937, and although he played fairly well each time up, he did not stick until 1938. Jeff hit .341 in 12 games with the Indians in 1936 and .230 in 20 games in 1937. He also smashed four triples in only 61 at-bats during 1937, and he would eventually lead the American League twice in that batting category. His Cleveland manager in his rookie season of 1938 was Ossie Vitt, who had taken over from the popular Steve O'Neill that year. Heath often had trouble getting along with management during his career, and he would become renowned for leading a player revolt against Vitt a few years later.

Heath started slowly in 1938, and shared the outfield duties with aging slugger Moose Solters during the first couple months of the season. Beginning to sting the ball with regularity, Heath took over the left-field duties on a permanent basis in late June. His batting marks continued to rise as the year progressed, and he would go on to have one of the finest seasons for any rookie batter in American League history. Heath finished the year as runner-up in the batting race to Boston's Jimmie Foxx. Heath wound up at .343 and also contributed 21 home runs. He lead the AL with 18 triples and finished third in slugging average behind Hall of Famers Foxx and Hank Greenberg. Heath's .602 figure was the best mark by a Canadian-born batter in this century until Larry Walker blasted away at a .607 clip in 1995. Heath also had 112 runs batted in and scored 104 runs himself, all this while getting only 502 at bats in 126 games. The Baseball Writers Association of America did not institute the Rookie of the Year Award until 1947, but Heath almost surely would have won had it existed back in 1938.

Heath's batting marks fell off significantly during the next two seasons, as he suffered a series of nagging injuries. He slipped to a .292 batting average with only 14 homers in 1939, and hit .219 in 1940 while seeing action in just 100 games. During that 1940 season, Heath was one of the leaders in a player revolt against manager Ossie Vitt. A number of Cleveland players harboured ill-feeling for Vitt, despite the fact that the team was in a race for the AL pennant with Detroit. In June, the players presented the Cleveland owners with a petition asking that Vitt be removed. While a move like this might seem commonplace for today's athletes, it showed remarkable courage (or audacity) in 1940. The Cleveland owners refused to give in to the players' demand during the season, but would later drop Vitt in the fall. The Cleveland fans had to watch a dispirited club make a half-hearted stretch run that saw them finish just one game behind the front-running Tigers.

In 1941, Jeff enjoyed perhaps the finest year at bat that any Canadian slugger has produced. Unfortunately, 1941 was the year of Joe DiMaggio's 56-game hitting streak and Ted Williams' lofty .406 batting average, so Heath did not get the recognition that he might have otherwise received. He made 199 hits in 585 at-bats, good for a .340 average. He also smashed 32 doubles, 20 triples (to lead the league) and 24 home runs, while accumulating 123 RBI. It was the first time that an American League player totaled 20 or more doubles, triples and homers in the same year; only George Brett has done it since. Heath finished just two RBI behind Joe DiMaggio for the AL lead in that category. He played in the 1941 All-Star game (alongside Ted Williams and Joe DiMaggio in the outfield) and again in the 1943 midseason classic.

Heath's batting cooled down somewhat after 1941, but he still displayed flashes of power for the Indians. He blasted 18 home runs in 1943 and hit over .300 in both 1944 and 1945, although he missed a number of games each year with a knee injury. In a surprise move, Cleveland traded Heath to Washington in December of 1945. He did not last long there, however, as he found himself a St. Louis Brown after failing to run out a ground ball. In 1947 while with the Browns, Heath slugged 27 home runs, which remained the standard for a Canadian-born player for nearly 50 years. Still, St. Louis couldn't have been all that enamoured with Heath's slugging (he was involved in a number of fights off the field), because they sold him to the National League's Boston Braves for 1948.

Playing in the National League, Heath enjoyed another productive year with the bat, but he suffered a serious injury that led to his career ending prematurely shortly thereafter. Heath batted .319 and slugged 20 homers in Boston. He even led all NL outfielders with a .991 fielding average that year. Boston wound up capturing the National League pennant, and Heath looked forward to playing against his former Cleveland Indians in the World Series. But before that could happen, Jeff broke his ankle while sliding in to home plate in a game against the Brooklyn Dodgers. The injury, which was quite serious, happened in the last week of the season, so Heath failed to join the short list of Canadians who have played in a World Series game. Cleveland would go on to defeat the Braves in the Series, four games to two. Heath was slow to come back in 1949, but he displayed great power in the few at-bats he did manage. Unfortunately, another broken ankle in September of that year finished his career as a major league player.

Heath later worked as a radio play-by-play broadcaster, calling games for the Seattle Rainiers of the Pacific Coast League. He died of a heart attack in Seattle in 1975, at age 60. He was inducted into the Canadian Baseball Hall of Fame in 1988. Heath still holds most of the career batting marks for

Canadians. He played in 1383 games getting 1447 hits for a .293 batting average. He is one of the few major league players with a slugging percentage better than .500 (he finished at .509) on the basis of 279 doubles, 102 triples and 194 home runs. He was the only Canadian with a .500 career slugging average until Walker moved above that mark and finished 1995 at .504. Heath's hits, doubles, triples, home runs as well as his 887 career RBI set the standard for Canadian-born sluggers, exceeding even the marks set by Tip O'Neill. It remains to be seen whether Larry Walker will be successful in his bid to overhaul those records during the next decade.

John Hiller   1965-1970, 1972-1980

Most of the players who have had an interruption in their big-league careers either served in the military during one of the wars fought in this century or were sent down to the minor leagues to recover their major league form. John Hiller may well be the only player whose career was interrupted by a heart attack. In the first place, you don't think of a strapping professional athlete as even being a candidate for a heart attack, at least when he is only 27 years old. Nonetheless, it happened to Hiller.

John probably didn't take his baseball career as seriously as he might have before the heart attack. He was a relief pitcher with the Detroit Tigers who had been in the big leagues six years because every team is in need of a lefthander who can throw a fastball with control. But Hiller also was a three-packs-a-day smoker who never really made his fitness a serious priority the way many professional athletes do today. On January 11, 1971, he suffered a heart attack right after having his morning coffee and cigarette. He managed to get to the local hospital by himself and, after a preliminary examination, was quickly taken to the coronary unit. Although his major arteries had severe blockage, Hiller decided to have a portion of his large intestine removed instead of bypass surgery. This rather unusual procedure was intended to reduce the amount of his cholesterol, and possibly leave him with a better shot at coming back as a major league pitcher. He eventually lost 70 pounds, going from 210 to 140 by the time he was released from the hospital. Of course he missed the entire 1971 season, and the only way he could make it back with the Tigers was to report to training camp in 1972 as a pitching coach. The Detroit management, along with everyone else, never believed for a moment that Hiller would ever pitch in the major leagues again.

The Tigers had not officially released him as a player yet, but Hiller started the 1972 season as a scout. When Hiller convinced the team physician that he was back in shape, he was allowed to pitch batting practice. Finally, the Tigers made room for John on their roster, and he actually had a pretty decent season in the last three months, as he posted a 2.05 ERA in 24 games pitched. He even started three games that year and completed one of those starts. Not only was Hiller back as a major league pitcher, but he would have the best years of his career *after* the heart attack.

John Hiller was born in Toronto in 1943 and grew up in Scarborough, thinking more of being a hockey star than a major league pitcher. He had a tryout with the Toronto Maple Leafs (the Triple-A baseball team, that is) before he was spotted and signed by Bob Prentice, then a scout for Detroit. He was sent to pitch for Class-A Jamestown in 1963. He moved up through the chain, getting brief tryouts with Detroit in both 1965 and 1966. In 1967 he was called up from Toledo of the International League to finish the season with Detroit. In 1968, Hiller had a pretty good year as Detroit won the American League pennant for the first time since 1945. He had a 9-6 record with a 2.39 ERA in 128 innings. John pitched in two games in the 1968 World Series, without a decision or a save, as the Tigers topped the Cardinals in seven games. Hiller was used primarily in relief during his career, but he did start 31 contests in his first six seasons, and even pitched five shutouts.

In 1973, in his first full season after suffering the heart attack, Hiller turned in what may be the best season for a relief pitcher in baseball history. He led the AL in games pitched (65) and games finished (60). His ERA was a microscopic 1.44, while he yielded just 89 hits in 125 innings. He won 10 games, lost five, and struck out 124 batters against only 39 walks. More importantly, he set what was then a major league record of 38 saves. Hiller placed fourth (tied) in the vote for Most Valuable Player. Relief pitchers were used differently in the 1970s than they are today, so it is difficult to compare the records of the top closers of 1995 with those of 20 years earlier. Still, it is hard to find another relief pitcher who was as dominating as was John Hiller in 1973.

While his ERA rose to 2.64 in 1974, Hiller pitched 150 innings in relief while setting a league record of 17 wins for a relief pitcher. This mark has been tied (by Minnesota's Bill Campbell in 1976) but never broken. He was limited to just 36 games in 1975, but still recorded a 2.15 ERA that year. In 1976, he had another fine season, pitching 121 innings in 56 games (which included one complete-game shutout), winning 12 while losing eight. He struck out 117 batters and posted a 2.38 ERA. After dropping to an 8-14 record in 1977, he came back with a 9-4 record and a 2.35 ERA in 1978. By the time his career ended in 1980, Hiller had pitched in 545 games, posting a record of 87 wins against 76 losses, while fashioning an ERA of 2.83. He also had 125 saves for Detroit. Hiller still holds the records for games pitched in relief, games finished, and saves for a Canadian pitcher. As well, his 1036 career strikeouts place him second only to Ferguson Jenkins in that category. He is not only Canada's greatest relief pitcher, he is also the top lefthander from north of the border. Hiller, a member of the Canadian Baseball Hall of Fame, was also voted by Tiger fans to Detroit's all-time all-star team as the relief pitcher. He now operates a farm in the upper peninsula of Michigan.

Arthur Irwin   1880-1891, 1894

Arthur "Doc" Irwin played his last game in the major leagues more than one hundred years ago, but no Canadian has yet been his equal as a shortstop. Arthur was born in Toronto in 1858. His brother John, who would also become a major league ball player, was born three years later, also in Toronto. When the Irwin brothers were still youngsters, their family moved to Boston, where Arthur eventually attracted some attention as an amateur baseball player. He played with Aetna in 1873 and 1874 and with the Amateurs (of Boston) from 1875 to 1879. In 1879 he joined an independent professional baseball team in Massachusetts, the Worcester Brown Stockings. In 1880, Arthur became a major league shortstop when Worcester was admitted to the National League to replace the Syracuse Stars, who folded at the conclusion of their 1879 campaign. Irwin's team finished a respectable fourth place in its inaugural year in the league.

The National League schedule was just 85 games in 1880, and Arthur played in every game, appearing in 82 games at shortstop and three at third base. He even donned the limited catcher's gear of the day, finishing up one game behind the plate. Irwin was the top shortstop in the NL, leading the loop in assists, chances taken, and double plays. But he also made the most errors of any shortstop. Arthur was not an outstanding hitter, usually batting about .250, but he always was regarded as a very reliable fielder and an exciting baserunner. Many of the common batting statistics that are compiled today were not recorded in the first decade of major league baseball, so his career total in stolen bases is not known. Irwin continued with Worcester for two more years, spending some time at third base as well as shortstop. The team fared very badly, finishing in last place in both 1881 and 1882, and was eventually dropped from the NL in favour of a new team from Philadelphia. Irwin moved on to play with the Providence Grays in the National League in 1883, and it was there that he really earned his reputation as an innovative and daring baseball player. The Grays finished in third place in Arthur's first year with the club, and he had his best season at the plate. Irwin batted .286, collecting 116 hits in 98 games. In 1884 the Providence club won the NL pennant with an outstanding record of 84 wins against only 28 losses. That was the season that Providence's star pitcher, Charles "Old Hoss" Radbourne, set the all-time major league record with 60 wins in one season. (In a move typifying our penchant for accuracy and consistency, modern baseball analysts have since reduced Radbourne's 1884 victory total to 59.)

Following an exchange of boasts and challenges, Grays manager Frank Bancroft and Jim Mutrie, manager of the American Association's pennant-winning New York Metropolitans, arranged for a three-game "World Series" to determine the true champions of professional baseball for 1884. The Grays swept the series, with Radbourne earning all three victories. The records are incomplete for that series. Irwin played shortstop in all three games and was credited with three hits in 10 at-bats in contemporary accounts, but today he is listed with two hits in nine at-bats. In any case, Canadian Arthur Irwin was the regular shortstop of the very first World Series Championship club.

In 1885, Irwin achieved fame as the "inventor" of the infielder's glove. At the time, only catchers and first basemen wore padded mitts, while the rest of the players used only skimpy skintight gloves, if they wore anything at all. After he broke a finger, Irwin devised a padded infielder's glove for protection, allowing him to remain in the lineup. He liked it so much that he continued to use the glove even after the finger healed. Gradually, some other infielders began to wear a similar glove, and the trend quickly spread throughout organized baseball. However, in 1885 the Providence club slipped below .500, and fan support was dwindling. When the Grays were disbanded at the end of the season, Irwin moved on to play for the Philadelphia Phillies in 1886. He played in over 100 games for the Phillies in each of his three years there, batting .233, .254 and .219. His manager was the legendary Harry Wright, and Irwin picked up enough insights into managing strategy that he would soon join the ranks of the field generals. He left Philadelphia to play for the National League's Washington Senators in 1889. This team had been either last or next-to-last in every year of its existence, but after getting off to a terrible start, even for Washington, manager John Morrill was fired, and replaced by Irwin. The club fared a little better under Arthur, but still finished the year in last place, and he was not re-hired for 1890. One of his teammates on that 1889 club was brother John, who batted .289 while playing third base. In 1890, the baseball players, alarmed at a new proposal by the owners to severely limit their salaries, formed their own professional league, the Players League. The Players League attracted most of the best players in the game, and Irwin joined a fine Boston Red Stockings club which featured Dan Brouthers, Harry Stovey, Hardy Richardson, Irwin's old teammate Charles Radbourne, and manager King Kelly. The team finished first that season, in the league's only year of operation. Needless to say, the pennant winners from the National League and American Association wanted no part of this Boston powerhouse in the World Series of 1890. The Boston team, the only Players League club to make money in 1890, moved over to the American Association for the 1891 season. However, the popular Kelly jumped to the National League's Boston Beaneaters for the 1891 season, and the fans would not support the new AA club. The team still had a number of good players though, and Irwin, who had replaced Kelly as manager, brought the Red Stockings home in first place with a 93-42 record.

Irwin missed yet another chance to play in the World Series in 1891, as it was canceled that year because of squabbling between the NL and AA. It was also clear that 1891 would be the last gasp for the American Association. Four of its clubs joined the National League in 1892. Baltimore, Louisville, St. Louis, and Washington survived, while the rest folded. Because Kelly was firmly entrenched as the Boston manager, Irwin took over the reigns in Washington in 1892. By this time he was a non-playing manager. He had played in only six games with Boston in 1891 and would take the field for just one more brief appearance at shortstop while he was the managing the Philadelphia Phillies in 1894. Irwin was released by Washington near the end of 1892, but came back to manage the Phillies one year later. He continued managing teams in the NL for the rest of the decade, moving on to New York and then back to Washington. His best finish was third place with the Phillies in 1895.

Irwin continued to be active in professional baseball until his death in 1921. He managed or owned a string of minor league clubs, including Toronto in the Eastern League (which would later become the International League). Irwin was also a scout for the New York Highlanders from 1908 to 1912. He was voted a member of the Canadian Baseball Hall Fame of Fame in 1989, 98 years after he had been the last Canadian to manage a big-league pennant winner. Irwin's death is still shrouded in controversy and mystery. While he was a passenger on a ship traveling from New York to Boston, he disappeared overboard and drowned. Consequently, his place of death is listed as the Atlantic Ocean. He was reported to have been very depressed while on that trip. Whether he jumped, fell, or was pushed overboard is not clear, but after his death it was discovered that he had lived a double life, with wives in both Boston and New York. Irwin, quite possibly the best-known Canadian baseball figure of the 19th century, died at the age of 63.

Ferguson Jenkins   1965-1983

There are over 170 former players who have been inducted into the National Baseball Hall of Fame in Cooperstown; only one is a Canadian. To indicate just how far Ferguson Jenkins ranks ahead of all his fellow Canadians, consider the votes accumulated by our candidates for the Hall of Fame. Fergie's first year of eligibility was 1989, and he drew 234 votes that year. In 1990 he moved up to 296 votes, and he finally was elected in 1991, gathering 334 votes. While the rules for eligibility and the number of votes cast have changed periodically since the first vote was held in 1936, all other Canadians (even counting Jimmy Archer as a Canadian) have combined for just 35 votes. John Hiller, with 11 votes in 1986, is second. At first, it was feared that Jenkins might not win the approval of the voting writers. In 1980, while on a flight to Toronto (he was pitching with Texas as the time), customs officials found a small amount of cocaine and marijuana in his luggage. Jenkins said that he was carrying it for a teammate, but he was fined and suspended by baseball commissioner Bowie Kuhn. Jenkins was also convicted by the courts, but was given an absolute discharge with no criminal record. Thus, the Hall of Fame vote seemed tenuous at best. Many times the perceived character of a candidate carries more weight with the voters than does his won-lost record or batting average. Some other pitchers with records comparable to that compiled by Jenkins have also had to wait for their turn at being invited into baseball's most exclusive club. Gaylord Perry, with over 300 victories and two Cy Young Awards, was made to wait three years before going in the same year as Jenkins. Phil Niekro, another 300-game winner, is still waiting. So is Don Sutton, with 324 big league wins. Jim Kaat, with only one victory fewer than the 284 accumulated by Jenkins, has not come close in any of the eight years his name has been on the ballot. As well, Jenkins never pitched an inning in postseason play, and this is also often a factor which weighs in the minds of the judges. Thankfully, the worst fears of Jenkins, and of all Canadian baseball fans, were laid to rest when the doors of the baseball museum in Cooperstown were finally opened for Fergie in 1991.

How good was Jenkins as a pitcher? Among Canadian pitchers there is simply no contest for the number-one spot, but where does Fergie rank among history's best pitchers? His 284 career victories rank 24th (tied) on the all-time list; he is 17th best among 20th century pitchers. His 3,192 strikeouts stand ninth best, his 594 games started ranks 18th, and his 49 shutouts tie him for the 21st spot (with Don Drysdale, Luis Tiant, and Early Wynn). Jenkins is the only pitcher in history to strike out more than 3,000 batters but give up fewer than 1000 walks (he was close, with 997). One age-old standard for pitching greatness is winning 20 games in a season. Fergie won 20 or more games seven times, with an amazing six years in a row from 1967 to 1972 while he was with the Cubs. Only Warren Spahn, Lefty Grove and Robin Roberts have had six or more consecutive 20-win seasons in the modern era (since 1920). Few pitchers in baseball history have been able to consistently ring up 40 starts and 300 innings pitched. In the five-year stretch between 1967 and 1971, Fergie averaged 21 wins, 40 starts, 23 complete games, 309 innings and 261 strikeouts, against just 65 walks.

He won the Cy Young Award with a 24-13 record with the fourth-place Cubs in 1971 (despite the best efforts of Tom Seaver to campaign for the award that year). Fergie's control was astounding as walked only 37 batters in 325 innings. He struck out 263 and completed 30 of his 39 starts. He even belted six home runs as a batter that year. With Texas in 1974, his first season in the AL, he turned in a 25-12 record with 29 complete games in 41 starts. He also reached a career-high 328 innings pitched that year. Furthermore, he accomplished much of this while pitching in Wrigley Field, home of the Chicago Cubs. Batters still look forward to getting to bat in Wrigley, especially when the wind is blowing out. If Jenkins had pitched for the Dodgers in Chavez Ravine, his very respectable 3.34 career ERA might have been 50 points lower. Jenkins earned his place as one of the very best pitchers of all time.

Ferguson Jenkins was born in Chatham, Ontario, in 1943. Fergie got his love for baseball from his father, who had been a star outfielder for several Chatham baseball teams a generation earlier. Ferguson was himself a local sports hero, in hockey and basketball as well as baseball. He once barnstormed with the Harlem Globetrotters, and he also played junior B hockey. Jenkins began his minor league career in 1962, with Miami of the Florida State League, in the Phillies organization. After a good season at the Triple-A level with Arkansas, he was called up to pitch for Philadelphia in the closing weeks of 1965. Fergie had been both a reliever and starter throughout his minor league career, and he started out as a reliever in the majors. With Philadelphia, Jenkins was 2-1 in seven games, with a 2.19 ERA in 12.1 innings. This earned him a spot with the Phillies for 1966. However, after making only one relief appearance for Philadelphia, Fergie was traded to the Cubs (along with two outfielders) for two former All-Star pitchers, Bob Buhl and Larry Jackson. The Cubs, despite their last-place finish in 1966, were pretty deep in starting pitchers, so Jenkins had a tough time cracking the rotation. He finished the 1966 season with an ERA of 3.32, making just 12 starts in 61 games. His record was 6-8, and he pitched one shutout and earned five saves.

As he prepared for the 1967 season, no one would have predicted that Fergie would begin a string of six consecutive seasons with at least 20 wins. Yet Jenkins, and the Cubs in general, surprised a lot of people. The Cubs made a dramatic improvement from last place to third, and Jenkins became such a fixture in the starting rotation he was named to the National League All-Star team. In the actual game, he tied a record by striking out six American League batters.

After his six straight 20-victory seasons, Fergie slipped to a 14-16 record with the Cubs in 1973. The Cubs reacted to Jenkins' first off-year by trading him to Texas for rookie Bill Madlock. Madlock would go on to win two batting crowns for the Cubs, but Jenkins certainly paid dividends for the Rangers. He rebounded with a 25-win season in 1974, and as it turned out, he had almost exactly the same statistical record as Oakland's Cy Young winner, Catfish Hunter. Both pitchers were 25-12, both had six shutouts, and both made 41 starts that year. Jenkins completed 29 games and pitched 328 innings, to Hunter's 23 and 318. Jenkins struck out 225 batters, Hunter 143, but Catfish won the ERA title with a 2.49 mark. Jenkins' ERA was 2.82, and he finished behind Hunter in the Cy Young Award voting, 90 to 75. He just failed to become the first pitcher to win the award in both leagues—Gaylord Perry would wind up accomplishing that feat four years later.

Jenkins pitched for both Texas and Boston in his eight years in the American League, before returning to the Cubs for his last two years in 1982 and 1983. His full record for Chicago was 167-132. With Texas he finished at 93-72; he was 22-21 with the Red Sox, and 2-1 with the Phillies. Jenkins was noted for his fastball, curve and slider, but most of all for his pinpoint control. Needless to say, he owns virtually every career pitching record for Canadians. When his major league career ended, he actually returned to Canada to pitch in Ontario's Inter-County League in 1984 (he donated his earnings to the CNIB and the Cancer Society). Jenkins has been the recipient of a number of honours, besides being a Hall of Fame member in two countries. In 1974, he won the *Lou Marsh Trophy*, emblematic of Canada's outstanding sports figure. He was Canada's male athlete of the year four times, and was recipient of the Order of Canada. One of Canada's best-loved athletes, all baseball fans were certainly disappointed that the Blue Jays chose not to sign Fergie after his last year with the Cubs, and give him a shot at 300 wins. As it turned out, 284 wins were enough to secure him a place in Cooperstown, alongside baseball's immortals.

Phil Marchildon   1940-1942, 1945-1950

Perhaps Phil Marchildon should be remembered as a World War II hero rather than as a baseball star. His pitching accomplishments, though formidable, seem to pale alongside the incredible events of his three years in the military. Phil was born in Penetanguishene, on the shores of Georgian Bay in Ontario, in 1913. He was a pitcher for his hometown against the other community teams of the area. While pitching for Creighton Mines of the Nickel Belt League, he attended a tryout camp in Barrie and was shortly thereafter signed to a contract by the Toronto Maple Leafs. Following a short stint with Cornwall and then two years in Toronto, he was a starting pitcher with Connie Mack's Philadelphia Athletics in 1941. He had been briefly up with Philadelphia at the end of the 1940 season, losing both of his two starting assignments.

His days as a pitcher with the Athletics must have been almost as trying for Phil as his time spent in the war; the A's were a last-place club in each of his first five years with them. They were near the bottom of the AL in most offensive categories, and were also burdened by a porous infield. He had a fine rookie campaign, compiling a 10-15 record with a respectable 3.57 ERA in 204 innings. He was even better in 1942, winning 17 games for the last-place team. Only Tex Hughson and Ernie Bonham won more games than Marchildon that season, and they played for the top two teams in the league. He lost just 14 games (the Athletics dropped 99 decisions in 1942), completing 18 of his 31 starts and striking out 110 batters in 244 innings. He pitched well enough that the New York Yankees tried to made a trade for him on more than one occasion. But this was also the year after the Japanese bombed Pearl Harbor, so it was clear that many players, including Marchildon, would soon be serving on a different battlefield than the baseball diamond.

Marchildon had been ordered to report for duty with the Canadian Army in midseason of 1942, but was granted an extension until the end of September. He needed the time to support his family, not that Phil would get rich on his $4,300 baseball salary. When he did enlist at the end of September of 1942, Marchildon chose the Royal Canadian Air Force over the army, recalling the horror stories his father had told of trench warfare during the First World War. Little did he realize what lay ahead for him. A publicity stunt was staged as Marchildon and hockey star Roy Conacher were welcomed into the air force. He turned down the chance to be a fitness instructor and play ball during the war, instead volunteering for overseas duty. Before going to Britain, Marchildon pitched an exhibition inter-service game against Dick Fowler, his old Philadelphia A's roommate. Appropriately, the game ended in a 2-2 tie. Phil became a tail-gunner on a Halifax bomber with the RCAF, making 25 successful, but always dangerous, bombing missions over Europe. In August of 1944, on his 26th mission, Marchildon's plane was shot down over the Baltic Sea. Marchildon hurriedly put on his parachute and pushed himself through the turret's sliding glass doors. He was picked up by the Germans in Denmark and shipped off to a POW camp, Stalag Luft III. Marchildon spent most of the rest of the war in this camp, but as the Russian army closed in near the end of the war, the prisoners were taken on a long series of marches to avoid being freed by the Soviets. They were finally liberated by the British Army in May of 1945. The popular book *Ace, Phil Marchildon*, by Marchildon and Brian Kendall, gives the frightening and detailed accounts of the horrors that Phil experienced, and the psychological impact these held for him in his later years.

Back with Connie Mack's Athletics before the 1945 season had concluded, Marchildon showed few ill effects of the three lost seasons. He had another good year in 1946, even though his team was again dead last. While Phil and Dick Fowler tied for the A.L. lead with 16 losses, Marchildon won 13 games while pitching 227 innings, and his ERA was 3.49. In 1947, he had his best year, winning 19 games as the Athletics moved up to fifth place. His ERA was 3.22 and he completed 21 of his 35 starts. He ranked third in the league in innings pitched with 277, behind only future Hall of Famers Bob Feller and Hal Newhouser. Marchildon lost his chance to be a 20-game winner when was beaten 1-0 by the lowly St. Louis Browns in early September. Jeff Heath drove in the only run of that game. He slipped a little in 1948, dropping to a 9-15 record with a 4.53 ERA. As it turned out, those would be his last big league victories. In 1949, he was limited to 16 innings because of a sore arm. During spring training in 1950, Marchildon was sold to Buffalo of the International League. Connie Mack, who owned the A's as well as managed them, was constantly pleading poverty. War hero or not, Marchildon was disposed of while he could still bring Mack a few dollars. After a brief stay in Buffalo, Phil was given a chance with the Boston Red Sox, but pitched in only one game with them in July of 1950. That was his last fling.

Marchildon finished with a career record of 68 wins and 75 losses. If not for the war and the fact that he toiled for the lowly Athletics, he might easily have registered 100 wins. He completed 82 games, a little over half of his 162 starts. He also pitched six shutouts and struck out 481 batters in 1,214 innings. At his best, the man with the blazing fastball and big-breaking curveball was the equal of any pitcher of his day. Marchildon, along with Tip O'Neill and George Selkirk, were the first major league ball players elected to the Canadian Baseball Hall of Fame. He worked in various jobs in Toronto after his baseball career was over, and was once part of the Avro project that, in a questionable move, was cancelled by the Canadian government. He still lives in Toronto today.

Kirk McCaskill   1985-1995

Kirk McCaskill was one of nine Canadian-born players who appeared in the major leagues during the 1995 baseball season. The others were Phil Quantrill, Rheal Cormier, Mike Gardiner, Vince Horsman, Matt Stairs, Joe Siddall, Nigel Wilson, and of course Larry Walker. McCaskill's career typifies that of many major league pitchers. He relied on overpowering stuff during his early years, then suffered an injury but survived with guile, pitch location, and speed variation. Once a starting pitcher with the Angels, he is used almost exclusively as a set-up man in relief with the Chicago White Sox today. His six wins in the 1995 season made him the third Canadian-born pitcher to crack the century mark in wins. McCaskill now has 101 career victories in the majors.

Kirk was born in Kapuskasing in 1961, but his family moved to Nashville, Tennessee, when he was just two years old. He grew up in Burlington, Vermont. Kirk is an American citizen and that is where he learned to play baseball and hockey. While still in college, he began his minor league career pitching for Salem of the Northwest League, in the summer of 1982. The next year, still under contract with the California Angels and pitching for Nashua, their Double-A farm team of the Eastern League, he left baseball to try out with the NHL Winnipeg Jets at their training camp. McCaskill had been a star centre with the University of Vermont and had been selected by the Jets in the 1981 amateur hockey draft. In 1983, McCaskill began what he believed would be the career of a professional hockey player, and was assigned to Sherbrook of the AHL. However, after he scored just 10 goals in 78 games, he decided that his future would be in baseball after all.

The Angels had Kirk on their suspended list while he played hockey, but they reinstated him and sent him to pitch for their Triple-A team in Edmonton of the Pacific Coast League, early in the 1984 season. His pitching record there reflected the fact that he had been away for nearly a full season, as he won 7 games, lost 11 and was roughed up for an ERA of 5.73 in 143 innings. Kirk was back with Edmonton for the 1985 season, and after splitting his first two decisions he was called up to the Angels to pitch in the American League. His very first game was against the Toronto Blue Jays in Anaheim Stadium. He lost, 6-3. Still, Kirk was inserted into the Angels' starting rotation, and responded with a 12-12 record. He pitched in 30 games and started 29 of those, accumulating 102 strikeouts in 189.2 innings. In 1986, McCaskill was one of the best pitchers in the American League, as he helped the Angels capture the A.L. West title. Kirk won 17 games, lost only 10, and struck out 202 batters in 246.1 innings. He completed 10 of his 33 starts and tossed two shutouts. His ERA was a very respectable 3.36. In the ALCS against Boston, the young McCaskill lost both of his starting assignments, as the Angels dropped the last three games to fail in their quest for a World Series berth.

Kirk started the 1987 season just where he had left off in 1986, with two straight wins, one of them a shutout. Then he injured his arm and missed most of the rest of the season, finally submitting to elbow surgery. After a brief rehabilitation assignment back with Edmonton, he finished 1987 with a 4-6 record for the Angels. He continued to struggle in 1988, posting eight wins against six losses in just 146.1 innings. His strikeout ratio also began to drop significantly during those two years, indicating that he would have to make an adjustment, or lose his spot on the major league roster. But McCaskill responded with another great year in 1989, winning 15 games while losing 10. While his strikeouts were no longer impressive (he struck out only 107 batters in 212 innings), his control was better than ever. He walked only 59 batters while lowering his ERA to a career-best 2.93. He was tied for second in the American League in shutouts with four, and he ranked fifth in the league in earned-run average. One of those wins was a one-hit shutout pitched against the Toronto Blue Jays.

McCaskill had another good year in 1990, with a 12-11 record and a 3.25 ERA. Included in his 12 victories was a four-hit shutout against Nolan Ryan. He then signed a contract worth more than two million dollars for 1991, making him, at the time, the highest-paid Canadian-born player ever. However, 1991 was a terrible disappointment for Kirk, and for the Angels. Despite finishing with an 81 and 81 record, the Angels placed last in the West. McCaskill lost more games (19) than any other American League pitcher, and he saw his ERA balloon to 4.26. He received little offensive support from his teammates, and he won just 10 games. A free agent after that season, McCaskill signed a three-year contract with the Chicago White Sox. He still was earning more than two million dollars per season.

The 1992 season was McCaskill's last as a full-time starting pitcher. He started 34 games (with none complete however) and pitched 209 innings. His record was 12-13 and he struck out 109 batters. In 1993, McCaskill was forced into a swing role with the Sox, because of the number of fine young starting pitchers with the club. He started 14 games while pitching 16 in long relief. He even earned his first two big league saves as the White Sox took the American League West Championship, winning 94 games. The Sox then faced the Toronto Blue Jays in the ALCS. The Jays rolled over the White Sox in six games, on the way to their second straight World Series victory. McCaskill pitched three games in relief, and did not allow a run in 3.2 innings of work. Kirk was used exclusively in relief in 1994, and he pitched 52.2 innings in 40 games before the strike in August wiped out the rest of the season.

It looked for a while like 1994 would be McCaskill's last year, but he re-signed with the White Sox in April of 1995, inking a two-year deal worth $1.5 million. Last season he again was used in a set-up relief role and pitched in 55 games, winning six while losing only four. McCaskill wants to spend more time with his family, and it remains to be seen whether he will be back after 1996. In his career to date, he has won 101 games while losing 103. He has pitched 1,677 innings in 351 games, starting 238 of those. On the all-time list of Canadian-born pitchers, he now ranks sixth in games, third in innings pitched, strikeouts, and victories as well as losses, and he is second in games started. Those are pretty impressive pitching statistics for the man who wanted to play hockey alongside Dale Hawerchuck.

James "Tip" O'Neill   1883-1892

Tip O'Neill set a number of batting records for Canadians that will never be broken, unless the rules of the game are dramatically revised. James Edward O'Neill was born to second generation Irish-Canadians in Woodstock, Ontario, in 1858, and was one of a number of men who were successful in the major leagues after developing their skills in southwestern Ontario. "Tip" pitched amateur baseball for Harrison and Woodstock, Ontario, and after he led Woodstock to the Canadian national championship in 1880, he signed to play professional baseball with the Hiawatha Grays in Detroit. After one year of barnstorming with that team, he was picked up by the New York Metropolitans, then the top independent baseball club in the eastern U.S.

In 1883, the ownership of the Mets acquired major league franchises in both the National League and the American Association. O'Neill, thought to be a promising pitcher, was placed on the National League squad. However, the New York Nationals already had two outstanding pitchers in John Montgomery Ward and Mickey Welch. Welch would go on to win over 300 games in his career, and Ward was probably even a better pitcher until he hurt his arm and switched to playing the outfield and then shortstop. Consequently, O'Neill pitched in only 19 games, winning five while losing

12. He also appeared in seven games in the outfield but batted just .197 for the season. In July of 1883, O'Neill and Ontario-born catcher John Humphries formed the first all-Canadian battery to work in a major league game. They lost to the Buffalo Bisons, 11-7.

At the end of the 1883 season, the New York management decided to move O'Neill over to their American Association franchise, but the move was voided by Jimmy Williams, then secretary of the A.A., and Tip was given his release, freeing him to sign with any team he wished. O'Neill signed with the Browns of St. Louis in the American Association, which by now had engaged the very same Williams as their field manager. Tip was the Opening Day pitcher for St. Louis, but he soon developed a sore arm, and despite his pitching record of 11 wins and four losses, O'Neill was playing in left field by midseason. He had begun to demonstrate some batting prowess, and finished the 1884 season with .276 average and decent power. O'Neill never pitched again, and by June of 1885 he was pounding A.A. pitching at a .370 clip when he hurt his leg in a collision on the basepaths. He did not return until September, and then often needed a pinch runner when he made it on base. He finished with a .350 batting average, but saw action in only 52 games. St. Louis captured the pennant, and O'Neill played in the World Series against the N.L. champions, Cap Anson's Chicago White Stockings. O'Neill batted only .208 with five hits in seven games, as the two teams played to a tie (three wins apiece, plus a tie).

Beginning in 1886, O'Neill would lead the St. Louis Browns to three more A.A. pennants, as he became one of the dominant players in the league. He had developed into a fine outfielder and displayed a strong arm. He even recovered from his leg injury enough to be considered a fast baserunner, but it was for his hitting that O'Neill would best be remembered. In 1886, O'Neill was fifth in the league in batting (.328), second in hits (190), and second in total bases (255). (Runs batted in were not recorded at the time, and have not been completely compiled for the American Association by historical researchers for the years before its 1888 season.) This time in the World Series, the Browns defeated the White Stockings, four games to two. O'Neill batted .400 in the six-game series, smashing two home runs in one game.

In 1886, batters needed six balls for a walk and three strikes for an out, but this rule was changed for the 1887 season, when just five balls would earn a batter a free pass, and it would require four strikes for an out. Furthermore, a batter would be given credit for a "hit" whenever he received a base on balls. Needless to say, there was a big increase in scoring, and batting averages reached an all-time high in 1887.

Under the new rules in 1887, O'Neill finished with a whopping .492 average after being around the .500 mark all season. Today, after removing his 50 "hits" which were really walks, his batting average has been reduced to a "mere" .435. This is still the second-highest batting average ever recorded, behind only the .440 posted by Hugh Duffy in 1894. O'Neill also became the first and only batter in history to lead his league in doubles (52), triples (19) and homers (14) in the same season. He was the unofficial RBI leader, knocking in a career-high 123 runs. He also led the league in runs scored with 167, and this figure remains the fourth-best mark ever. Only Babe Ruth's 177 runs in 1921, Tom Brown's 177 runs while playing for Arthur Irwin's 1891 A.A. Boston champs, and Billy Hamilton with his record 192 runs scored in 1894, have surpassed O'Neill's 167 runs. As well, he led the A.A. with 225 hits, 357 total bases, and a .691 slugging average. These all remain unchallenged as the best single-season marks for Canadian batters. O'Neill cooled off to a paltry .200 in the World Series as the Browns lost to Canadian manager Bill Watkin's Detroit Wolverines in fifteen games.

In 1888, O'Neill fell off exactly 100 batting points, but still captured his second batting crown with a .335 mark. That year, the leagues were back to the three-strike rule and dropped the idea of counting walks as base hits, so batting averages returned to normal levels. He again led the league in hits (177) and he finished third in total bases (236). In their fourth straight World Series appearance, the Browns lost once more, six games to three, this time to O'Neill's former team, the New York Giants (as they were called by then). O'Neill was one of the game's most popular players, and he was idolized in St. Louis. Small boys vied for the privilege of carrying his bag as he made his way to the ballpark each day. After another fine year in 1889, when his .335 average was second best in the league, O'Neill followed his manager Charles Comiskey to the new Players League in 1890. After its one year of existence (O'Neill batted .302), he returned with Comiskey to the St. Louis Browns for 1891, where he had his last good year, batting .321. When the American Association folded after the 1891 season, the St. Louis team was one of only four clubs admitted to the National League, but O'Neill chose to leave the Browns (again following Comiskey) to sign with the Cincinnati Reds. That would be his last season, as his batting average fell sharply. He missed the last six weeks of the 1892 season because of illness, and wound up hitting only .251.

O'Neill returned to Canada after his playing days were over, moving to Montreal with his mother and brothers. He tried brief comebacks at the minor league level on a couple of occasions, but met with little success. Back in Montreal, he served as president of Montreal's Eastern League team for a few years, and also as an umpire in that league. His main occupation for the rest of his life was operating a restaurant and saloon with his brothers in Montreal. He died of a heart attack on a Montreal street in 1915.

While Tip O'Neill was one of the three baseball players elected to the Canadian Hall of Fame in the first vote in 1983, he did not receive any serious consideration in elections for entry into the National Baseball Hall of Fame (in Cooperstown). The baseball establishment never really accepted the American Association as the equal of the National League, and former Association players have been regularly shunned by the voters. O'Neill and Harry Stovey were probably the best hitters in the A.A. during its 10-year run as a major league, but Stovey has garnered a total of just six votes for the Hall of Fame, while O'Neill has been completely shut out, never getting even a single vote. His legacy to baseball is the standard he set for Canadian sluggers: a .326 lifetime batting average, based on 1386 hits in 1054 games. While many of his career marks have since been surpassed, that batting average will likely remain as the best ever produced by a Canadian.

Frank O'Rourke 1912, 1917-1918, 1920-1931

Frank "Blackie" O'Rourke must have had the longest association with professional baseball of any Canadian. He served 70 years as a player, minor league manager, coach, and scout. Born in Hamilton, Ontario, in 1894, he became the youngest Canadian, and one of the youngest players ever, to reach the major leagues. At the tender age of 17, he was called up to play shortstop for the Boston Braves, after just one month with Bridgeport of the Connecticut League. He had played a little bit with Lawrence of the New England League in 1911 and impressed everyone with his agile moves as an minor league infielder, despite his age. Boston must have needed all the help they could get, because they finished dead last in the N.L. in 1912, losing over 100 games. Braves manager Johnny Kling stuck with his young shortstop for 61 games before sending him back to the minors for more seasoning. Frank was batting only .177 with 50 strikeouts at the time, and while showing good range in the infield, he had made too many errors. The Braves replaced O'Rourke with Rabbit Maranville that September, and the Rabbit was a fixture there for the rest of that decade. O'Rourke would either have to make his mark at another position or with another club.

Frank played four seasons with Wilkes-Barre of the New York State League, usually hitting in the .280 range, and seeing action at shortstop, third base, and second base. The Brooklyn Dodgers purchased his contract and brought him up for the 1917 season to play third base. The Dodgers were coming off a pennant-winning season, but fell all the way to seventh place in 1917.

O'Rourke shared hot-corner duties with Mike Mowrey. He raised his batting average to .237, stole 11 bases, and cut down on his strikeouts, while giving a steady performance in the field. In 1918, the Dodgers used Ollie O'Mara at third and sent O'Rourke back to the minors after giving him a very brief look at second base. Frank played for New London of the Eastern League for the rest of 1918, and produced his best batting average in professional baseball, hitting .335. He moved on to Birmingham of the International League in 1919, batting .291, and then returned closer to home, to Toronto, for the following season. With the Toronto Maple Leafs in 1920, he enjoyed his best year in any league, batting .327 with 201 hits and 130 runs scored. He led all International League shortstops in putouts and fielding average.

O'Rourke was then sold to the Washington Senators, who called him up for the last two weeks of the 1920 season. He batted .296 in 14 games and played his usual stellar defense, thus ensuring a roster spot for himself in 1921. Playing his first full season, O'Rourke batted just .234 in 123 games. He did hit his first major league home runs, banging out three that year. But Frank led American League shortstops in errors with 55, and once again he was sent to a new club, this time the Boston Red Sox. In January of 1922, the Senators traded O'Rourke and third baseman "Jumping Joe" Dugan as part of a three-way deal involving Boston, Philadelphia and Washington. Neither O'Rourke nor Dugan would last long in Boston, however. Dugan was sent to the Yankees before the 1922 season was over, and O'Rourke was on his way back to Toronto after playing only one year with the Red Sox. With Boston, he had played at shortstop and third base and raised his average to .264 in limited action (67 games). O'Rourke regained his batting touch with the Maple Leafs, and hit .321 in both 1923 and 1924. Then he was picked up on waivers by the Detroit Tigers, and on the move once more. They brought him back to the American League for the last six weeks of the 1924 campaign. His manager at Detroit was none other than Ty Cobb.

Cobb's batting touch seemed to rub off on Frank, as he hit .276 in 47 games in 1924, and then enjoyed his best major league season in 1925. That year he hit .293 and banged out 40 doubles. In 1924, the Tigers had moved him to second base after he had played only a few games at shortstop (Detroit had .300-hitter Topper Rigney at short). In 1925, in his first full season at second base, O'Rourke led A.L. second sackers with a .971 fielding average. Frank's tenure at second base in the Motor City did not last long, however, because Cobb installed Charlie Gehringer as the regular second sacker early in 1926. (First Maranville, now Gehringer; O'Rourke had lost his job to two future Hall of Famers.) So Frank was used in a utility role, playing second, shortstop and third base, while batting .242 in 111 games. Once again he was traded, this time to the St. Louis Browns, along with three other players for Marty McManus, Bobby LaMotte and Pinky Hargrave. O'Rourke played third base for the Browns for the next four seasons and was steady, if not spectacular, at the plate. In 1929 he played in every one of the Browns' 154 games, and led A.L. third basemen in double plays. In 1927 he led the league in getting hit by a pitch (12), the only Canadian to ever achieve this somewhat painful accomplishment.

In 1931, at the age of 36, O'Rourke reached the end of his playing days as a major leaguer. After he batted just .222 in eight games with the Browns, he left the club and returned to the minors. He played third base and managed Milwaukee of the American Association, batting .304 in 50 games. He continued as Milwaukee's player-manager from 1931 to 1933 before moving on to play with Montreal of the International League in 1934. O'Rourke was a minor league player-manager with Charlotte (Piedmont League) in 1935, and then with El Dorado (Cotton States League) until the end of the 1939 season. In 1938, at 43, he batted .327 in 29 games. His record managing in the minor leagues was just a shade above .500, at 536 wins and 534 losses.

In 1941, O'Rourke became a scout for the Cincinnati Reds, and in 1952 he joined the Yankee scouting staff and remained there until 1983, when he was 89 years old. He died three years later. In his major league career, O'Rourke had played in 1,131 games, collecting 1,032 hits in 4,069 at-bats. Although he did not hit for power or average, he did the little things that managers always appreciate, moving runners along and taking one for the team in order to reach base. His 170 career sacrifice hits are easily the most by a Canadian. He was also hit by 53 pitches. If there is a place for a utility infielder on the Canadian all-star team, then surely Frank O'Rourke deserves to be that player.

Bill Phillips   1879-1888

In 1879, Bill Phillips became the first Canadian to play in the major leagues. He was also the first to smash a home run, but he would have to wait until 1880 to accomplish that feat. While most Canadians who made their mark in baseball in the 1880s came from southwestern Ontario, the first Canadian major leaguer was a maritimer. Phillips was born in St. John, New Brunswick in 1857. In St. John, as in other Canadian maritime cities and towns, the dominant baseball game before 1873 was the Massachusetts game, more closely resembling town ball. The details of Bill Phillips' youth, and even the date of his birth, remain a mystery today, but he did move to Chicago when he was a youngster and probably learned to play baseball there.

In its first few years as a professional circuit, the National League had difficulty keeping its franchises intact. After losing the teams which played in Indianapolis and Milwaukee in 1878, the league would have been left with just four clubs, so it admitted four new teams for the 1979 season. One of these clubs was the Cleveland Blues, which featured Bill Phillips at first base.

Cleveland possessed an outstanding pitcher in Jim McCormick, and its standing in the N.L. for the next six years would pretty much rest with his success, or lack of it, on the mound. In 1879, Phillips played in all but one of Cleveland's 82 scheduled games, collecting 99 hits and batting .271. He was the team's regular first baseman, but also saw limited action as a catcher (11 games) and outfielder (2). Cleveland would finish in sixth place in 1879, as McCormick lost 40 games. In 1880, the Blues moved up to third place as McCormick won 45, but Phillips slipped to a .254 batting mark. He did hit his first major league home run, not a common achievement in those days, as there were only 62 homers hit by the entire league in 1880. In 1881, Phillips raised his batting average to .272 and hit his second homer, but McCormick lost 30 games that year and Cleveland dropped to seventh. Phillips improved his fielding average in each of his first four years in the league, and also led the N.L. in double plays from 1880 to 1882. Bill hit .260 in '82, but he slipped to .246 in 1883. In 1884, he came back to have his best year with Cleveland, batting .276, collecting 128 hits in 111 games.

That would be his last year in Cleveland, however, as the Blues faced increasing financial difficulties. In 1884 the club had fallen back to seventh place when many of its players jumped to the newly-formed Union Association. Included among the jumpers was Jim McCormick, who left for Cincinnati in midseason. The Cleveland franchise folded at the end of the season, and Phillips hooked up with the American Association's Brooklyn Bridegrooms. Brooklyn had won the Inter-State Association championship in 1883, then joined the A.A. in 1884.

Phillips batted .302 in 99 games in his first year in the A.A., a league generally not regarded as having the same caliber of pitching as the N.L. He also had the best slugging average of his career (.422), and led A.A. first basemen in putouts and fielding average. In 1886, Phillips played the role of iron man again, working at first base in all 141 of Brooklyn's games. He hit .274 and posted career highs with 160 hits and 15 triples. In his final season with Brooklyn in 1887, Phillips batted .266 (not counting walks as hits, as the league did that year), and this time established career highs in runs scored (82) and doubles (34). Once again, he led the N.L. in fielding with a .982 percentage, his highest for any year.

Before the start of the 1888 season, Brooklyn management made a number of changes. Most notably for Phillips, Brooklyn purchased two star players from the champion St. Louis Browns, pitcher Bob Caruthers and first baseman Dave Foutz. As a result, Phillips was sold to the Kansas City Blues, a newly-formed A.A. team which was added to replace the dismantled New York club. Kansas City lasted only two years in the league, finishing last in 1888 and next to last in 1889. Phillips was there for just the first of those seasons. He was still a dependable fielder at first base, but his batting fell significantly. He hit only .236, managing 120 hits in 129 games in 1888. He still hit 10 triples, his fifth straight year in double figures in that category.

The details of Bill Phillips' life after he left baseball remain pretty sketchy. He did not catch on with any major league team in 1889 or even in 1890, when there were three major leagues searching for players. He probably returned to Chicago, and it is known that he died there in 1900.

Phillips was a big man for his time; most sources list him as being over six feet tall and weighing at least 200 pounds. He was always considered to be the prototype first baseman of his day, offering a large target for the other infielders to throw at while remaining glued to the bag. His career batting average was .266, and he was the first Canadian to play in more than 1,000 games and collect over 1,000 hits. He also legged out 98 career triples, a figure second among Canadians only to Jeff Heath's 102. Although first base is often thought to be the position requiring the least amount of skill, very few Canadians followed Phillips to the majors as first sackers. Tim Harkness is the only other Canadian to spend much time at first base, and his 199 games there are far behind the 1,032 played by Phillips. Bill Phillips was inducted into the Canadian Baseball Hall of Fame in 1988.

Terry Puhl   1977-1991

Terry Puhl had a tryout with the Montreal Expos in Regina when he was just 16 years old, but Canada's only team at the time passed him over. He was actually a pitcher then, and just played in the outfield on the days he wasn't starting. Puhl was born in Melville, Saskatchewan, in 1956, and he learned to play baseball in the communities of western Canada. His big break came the year after his tryout in Regina, when a scout for the Houston Astros saw him play in a national baseball tournament in Alberta. The Astros weren't impressed with Puhl as a pitcher, but liked what they saw of him as an outfielder. He was big, strong and fast, and had always been a good hitter. The Astros signed Puhl to a contract and sent him to Covington, Virginia, in the rookie-level Appalachian League.

Puhl batted .284 and stole 17 bases in 59 games, and the next year he was promoted to Class-A ball with Dubuque (Midwest League). After batting .332 and stealing 30 bases, he moved up to Double-A Columbus (Southern League). He batted .286 in 28 games and was promoted again, this time to Triple-A Memphis (International League). Beginning the 1977 season at Charleston, Puhl was called up to Houston only four days after his 21st birthday. He made such an impression for the remainder of the year that the Astros felt he would be a superstar one day. He batted .301 in 60 games, and stole 10 bases in 11 attempts. He was nearly flawless in the outfield (as would frequently be the case), making just one error in 123 chances. He would not hit a home run until 1978, but of course the Astrodome was not a ballpark designed for power hitters.

The Astros were an exciting club in the late 1970s, and they expected Puhl, along with Cesar Cedeno, Jose Cruz, Enos Cabell, Art Howe and Craig Reynolds, to take them to postseason play on a regular basis. Their pitching staff of J. R. Richard, Joe Niekro, Ken Forsch, Joaquin Andujar, and later Nolan Ryan, was also one of the best in the game. Puhl would play a number of games at all three outfield spots over his career, but he began in left field. He could cover a lot of ground, and he had an accurate, if not overpowering, arm. When he finished his career, Terry Puhl owned the major league record for the highest fielding average by any outfielder playing in more than 1,000 games. In 1979, he recorded his first perfect-fielding season, accepting 392 chances in 157 games without making an error. He duplicated that feat in 1981, fielding 1.000 in 190 chances. That was the first strike year, of course, so he appeared in only 88 games in the outfield that season. He would also play errorless ball in the outfield for Houston on three other occasions, but did not qualify for fielding honours because he was a part-time player by then. Between 1977 and 1991, Puhl played in exactly 1,300 games in the outfield and committed only 18 errors in 2,651 chances, for a .993 fielding average. Just for good measure, he was also perfect in the nine games he played in the outfield during postseason play.

Puhl usually batted near the top of the order, slashing the ball to all fields. Hitting in the leadoff spot, he batted .289 in 1978 and .287 in 1979, scoring 87 runs each year. He was selected to the National League All-Star team in 1978, his first full year in the majors, but he did not see action in that contest. In 1980, the Astros finally did win the NL West Division, but not without a serious challenge from the Los Angeles Dodgers. Houston could have wrapped up the title in their final series against the Dodgers, but lost three straight games to finish the regular season in a tie. The Astros rebounded to take the one-game playoff, 7-1, and earn the team's first appearance in postseason play.

Their opponents were the Philadelphia Phillies, led by Mike Schmidt and Pete Rose. The 1980 NLCS turned out to be one of the most exciting ever staged, but the Astros lost a heart-breaking fifth and final game, 8-7 in ten innings. The lead would change hands three times in that deciding contest. Puhl was simply outstanding in the playoffs, hitting a league playoff record .526 (10 hits in 19 at-bats) in the five games. He doubled twice, stole two bases, and drove in three runs. Puhl was at his best in Game 5, collecting four hits. Houston would capture the NL West title again in 1986, but by then Puhl's role was reduced to pinch-hitter. Still, he managed to collect two hits in three tries, so his NL Championship Series ledger is 12 hits in 22 at-bats, good for a stunning .545 batting average.

Puhl hit 13 home runs in 1980, while keeping his batting average at .282. He probably would have hit 20-odd if his team had played in a typical major league ballpark. The Houston management never seemed to understand the effect that the Astrodome had on major league batters and pitchers. They spent years trading for power hitters only to see them fizzle in Houston, yet they could not figure out why their pitchers sported sparkling earned-run averages but didn't win more often. And they were convinced that Puhl could increase his home-run output, if only he would change his swing. Puhl's batting figures might have been even more impressive, had they just let him play his game. However, Puhl hit just .251 in 1981 and then .262 in 1982, and his power output did not improve. In 1981, the Astros won the second-half championship (in a split-season format made necessary by the strike) but this time lost to the Dodgers in the five-game division playoff. Puhl hit just .190 in the series.

Terry was allowed to go back to his natural batting form in 1983 (the Astros had a new batting coach then, Dennis Menke, who had played in Houston). As a result, he hit .292 in 1983 and .301 in 1984. Puhl had been a fine baserunner for the Astros as well. He would swipe more than 20 stolen bases six times, getting 32 in 1978 and 30 in 1979. Only two other Canadians have reached 30 steals in the 20th century: Doc Miller stole 32 bases for the Boston Braves in 1911, and Bill O'Hara 31 with the New York Giants in 1909. Terry was held back by injuries in 1985, so 1984 was his last year as a regular. He pulled a hamstring early in the season, then damaged it further trying to come back too soon. He was on the disabled list four times in 1985 and appeared in only 57 games, but still batted .284. He spent more time on the disabled list the next year, tearing up his ankle while sliding. The ankle bothered him in 1987 as well, and he finished below .250 both seasons, seeing only limited duty each year.

By the 1988 season, Puhl was Houston's fourth outfielder, behind Billy Hatcher, Gerald Young and Kevin Bass. Still he turned in two more fine years in a part-time role. In 1988, he batted .303 in 113 games, and in 1989 he hit .271 in 121 games. Even more amazing was the fact that he stole 22 bases in 1988 (in 26 attempts). However, in 1990 a serious shoulder injury pretty well spelled the end for Puhl. He needed surgery during the year and was able to play only 37 games, mostly as a pinch hitter. The Astros did not offer him a contract for the 1991 season, so he became a free agent. Puhl was invited to the New York Mets' spring training camp, but was released on waivers before the season started. Back home in Houston, Terry assumed that his major league career was over, but he then was offered a contract by the Kansas City Royals of the American League, after they lost George Brett to injuries. Puhl played two games as a DH, and made one brief appearance (with no chances) in left field, but was used primarily as a pinch hitter in Kansas City. He was released after appearing in only 15 games, and now his baseball career was over for good.

Puhl had worked in Houston as a stockbroker for some years in the offseason, and he now works full time in that profession. Although he has played in more major league games (1,531) than any other Canadian, he might have had a much longer career if not for his injuries. Puhl ended up with 1,361 hits in 4,855 at bats, good for a .280 career batting average. He slugged 226 doubles, 56 triples and 62 homers, and he stole 217 bases, more than any other Canadian. Before Larry Walker arrived, Puhl was perhaps the best Canadian all-around position player of this century. He was a fine baserunner and an exceptional outfielder. Although his batting marks are impressive, they would have been significantly better if he had been with any other club, and didn't have to play half of his games in the Houston Astrodome. Terry is the most recent addition to the Canadian Baseball Hall of Fame, being elected in the fall of 1995. The best baseball player ever to come out of Saskatchewan (we would have to concede that Gordie Howe was the best athlete from that province), Puhl made a lasting impression with teammates and opponents alike, with his day-in and day-out quality service.

Claude Raymond   1959, 1961-1971

There have been several fine major league pitchers to come out of Quebec, including Paul Calvert, Joe Krakauakas, Dick Lines, and Ron Piche, but the best would have to be relief specialist Claude Raymond. Appropriately enough, both his teammates and the fans called him "Frenchy." Claude was born in St. Jean (a suburb of Montreal) in 1937. At the age of 12, Raymond was pitching against men, relying on a surprising fastball. Raymond tossed two no-hitters while playing junior ball in Montreal. When he was just 16, his games against another future major league pitcher, Ron Piche, were popular events at Parc Jarry. Claude was signed by the Dodgers for $250, but the commissioner's office voided the contract, because Raymond was still in high school.

Later, Raymond was scouted and signed by another Canadian (former player Roland Gladu, also from Montreal) for the Milwaukee Braves organization. He was 17 when they sent him to pitch for West Palm Beach in the Florida State League. He could not speak English at the time, but he picked it up quickly. The first English words he learned were "strike," "ball," and "hot dog." He tossed a two-hitter in his first outing (but lost the game), and wound up with a 13-12 record and a 2.60 ERA in 194 innings. He also learned to throw the curveball, allowing him to set up his blazing fastball. He moved through the Braves' farm system, pitching in Class-B ball at Evansville in 1956 (9-3 with a 2.57 ERA), Class-A Jacksonville in 1957 (12-6 with a 2.50 ERA in league-leading 54 games), and at Wichita, in the American Association in 1958. The Braves were developing him as a relief specialist. Then, it was still relatively uncommon for pitchers to begin their career in the bullpen; most relief pitchers began as starters.

The White Sox put in a draft for Raymond after the 1958 season, and he spent part of 1959 on the major league roster. He pitched just three games in relief for Chicago (he gave up four runs in four innings), and was soon returned to the Braves. In his brief stay with the White Sox, he roomed with second baseman Nellie Fox. Raymond pitched in Atlanta (Southern League) and Louisville (American Association) for the rest of the 1959 season. Ron Piche was briefly his teammate in Louisville, as was Ken MacKenzie, another Canadian who would soon be pitching in the major leagues. In 1960, Raymond went 9-9 in the Pacific Coast League with Sacramento, and returned to the majors in 1961, this time with the Braves. Milwaukee used him sparingly in relief, but he did win his only decision in 13 games. When the Braves acquired veteran pitcher Johnny Antonelli from Cleveland, Raymond was optioned out to Vancouver (Pacific Coast League). He pitched very poorly in Vancouver, (3-5, 5.37), and began to wonder if he would ever make it back to the big leagues.

The Braves optioned him to Toronto of the International League for 1962, and after a good showing there (2.63 ERA in 14 games), he was back in Milwaukee to stay. In his first appearance in 1962, he saved a game for Warren Spahn. Raymond pitched well the rest of the way, and finished with a 2.74 ERA and 10 saves. (The "save" was not an official stat until the 1969 season, but was kept unofficially at the time. The top pitchers still completed more than half their starts, and no relief pitcher accumulated the number of saves that are commonplace today.) In 1963, Claude was roughed up for a 4-6 record and an ERA of 5.40 in 45 games. Left unprotected by Milwaukee, he was claimed by Houston for the waiver price of $30,000.

Raymond had three good years with Houston, recording a 5-5 record with a 2.82 ERA in 1964, 7-4 with a 2.90 ERA in 1965, and 7-5 with a 3.13 ERA in 1966. He even started seven games and completed two of those in 1965. Raymond got off to a great start in 1966, and had one of the lowest earned-run averages in the National League at midseason. He was named to the National League All-Star roster, but didn't pitch in the game. By season's end, Claude had registered 16 saves, 62 games pitched and 42 games finished, the best marks in those categories for any Canadian pitcher up until that time. By then, Raymond had developed a number of pitches with which he could complement his fastball: forkball, slider and curve. During the 1967 season, the Braves (now playing in Atlanta) reacquired Claude, when they traded Wade Blasingame for him. His combined record for the two teams was 4-5 with an ERA of 2.89. In 1968, he was 3-5 with a 2.83 ERA for Atlanta. He recorded 10 saves in both 1967 and '68.

In 1969, the Braves finished first in the new National League West Division. Raymond was not around to participate in postseason play, however, because he was sold to the expansion Montreal Expos during that season. While still with Atlanta on May 16, Raymond pitched and won a game in relief (back in Jarry Park, site of his teenage exploits 15 years before). It was the first major league appearance by a French Canadian on his home turf and, for that game, all of the Expo faithful were cheering wildly for Montreal to lose (which they did on a Tito Francona home run in the 12th inning). When he joined the Expos, Raymond was not only the first Quebecois, but also the first person from all of Canada to play major league baseball for a Canadian team. He said later that he regretted that he did not have his good stuff anymore, but was determined to make a creditable showing. He pitched in 16 games for the Expos in the remainder of that season, saving just one. Montreal lost 110 games that year, which of course didn't leave many save chances.

In his first full year with Montreal, 1970, Claude made 59 relief appearances, accumulating a 6-7 record with a 4.43 ERA in 83.1 innings. He also saved 23 games, the fourth-best total in the National League that year. By 1971, however, Raymond didn't have much left. Indeed, his effort the year before may have been the result of sheer willpower. In 1971, the Expos acquired workhorse reliever Mike Marshall. Raymond pitched in 37 games and could manage only a 1-7 record. He was one game over .500 for his career before he joined the Expos, but pitching for an expansion team dropped his final won-lost record to 46-53.

After his playing career ended, Claude moved into the Expo broadcasting booth, and soon became the most popular play-by-play man in Montreal. In his career, Raymond pitched 721 innings while appearing in 449 games (all but seven in relief). He saved 83 games while fashioning an ERA of 3.66. His strikeout-to-walk ratio was an excellent 497 to 225. He stands fourth in games pitched among Canadians (behind Jenkins, John Hiller, and Ron Taylor) and is second only to Hiller in saves. He was elected to the Canadian Baseball Hall of Fame in 1984, and was only the second pitcher to be inducted.

Goodwin "Goody" Rosen   1937-1939, 1944-1946

They called Paul Waner (155 pounds) "Big Poison" and his brother Lloyd (150 pounds) "Little Poison," so perhaps the most appropriate nickname for Goodwin George Rosen (often under 140 pounds) would have been "Micro Poison." It ended up just being "Goody." That's better than "The Toronto Tidbit" or the "Stumpy Canadian," which some writers tried to hang on him. Goody Rosen was born in Toronto in 1912. His Jewish parents had arrived in Canada just two years earlier, fleeing the persecution of czarist Russia. Goody's first real experience with professional baseball was shagging fly balls for the Toronto Maple Leafs. He had unsuccessful stints with teams in Little Rock and Memphis, and finally signed to play for the Louisville Colonels of the American Association. One wonders why the Maple Leafs would not be interested in a local player possessing Rosen's obvious skills, but his small stature might have been a factor. Goody would actually play his last year of professional baseball with Toronto in 1947.

Rosen played with the Colonels from 1933 through 1937 before he finally made to the major leagues. He was a star and local favourite in Louisville, almost from the start. His only sub-.300 average there was a respectable .293 in 1935. He scored more than 100 runs four times and he made 200 hits in 1937, before moving up to the National League to play for the Dodgers. He was also a very fine outfielder, running down everything hit in his direction. He led the American Association in putouts and chances twice, with a high of 444 putouts in 1937. His manager with the Colonels was ex-spitballer Burleigh Grimes, and when Grimes was signed to manage the Brooklyn Dodgers in 1937, he persuaded them later that year to spend $125,000 on Rosen's Louisville contract. Rosen debuted with Brooklyn that September. The Dodgers of the 1930s were called the "Daffiness Boys," and were known more for their colourful characters than their talent. A few years later the Dodgers would become one of baseball's best teams, but in 1937 they were mired in the second division.

In 1938, Rosen's first full year in Brooklyn, Babe Ruth joined the team as a coach. Goody was a free spirit, known as a bit of a rebel himself, so he hit it off quite well with the former home run king. They must have been a pair to see. Rosen was only 145 pounds at best, and Ruth, whose weight exceeded 250 pounds in his final years as a player, probably doubled Goody's weight by then. Rosen batted .312 in 22 games with the Dodgers in 1937, and he hit .281 in 1938. Rosen had many skills as a player, collecting 11 triples and taking 65 walks. He led National League outfielders in assists (19) and fielding average (.989), making just three errors all season. Still only 25 years old at the time, Rosen, a Jewish ballplayer in Flatbush, should have been a fan favourite and productive outfielder for the next decade. It did not turn out that way at all.

Early in the 1939 season, Rosen hurt his leg while attempting to slide back into first base. Showing a toughness and willingness to put up with pain all too common during the Depression years, Rosen stayed in the lineup. Unfortunately, the leg injury interfered with his fluid swing at the plate. While his outfield play did not seem to suffer, his batting average dropped over 50 points in a month. Leo Durocher, by then the Brooklyn manager, informed Rosen that he was being sent down to Montreal (their International League farm team). Rosen maintains that it was Durcher who urged him to play hurt, saying that the Dodgers would not worry about the effect on his hitting. While his batting average had fallen to .251 with Brooklyn, Rosen recovered in Montreal and his average bounced back to the .300 level. The Dodgers sold him to the St. Louis Cardinals in the offseason, and they sent him to play in Columbus rather than the big leagues. There, Gooden clashed with manager Burt Shotton, and he was sent back to the Dodgers after batting only .212 in 10 games. Dodgers GM Larry MacPhail then peddled him to the Syracuse Chiefs of the International League.

While it looked like he would never be back to the major leagues, life in the high minors was different than it is today. Without television and all of the other professional sports to compete with, many minor league franchises served as the recreation and entertainment hub of their community. Rosen would star for the Syracuse Chiefs for five more years, leading them to two Little World Series Championships (the postseason playoff staged for the Triple-A leagues). He batted near the .300 mark each year, leading the league in walks in 1942, and again leading outfielders in putouts twice. Rosen might have finished his playing career in Syracuse, but for the shortage of able-bodied players to serve the needs of the major leagues during World War Two. In 1944, Syracuse made a deal to sell Rosen back to a major league club, but he was reluctant to leave. Branch Rickey was president of the Dodgers by then, and although he was never known as a spendthrift, Rickey offered Rosen enough money that he agreed to put up with the belligerent "Leo the Lip" once again. Rosen reported to Brooklyn in May of 1944, but Durocher used him only in a platoon role in center field for the remainder of the season. Although he batted just .261 in 89 games (with no home runs), his outfield play was sparkling. He averaged three putouts per game, while throwing out 12 baserunners in 65 games. His fielding average was an excellent .991.

The Dodgers had lost many of their star players to military service during the war years; after winning 104 games in 1942, they dropped to seventh place in 1944. Durocher's starting outfield for the 1945 season consisted of Luis Olmo in left, Brooklyn idol Dixie Walker in right, and rookie Red Duvrett in center field. When Duvrett became seriously ill, Leo inserted Rosen in the lineup, and he hit so well for the remainder of the year that his popularity rivaled even Walker's. The Dodger's rebounded to third place in 1945, thanks to the best-hitting lineup in the majors. Rosen, who had "bulked up" to over 160 pounds by then, had a spectacular year. He collected 197 hits in 145 games, good for a .325 batting average. He also scored 126 runs, and hit 11 triples and 12 home runs. His runs scored total has only been exceeded by Tip O'Neill among all Canadian batters. Goody was still spectacular in center field, making terrific catches day after day. He made 392 putouts and only three errors, so his fielding average was a fine .993. That year, Dixie Walker led the league with 124 RBI while batting an even .300, and Olmo was third in RBI with 110. Eddie Stanky, Brooklyn's scrappy second baseman, edged out Rosen for the league lead in runs scored, 128 to 126, while collecting a league record 148 walks. Rosen was named to the National League All-Star team, but the game was canceled in 1945 because of restrictions on wartime travel.

In 1946, most of the regulars returned to the major leagues from military service. For Brooklyn, Pete Reiser replaced Olmo in left and rookie star Carl Furillo took over in center field. Rosen was sold to the crosstown rival New York Giants on April 27, after three brief appearances with the Dodgers. Goody was stationed in right field by Giants manager Mel Ott. He was still productive at the plate and an effective outfielder, but when he crashed into a wall chasing a fly ball, his season and major league career were finished. He had batted .281 in 100 games with the Giants. After he returned home to Toronto, the Maple Leafs pressured him to play one more year in his home town, and Rosen was persuaded to take one last fling in 1947. While he batted just .274 for Toronto, he was still a brilliant outfielder, with a .993 average and 16 assists.

Goody had worked for Biltrite Industries in Toronto during his offseasons, and after retiring as a player he accepted a full-time position with them. Rosen became a successful business executive and was a big Blue Jays booster after the American League expanded to Toronto. He died in 1994, at the age of 81. Rosen's career totals were not what they might have been because of the interruption in his career, but he still finished with a .291 batting average in 551 games. His .989 career fielding average is second only to Terry Puhl among Canadians, and of course Puhl's percentage is the best ever. Rosen handled the most chances per game of any outfielder from Canada. Always very popular back in his hometown, he was elected to the Canadian Baseball Hall of Fame in 1984.

George "Twinkletoes" Selkirk   1934-1942

The job of being the man to replace Babe Ruth in right field in Yankee Stadium, was given to a Canadian, George Selkirk. George had spent eight long years in the minor leagues, waiting for a chance at the big time. When he became the New York Yankee right fielder in 1935, he even got to wear Ruth's uniform number three. After finally being given this opportunity, Selkirk played nine seasons with the Yankees, appearing in six World Series. The Yankees won five of those six, including four straight (1936-1939). Batting alongside Joe DiMaggio, Bill Dickey, and Lou Gehrig, George was a productive member of some of the finest baseball teams ever assembled.

George Selkirk was born in Huntsville, Ontario, in 1908, but his family moved to Rochester, New York, when he was just five years old. George developed in the strong high school baseball program there (he actually was a catcher when first scouted), then pursued a career in the minor leagues. After a brief stop at Rochester of the International League, where he batted only .222 in four games, he found his batting stroke in Cambridge (Eastern Shore League) in 1927. There, he hit .349 and connected for his first home runs as a professional ballplayer. George hit only three homers that year, while at the same time, that other George, George Herman Ruth, belted 60 for the Yankees. Selkirk was promoted to Jersey City of the International League for the 1928 season, and he then would play seven years for four different International League teams: Newark, Toronto, his hometown Rochester, and of course Jersey City. He made gradual progress over that time, batting .261 in 1928 and then .285 in 1929 while hitting 13 home runs, his first year in double figures. Still with Jersey City in 1930, he had one of his best years in the minors, batting .324 with 16 homers and 88 RBI. In 1931, Selkirk's final season at Jersey City, he batted .311 with 14 homers and 84 RBI. He split the 1932 season with three teams, Newark and Toronto of the International League, and Columbus of the American Association. He was back in the International League in 1933, where he hit 22 home runs and drove in 108 runs, while dividing his time between Rochester and Newark.

Still with Newark in 1934, he was batting .357 in early August, which finally earned him a call from the Yankees. His first game in the majors was on August 12, when he was inserted in right field for a doubleheader against the Boston Red Sox. Selkirk played in 46 games in what remained of the 1934 season, batting .313. He hit five home runs and drove in 38 runs while making just one error in 94 chances in the outfield. That was Ruth's last year with the Yankees; he still was good for 22 home runs and 84 RBI in 125 games in 1934. Disgruntled at not being given a chance to manage the Yankees, the Babe finished his career with the National League's Boston Braves in 1935. Selkirk became the Yankees' permanent right fielder in 1935, his first full year with the club. He responded by batting .312 in 128 games. "Twinkletoes" hit 11 homers and 12 triples, and knocked in 94 runs. George was given his nickname by a New Jersey sportswriter years earlier. He was a fast baserunner and could leg out his share of doubles and triples, but he also had a unique running style for a baseball player, rising high on his toes when in full flight. Actually, this is the normal form used by sprinters when competing in track events.

New York did not make it into the World Series in either of Selkirk's first two seasons with the club (unusual for them at the time), but by 1936, they had developed a powerhouse to rival even the famed 1927 Yankees. That '36 squad featured four Hall of Famers in Bill Dickey, Lou Gehrig, Tony Lazzeri, and rookie Joe DiMaggio. Selkirk, of course, was in right field, and he had one of his best years in 1936: 18 home runs, 107 RBI, and a .308 batting average in 137 games. The Yankees blasted 182 home runs and scored 1,065 runs, both figures exceeding the standards set by the 1927 club. It was also the only team in history that ever had five players with 100 or more RBI. The pitching staff was led by Red Ruffing and Lefty Gomez.

In the World Series that year, the Yankees faced the New York Giants, led by future Hall of Famers Mel Ott, Bill Terry, and pitcher Carl Hubbell. In his very first World Series at-bat, Selkirk blasted a home run into the upper right-field stands at the Polo Grounds off none other than Carl Hubbell. The Yankees lost anyway, 6-1. The Yankees came back with a vengeance, and took the Series by winning four of the next five games. Selkirk hit another home run to begin a comeback victory in Game 5. In the six-game Series, Selkirk batted .333 with six runs scored, three RBI and two home runs. Those homers, by the way, are the only ones hit by a Canadian in the World Series this century. In June of 1937, George was having his best season yet before breaking his collarbone diving for a catch in the outfield. He was batting .344 and tied for the AL lead in home runs at the time. After missing the next two months because of his injury, he returned to see his batting average drop to .328, and he would hit only one more home run to finish the year with 18 round trippers. In 1938, Selkirk was moved to left field when Tommy Henrich took over in right, and he could manage only a .254 batting average with 10 homers in 99 games. He bounced back in 1939 to enjoy what was probably his best year, as the Yankees took their fourth straight World Series title, this time in four straight games over Cincinnati. Selkirk batted .306 and hit 21 home runs. He drove in and scored more than one hundred runs (103 runs and 101 RBI), while drawing 103 walks. That made his on-base average .452, second in the league to Jimmie Foxx and just ahead of third place Joe DiMaggio (pretty good company!). George also led the league in fielding average by outfielders with a .989 mark.

After that, he began to fade, dropping to a .269 average and 19 homers in 118 games in 1940, just a .220 average in 70 games in 1941, and finally down to a .192 batting average (mostly as a pinch hitter) in his last year, 1942. George served in the U.S. Navy for the next three years, but he was not going to crack the outfield of DiMaggio, Henrich, and Charlie Keller in any case. When the war was over, the Yankees installed Selkirk as player-manager of their Newark farm club in the International League. George was still able to bat .300 in 31 games, but his team did not fare as well, finishing in fourth place. After several more years of managing five different clubs in the minor leagues, he returned to the American League to assume front-office duties with three different teams. He served as the general manager of the Washington Senators from 1962 to 1969, before going into semi-retirement as a scout for the New York Yankees in 1970. After a prolonged illness, he died in Fort Lauderdale, Florida, in 1987.

George finished his big league career with a .290 batting average in 846 games. His 108 home runs rank third among Canadians, behind Jeff Heath and Larry Walker. Because he drew so many walks, his on-base average (an even .400) is the best by any Canadian. Selkirk batted .265 in 21 World Series games, and he also played in two All-Star games. George was one of the first three ballplayers elected to the Canadian Hall of Fame (Phil Marchildon and Tip O'Neill being the other two) in the inaugural vote in 1983.

Charles "Pop" Smith   1880-1891

Charles Marvin Smith was born in Digby, Nova Scotia, in 1856. Like many other ballplayers of the 19th century, most details of his life outside of baseball are yet to be uncovered through investigative research. Having grown up in eastern Canada, the first "baseball" Smith learned to play was probably a game more closely resembling rounders, the "Massachusetts game." He came to the major leagues at the rather advanced age of 23, in 1880, playing second base for the Cincinnati Red Stockings of the National League. He and Arthur Irwin, who also began his career in 1880, were the second and third Canadian-born major league baseball players after Bill Phillips, who broke in the year before. Smith was frequently referred to as an agile infielder, with sure hands and an accurate arm. He was called "Pop" throughout his major league career.

Cincinnati was one of the founding members of the National League in 1876. After challenging for the pennant in 1878, the team dropped into the second division by 1879. After that, most of its top stars either transferred to other clubs or retired from baseball. Among those dropped from the 1879 team was second baseman Joe Gerhardt. Gerhardt had been a dependable batter, near .300 in the previous two seasons, but he slumped to .198 in 1879. That opened up a spot for Pop Smith, and he played every one of the team's 83 games at second base in his rookie 1880 campaign. Smith batted only .207 and he led NL second baseman with 87 errors. While this number of errors is unheard of today, several infielders made over 100 errors in the 19th century. Smith would never be known as a great hitter during his baseball career, but the scrappy infielder did hit the occasional long ball and he was a fine basestealer.

After finishing dead last in 1880, and trying to pay its bills by selling beer at its home games (which was against league rules then), the Cincinnati club was expelled from the NL at the end of the season. It would resurface again in 1882 in the newly formed American Association to capture that league's first pennant, but in the meantime Smith was in search of a new baseball job. He saw limited action with Cleveland, Worcester and Buffalo in 1881, and then with Baltimore and Louisville of new American Association in 1882. He totaled only 100 at-bats in those two seasons while playing a number of positions. However, when the American Association expanded from six teams to eight in 1883, Smith earned a regular job with the new Columbus Colts. Pop had his best year at the plate in 1883, leading the A.A. with 17 triples, and batting .262 while seeing action in every one of the Colts' 97 games. He continued in his role as a utility player, playing in 73 games at second and 24 games at third base. He even appeared in three games as a relief pitcher, allowing seven runs in five-plus innings. In 1884, Columbus made a serious challenge for the 1884 pennant, finishing in second place behind the New York Metropolitans. That year, Smith was used exclusively at second base, batting .238 in 108 games while leading the loop's second basemen in assists.

At the conclusion of the 1884 season, the AA cut back to eight teams, and Columbus was dropped from the league. In another bizarre move that seemed all too common at the time, most of the Columbus players, including Pop Smith, were picked up by the Pittsburgh Allegheny club. The Allegheny team was one of the original six 1882 American Association clubs, but they had finished near the bottom of the league in each of their first three seasons. The team hired Horace Phillips as its manager near the end of 1884 season. Phillips had managed Columbus in 1883, and in 1885 he brought many of his former players to Pittsburgh. The move worked for Phillips, as Pittsburgh immediately challenged for the AA pennant, finishing third in 1885 and second in 1886. Pop Smith was the regular second baseman for the Allegheny club in 1885, batting .249 in 106 games, while leading the league in both putouts and assists. In 1886, Pittsburgh picked up Sam Barkley to play second base, so Smith shifted to shortstop. Barkley had been the second baseman for the league champion St. Louis Browns in 1885, and was a better hitter than Smith, but probably not as skilled in the field. The move didn't seem to bother Smith much, as he led American Association shortstops in fielding percentage in 1886. He batted just .217, but stole 38 bases. This was the first season in which stolen bases were recorded, so Smith's known career total of 169 steals underestimates his real value in that department. Smith would steal 30 or more bases in four of his last six years.

Following their near miss in the 1886 pennant race, the Pittsburgh team left the American Association to join the more established National League for 1887. They found the competition a little stiffer in the NL, and dropped to sixth place. Barkley switched positions to play first base for the Allegheny club, so Smith was shifted back to second base in '87. He batted just .215 (he was "officially" listed as batting .263 because his 30 walks were counted as base hits in 1887). He also stole 30 bases and was hit by a pitch 13 times, the most ever for a Canadian in one season until Larry Walker was plunked 14 times in 1995. In 1888, Smith's batting average dropped to .206 as he saw infield duty at both shortstop and second base. He still managed to steal 37 bases, however. Mired near the .200 batting mark in 1889, Smith was sold to the National League Boston Beaneaters halfway through the season. This was actually a break for Smith, because Boston had assembled a good team in 1889 and finished a scant one game behind New York in the pennant race. Pop must have found the hitting infectious at Boston, because he batted

.260 after joining the club. He played shortstop for both Pittsburgh and Boston in 1889.

In 1890, most of the best Beaneaters moved to the new Boston Players League entry, and the National League club fell back into the second division. Smith remained loyal to the National League team (or else was not given the chance to play with the Players League club), and put in his last full year of major league ball. Herman Long, an outstanding shortstop, had joined the Boston team for 1890, so Smith was a second baseman again (he led the NL with 57 errors at that position). Pop batted .229, and as always, he found other ways to contribute to the team, drawing 80 walks, stealing 39 bases, and getting hit by nine pitches. In 1891, with the Players League just a memory and the regulars back in the NL, Smith found himself the victim of a youth movement in Boston. He caught on with Washington (American Association) in 1891, but was released after hitting .178 in 27 games. His major league career had spanned 12 seasons.

Pop Smith played in 1,093 games in the big leagues, batting just .224. He scored 633 runs while collecting 935 hits and 87 triples. He owns the dubious distinction of being hit by a pitch 60 times, a record for Canadian ball players. Actually, he was undoubtedly hit more often than that, but a batter was not awarded first base after being hit by a pitch until the 1884 season in the A.A. Remembered more for his fielding and baserunning than for his batting, Smith was also known to use "California tactics" against both umpires and opposing players. This referred to his attempts to upset opponents by shouting còlourful or insulting comments at them during the game. Smith died in 1927, while residing in Boston, Massachusetts.

Ron Taylor   1962-1972

Ron Taylor was Canada's best postseason pitcher. In two different World Series and one division playoff series, he did not allow a run in seven relief appearances. He also played key roles in two of the most exciting pennant races in National League history. Ron learned to pitch while growing up in Toronto. He was born there in 1937, and at the tender age of 17 was given a tryout with the Cleveland Indians. The year was 1955, and one of the people that took a turn catching Ron was Indians manager, former catcher, and future Hall of Famer Al Lopez. Taylor accepted a $4,000 bonus, signed a contract with Cleveland, and was told to report to their minor league spring training camp in Daytona Beach for 1956. With that club in the Florida State Instructional League, Taylor compiled a 17-11 won-lost record. He struck out 184 batters, while walking only 74 in 227 innings. That was quite a workload for an 18-year-old. Ron had dropped out of his final year of high school.

Up until that point, his story was not unlike that of thousands of other baseball prospects from across Canada and the USA. Then Taylor did something that did distinguish him from most would-be major leaguers. He received permission from the Indians to report late to his designated minor league assignment each year, while he finished his education. Thus Ron not only completed his high school education, but earned a degree in engineering from the University of Toronto. Even more amazing was the fact that he stood third in his graduating class in 1961. While doing that, he worked his way slowly through Cleveland's farm system. With Fargo-Moorhead (Class C) in 1957, he went 9-7 with a 3.40 ERA. The next season, with Minot of the Eastern League, he won 14 games, struck out 146 batters in 187 innings and led the league with five shutouts. While he would later be a relief pitcher in the majors, Ron was a starting pitcher everywhere he worked in the minors. The next three years would see only limited success for Taylor, as he was a .500 pitcher with earned-run averages near or above 4.00.

In 1962, Ron was invited to the Indians' major league training camp. There, his 21 innings of scoreless ball earned him a spot with Cleveland. His major league debut with the Tribe on April 11 may have been the best pitching performance of his whole career. After he had pitched 11 innings of a scoreless tie against the Boston Red Sox, the Indians left him on the mound for the 12th. One has to wonder what the effect from such an effort was on his pitching arm, but the effect in that one game was immediately apparent—he was rocked for a triple by the first batter, Carl Yastrzemski. After intentionally walking the next two batters, he served up a grand slam home run to Carroll Hardy. That game would be the high point of his rookie campaign. With the Indians, he gave up 36 hits and 23 runs in just 33 innings. He was sent down to regain his form with Jacksonville of the International League.

In Jacksonville, Taylor posted an excellent 12-4 record with a 2.62 ERA. Although he was ready for major league batters in 1963, it would not be with the Indians; they traded him and Jack Kubiszyn to the St. Louis Cardinals for rookie first baseman Fred Whitfield. The Cardinals had Bill White at first base, so Whitfield was expendable, but the Tribe would suffer for lack of pitching for decades to come. Ron joined a fine St. Louis team that would challenge the Sandy Koufax-led Dodgers for the NL championship. The Cardinals had Bob Gibson, Ernie Broglio, Curt Simmons, and Ray Sadecki in their starting rotation, so they converted Taylor to a relief pitcher. He appeared in 54 games in 1963 (all but nine in relief), posting a 9-7 record with an ERA of 2.84. He also had 11 saves, which tied for the club lead. In 1964, the Cardinals won an exciting three-way pennant race, clinching the title on the last day of the regular season. That was the year that Philadelphia blew a six-game lead with only 11 to play. Taylor and Barney Schultz were the top Cardinal relievers. While his ERA ended up at 4.62, Ron still managed an 8-4 record with seven saves in 63 games.

St. Louis was going against the New York Yankees in the 1964 World Series. The Yankee team, featuring Mantle, Maris, and Whitey Ford, was making its fifth straight appearance in the fall classic, so they were experienced in pressure situations, and confident of victory. However, this turned out to be the first of three outstanding World Series performances for Bob Gibson. He struck out a Series-record 31 batters in 27 innings, winning two games. For his part, Taylor was just about perfect. A walk to Mickey Mantle was the only baserunner that he permitted in the 4.2 innings he worked in his two relief appearances. Taylor earned a save in Game 4 by pitching 4 scoreless innings after St. Louis had taken a 4-3 lead in the top half of the sixth inning on Ken Boyer's grand slam home run. He was the second of five pitchers for the Cards in Game 6, and recorded two outs on one pitch as his mound opponent, Jim Bouton, lined into a double play to end the seventh inning. Although St. Louis lost that game 8-3, they came back to claim the championship with a 7-5 win in the deciding game, as Bob Gibson tossed a complete-game victory.

In 1965, Taylor was hospitalized for six weeks with a herniated disk. Then, along with Mike Cuellar, he was traded to the Houston Astros for Chuck Taylor and Hal Woodeshick. His combined record for both clubs was 3-6, with an ERA of 5.60. In Houston, he joined Canadian Claude Raymond in the bullpen for a year and a half. But he was even worse the next year, surrendering a 5.71 ERA in 36 games. He had no saves in 1966, the only time that would happen between 1963 and 1971. After Houston gave up on him, Taylor cleared waivers and was picked up by the New York Mets for the 1967 season. This team would not transform itself into the Miracle Mets for two more years. It was still a club that had never climbed higher than ninth place, and whose best record was 95 losses in 1966. They were in the NL basement in 1967, losing 101 games, but somehow Taylor managed to come back and have a good year. Although his record was 4-6, he had a sparking 2.34 ERA and saved eight games. In 1968 the Mets brought up Jerry Koosman (who would be Taylor's roommate) to go with Tom Seaver, who was the Rookie of the Year in 1967. Gary Gentry arrived in 1969, and now with a young Tug McGraw joining Taylor in the bullpen, the Mets' pitching could hold their own with anybody. Ron was 1-5 in 1968, but still had an impressive 2.70 ERA with 13 saves.

Although 1969 will always be remembered as the year that the Cubs folded in the stretch drive, maybe the Mets should be given more credit for their fine season. After all, they did win 100 contests, an improvement of 27 games, in going from ninth to first. For his part, Taylor posted a 9-4 record with a 2.72 ERA, while again saving 13 games. In the League Championship Series, the Mets swept the Atlanta Braves in three straight games. Taylor was outstanding in postseason play once again, saving a victory for Tom Seaver in Game 1, and earning a win in relief of Jerry Koosman in Game 2. In the World Series, the Baltimore Orioles were heavily favoured. Besides having the Robinson boys, Frank and Brooks, and an All-Star at almost every position, the Oriole pitching staff—including Cuellar, Jim Palmer and Dave McNally—looked to be every bit the equal of the Mets. Many observers considered the Baltimore club, which had won 109 games in the regular season, as one of the best of all time. However good they were, the Orioles were not miracle workers like the Mets, and they fell in five games. In addition to fine pitching, this series featured a daily outstanding outfield catch, typically made by players whose reputations suggested only a defensive liability. Taylor was unhittable once more, giving up only a harmless walk to Paul Blair in 2.1 innings. . . and then he picked Blair off first base. Taylor pitched the last two innings of the first game, and then saved Game 2 for Jerry Koosman by getting Brooks Robinson to ground out in the ninth with the winning runs on base. Ron had not given up a single hit in seven pressure-packed innings of World Series play.

Ron had two more productive seasons pitching in relief for the Mets, but the end was near. He was sold to the Expos in October, 1971, but after being released in spring training he was picked up by the San Diego Padres. He pitched only four games for them, and was released once more. After his baseball career was over, Taylor could of course fall back on his engineering degree, but the only offers for jobs that he received were for Ron Taylor, World Series hero, to go into sales. Then he did something that was probably more difficult than pitching against major league batters. At age 34 he decided to get another degree, this time in medicine. First he had to complete a make-up year, taking four difficult science courses. Remember, he had been away from his studies for a dozen years, and organic chemistry was never a popular topic of conversation among ball players. He was managing an amateur baseball team in Alberta, while waiting to hear from Toronto on his grades in those make-up courses. It turned out that his marks were the same as his World Series pitching; perfect, straight A's. Taylor completed his medical degree in 1977, and now serves as one of the team doctors for the Blue Jays. In addition to having his own practice, Taylor runs a sports medicine clinic in Toronto. It must seem almost dull to a World Series hero.

Taylor's career record as a pitcher reads: 491 games, exactly 800 innings, 3.93 ERA. He also posted 72 saves. The games pitched and saves both rank third among Canadian pitchers. Taylor was elected to the Canadian Baseball Hall of Fame in 1985, the same year that John Hiller went in. In 1993, Taylor was elected to the Canadian Sports Hall of Fame. Along with Jenkins and Phil Marchildon, he is one of only three baseball pitchers to be honoured with such a selection.

Larry Walker   1989-1995

On August 24, 1995, Larry Walker crushed a pinch-hit, three-run home run off Jason Christiansen to help his new team, the Colorado Rockies, defeat Pittsburgh 8-6. That was his 28th home run of the year, and a new single-season record for Canadian sluggers. Walker was just getting started, and would wind up with 36 homers for the season. In April of 1995, after becoming a free agent, Larry had signed a four-year deal with the Rockies. Walker will be playing half his games in the rarefied atmosphere of Denver's Coors Field, which should just about guarantee that Larry will one day own the career mark for home runs by a Canadian as well. Jeff Heath still has that record, having finished his career with 194 round trippers. However, Larry Walker should be remembered as far more than a slugger who benefited from playing in Colorado's thin air. He is a fine all-around player, and is in fact the only Canadian to have won a Gold Glove Award for his fielding at any position. He garnered Gold Gloves for his right-field play in both 1992 and '93. He was also named an outfielder on the National League Silver Slugger Team in 1992 while with the Expos.

Larry was born in Maple Ridge, British Columbia, in 1966. He excelled at hockey, playing as a goalie, and even had a tryout with the Regina Pats. When he took up baseball in a serious way at age 17, he looked like a natural. Walker was scouted and signed in 1984 by Jim Fanning, at that time director of scouting for the Expos. Even then, Walker had all the requirements to make it as a big leaguer: power, speed, a strong throwing arm, and that smooth, quick batting stroke that you can witness today. He began his minor league apprenticeship at Utica of the New York-Pennsylvania League. He played first and third base there, batting only .223 with little power. In 1986, he divided his season between Burlington of the Midwest League and West Palm Beach of the Florida State League, both Class-A designations. In 95 games at Burlington, he walloped 29 home runs and led the league in slugging average (.623). He also shifted to the outfield that year. In 1987, he played for Jacksonville of the Southern League, and continued to progress. He slugged 26 home runs, stole 24 bases, and batted in 83 runs.

Walker was touted as a genuine prospect with a chance to play for Montreal in 1988, but instead he ended up missing the entire season after he tore up his knee while playing winter ball in Mexico. He needed surgery to repair a mangled anterior cruciate ligament, and spent most of the year in rehabilitation. In 1989, Walker rebounded strongly from the mishap. Playing with Indianapolis of the American Association, he batted .270 with 12 home runs in 114 games. He led the league in outfield assists (18) and, most surprisingly, even managed to steal 36 bases. Apparently he had regained his full mobility. Larry was called up to Montreal in August, but there he batted only .170 in 20 games against National League pitching.

In 1990, Walker, along with Delino DeShields and Marquis Grissom, gave the Expos fans three exciting young rookies to watch. DeShields batted .289 and stole 42 bases while holding down second base; Grissom batted .257 and stole 22 bases while playing in centre alongside Walker, who was stationed in right field. Larry stole 21 bases and hit 19 home runs, just missing becoming the first Canadian to reach 20 homers and steals in the same season. On the other hand, he batted only .241 while striking out 112 times, and that still stands as the single-season high for a Canadian batter. Since Tim Raines was still playing left field for the Expos then, Montreal had the most stolen bases (235) of any team in the NL. Walker showed improvement in almost all facets of the game in 1991, raising his batting average to .290, while hitting 16 homers and 30 doubles in only 487 at-bats. In the outfield, his two errors left him with an excellent .991 fielding average. However, the team dropped to last place in the NL East. Things would get better, both for Montreal and for Walker, the following season.

The Expos started slowly in 1992, and the team changed managers after losing 20 of their first 37 games, hiring Felipe Alou. The Expos responded with a complete turnaround, climbing all the way to second place by season's end. Larry had probably the best overall season of any Canadian playing in this century; only Jeff Heath's 1941 campaign, and Walker's own 1995 performance, can compare with it. Larry batted .301, belted 23 home runs, knocked in 93 runs, and stole 18 bases. In the outfield he was a thrill to watch, making impossible catches while showing off perhaps the best throwing arm in the league. Some observers even compared Walker's cannon to that of Roberto Clemente. Walker threw out 16 enemy baserunners and compiled a .993 fielding average (two errors). His most exciting play was to charge in and fire the ball to first base when the opposing batter was jogging down the line after getting a "sure" base hit to right field. Walker once threw out Tony Gwynn on just this type of play in San Diego. He won the Gold Glove Award for his fielding, and was a member of the Silver Slugger Team, the only Canadian ever to claim either award. (However, it should be noted that the Gold Glove Award was first instituted in 1957 and the Silver Slugger Team presented only since 1980. More than likely, George Gibson or Goody Rosen would have won a Gold Glove had the award existed when they were playing.) Needless to say, Walker was also selected to play in the All-Star game; he pinch hit for Greg Maddux, and singled. To top his season off, Walker placed fifth in the NL MVP vote.

In 1993, the Expos finished second once more, just three games behind the Philadelphia Phillies. Walker's batting average dropped to .265, but he still hit 22 home runs and stole 29 bases. Now he was the first Canadian 20-20 man. He also drew a career-high 80 walks and repeated as a Gold Glove outfielder. In 1994, Walker and the Expos were poised to climb to even greater heights, when the player's strike ended a year of promise in Montreal. By August, the Expos' 74-40 record was the best in the majors. Walker was batting .322 with 19 homers, 86 RBI, and 15 steals (in just 103 games). He had hit an incredible 44 doubles as well, and was on pace to break the National League's all-time record of 64 two-baggers in a season. Teammate Moises Alou, manager Felipe's son, was batting .339 with 22 home runs. Grissom had 36 steals and 96 runs scored (second in the NL). Pitcher Ken Hill was leading National League pitchers with 16 wins. But on August 12, it was all over, as the players went on strike once again. The World Series was cancelled for 1994, and no team was hurt more than Montreal. By the start of the 1995 season, Walker, Grissom, Hill, and relief ace John Wetteland were no longer Expos. The "new economic realities" left the Montreal team in intensive care, and rumours abounded that the franchise would have to be relocated.

After signing with the Colorado Rockies, Walker found himself part of a record-breaking wrecking crew. In addition to his 36 home runs and 101 RBI, Andres Galarraga belted 31 home runs with 106 RBI. Dante Bichette led the NL with 40 homers and 128 RBI, while Vinny Castilla blasted 32 round trippers and drove in 90 runs (his previous major league high in home runs was only nine). Colorado became just the second team in history to have four players with 30 or more home runs (the Dodgers in 1977 were the first club to accomplish this). Walker had perhaps his best year to date, placing second in the NL in six batting categories, including home runs (36), slugging average (.607) and total bases (300). Still the complete ballplayer, he also stole 16 bases and made only three errors while displaying one of the most feared outfield arms in baseball. The Rockies battled with the Dodgers for the Western Division lead all season, with Los Angeles finally winning out by a single game. There were now three division winners in the NL, with one wild-card entry also going to the playoffs. Walker led the Rockies to that wild-card spot by hitting home runs in each of the last two games of the season as Colorado beat out Houston by one game. However, the Rockies fell to the pitching-rich Atlanta Braves in the Divisional Play-offs, three games to one.

Walker now seems ready to fulfill his promise and become the greatest Canadian non-pitcher ever to play major league baseball. The one blemish on his sparkling record has been the games he has missed each year from the nagging injuries he sustains from playing the game so aggressively. It would seem that only a prolonged player strike or a serious injury can deny him most of the Canadian career batting records. He already holds the single-season 20th-century standards for home runs (36), doubles (44, in the abbreviated 1994 season), slugging average (.607) and intentional walks (20). He even set the Canadian-born record for the most times being hit by a pitch, with 14 in 1995. His career totals have already reached 135 home runs, 485 RBI, and 114 stolen bases. All of Canada's baseball fans will watch the pride of Maple Ridge, British Columbia with eager anticipation as he roughs up NL pitching for the next decade. If he plays in Coors Field long enough, Walker might even be a serious candidate for the National Baseball Hall of Fame in Cooperstown.

Pete Ward   1962-1970

Pete Ward picked the wrong place and the wrong time to demonstrate his hitting prowess in major league baseball. Ward, who played briefly with the Baltimore Orioles in 1962 and the New York Yankees in 1970, was a fixture in the Chicago White Sox lineup in the intervening years. At the urging of commissioner Ford Frick, the owners implemented two new rules for the 1963 season, after a few of baseball's most cherished records had tumbled in 1961 and 1962. First, they increased the size of the strike zone. It had been between the batter' knees and armpits before 1963 (and was changed back to that again for the 1969 season), but from 1963 through 1968 it was between the batter's knees and shoulders. Second, they raised the height of the pitcher's mound from 10 inches to 15. The combined effects of these changes would cause batting averages, home-run totals, and run production to plummet. The levels of offensive production reached historic lows by 1968, when Carl Yastrzemski won the AL batting crown with just a lowly .301 batting average. At the same time, baseball's attendance figures and revenue were going in the same direction as the game's offensive statistics. Finally, the rule changes of 1963 were reversed, and .300 batting averages and 40-homer seasons returned to major league baseball.

However, Pete Ward had spent his best years playing in this period when the hitters were on the endangered species list. Furthermore, he plied his trade for the White Sox, a team which did not have a single player reach 30 home runs in one season until 1970. Given the dimensions of their home, Comiskey Park, home runs were merely a dream for most players. It was 350 feet down the lines and nearly 380 feet in the power alleys. For years, the White Sox stars would be singles and doubles hitters like Luke Appling and Nellie Fox. If Pete Ward had remained with the Baltimore Orioles, with whom he had originally signed, it would have been his Canadian home-run record that Larry Walker was chasing, and not Jeff Heath's. However, a great natural hitter like Pete Ward can't be kept down forever, and he still managed to have a few good seasons with the bat in Chicago.

Pete's dad, a forward in the National Hockey League, was a hockey star for twelve years. Jimmy Ward spent all but one of those seasons with the Montreal Maroons, including 1934-35 when they won the Stanley Cup. Playing in the 1930s, when hockey had its own period of low-scoring games, the elder Ward collected 147 goals and 127 assists in his 532-game career. Pete was born in Montreal in 1939, his dad's final year in the NHL. When he was just eight years old, the Wards moved to Portland, Oregon, where father Jimmy organized a high school hockey program. Pete's older brother, Jimmy Jr., was a hockey star in high school and also at Michigan State University, but Pete excelled at baseball and basketball.

Pete signed to play baseball for the Baltimore Oriole organization, and was sent to Vancouver of the Pacific Coast League to try out with them at the conclusion of the 1958 season. Despite the fact that he batted .353 in 11 games there, it was clear that he needed more playing time in the lower minors. Ward went to Stockton of the California League (Class C ball) for 1959, and hit 16 homers while batting .321 there. He divided his playing time between third base and shortstop. In 1960 he moved up to the Three-I league with Fox Cities, where he won the batting crown with a .345 average. He also scored 109 runs and batted in 105, but he led third basemen with 32 errors. In 1961, he split the season between Little Rock, Arkansas, and Ardmore, Texas. That year, he spent most of his time in the outfield. Finally he broke through and earned a shot at the big leagues in 1962. That year, with Rochester of the International League, Pete batted .328 and hit 22 home runs. He led the league in runs scored (114) and doubles (34), while splitting his time between the outfield and third base. He was summoned to Baltimore, and made his debut on September 21, 1962. He played in the outfield and batted just .143 in eight games before season's end.

The Orioles knew that Ward would be a good hitter at whatever position he played, but it was obvious that it wouldn't be third base, not with Brooks Robinson around. In January of 1963, the Orioles pulled off a huge deal with the Chicago White Sox. They sent Pete, along with Hoyt Wilhelm, shortstop Ron Hansen and outfielder Dave Nicholson, to the Sox for Luis Aparicio and outfielder Al Smith. Both Hansen and Smith were former All-Stars, but Wilhelm and Aparicio were the most significant players in the deal. Hoyt Wilhelm was probably the greatest relief pitcher of all time, while Luis Aparicio was regarded as the best shortstop in baseball. Both are now in the Hall of Fame. So Pete could look forward to going to spring training camp with the White Sox, and not the Orioles. He was inserted into the Chicago lineup at third base right from the start, and he immediately began to wear out American League pitching. In fact, on Opening Day, Ward hit a game-winning home run. By the end of the 1963 season, Ward had belted 22 home runs, driven in 84 runs and batted .295. He ranked fifth in the AL in batting, and he placed second in hits (177), doubles (34), and total bases (289). He also played 154 games at third base, where he led the league in errors with 38. In June of that year, he had an 18-game hitting streak, the longest in the AL in 1963. For his outstanding season, Pete was voted the American League's Rookie Player of the Year by *The Sporting News*. Despite his great year, he had some strong competition for the award in the person of Jimmy Hall, who belted 33 home runs as a rookie for the Minnesota Twins.

In 1964, Ward continued his assault on American league hurlers. His batting average dropped slightly to .282, but he increased his home runs and RBI to 23 and 94, respectively. He also cut down his errors at third base to 19, and among AL third basemen was near the leaders in putouts, assists, and chances per game. However, the 1964 season also demonstrated the effect that playing in Comiskey Park would have on a slugger like Ward. That season he hit 14 home runs on the road, only nine at home. If he had been playing with the Cubs on the North Side of Chicago, he almost certainly would have hit 30-odd homers that year. The White Sox were in first place going into the last week of that season, but in the end they fell one agonizing game short, as the New York Yankees won 11 straight games to nose out the Sox. The Sox were second again in 1965, their third straight year as runners-up, despite Ward's slump at the plate. He batted only .247, with 10 home runs and 57 RBI. While he and Tommy John were driving to a Chicago Black Hawks game, they were involved in an automobile accident. Pete suffered neck and back injuries that were to plague him for the rest of his career.

In 1966, Ward developed a hernia problem and had to undergo surgery in June. He missed half of his team's games that year, and saw his batting average fall to .219. His back problems could probably be traced back to that auto accident, and he was never really the same player. Still, he did rebound to hit 18 home runs in 1967, as the White Sox were involved in a tight four-way pennant race. After two more seasons with limited production (he hit 15 homers in 1968 but never lifted his batting average back to the .250 level), Ward was dispatched to the New York Yankees. In December of 1969, he was traded for pitcher Mickey Scott and an undisclosed amount of cash. In his last seasons with the White Sox, Ward saw significant action at first base and in the outfield as well as at third base. In 1970 with New York, he appeared in just 66 games, primarily as a pinch hitter. It would be his last year in the major leagues. Pete was always a fine hitter coming off the bench, and in fact he led the American League with 17 pinch hits in 1968. His career average as a pinch hitter was an outstanding .280 (35 hits in 125 at-bats), 26 points better than his lifetime batting average.

When his big league career was over, Pete spent seven years working in the Yankees farm system. He was a minor league coach at Rochester and then managed Fort Lauderdale of the Florida State League for three years. Next he managed at West Haven of the Eastern League in 1975 and 1976. Ward's teams won two pennants. Finally he became a coach with the Atlanta Braves for the 1978 season. Ward then returned "home" to Oregon, where he now operates a travel agency. Pete had obtained his bachelor of science degree in business administration in Portland during the offseason while he was a player. In his nine-year major league career, he belted 98 home runs and collected 776 hits in 973 games. He stands fourth in homers among Canadians, behind only Heath, Walker, and George Selkirk. If he had played in a different ballpark at a different time, or had avoided injuries, Pete Ward would have had a better chance to reach his full potential as a talented hitter. He was elected to the Canadian Baseball Hall of Fame in 1991.

The All-Stars

Selecting an all-star team from the 179 Canadians who played in the major leagues may at first appear to reflect an inappropriate use of the term "all-star." A lineup of even the best of the Canadians certainly pales next to the great baseball stars who were born in America. Only one Canadian pitcher has won more than 110 games, and no Canadian batter this century has finished with either a career average of .300 or as many as 200 home runs. Our baseball stars also seem to fall well short of the standards of excellence set by the Canadians who have dominated the NHL for many decades. Gordie Howe, Jean Beliveau, Bobby Orr and Wayne Gretzky, to name just a few Canadian hockey giants, were clearly the best in the world at their profession. Except for Fergie Jenkins winning a single Cy Young Award, no Canadian baseball player was ever voted as the best in any league for even one season. Nevertheless, the exercise of selecting the Canadian baseball all-stars is a worthwhile venture, and the players chosen are deserving of our highest accolades and deepest respect. We sometimes sour on the arrogance and greed displayed by too many of today's professional sports figures, but we should not lose sight of the fact that any baseball player who makes it to the major leagues, even for a couple of at-bats or innings pitched, is an outstanding athlete. These Canadians have had to overcome still longer odds to make it there.

Some of the choices for a position on this mythical team of all-stars are easy ones. Bill Phillips played more than five times as many games at first base than the number-two Canadian on the list, and selecting Ferguson Jenkins as our best starting pitcher is akin to proclaiming that Mario Lemieux is a better hockey player than Mario Andretti. However, some choices for positions are open to endless debate, and in the end, come down to subjective opinions. Thus, the following all-star selections are reasonable, but not necessarily definitive.

First Base

Let's start with an easy spot. Bill Phillips will not be known to most baseball fans today, but he is fully deserving of the selection. Phillips was recognized as a fine fielder and reliable batter in his day. The very first Canadian big-leaguer, he was also the first to collect 1,000 base hits. Bill played 1,032 games at first base and led the league in many fielding categories at that position during his 10-year career. Tim Harkness is second in games played at first base with 199. It seems appropriate that the first Canadian big leaguer is also the first-base all-star. Just write the name Bill Phillips of New Brunswick on the all-star scorecard, then move to the next position.

Second Base

Pop Smith leads Canadian second basemen in all categories but fielding average (Dave McKay holds down the top spot there), but fielding averages were of course much lower in the nineteenth century. Smith leads John O'Brien, the number-two man in games played at second base, 711 to 498. Smith's career batting average was just .224, but he was a good baserunner and even showed a little power for that era. He was also a versatile fielder, playing at shortstop and third base. O'Brien could not carry Smith's glove, and although he played in the 1890s when batting averages were the highest in the history of the game, he hit just .254. Dave McKay was the first Canadian to play for the Toronto Blue Jays, and he helped Oakland win a division championship in 1981. He was also the only Canadian to hit a home run in his very first major league at-bat. While it is very difficult to compare a player from the 1880s with one from the 1980s, McKay was no better when compared to his contemporaries than was Smith, and he played 400 fewer games, even though his schedule was much longer each season. Hence, the selection for our second baseman must go to another nineteenth-century Maritimer, Nova Scotia's Charles "Pop" Smith.

Third Base

Here we have the first real competition for a place on the team. The top candidates at third base are Frank O'Rourke and Pete Ward. O'Rourke played 598 games at the hot corner to Ward's 562, and he was clearly a better fielder than Ward. He leads Canadian third basemen in all fielding categories except assists (Ward leads, 1182-1101). Frank even compiled a higher fielding average than Pete did, and he played 40 years earlier, when fielding averages were generally lower. O'Rourke also played many games at shortstop and second base and he had more games played and hits in his career than did Ward. However, when it comes to batting, there is simply no comparison. Both men posted .254 career batting averages, but Ward played in Comiskey Park at a time when hitters were setting records for futility. On the other hand, O'Rourke performed in the 1920s when pitchers were routinely battered by the hitting onslaught. Pete was a fine power hitter and run-producer who could have been one of the most productive Canadian batters to play the game if not for the injuries which he sustained in an auto accident. If he had played for Detroit and St. Louis in the 1920's, as O'Rourke did, he might have driven in 120 runs a year. So the all-star third baseman is Pete Ward from Quebec.

Shortstop

Frank O'Rourke is back again for consideration as the best shortstop too. His 288 games played at that position ranks third among Canadians, while Pop Smith, the man in second place with 332 games, is already our all-star at second base. But the player with the most games at shortstop is really the only reasonable selection here. Arthur Irwin, another nineteenth century player, was not only a flashy performer with the glove (and the fielder's glove was probably his invention) but was also steady with the bat. Of Irwin's 1,010 games in the major leagues, 947 were at shortstop. He batted .241 and was regarded as a daring baserunner. His knowledge of baseball was also well-respected by his peers. Irwin managed 863 major league games, winning a pennant in 1891. Arthur was from a baseball family, and his brother John, also born in Toronto, played in over 300 big-league games. With Ontario's Irwin selected as the shortstop on our all-star team, we now have four provinces represented.

Catcher

Possibly the best Canadian catcher is not eligible for selection by our rules because he was born in Ireland. However, Jimmy Archer deserves a mention here. He was a very good fielder (the catcher to throw effectively from the squat position) and a steady hitter for his 847-game career. Of the catchers born in Canada, three must be considered: George "Moon" Gibson, Jay "Nig" Clarke, and John "Larry" McLean. All were outstanding fielders and hit just enough to hold down a regular spot in the lineup. Still, Gibson gets the nod here. He caught more games than any of the others (1,194), and set significant major league fielding records during his playing days. George was one of the leaders on a great team, and respected throughout major league baseball. He is best remembered for taming Ty Cobb on the basepaths during the 1909 World Series, when his Pirates became world champions. Gibson also managed in the big leagues and brought home three second-place finishes during his seven years at the helm. Since Gibson was born in London, he is the second all-star selected from Ontario.

The Outfielders

Because none of Canada's best outfielders played very many games in centre field (with apologies to Goody Rosen, who did), we will pick the outfield all-star spots the same way that major league managers and coaches select Gold Glove winners, and simply choose any three outfielders, regardless of whether they played left, centre or right field.

Six Canadians must be considered here, and it is a shame that three of them won't make the team, because they were all probably better ballplayers than any of the infield all-stars. The six finalists are Tip O'Neill, Jack Graney, George Selkirk, Jeff Heath, Terry Puhl and Larry Walker. As intimated above, Goody Rosen, and also Doc Miller, were also very good outfielders, but not in the same class as these six.

Tip O'Neill was consistently one of the best hitters in the American Association during the 1880's, and was also a steady left fielder. Whether the American Association featured competition that compared with the National League can be debated, but a .400 hitter with power, in any league, must have been a pretty frightening sight at the plate for the pitcher that had to face him. Jack Graney was a fine leadoff batter, twice leading the American League in walks, and was a solid left fielder and steady baserunner. Graney spent most of his career in the dead-ball era, so his batting statistics are not as impressive as Selkirk's or Heath's, but if he had been born 10 years later, he might well have compared favourably with either of those players.

Selkirk's career was not as long as Graney's or Heath's, but then again, he had to wait for Babe Ruth to vacate his position before he got to wear a Yankees uniform. Selkirk was the complete player: good power, speed, and fielding skills. His ability to draw walks earned him the highest on-base average of any Canadian. Jeff Heath has the most impressive batting statistics of any Canadian since the glory days of Tip O'Neill. In 1941 his production was not far behind that of Ted Williams and Joe DiMaggio, when they were at the top of their games. Heath was not the most respected player on any of the teams for which he starred, but the left fielder was a batting force to be reckoned with throughout his career. Two serious injuries in his last two seasons prevented him from accumulating even more impressive career statistics.

Terry Puhl was another player who excelled in all aspects of the game. He was a fine outfielder with a picture-perfect swing. He may have been the best baserunner of any Canadian to play the game. His batting statistics were seriously diminished by having to play half of his games in the Houston Astrodome. During his career, Puhl hit nearly twice as many home runs on the road as he did at home, 41-21. If Puhl had played with the Cubs or Red Sox, he would have batted .300 with 15 homers each year. His career was also cut short by injuries, but he was an exciting player to watch and he earned the respect of his teammates and opponents. Larry Walker has played in just 805 games through 1995, so part of his ranking must be based on his potential. Still, Walker has already reached some lofty accomplishments that no other Canadian has. His two Gold Glove Awards attest to his fielding skills, and his throwing arm is one of the best in the game. Walker has now established himself as a .300 hitter with excellent power who can steal a base when required. If he can avoid serious injuries, he should finish up with 300 home runs and 200 stolen bases. He is also a threat to win an MVP award one of these years.

It is indeed a shame that three of these six players won't be on the all-star team, but Tip O'Neill, Jeff Heath, and Larry Walker are our chosen three to patrol the outfield. That adds two more players from Ontario (O'Neill and Heath) and the first from the west, British Columbia's Larry Walker.

The Pitchers

We will select one starting pitcher and one relief pitcher to round out the all-star team. Reggie Cleveland, Russ Ford, and Kirk McCaskill were fine major league pitchers, and Phil Marchildon and Dick Fowler, who lost three of their peak years to war service and toiled for last-place teams much of their careers, never did receive the recognition they each deserved. However, there simply is no contest for Canada's best starting pitcher. Ferguson Jenkins' outstanding accomplishments do not need to be recounted here, but it is important to remember that his statistics were hurt by his home ballpark as much as those of Terry Puhl and Pete Ward. Jenkins spent over half of his career pitching in Wrigley Field, and then two more seasons in Boston's Fenway Park. If he had played in the Astrodome or Dodger Stadium, his career ERA would have been about 2.80, and then he might have been recognized as being the equal of Tom Seaver. Hall of Famer Fergie Jenkins put Canada firmly and proudly on the baseball map.

There is a little more competition for our all-star relief pitcher. Although the bullpen stopper did not come into his own until after 1940, and very few pitchers specialized in this role before the 1960s, there are still three good candidates here. John Hiller, Claude Raymond and Ron Taylor all were impressive relief pitchers for many years. Taylor was easily Canada's best pitcher in postseason play, and was a highly-regarded pitcher for a decade. Claude Raymond was not only the first Canadian to play major league ball for a Canadian team, but he had five seasons in which his ERA was under three. However, John Hiller was not only a fine Canadian relief pitcher, but was one of the greatest from any country. His record-smashing 1973 season may have been the best ever posted by any relief pitcher. After recording an ERA under three for eight different seasons, he retired with a career mark of 2.83. He saved 125 games and stands second only to Jenkins in games pitched and strikeouts. Hiller is our all-star relief pitcher. The selection of these two Ontario pitchers brings the total number from that province to six.

These all-stars seem to epitomize the Canadian character, at least as we perceive it. The players show more dependability than brilliance, more dignity than bravado, and perhaps, just more survival than splendor. How long it will be until a future Canadian is able to replace one of these all-stars remains to be seen. No immediate threats are on the horizon, but since these players starred in every era of baseball's first 120 years, it should not be long before some other Canadian all-star makes his presence felt.

For now, you may examine all of the written evidence and make your own selections. The most complete records ever published, for all of the 179 Canadian ball players, are presented here. Their full batting, pitching, and fielding statistics are given for regular and postseason play. In addition there are extensive lists of leaders in all significant single season and career categories. If a Canadian recorded it in a major league game, it is shown in the pages that follow.

The Canadian All-Stars

CENTRE FIELD: JEFF HEATH

LEFT FIELD: TIP O'NEILL   RIGHT FIELD: LARRY WALKER

SHORTSTOP: ARTHUR IRWIN   SECOND BASE: POP SMITH

THIRD BASE: PETE WARD   FIRST BASE: BILL PHILLIPS

STARTING PITCHER: FERGUSON JENKINS

RELIEF PITCHER: JOHN HILLER

CATCHER: GEORGE GIBSON

The Complete List Of Major League Baseball Players Born In Canada

Players in **boldface** were active in 1995

Player	Years in Major Leagues	Games	Positions
Alexander, Bob	1955, 1957	9	P
Andrus, Wiman	1885	1	3B
Atkinson, Bill	1976 - 1979	99	P
Bahr, Ed	1946 - 1947	50	P
Balaz, John	1974 - 1975	59	OF DH
Barton, Vince	1931 - 1932	102	OF
Boucher, Denis	1991 - 1994	35	P
Bowsfield, Ted	1958 - 1964	235	P
Burgess, Tom "Tim"	1954, 1962	104	1B OF
Butler, Rob	1993 - 1994	58	OF
Buxton, Ralph	1938, 1949	19	P
Calvert, Paul	1942 - 1945, 1949 - 1951	110	P
Cameron, Jack	1906	1906	P OF
Casey, Orrin "Bob"	1882	9	3B 2B
Clarke, Jay "Nig"	1905 - 1911, 1919 - 1920	506	C 1B
Cleveland, Reggie	1969 - 1981	428	P
Cockman, Jim	1905	13	3B
Collins, "Chub"	1884 - 1885	97	2B SS
Colman, Frank	1942 - 1946	271	OF 1B
Congalton, "Bunk"	1902, 1905 - 1907	310	OF
Cook, Earl	1941	1	P
Cormier, Rheal	**1991 - 1995**	**135**	**P**
Cort, Barry	1977	7	P
Craig, Pete	1964 - 1966	6	P

Player	Years in Major Leagues	Games	Positions
Crosby, Ken	1975 - 1976	16	P
Currie, Clarence	1902 - 1903	54	P
Daly, Tom	1913 - 1916, 1918 - 1921	243	C OF 3B 1B
Daviault, Ray	1962	36	P
Dee, Maurice	1915	1	SS
Demarais, Fred	1890	1	P
Dorsey, Jerry	1884	1	P
Doyle, John	1882	3	P
Ducey, Rob	1987 - 1994	252	OF DH
Dugas, Gus	1930, 1932 - 1934	125	OF 1B
Dunn, Steve	1884	9	1B 3B
Emslie, Bob	1883 - 1885	95	P OF
Erautt, Joe "Stubby"	1950 - 1951	32	C
Fisher, Harry	1951 - 1952	18	P PH
Ford, Gene	1905	7	P
Ford, Russ	1909 - 1915	206	P 2B OF
Fowler, Dick	1941 - 1942, 1945 - 1952	226	P
Frisk, Emil	1899, 1901, 1905, 1907	160	OF P
Frobel, Doug	1982 - 1987	268	OF DH
Gardiner, Mike	**1990 - 1995**	**136**	**P**
Gardner, Alex	1884	1	C
Gibson, George	1905 - 1918	1213	C 1B
Gillespie, Jim	1890	1	OF
Gladu, Roland	1944	21	3B OF
Gorbous, Glen	1955 - 1957	117	OF
Graney, Jack	1908, 1910 - 1922	1402	OF P
Handrahan, Vern	1964, 1966	34	P
Hannifin, Pat	1897	10	OF 2B
Hardy, Alex "Dooney"	1902 - 1903	7	P
Harkness, Tim	1961 - 1964	259	1B
Harris, Bill	1957, 1959	2	P
Harrison, Tom	1965	2	P
Heath, Jeff	1936 - 1949	1383	OF
Hiller, John	1965 - 1970, 1972 - 1980	546	P

Player	Years in Major Leagues	Games	Positions
Hodgson, Paul	1980	20	OF DH
Hogg, William	1905 - 1908	118	P
Hooper, Bob	1950 - 1955	194	P
Horsman, Vince	**1991 - 1995**	**141**	**P**
Hoy, Peter	1992	5	P
Humphries, John	1883 - 1884	98	C OF 1B
Hunter, Bill	1884	2	C
Hyndman, Jim	1886	1	OF P
Irwin, Arthur "Doc"	1880 - 1891, 1894	1010	SS 3B 2B P C
Irwin, John	1882, 1884, 1886 - 1891	322	3B SS OF 1B 2B
Jenkins, Ferguson	1965 - 1983	665	P
Johnson, Albert "Abbie"	1896 - 1897	73	2B SS
Johnson, John "Spud"	1889 - 1891	331	OF 3B 1B SS
Jones, Bill "Midget"	1911 - 1912	27	OF
Jones, Mike	1890	3	P
Judd, Oscar "Ossie"	1941 - 1948	206	P
Kellum, Win	1901, 1904 - 1905	53	P OF
Kerr, Mel	1925	1	PR
Kilkenny, Mike	1969 - 1972	135	P
Knight, Jonas "Joe"	1884, 1890	133	OF P
Knowles, Jimmy	1884, 1886 - 1887, 1890, 1892	357	3B 2B 1B SS
Korince, George	1966 - 1967	11	P
Krakauskas, Joe	1937 - 1942, 1946	149	P
Kyle, Andy	1912	9	OF
LaForest, Byron "Ty"	1945	52	3B OF
Lake, Fred	1891, 1894, 1897 - 1899	48	C 2B SS 1B OF
Landreth, Larry	1976 - 1977	7	P
LaRoque, Sam	1888, 1890 - 1891	124	2B SS 1B 3B OF
Law, Ron	1969	35	P
Lawrence, Jim	1963	2	C
LePine, Louis "Pete"	1902	30	OF 1B
Lines, Dick	1966 - 1967	107	P
Lisi, Rick	1981	9	OF
Long, Nelson "Red"	1902	1	P

Player	Years in Major Leagues	Games	Positions
Lyons, Pat	1890	11	2B
MacKenzie, Eric	1955	1	C
MacKenzie, Ken	1960 - 1965	129	P
Magee, Bill	1897 - 1899, 1901 - 1902	106	P
Maranda, Georges	1960, 1962	49	P
Marchildon, Phil	1940 - 1942, 1945 - 1950	185	P
Maysey, Matt	1992 - 1993	25	P
McCabe, Ralph	1946	1	P
McCaskill, Kirk	**1985 - 1995**	**351**	**P**
McGovern, Art	1905	15	C
McKay, Dave	1975 - 1982	645	2B 3B SS DH
McKeever, Jim	1884	16	C OF
McLean, John "Larry"	1901, 1903 - 1904, 1906 - 1915	862	C 1B
Mead, Charlie	1943 - 1945	87	OF
Miller, Roy "Doc"	1910 - 1914	557	OF SS
Morrison, Jon	1884, 1887	53	OF
Mountjoy, Bill	1883 - 1885	59	P OF
Mullin, Henry	1884	36	OF 3B
O'Brien, John	1891, 1893, 1895 - 1897, 1899	501	2B 1B
O'Connor, Dan	1890	6	1B
O'Halloran, Greg	1994	12	C
O'Hara, Bill	1909 - 1910	124	OF P 1B
O'Neill, Bill	1904, 1906	206	OF 2B SS
O'Neill, Fred	1887	6	OF
O'Neill, Harry	1922 - 1923	4	P
O'Neill, James "Tip"	1883 - 1892	1054	OF P 1B
O'Rourke, Frank	1912, 1917 - 1918, 1920 - 1931	1131	3B SS 2B 1B OF
Osborne, Fred	1890	41	OF P
Ostrosser, Brian	1973	4	SS
Owens, Frank	1905, 1909, 1914-1915	222	C
Oxley, Henry	1884	4	C
Pagan, Dave	1973 - 1977	85	P
Payne, Harley	1896 - 1899	85	P OF
Pfann, Bill	1894	1	P

Player	Years in Major Leagues	Games	Positions
Phillips, Bill	1879 - 1888	1038	1B C OF
Piche, Ron	1960 - 1966	136	P
Pinnance, Ed	1903	2	P
Pirie, James	1883	5	SS
Plasdon, Gordie	1979 - 1982	20	P
Puhl, Terry	1977 - 1991	1531	OF 1B DH
Quantrill, Paul	**1992 - 1995**	**144**	**P**
Randall, Newton	1907	97	OF
Raymond, Claude	1959, 1961 - 1971	456	P
Reid, Billy	1883 - 1884	43	2B OF SS 3B
Riley, Jim	1921, 1923	6	2B 1B
Robertson, Sherry	1940 - 1941, 1943, 1946 - 1952	597	OF 2B 3B SS
Rosen, Goody	1937 - 1939, 1944 - 1946	551	OF
Ross, Ernie "Curly"	1902	2	P
Rowan, Dave	1911	18	1B
Roy, Jean-Pierre	1946	3	P
Rutherford, Johnny	1952	22	P
Scannell, Patrick	1884	6	OF
Selkirk, George	1934 - 1942	846	OF
Shank, Harvey	1970	1	P
Shields, Vince	1924	2	P
Shipanoff, Dave	1985	26	P
Siddall, Joe	**1993 - 1995**	**26**	**C 1B OF**
Sincock, Bert	1908	1	P
Sketchley, Harry "Bud"	1942	13	OF
Smith, Charles "Pop"	1880 - 1891	1093	2B SS 3B OF P C
Smith, Frank	1884	10	C OF
Smith, Tom	1882	20	3B SS OF 2B
Snyder, Frank	1898	17	C
Spoljaric, Paul	1994	2	P
Stairs, Matt	**1992 - 1995**	**58**	**OF**
Steele, Bob	1916 - 1919	97	P
Summers, William	1893	2	OF C
Taylor, Ron	1962 - 1972	491	P

Player	Years in Major Leagues	Games	Positions
Thompson, John "Tug"	1882	25	OF C
Upham, John	1967 - 1968	7	P OF
Vadeboncoeur, Gene	1884	4	C
Van Brabant, Ozzie	1954 - 1955	11	P
Vickers, Harry "Rube"	1902 - 1903, 1907 - 1909	163	P C OF
Wainhouse, Dave	1991, 1993	5	P
Walker, George	1888	4	P
Walker, Larry	**1989 - 1995**	**805**	**OF 1B**
Ward, Pete	1962 - 1970	973	3B OF 1B 2B SS
Watkins, Bill	1884	34	3B 2B SS
Weber, Joe	1884	2	OF
Whitehead, Milt	1884	104	SS OF P 2B 3B C
Wilkie, Lefty	1941 - 1942	1946	69
Wilson, Nigel	**1993, 1995**	**12**	**OF**
Wilson, Steve	1988 - 1993	206	P
Wingo, Ed	1920	1	C
Wood, Fred	1884, 1885	13	C OF SS
Wood, Pete	1885, 1889	31	P OF 1B
Yost, Gus	1893	1	P

Players Who Were Born Elsewhere But Raised In Canada

Player	Years in Major Leagues	Games	Positions
Archer, Jimmy	1904, 1907, 1909 - 1918	847	C 1B 2B 3B OF
Bertoia, Reno	1953 - 1962	612	3B 2B SS OF
Biasatti, Hank	1949	54	1B
Burnside, Sheldon	1978 - 1980	19	P
Reimer, Kevin	1988 - 1993	488	OF DH

Members Of The Canadian Baseball Hall Of Fame

Player	Years Played	Career Highlights
Bill Phillips	1879 - 1888	First Canadian-born player to hit home run. Batted .266 in 1038 games played in major leagues.
Arthur Irwin	1880 - 1891, 1894	Manager for 8 seasons in major leagues. Credited for being first fielder (other than catcher and first base) to use a glove.
Tip O'Neill	1883 - 1892	Career batting average of .326 in 1054 games. Registered second highest batting mark in major league history (.435 in 1887).
Bob Emslie	1883 - 1885	Won 32 games (most by any Canadian) and pitched 455 innings in 1884 season with Baltimore of American Association.
Jimmy Archer	1904, 1907, 1909 - 1918	Born in Ireland but raised in Canada. He was the first major league catcher to make throws from a squat position.
George Gibson	1905 - 1918	First catcher to appear in 150 games in a season (1909) when he played for World Champion Pittsburgh Pirates.
Nig Clarke	1905 - 1911 1919 - 1920	Known as a top flight defensive catcher in the American League for many years, he batted .358 in 57 games for Cleveland in 1906.
Jack Graney	1908, 1910 - 1922	Lead A.L. in walks in 1917 and 1919. First player to wear a number (1916) and first former player to become a broadcaster.
Russ Ford	1909 - 1915	Compiled record of 26 wins and 6 losses with 8 shutouts in rookie season. Credited with discovering the emery ball.
George Selkirk	1934 - 1942	He replaced Babe Ruth in right field for Yankees in 1935. Selkirk played in 6 World Series and 2 All-Star games.
Jeff Heath	1936 - 1949	Batted .343 as rookie in 1938 and .340 in 1941. First A.L. player with 20 doubles, triples and homers in same season (in 1941).
Goody Rosen	1937 - 1939, 1944 - 1946	Batted .325 with 126 runs scored, 197 hits in 1945. Had .291 career average in 551 games.

Phil Marchildon	1940 - 1942, 1945 - 1950	Compiled 19 - 9 record in 1947 and won 17 games for last place Philadelphia A's in 1942.
Oscar Judd	1941 - 1948	Posted 11 - 6 record with 2.90 ERA with Boston (A.L.) in 1943. Won 11 games with Philadelphia (N.L.) in 1946.
Dick Fowler	1941 - 1942, 1945 - 1952	Pitched only no-hitter by Canadian on September 9, 1945. Won 15 games in 1948 and 1949 for Philadelphia Athletics.
Reno Bertoia	1953 - 1962	Born in Italy but raised in Canada. Batted .265 in 121 games with Washington in 1960 and .275 with Detroit in 1957.
Tom Burgess	1954, 1962	Had eight-year gap in major league career between seasons.
Ted Bowsfield	1958 - 1964	Pitched 235 games in his seven-year American League career, winning 37. He was 11-8 with the expansion 1962 Angels.
Claude Raymond	1959, 1961 - 1971	Saved 23 for Montreal Expos in 1971 and 83 games in all as relief pitcher. Had 5 seasons with sub-3.00 ERA in major league career.
Ken MacKenzie	1960 - 1965	Posted 5 - 4 with expansion New York Mets in 1962. Pitched 129 games in major league career.
Ron Piché	1960 - 1963, 1965 - 1966	Relief pitcher with the Milwaukee Braves from 1960 to 1963 and with California and St. Louis in 1965 and 1966.
Ron Taylor	1962 - 1972	Pitched 9 - 4 record with 13 saves and 2.72 ERA with World Champion New York Mets in 1969. Posted 72 career saves.
Pete Ward	1962 - 1970	Named A.L. Rookie of the Year by TSN in 1963 when he batted .285 with 22 homers. Hit .282 with 23 home runs in 1964.
John Hiller	1965 - 1970, 1972 - 1980	Set major league record (since broken) with 38 saves in 1973 and was named Fireman of the Year. Won 17 games in relief in 1974.
Fergie Jenkins	1965 - 1983	Won N.L. Cy Young Award in 1971. Posted seven 20-win seasons including 6 consecutive years (1967 - 1972) with Cubs. Won 284 games in 664 games in major league career. He is the only Canadian-born member of National Baseball Hall of Fame.
Reggie Cleveland	1969 - 1981	Named Rookie of the Year in 1971. Won 10 or more games for seven consecutive years. Posted 105 career wins in major leagues.
Terry Puhl	1977 - 1991	Played in 1531 career games, the most by a Canadian. He holds the major league record for fielding average by an outfielder (.993).

Canadian-Born Single-Season Major League Baseball Records

Twentieth Century Batters

Games Played	157	Terry Puhl	Houston (NL)	1979
		Pete Ward	Chicago (AL)	1963
At-Bats	606	Goody Rosen	Brooklyn (NL)	1945
Plate Appearances	702	Jack Graney	Cleveland (AL)	1916
Runs Scored	126	Goody Rosen	Brooklyn (NL)	1945
Hits	199	Jeff Heath	Cleveland (AL)	1941
Singles	150	Goody Rosen	Brooklyn (NL)	1945
Doubles	44	Larry Walker	Montreal (NL)	1994
Triples	20	Jeff Heath	Cleveland (AL)	1941
Home Runs	36	Larry Walker	Colorado (NL)	1995
Total Bases	343	Jeff Heath	Cleveland (AL)	1941
Extra Base Hits	76	Jeff Heath	Cleveland (AL)	1941
Extra Bases	149	Larry Walker	Colorado (NL)	1995
Runs Batted In	123	Jeff Heath	Cleveland (AL)	1941
Bases on Balls	105	Jack Graney	Cleveland (AL)	1919
Intentional Walks	20	Larry Walker	Montreal (NL)	1993
Strikeouts	112	Larry Walker	Montreal (NL)	1990
Stolen Bases	32	Terry Puhl	Houston (NL)	1978
		Doc Miller	Boston (NL)	1911
Caught Stealing	22	Terry Puhl	Houston (NL)	1979
Sacrifice Hits	24	Bunk Congalton	Cleveland (AL)	1906
Sacrifice Flies	8	Larry Walker	Montreal (NL)	1992
Sacrifices (both)	29	Frank O'Rourke	Detroit (AL)	1925
Hit by Pitch	14	Larry Walker	Colorado (NL)	1995
Grounded into DP	17	Dave McKay	Toronto (AL)	1978
Batting Average	.343	Jeff Heath	Cleveland (AL)	1938
On-Base Average	.452	George Selkirk	New York (AL)	1939
Slugging Percentage	.607	Larry Walker	Colorado (NL)	1995

Nineteenth Century Batters

Games Played	141	Bill Phillips	Brooklyn (AA)	1886
At-Bats	585	Bill Phillips	Brooklyn (AA)	1886
Plate Appearances	647	Tip O'Neill	Chicago (PL)	1890
Runs Scored	167	Tip O'Neill	St. Louis (AA)	1887
Hits	225	Tip O'Neill	St. Louis (AA)	1887
Singles	145	Tip O'Neill	St. Louis (AA)	1886
Doubles	52	Tip O'Neill	St. Louis (AA)	1887
Triples	19	Tip O'Neill	St. Louis (AA)	1887
Home Runs	14	Tip O'Neill	St. Louis (AA)	1887
Total Bases	357	Tip O'Neill	St. Louis (AA)	1887
Extra Base Hits	85	Tip O'Neill	St. Louis (AA)	1887
Extra Bases	132	Tip O'Neill	St. Louis (AA)	1887
Runs Batted In	123	Tip O'Neill	St. Louis (AA)	1887

(listed by Canadian Hall of Fame but not other sources)

Bases on Balls	80	Pop Smith	Boston (NL)	1890
Strikeouts	81	Pop Smith	Boston (NL)	1890
Stolen Bases	55	Jimmy Knowles	Rochester (AA)	1890
Sacrifice Hits	18	John O'Brien	Louisville (NL)	1895
Hit by Pitch	13	Pop Smith	Pittsburgh (NL)	1887
Batting Average	.435	Tip O'Neill	St. Louis (AA)	1887
On-Base Average	.490	Tip O'Neill	St. Louis (AA)	1887
Slugging Percentage	.691	Tip O'Neill	St. Louis (AA)	1887

Twentieth Century Pitchers

Games Pitched	65	John Hiller	Detroit (AL)	1973
Games Started	42	Ferguson Jenkins	Chicago (NL)	1969
Complete Games	30	Ferguson Jenkins	Chicago (NL)	1971
		Russ Ford	New York (AL)	1912
Games Finished	60	John Hiller	Detroit (AL)	1973
Shutouts	8	Russ Ford	New York (AL)	1910
Saves	38	John Hiller	Detroit (AL)	1973
Innings Pitched	328.1	Ferguson Jenkins	Texas (AL)	1974
Batters Facing Pitcher	1305	Ferguson Jenkins	Texas (AL)	1974

Games Won	26	Russ Ford	New York (AL)	1910
Games Lost	21	Russ Ford	New York (AL)	1912
Winning Percentage	.813	Russ Ford	New York (AL)	1910
Hits Allowed	327	Russ Ford	New York (AL)	1912
Runs Allowed	165	Russ Ford	New York (AL)	1912
Earned Runs Allowed	112	Ferguson Jenkins	Chicago (NL)	1970
		Ferguson Jenkins	Texas (AL)	1975
Bases on Balls	141	Phil Marchildon	Philadelphia (AL)	1947
Intentional Walks	19	John Hiller	Detroit (AL)	1974
Strikeouts	274	Ferguson Jenkins	Chicago (NL)	1970
Hit Batters	11	Rube Vickers	Philadelphia (AL)	1908
Wild Pitches	13	Phil Marchildon	Philadelphia (AL)	1942
		Kirk McCaskill	California (AL)	1988
Balks	4	Ferguson Jenkins	Chicago (NL)	1971
		Denis Boucher	Toronto-Cleveland (AL)	1991
Sacrifice Hits Allowed	22	Phil Marchildon	Philadelphia (AL)	1942
Sacrifice Flies Allowed	13	Ferguson Jenkins	Chicago (NL)	1982
Sacrifices (both)	29	Bob Steele	St. Louis-Pittsburgh (NL)	1917
		(6 with St. Louis, 23 with Pittsburgh)		
Sacrifices (both)	50	Rube Vickers	Philadelphia (AL)	1908
		(unofficial record)		
Home Runs Allowed	40	Ferguson Jenkins	Texas (AL)	1979
Earned-Run Average	1.65	Russ Ford	New York (AL)	1910

Nineteenth Century Pitchers

Games Pitched	50	Bob Emslie	Baltimore (AA)	1884
Games Started	50	Bob Emslie	Baltimore (AA)	1884
Complete Games	50	Bob Emslie	Baltimore (AA)	1884
Games Finished	6	Harley Payne	Brooklyn (NL)	1896
		Bill Magee	Louisville (NL)	1897
Shutouts	4	Bob Emslie	Baltimore (AA)	1884
Saves	0	(none in nineteenth century)		
Innings Pitched	455.1	Bob Emslie	Baltimore (AA)	1884
Batters Facing Pitcher	1971	Bob Emslie	Baltimore (AA)	1884
Games Won	32	Bob Emslie	Baltimore (AA)	1884
Games Lost	17	Bob Emslie	Baltimore (AA)	1884
		Harley Payne	Brooklyn (NL)	1897

Winning Percentage	.653	Bob Emslie	Baltimore (AA)	1884
Hits Allowed	419	Bob Emslie	Baltimore (AA)	1884
Runs Allowed	241	Bob Emslie	Baltimore (AA)	1884
Earned Runs Allowed	139	Bob Emslie	Baltimore (AA)	1884
Bases on Balls	129	Bill Magee	Louisville (NL)	1898
Strikeouts	264	Bob Emslie	Baltimore (AA)	1884
Hit Batters	23	Bill Magee	Lou-Phi-Was (NL)	1899
Wild Pitches	43	Bob Emslie	Baltimore (AA)	1884
Balks	1	Harley Payne	Brooklyn (NL)	1897
		Harley Payne	Pittsburgh (NL)	1899
		Bill Magee	Louisville (NL)	1898
		Bill Magee	Philadelphia (NL)	1899
Sacrifice Hits Allowed	26	Bill Magee	Louisville (NL)	1898
Home Runs Allowed	8	Pete Wood	Buffalo (NL)	1885
		Harley Payne	Brooklyn (NL)	1897
		Bill Magee	Louisville (NL)	1898
Earned-Run Average	2.75	Bob Emslie	Baltimore (AA)	1884

Canadian-Born Career
Major League Baseball Records

All Batters

Games Played	1531	Terry Puhl	15 Years	1977 - 1991
At-Bats	4937	Jeff Heath	14 Years	1936 - 1949
Plate Appearances	5576	Jack Graney	14 Years	1908 - 1922
Runs Scored	880	Tip O'Neill	10 Years	1883 - 1892
Hits	1447	Jeff Heath	14 Years	1936 - 1949
Singles	1020	Tip O'Neill	10 Years	1883 - 1892
Doubles	279	Jeff Heath	14 Years	1936 - 1949
Triples	102	Jeff Heath	14 Years	1936 - 1949
Home Runs	194	Jeff Heath	14 Years	1936 - 1949
Total Bases	2512	Jeff Heath	14 Years	1936 - 1949
Extra Base Hits	575	Jeff Heath	14 Years	1936 - 1949
Extra Bases	1065	Jeff Heath	14 Years	1936 - 1949
Runs Batted In	887	Jeff Heath	14 Years	1936 - 1949
Bases on Balls	712	Jack Graney	14 Years	1908 - 1922
Intentional Walks	55	Larry Walker	7 Years	1989 - 1995
Strikeouts	670	Jeff Heath	14 Years	1936 - 1949
Stolen Bases	217	Terry Puhl	15 Years	1977 - 1991
Caught Stealing	99	Terry Puhl	15 Years	1977 - 1991
Sacrifice Hits	66	Ferguson Jenkins	19 Years	1965 - 1983
Sacrifice Flies	36	Terry Puhl	15 Years	1977 - 1991
Sacrifices (both)	170	Frank O'Rourke	14 Years	1912 - 1931
Hit by Pitch	60	Pop Smith	12 Years	1880 - 1891
Grounded into DP	59	Jeff Heath	14 Years	1936 - 1949
		Terry Puhl	15 Years	1977 - 1991
Batting Average	.326	Tip O'Neill	10 Years	1883 - 1892
On-Base Average	.400	George Selkirk	9 Years	1934 - 1942
Slugging Percentage	.509	Jeff Heath	14 Years	1936 - 1949

All Pitchers

Games Pitched	664	Ferguson Jenkins	19 Years 1965 - 1983
Games Started	594	Ferguson Jenkins	19 Years 1965 - 1983
Complete Games	267	Ferguson Jenkins	19 Years 1965 - 1983
Games Finished	363	John Hiller	15 Years 1965 - 1980
Shutouts	49	Ferguson Jenkins	19 Years 1965 - 1983
Saves	125	John Hiller	15 Years 1965 - 1980
Innings Pitched	4500.2	Ferguson Jenkins	19 Years 1965 - 1983
Batters Facing Pitcher	18400	Ferguson Jenkins	19 Years 1965 - 1983
Games Won	284	Ferguson Jenkins	19 Years 1965 - 1983
Games Lost	226	Ferguson Jenkins	19 Years 1965 - 1983
Winning Percentage	.582	Russ Ford	7 Years 1909 - 1915
Hits Allowed	4142	Ferguson Jenkins	19 Years 1965 - 1983
Runs Allowed	1853	Ferguson Jenkins	19 Years 1965 - 1983
Earned Runs Allowed	1669	Ferguson Jenkins	19 Years 1965 - 1983
Bases on Balls	997	Ferguson Jenkins	19 Years 1965 - 1983
Intentional Walks	116	Ferguson Jenkins	19 Years 1965 - 1983
Strikeouts	3192	Ferguson Jenkins	19 Years 1965 - 1983
Hit Batters	84	Ferguson Jenkins	19 Years 1965 - 1983
Wild Pitches	70	Bob Emslie	3 Years 1883 - 1885
Balks	18	Ferguson Jenkins	19 Years 1965 - 1983
Sacrifice Hits Allowed	176	Ferguson Jenkins	19 Years 1965 - 1983
Sacrifice Flies Allowed	124	Ferguson Jenkins	19 Years 1965 - 1983
Home Runs Allowed	484	Ferguson Jenkins	19 Years 1965 - 1983
Earned-Run Average	2.59	Russ Ford	7 Years 1909 - 1915

Canadian Leader Boards

This section lists the Canadian leaders in single-season and career batting, pitching and fielding performance. Active players are denoted in **bold** type. Players who were raised in Canada but born elsewhere are not included in the Leader Boards, but are included in the Player Register.

The minimum qualifications for the batting Leader Boards are:

Single Season: 3.1 Plate Appearances for each team game played
Career: 1000 or more At-Bats

Note: For batting totals, sacrifice hits (SH), sacrifice flies (SF), times hit by pitch (HBP), runs batted in (RBI), strikeouts (SO) and stolen bases (SB) were not kept in some years.

The minimum qualifications for the pitching Leader Boards are:

Single Season: 15 wins for Win-Loss Percentage; 1 inning pitched per team game played for ERA

Career: 40 pitching decisions

The minimum qualifications for the Fielding Leader Boards are:

Single Season: 80 games for catchers; 100 games for first basemen, second basemen, third basemen and shortstops; 120 games for outfielders; 25 chances for pitchers

Career: 100 games for first basemen; 200 games for second basemen, third basemen, shortstops, outfielders and catchers; 100 chances for pitchers.

Note: Chances Accepted or Successful Chances *excludes* Errors, while Total Chances *includes* Errors

The Top 15 Batting Performances in a Season

	Games	Year	Team-League	G		At-Bats	Year	Team-League	AB
1	Terry Puhl	1979	Houston NL	157	1	Goody Rosen	1945	Brooklyn NL	606
1	Pete Ward	1963	Chicago AL	157	2	Pete Ward	1963	Chicago AL	600
3	Jack Graney	1916	Cleveland AL	155	2	Terry Puhl	1979	Houston NL	600
4	Frank O'Rourke	1929	St. Louis AL	154	4	Jack Graney	1916	Cleveland AL	589
5	Jeff Heath	1941	Cleveland AL	151	5	Jeff Heath	1941	Cleveland AL	585
6	George Gibson	1909	Pittsburgh NL	150	5	Frank O'Rourke	1929	St. Louis AL	585
7	Terry Puhl	1978	Houston NL	149	5	Terry Puhl	1978	Houston NL	585
8	Jack Graney	1913	Cleveland AL	148	5	Bill Phillips	1886	Brooklyn AA	585
9	Jeff Heath	1942	Cleveland AL	147	9	Tip O'Neill	1890	Chicago PL	579
10	Pete Ward	1967	Chicago AL	146	10	Tip O'Neill	1886	St. Louis AA	577
10	Jack Graney	1917	Cleveland AL	146	10	Doc Miller	1911	Boston NL	577
10	Doc Miller	1911	Boston NL	146	12	Jeff Heath	1942	Cleveland AL	568
13	Three Times			145	13	John O'Brien	1895	Louisville NL	539
					14	Frank O'Rourke	1927	St. Louis AL	538
					14	Spud Johnson	1890	Columbus AA	538

The Top 15 Batting Performances in a Season

	Runs Scored	Year	Team-League	R		Hits	Year	Team-League	H
1	Tip O'Neill	1887	St. Louis AA	167	1	Tip O'Neill	1887	St. Louis AA	225
2	Goody Rosen	1945	Brooklyn NL	126	2	Jeff Heath	1941	Cleveland AL	199
3	Tip O'Neill	1889	St. Louis AA	123	3	Goody Rosen	1945	Brooklyn NL	197
4	Tip O'Neill	1890	Chicago PL	112	4	Doc Miller	1911	Boston NL	192
4	Tip O'Neill	1891	St. Louis AA	112	5	Tip O'Neill	1886	St. Louis AA	190
6	Spud Johnson	1890	Columbus AA	106	6	Spud Johnson	1890	Columbus AA	186
6	Jack Graney	1916	Cleveland AL	106	7	Tip O'Neill	1889	St. Louis AA	179
6	Tip O'Neill	1886	St. Louis AA	106	8	Pete Ward	1963	Chicago AL	177
9	Jeff Heath	1938	Cleveland AL	104	8	Tip O'Neill	1888	St. Louis AA	177
10	George Selkirk	1939	New York AL	103	10	Tip O'Neill	1890	Chicago PL	174
11	**Larry Walker**	**1995**	**Colorado NL**	**96**	11	Terry Puhl	1979	Houston NL	172
11	Tip O'Neill	1888	St. Louis AA	96	11	Jeff Heath	1938	Cleveland AL	172
13	George Selkirk	1936	New York AL	93	13	Terry Puhl	1978	Houston NL	169
14	Jeff Heath	1941	Cleveland AL	89	14	Tip O'Neill	1891	St. Louis AA	167
15	Frank O'Rourke	1925	Detroit AL	88	15	Bill Phillips	1886	Brooklyn AA	160

The Top 15 Batting Performances in a Season

	Total Bases	Year	Team-League	TB		Doubles	Year	Team-League	2B
1	Tip O'Neill	1887	St. Louis AA	357	1	Tip O'Neill	1887	St. Louis AA	52
2	Jeff Heath	1941	Cleveland AL	343	**2**	**Larry Walker**	**1994**	**Montreal NL**	**44**
3	Jeff Heath	1938	Cleveland AL	302	3	Jack Graney	1916	Cleveland AL	41
4	**Larry Walker**	**1995**	**Colorado NL**	**300**	4	Frank O'Rourke	1925	Detroit AL	40
5	Pete Ward	1963	Chicago AL	289	5	Jeff Heath	1942	Cleveland AL	37
6	Goody Rosen	1945	Brooklyn NL	279	6	Doc Miller	1911	Boston NL	36
7	**Larry Walker**	**1992**	**Montreal NL**	**267**	7	Pete Ward	1963	Chicago AL	34
8	Pete Ward	1964	Chicago AL	255	7	Bill Phillips	1887	Brooklyn AA	34
8	Doc Miller	1911	Boston NL	255	9	Tip O'Neill	1889	St. Louis AA	33
8	Tip O'Neill	1886	St. Louis AA	255	10	Jeff Heath	1941	Cleveland AL	32
8	Tip O'Neill	1889	Chicago AA	255	10	Jeff Heath	1946	Wash-St.L AL	32
12	George Selkirk	1936	New York AL	252	**12**	**Larry Walker**	**1992**	**Montreal NL**	**31**
13	Jeff Heath	1942	Cleveland AL	251	**12**	**Larry Walker**	**1995**	**Colorado NL**	**31**
14	Spud Johnson	1890	Columbus AA	248	12	Jeff Heath	1938	Cleveland AL	31
15	George Selkirk	1935	New York AL	239	12	Jeff Heath	1939	Cleveland AL	31

The Top 15 Batting Performances in a Season

	Triples	Year	Team-League	3B		Home Runs	Year	Team-League	HR
1	Jeff Heath	1941	Cleveland AL	20	**1**	**Larry Walker**	**1995**	**Colorado NL**	**36**
2	Tip O'Neill	1887	St. Louis AA	19	2	Jeff Heath	1947	St. Louis AL	27
3	Spud Johnson	1890	Columbus AA	18	3	Jeff Heath	1941	Cleveland AL	24
3	Jeff Heath	1938	Cleveland AL	18	**4**	**Larry Walker**	**1992**	**Montreal NL**	**23**
5	Pop Smith	1883	Columbus AA	17	4	Pete Ward	1964	Chicago AL	23
6	Tip O'Neill	1890	Chicago PL	16	**6**	**Larry Walker**	**1993**	**Montreal NL**	**22**
7	Bill Phillips	1886	Brooklyn AA	15	6	Pete Ward	1963	Chicago AL	22
8	Jack Graney	1916	Cleveland AL	14	8	George Selkirk	1939	New York AL	21
8	Tip O'Neill	1886	St. Louis AA	14	8	Jeff Heath	1938	Cleveland AL	21
10	Jeff Heath	1942	Cleveland AL	13	10	Jeff Heath	1948	Boston NL	20
10	Pop Smith	1885	Pittsburgh AA	13	**11**	**Larry Walker**	**1990**	**Montreal NL**	**19**
12	George Selkirk	1935	New York AL	12	**11**	**Larry Walker**	**1994**	**Montreal NL**	**19**
12	Jack Graney	1913	Cleveland AL	12	11	George Selkirk	1940	New York AL	19
12	Bill Phillips	1884	Cleveland NL	12	14	Four Times			18
12	Pop Smith	1890	Boston NL	12					

The Top 15 Batting Performances in a Season

	RBI	Year	Team-League	RBI		Batting Avg	Year	Team-League	BA.
1	Jeff Heath	1941	Cleveland AL	123	1	Tip O'Neill	1887	St. Louis AA	.435
1	Tip O'Neill	1887	St. Louis AA	123	2	Spud Johnson	1890	Columbus AA	.346
3	Jeff Heath	1938	Cleveland AL	112	3	Jeff Heath	1938	Cleveland AL	.343
4	Tip O'Neill	1889	St. Louis AA	110	4	Jeff Heath	1941	Cleveland AL	.340
5	George Selkirk	1936	New York AL	107	5	Tip O'Neill	1889	St. Louis AA	.335
6	**Larry Walker**	**1995**	**Colorado NL**	**101**	6	Tip O'Neill	1888	St. Louis AA	.335
6	George Selkirk	1939	New York AL	101	7	Doc Miller	1911	Boston NL	.333
8	Tip O'Neill	1888	St. Louis AA	98	8	Tip O'Neill	1887	St. Louis AA	.328
9	Tip O'Neill	1891	St. Louis AA	95	9	Goody Rosen	1945	Brooklyn NL	.325
10	George Selkirk	1935	New York AL	94	**10**	**Larry Walker**	**1994**	**Montreal NL**	**.322**
10	Pete Ward	1964	Chicago AL	94	11	Tip O'Neill	1887	St. Louis AA	.321
12	**Larry Walker**	**1992**	**Montreal NL**	**93**	12	Bunk Congalton	1906	Cleveland AL	.320
13	Doc Miller	1911	Boston NL	91	13	Joe Knight	1890	Cincinnati NL	.312
14	**Larry Walker**	**1993**	**Montreal NL**	**86**	14	George Selkirk	1935	New York AL	.312
14	**Larry Walker**	**1994**	**Montreal NL**	**86**	15	George Selkirk	1936	New York AL	.308

The Top 15 Batting Performances in a Season

	Slugging Avg	Year	Team-League	SP.		On-Base Avg	Year	Team-League	OBA
1	Tip O'Neill	1887	St. Louis AA	.691	1	Tip O'Neill	1887	St. Louis AA	.490
2	**Larry Walker**	**1995**	**Colorado NL**	**.607**	2	George Selkirk	1939	New York AL	.452
3	Jeff Heath	1938	Cleveland AL	.602	3	George Selkirk	1936	New York AL	.420
4	**Larry Walker**	**1994**	**Montreal NL**	**.587**	4	Tip O'Neill	1889	St. Louis AA	.419
5	Jeff Heath	1941	Cleveland AL	.586	5	Spud johnson	1890	Columbus AA	.409
6	George Selkirk	1939	New York AL	.517	6	Tip O'Neill	1891	St. Louis AA	.402
7	George Selkirk	1936	New York AL	.511	7	**Larry Walker**	**1994**	**Montreal NL**	**.399**
8	**Larry Walker**	**1992**	**Montreal NL**	**.506**	8	Jeff Heath	1941	Cleveland AL	.396
9	Jeff Heath	1939	Cleveland AL	.494	9	Tip O'Neill	1888	St. Louis AA	.390
10	George Selkirk	1935	New York AL	.487	10	Terry Puhl	1984	Houston NL	.383
11	Jeff Heath	1947	St. Louis AL	.485	11	Jeff Heath	1938	Cleveland AL	.383
12	Pete Ward	1963	Chicago AL	.482	**12**	**Larry Walker**	**1995**	**Colorado NL**	**.381**
13	Jeff Heath	1943	Cleveland AL	.481	13	Jack Graney	1918	Cleveland AL	.380
14	Tip O'Neill	1889	St. Louis AA	.478	14	Goody Rosen	1945	Brooklyn NL	.379
15	Pete Ward	1964	Chicago AL	.473	15	Doc Miller	1911	Boston NL	.379

The Top 15 Batting Performances in a Season

	Walks	Year	Team-League	BB		Stolen Bases	Year	Team-League	SB
1	Jack Graney	1919	Cleveland AL	105	1	Jimmy Knowles	1890	Rochester AA	55
2	George Selkirk	1939	New York AL	103	2	Spud Johnson	1890	Columbus AA	43
3	Jack Graney	1916	Cleveland AL	102	3	Pop Smith	1890	Boston NL	39
4	George Selkirk	1936	New York AL	94	4	Pop Smith	1886	Pittsburgh AA	38
4	Jack Graney	1917	Cleveland AL	94	5	Pop Smith	1888	Pittsburgh NL	37
6	Jeff Heath	1947	St. Louis AL	88	6	Spud Johnson	1889	Columbus AA	34
7	George Selkirk	1940	New York AL	84	7	Doc Miller	1911	Boston NL	32
8	Pop Smith	1890	Boston NL	80	7	Terry Puhl	1978	Houston NL	32
8	**Larry Walker**	**1993**	**Montreal NL**	**80**	9	Bill O'Hara	1909	New York NL	31
10	Pete Ward	1968	Chicago AL	76	10	Tip O'Neill	1887	St.Louis AA	30
11	Jeff Heath	1946	Wash-St.L AL	73	10	Pop Smith	1887	Pittsburgh NL	30
12	Tip O'Neill	1889	St. Louis AA	72	10	Terry Puhl	1979	Houston NL	30
13	George Selkirk	1938	New York AL	68	**13**	**Larry Walker**	**1991**	**Montreal NL**	**29**
14	Jack Graney	1914	Cleveland AL	67	13	Tip O'Neill	1890	Chicago PL	29
15	Jack Graney	1911	Cleveland AL	66	15	Tip O'Neill	1889	St. Louis AA	28

The Top 15 Batting Performances in a Season

	Hit by Pitch	Year	Team-League	HP		SH plus SF	Year	Team-League	SH
1	**Larry Walker**	**1995**	**Colorado NL**	**14**	1	Frank O'Rourke	1925	Detroit AL	29
2	Pop Smith	1887	Pittsburgh NL	13	2	Frank O'Rourke	1929	St. Louis AL	28
3	Spud Johnson	1889	Columbus AA	12	3	Frank O'Rourke	1928	St. Louis AL	25
3	Pop Smith	1884	Columbus AA	12	4	Bunk Congalton	1906	Cleveland AL	24
3	Frank O'Rourke	1927	St. Louis AL	12	5	John O'Brien	1895	Louisville NL	18
3	Sam Laroque	1890	Pittsburgh NL	12	5	Doc Miller	1911	Boston NL	18
7	Pete Ward	1967	Chicago AL	11	7	Frank O'Rourke	1926	Detroit AL	17
7	Bill Phillips	1885	Brooklyn AA	11	8	Jack Graney	1911	Cleveland AL	16
7	John O'Brien	1897	Washington NL	11	8	Jack Graney	1919	Cleveland AL	16
7	Jack Graney	1911	Cleveland AL	11	10	George Gibson	1909	Pittsburgh NL	15
7	Frank O'Rourke	1925	Detroit AL	11	10	Frank O'Rourke	1930	St. Louis AL	15
7	Emil Frisk	1905	St. Louis AL	11	10	Jack Graney	1917	Cleveland AL	15
13	Four Times			10	13	Goody Rosen	1945	Brooklyn NL	14
					14	Five Times	1936		13

The Top 15 Performances in Career Batting Records

Rank	Games Played	Career	Games	Rank	At-Bats	Career	At-Bats
1	Terry Puhl	1977-1991	1531	1	Jeff Heath	1936-1949	4937
2	Jack Graney	1908-1922	1402	2	Terry Puhl	1977-1991	4855
3	Jeff Heath	1936-1949	1383	3	Jack Graney	1908-1922	4705
4	George Gibson	1905-1918	1213	4	Tip O'Neill	1883-1892	4255
5	Frank O'Rourke	1912-1931	1131	4	Bill Phillips	1879-1888	4255
6	Pop Smith	1880-1891	1093	6	Pop Smith	1880-1891	4176
7	Tip O'Neill	1883-1892	1054	7	Frank O'Rourke	1912-1931	4069
8	Bill Phillips	1879-1888	1038	8	Arthur Irwin	1880-1894	3871
9	Arthur Irwin	1880-1894	1010	9	George Gibson	1905-1918	3776
10	Pete Ward	1962-1970	973	10	Pete Ward	1962-1970	3060
11	Larry McLean	1901-1915	862	**11**	**Larry Walker**	**1989-1995**	**2860**
12	George Selkirk	1934-1942	846	12	George Selkirk	1934-1942	2790
13	**Larry Walker**	**1989-1995**	**805**	13	Larry McLean	1901-1915	2647
14	Ferguson Jenkins	1965-1983	665	14	Dave McKay	1975-1982	1928
15	Dave McKay	1975-1982	645	15	Goody Rosen	1937-1946	1916

Rank	Runs Scored	Career	Runs	Rank	Base Hits	Career	Hits
1	Tip O'Neill	1883-1892	880	1	Jeff Heath	1936-1949	1447
2	Jeff Heath	1936-1949	777	2	Tip O'Neill	1883-1892	1386
3	Jack Graney	1908-1922	706	3	Terry Puhl	1977-1991	1361
4	Terry Puhl	1977-1991	676	4	Jack Graney	1908-1922	1178
5	Pop Smith	1880-1891	633	5	Bill Phillips	1879-1888	1130
6	Bill Phillips	1879-1888	562	6	Frank O'Rourke	1912-1931	1032
7	Arthur Irwin	1880-1894	552	7	Pop Smith	1880-1891	935
8	Frank O'Rourke	1912-1931	547	8	Arthur Irwin	1880-1894	934
9	George Selkirk	1934-1942	503	9	George Gibson	1905-1918	893
10	**Larry Walker**	**1989-1995**	**464**	**10**	**Larry Walker**	**1989-1995**	**817**
11	Pete Ward	1962-1970	345	11	George Selkirk	1934-1942	810
12	Goody Rosen	1937-1946	310	12	Pete Ward	1962-1970	776
13	George Gibson	1905-1918	295	13	Larry McLean	1901-1915	694
14	Spud Johnson	1889-1891	246	14	Goody Rosen	1937-1946	557
14	John O'Brien	1891-1899	246	15	Doc Miller	1910-1914	507

The Top 15 Performances in Career Batting Records

Rank	Total Bases	Career	TB	Rank	Doubles	Career	2B
1	Jeff Heath	1936-1949	2512	1	Jeff Heath	1936-1949	279
2	Tip O'Neill	1883-1892	2048	2	Terry Puhl	1977-1991	226
3	Terry Puhl	1977-1991	1785	3	Tip O'Neill	1883-1892	222
4	Jack Graney	1908-1922	1609	4	Jack Graney	1908-1922	219
5	Bill Phillips	1879-1888	1591	5	Bill Phillips	1879-1888	214
6	**Larry Walker**	**1989-1995**	**1442**	6	Frank O'Rourke	1912-1931	196
7	Frank O'Rourke	1912-1931	1357	**7**	**Larry Walker**	**1989-1995**	**178**
8	George Selkirk	1934-1942	1347	8	George Gibson	1905-1918	142
9	Pop Smith	1880-1891	1322	9	Arthur Irwin	1880-1894	141
10	Pete Ward	1962-1970	1240	9	Pop Smith	1880-1891	141
11	Arthur Irwin	1880-1894	1180	11	Pete Ward	1962-1970	136
12	George Gibson	1905-1918	1178	12	George Selkirk	1934-1942	131
13	Larry McLean	1901-1915	854	13	Doc Miller	1910-1914	96
14	Goody Rosen	1937-1946	762	14	Larry McLean	1901-1915	90
15	Doc Miller	1910-1914	669	15	Dave McKay	1975-1982	70

Rank	Triples	Career	3B	Rank	Home Runs	Career	HR
1	Jeff Heath	1936-1949	102	1	Jeff Heath	1936-1949	194
2	Bill Phillips	1879-1888	98	**2**	**Larry Walker**	**1989-1995**	**135**
3	Tip O'Neill	1883-1892	92	3	George Selkirk	1934-1942	108
4	Pop Smith	1880-1891	87	4	Pete Ward	1962-1970	98
5	Jack Graney	1908-1922	79	5	Terry Puhl	1977-1991	62
6	Terry Puhl	1977-1991	56	6	Tip O'Neill	1883-1892	52
7	George Gibson	1905-1918	49	7	Sherry Robertson	1940-1952	26
8	Arthur Irwin	1880-1894	45	8	Pop Smith	1880-1891	24
9	Frank O'Rourke	1912-1931	42	9	Goody Rosen	1937-1946	22
10	George Selkirk	1934-1942	41	10	Dave McKay	1975-1982	21
11	Goody Rosen	1937-1946	34	11	Doug Frobel	1982-1985	20
12	Spud Johnson	1889-1891	31	12	Jack Graney	1908-1922	18
13	Jimmy Knowles	1884-1892	28	13	Bill Phillips	1879-1888	17
14	Larry McLean	1901-1915	26	14	Vince Barton	1931-1932	16
15	**Larry Walker**	**1989-1995**	**21**	15	Three Players		15

The Top 15 Performances in Career Batting Records

Rank	Runs Batted In	Career	RBI	Rank	Stolen Bases	Career	SB
1	Jeff Heath	1936-1949	887	1	Terry Puhl	1977-1991	217
2	George Selkirk	1934-1942	576	2	Pop Smith	1880-1891	169
3	Tip O'Neill	1883-1892	558	3	Tip O'Neill	1883-1892	161
4	**Larry Walker**	**1989-1995**	**485**	4	Jack Graney	1908-1922	148
5	Terry Puhl	1977-1991	435	**5**	**Larry Walker**	**1989-1995**	**114**
6	Frank O'Rourke	1912-1931	430	6	Frank O'Rourke	1912-1931	101
7	Pete Ward	1962-1970	427	7	Spud Johnson	1889-1891	93
8	Jack Graney	1908-1922	420	7	Arthur Irwin	1880-1894	93
9	Arthur Irwin	1880-1894	396	9	Jimmy Knowles	1884-1892	83
10	George Gibson	1905-1918	345	10	Doc Miller	1910-1914	64
11	Larry McLean	1901-1915	298	11	John Irwin	1882-1891	56
11	Bill Phillips	1879-1888	298	11	Jeff Heath	1936-1949	56
13	Pop Smith	1880-1891	264	13	George Selkirk	1934-1942	49
14	Doc Miller	1910-1914	235	14	John O'Brien	1891-1899	45
15	John O'Brien	1891-1899	229	15	Bill O'Neill	1904-1906	41

Rank	Bases On Balls	Career	Walks	Rank	Strikeouts	Career	SO
1	Jack Graney	1908-1922	712	1	Jeff Heath	1936-1949	670
2	Jeff Heath	1936-1949	593	**2**	**Larry Walker**	**1989-1995**	**546**
3	Terry Puhl	1977-1991	505	3	Pete Ward	1962-1970	539
4	George Selkirk	1934-1942	486	4	Terry Puhl	1977-1991	507
5	Tip O'Neill	1883-1892	421	5	Arthur Irwin	1880-1894	378
6	Pete Ward	1962-1970	371	6	Frank O'Rourke	1912-1931	377
7	Frank O'Rourke	1912-1931	314	7	Pop Smith	1880-1891	345
8	**Larry Walker**	**1989-1995**	**313**	7	Jack Graney	1908-1922	345
8	Pop Smith	1880-1891	313	9	Dave McKay	1975-1982	337
10	Arthur Irwin	1880-1894	309	10	Ferguson Jenkins	1965-1983	326
11	George Gibson	1905-1918	286	11	George Selkirk	1934-1942	319
12	Goody Rosen	1937-1946	218	12	Sherry Robertson	1940-1952	238
13	Sherry Robertson	1940-1952	202	13	Bill Phillips	1879-1888	215
14	Bill Phillips	1879-1888	178	14	Goody Rosen	1937-1946	166
15	John O'Brien	1891-1899	154	15	Doug Frobel	1982-1987	155

The Top 15 Performances in Career Batting Records

Rank	Sacrifices	Career	SH+SF	Rank	Batting Average	Career	B.A.
1	Frank O'Rourke	1912-1931	170	1	Tip O'Neill	1883-1892	.326
2	Jack Graney	1908-1922	119	2	Spud Johnson	1889-1891	.302
3	George Gibson	1905-1918	102	3	Doc Miller	1910-1914	.295
4	Terry Puhl	1977-1991	93	4	Jeff Heath	1936-1949	.293
5	Ferguson Jenkins	1965-1983	73	5	Goody Rosen	1937-1946	.291
6	Dave McKay	1975-1982	55	6	George Selkirk	1934-1942	.290
7	Doc Miller	1910-1914	47	7	Bunk Congalton	1902-1907	.290
8	Larry McLean	1901-1915	43	**8**	**Larry Walker**	**1989-1995**	**.286**
9	John O'Brien	1891-1899	42	9	Terry Puhl	1977-1991	.280
10	Bunk Congalton	1902-1907	41	10	Bill Phillips	1879-1888	.266
11	Pete Ward	1962-1970	40	11	Larry McLean	1901-1915	.262
12	**Larry Walker**	**1989-1995**	**38**	12	John O'Brien	1891-1899	.254
13	Phil Marchildon	1940-1950	36	13	Frank O'Rourke	1912-1931	.254
14	Nig Clarke	1905-1920	30	14	Nig Clarke	1905-1920	.254
15	Two Players		26	15	Pete Ward	1962-1970	.254

Rank	Slugging Pct	Career	S.P.	Rank	On-Base Avg	Career	OBA.
1	Jeff Heath	1936-1949	.509	1	George Selkirk	1934-1942	.400
2	**Larry Walker**	**1989-1995**	**.504**	2	Tip O'Neill	1883-1892	.392
3	George Selkirk	1934-1942	.483	3	Jeff Heath	1936-1949	.370
4	Tip O'Neill	1883-1892	.458	4	Spud Johnson	1889-1891	.368
5	Pete Ward	1962-1970	.405	5	Goody Rosen	1937-1946	.364
6	Goody Rosen	1937-1946	.398	**6**	**Larry Walker**	**1989-1995**	**.361**
7	Spud Johnson	1889-1891	.392	7	Jack Graney	1908-1922	.354
8	Doc Miller	1910-1914	.390	8	Terry Puhl	1977-1991	.351
9	Terry Puhl	1977-1991	.388	9	Doc Miller	1910-1914	.343
10	Bill Phillips	1879-1888	.374	10	Pete Ward	1962-1970	.342
11	Bunk Congalton	1902-1907	.351	11	Bunk Congalton	1902-1907	.326
12	Jack Graney	1908-1922	.342	12	Sherry Robertson	1940-1952	.323
13	Sherry Robertson	1940-1952	.342	13	John O'Brien	1891-1899	.322
14	Frank O'Rourke	1912-1931	.333	14	Nig Clarke	1905-1920	.318
15	Nig Clarke	1905-1920	.333	15	Frank O'Rourke	1912-1931	.315

The Top 15 Pitching Performances in a Season

	Games Won	Year	Team-League	W		Games Lost	Year	Team-League	L
1	Bob Emslie	1884	Baltimore AA	32	1	Russ Ford	1912	New York AL	21
2	Russ Ford	1910	New York AL	26	**2**	**Kirk McCaskill**	**1991**	**California AL**	**19**
3	Ferguson Jenkins	1974	Texas AL	25	2	Rube Vickers	1979	Philadelphia AL	19
4	Ferguson Jenkins	1971	Chicago NL	24	4	Ferguson Jenkins	1975	Texas AL	18
5	Ferguson Jenkins	1970	Chicago NL	22	4	Russ Ford	1913	New York AL	18
5	Russ Ford	1911	New York AL	22	6	Bob Emslie	1884	Baltimore AA	17
7	Ferguson Jenkins	1969	Chicago NL	21	6	Harley Payne	1897	Brooklyn NL	17
7	Russ Ford	1914	Buffalo FL	21	6	Joe Krakauskus	1939	Washington AL	17
9	Ferguson Jenkins	1967	Chicago NL	20	6	Paul Calvert	1949	Washington AL	17
9	Ferguson Jenkins	1968	Chicago NL	20	10	Ferguson Jenkins	1970	Chicago NL	16
9	Ferguson Jenkins	1972	Chicago NL	20	10	Ferguson Jenkins	1973	Chicago NL	16
12	Phil Marchildon	1947	Philadelphia AL	19	10	Harley Payne	1896	Brooklyn NL	16
12	Bill Mountjoy	1884	Cincinnati AA	19	10	Bill Magee	1899	Phi-Lou-Wsh NL	16
14	Ferguson Jenkins	1978	Texas AL	18	10	Phil Marchildon	1946	Philadelphia AL	16
14	Rube Vickers	1908	Philadelphia AL	18	10	Dick Fowler	1946	Philadelphia AL	16

The Top 15 Pitching Performances in a Season

	Shutouts	Year	Team-League	ShO		Saves	Year	Team-League	SV
1	Russ Ford	1910	New York AL	8	1	John Hiller	1973	Detroit AL	38
2	Ferguson Jenkins	1969	Chicago NL	7	2	Claude Raymond	1970	Montreal NL	23
3	Ferguson Jenkins	1974	Texas AL	6	3	John Hiller	1978	Detroit AL	17
3	Rube Vickers	1908	Philadelphia AL	6	4	Claude Raymond	1966	Houston NL	16
5	Ferguson Jenkins	1972	Chicago NL	5	5	John Hiller	1975	Detroit AL	14
5	Russ Ford	1914	Buffalo FL	5	6	John Hiller	1974	Detroit AL	13
7	Ferguson Jenkins	1975	Texas AL	4	6	John Hiller	1976	Detroit AL	13
7	Ferguson Jenkins	1978	Texas AL	4	6	Ron Taylor	1968	New York NL	13
7	Dick Fowler	1949	Philadelphia AL	4	6	Ron Taylor	1969	New York NL	13
7	Mike Kilkenny	1939	Detroit AL	4	6	Ron Taylor	1970	New York NL	13
7	**Kirk McCaskill**	**1989**	**California AL**	**4**	11	Reggie Cleveland	1978	Texas AL	12
7	Bob Emslie	1884	Baltimore AA	4	12	Ron Taylor	1963	St. Louis NL	11
13	Twelve Times			3	13	Claude Raymond	1962	Milwaukee NL	10
					13	Claude Raymond	1967	Hou-Atla NL	10
					13	Claude Raymond	1968	Atlanta NL	10

The Top 15 Pitching Performances in a Season

	Strikeouts	Year	Team-League	K		Walks	Year	Team-League	BB
1	Ferguson Jenkins	1970	Chicago NL	274	1	Phil Marchildon	1947	Philadelphia AL	141
2	Ferguson Jenkins	1969	Chicago NL	273	2	Phil Marchildon	1942	Philadelphia AL	140
3	Bob Emslie	1884	Baltimore AA	264	3	Phil Marchildon	1948	Philadelphia AL	131
4	Ferguson Jenkins	1971	Chicago NL	263	4	Bill Magee	1898	Louisville NL	129
5	Ferguson Jenkins	1968	Chicago NL	260	5	Phil Marchildon	1941	Philadelphia AL	118
6	Ferguson Jenkins	1967	Chicago NL	236	6	Phil Marchildon	1949	Philadelphia AL	115
7	Ferguson Jenkins	1974	Texas AL	225	7	Phil Marchildon	1946	Philadelphia AL	114
8	Russ Ford	1910	New York AL	209	7	Joe Krakauskus	1939	Washington AL	114
9	**Kirk McCaskill**	**1986**	**California AL**	**202**	9	Bill Hogg	1905	New York AL	101
10	Ferguson Jenkins	1972	Chicago NL	184	10	Bill Magee	1897	Louisville NL	99
11	Ferguson Jenkins	1973	Chicago NL	170	**11**	**Kirk McCaskill**	**1992**	**Chicago AL**	**95**
12	Ferguson Jenkins	1979	Texas AL	164	**12**	**Kirk McCaskill**	**1986**	**California AL**	**92**
13	Russ Ford	1911	New York AL	158	13	Bob Hooper	1950	Philadelphia AL	91
14	Ferguson Jenkins	1979	Texas AL	157	14	Oscar Judd	1942	Boston AL	90
14	Ferguson Jenkins	1979	Texas AL	157	14	Oscar Judd	1946	Philadelphia NL	90

The Top 15 Pitching Performances in a Season

	Innings	Year	Team-League	IP		Batters Faced	Year	Team-League	BFP
1	Bob Emslie	1884	Baltimore AA	455.1	1	Bob Emslie	1884	Baltimore AA	1971
2	Ferguson Jenkins	1974	Texas AL	328.1	2	Ferguson Jenkins	1974	Texas AL	1305
3	Ferguson Jenkins	1971	Chicago NL	325.0	3	Ferguson Jenkins	1971	Chicago NL	1299
4	Rube Vickers	1908	Philadelphia AL	317.0	4	Bill Magee	1898	Louisville NL	1293
5	Ferguson Jenkins	1970	Chicago NL	313.0	5	Harley Payne	1897	Brooklyn NL	1283
6	Ferguson Jenkins	1969	Chicago NL	311.1	6	Rube Vickers	1908	Philadelphia AL	1276
7	Ferguson Jenkins	1968	Chicago NL	308.0	7	Ferguson Jenkins	1969	Chicago NL	1275
8	Russ Ford	1910	New York AL	299.2	8	Ferguson Jenkins	1970	Chicago NL	1265
9	Bill Magee	1898	Louisville NL	295.1	8	Russ Ford	1912	New York AL	1265
10	Russ Ford	1912	New York AL	291.2	10	Ferguson Jenkins	1968	Chicago NL	1231
11	Ferguson Jenkins	1967	Chicago NL	289.1	11	Bill Mountjoy	1884	Cincinnati AA	1212
11	Ferguson Jenkins	1972	Chicago NL	289.1	12	Ferguson Jenkins	1972	Chicago NL	1176
13	Bill Mountjoy	1884	Cincinnati AA	289.0	13	Phil Marchildon	1947	Philadelphia AL	1172
14	Russ Ford	1911	New York AL	281.1	13	Russ Ford	1911	New York AL	1172
15	Harley Payne	1897	Brooklyn NL	280.0	15	Ferguson Jenkins	1967	Chicago NL	1156

The Top 15 Pitching Performances in a Season

	Games	Year	Team-League	G		Starts	Year	Team-League	GS
1	John Hiller	1973	Detroit AL	65	1	Bob Emslie	1884	Baltimore AA	50
2	Ron Taylor	1963	St. Louis NL	63	2	Ferguson Jenkins	1969	Chicago NL	42
3	Claude Raymond	1966	Houston NL	62	3	Ferguson Jenkins	1974	Texas AL	41
4	Ferguson Jenkins	1966	Phil-Chi NL	61	4	Ferguson Jenkins	1968	Chicago NL	40
5	Steve Wilson	1992	Los Angeles NL	60	5	Ferguson Jenkins	1970	Chicago NL	39
6	Claude Raymond	1959	Montreal NL	59	5	Ferguson Jenkins	1971	Chicago NL	39
6	Ron Taylor	1969	New York NL	59	7	Ferguson Jenkins	1973	Chicago NL	38
6	John Hiller	1974	Detroit AL	59	7	Ferguson Jenkins	1967	Chicago NL	38
9	**Vince Horsman**	**1992**	**Oakland AL**	**58**	7	Harley Payne	1897	Brooklyn NL	38
9	Ron Taylor	1968	New York NL	58	10	Ferguson Jenkins	1970	Chicago NL	37
11	Ron Taylor	1970	New York NL	57	10	Ferguson Jenkins	1973	Chicago NL	37
11	Ron Taylor	1965	St.L-Hou NL	57	12	Ferguson Jenkins	1972	Chicago NL	36
13	John Hiller	1976	Detroit AL	56	13	Russ Ford	1912	New York AL	35
14	**Kirk McCaskill**	**1995**	**Chicago AL**	**55**	13	Phil Marchildon	1947	Philadelphia AL	35
14	Bill Atkinson	1977	Montreal NL	55	15	Four Times			34

The Top 15 Pitching Performances in a Season

	Completed	Year	Team-League	CG		Finished	Year	Team-League	GF
1	Bob Emslie	1884	Baltimore AA	50	1	John Hiller	1973	Detroit AL	60
2	Bill Mountjoy	1884	Cincinnati AA	32	2	John Hiller	1974	Detroit AL	52
3	Ferguson Jenkins	1971	Chicago NL	30	3	John Hiller	1976	Detroit AL	46
3	Russ Ford	1912	New York AL	30	3	John Hiller	1978	Detroit AL	46
3	Harley Payne	1897	Brooklyn NL	30	5	Ron Taylor	1968	New York NL	44
6	Russ Ford	1910	Buffalo FL	29	5	Ron Taylor	1969	New York NL	44
6	Ferguson Jenkins	1974	Texas AL	29	7	Claude Raymond	1970	Montreal NL	43
6	Bill Magee	1898	Louisville NL	29	8	Claude Raymond	1966	Houston NL	42
9	Russ Ford	1911	New York AL	26	9	Reggie Cleveland	1978	Texas AL	41
10	Ferguson Jenkins	1970	Chicago NL	24	10	Ron Taylor	1970	New York NL	40
10	Harley Payne	1896	Brooklyn NL	24	11	John Hiller	1975	Detroit AL	34
12	Ferguson Jenkins	1969	Chicago NL	23	12	Claude Raymond	1967	Hous-Atla NL	33
12	Ferguson Jenkins	1972	Chicago NL	23	13	Ron Taylor	1964	St. Louis NL	31
14	Ferguson Jenkins	1975	Texas AL	22	13	Ron Taylor	1967	New York NL	31
14	Win Kellum	1904	Cincinnati NL	22	15	Two Times			30

The Top 15 Pitching Performances in a Season

	Hits	Year	Team-League	H		Runs	Year	Team-League	R
1	Bob Emslie	1884	Baltimore AA	419	1	Bob Emslie	1884	Baltimore AA	241
2	Harley Payne	1897	Brooklyn NL	350	2	Harley Payne	1897	Brooklyn NL	215
3	Russ Ford	1912	New York AL	317	3	Pete Wood	1885	Buffalo NL	170
4	Ferguson Jenkins	1971	Chicago NL	304	4	Russ Ford	1912	New York AL	165
5	Bill Magee	1898	Louisville NL	294	5	Bill Magee	1898	Louisville NL	163
6	Ferguson Jenkins	1974	Texas AL	286	6	Bill Magee	1899	Lou-Phi-Wsh NL	153
7	Ferguson Jenkins	1969	Chicago NL	284	7	Bob Emslie	1883	Baltimore AA	149
7	Harley Payne	1896	Brooklyn NL	284	8	Bill Mountjoy	1884	Cincinnati AA	148
9	Bill Mountjoy	1884	Cincinnati AA	274	9	Bill Magee	1897	Louisville NL	136
10	Ferguson Jenkins	1973	Chicago NL	267	10	Ferguson Jenkins	1973	Chicago NL	133
11	Ferguson Jenkins	1970	Chicago NL	265	10	Phil Marchildon	1948	Philadelphia AL	133
12	Rube Vickers	1908	Philadelphia AL	264	12	Ferguson Jenkins	1975	Texas AL	130
13	Ferguson Jenkins	1975	Texas AL	261	13	Tip O'Neill	1883	New York NL	129
14	Ferguson Jenkins	1968	Chicago NL	255	13	Harley Payne	1896	Brooklyn NL	129
15	Ferguson Jenkins	1972	Chicago NL	253	15	Ferguson Jenkins	1970	Chicago NL	128

The Top 15 Pitching Performances in a Season

	ERA	Year	Team-League	ERA		Won-Lost	Year	Team-League	Pct
1	Russ Ford	1910	New York AL	1.65	1	Russ Ford	1910	New York AL	.813
2	Russ Ford	1914	Buffalo FL	1.82	2	Russ Ford	1914	Buffalo FL	.778
3	Rube Vickers	1908	Philadelphia AL	2.21	3	Ferguson Jenkins	1978	Texas AL	.692
4	Russ Ford	1911	New York AL	2.27	4	Phil Marchildon	1947	Philadelphia AL	.679
5	Win Kellum	1904	Cincinnati NL	2.60	5	Ferguson Jenkins	1974	Texas AL	.676
6	Ferguson Jenkins	1968	Chicago NL	2.63	6	Russ Ford	1911	New York AL	.667
7	Russ Ford	1913	New York AL	2.66	7	Bob Emslie	1884	Baltimore AA	.653
8	Bob Emslie	1884	Baltimore AA	2.75	8	Dick Fowler	1948	Philadelphia AL	.652
9	Ferguson Jenkins	1971	Chicago NL	2.77	9	Ferguson Jenkins	1971	Chicago NL	.649
10	Ferguson Jenkins	1967	Chicago NL	2.80	**10**	**Kirk McCaskill**	**1986**	**California AL**	**.630**
11	Dick Fowler	1947	Philadelphia AL	2.81	11	Ferguson Jenkins	1972	Chicago NL	.625
12	Ferguson Jenkins	1974	Texas AL	2.82	12	Bill Mountjoy	1884	Cincinnati AA	.613
13	Bob Steele	1917	S.L.-Pitt NL	2.84	13	Ferguson Jenkins	1947	Chicago NL	.606
14	Oscar Judd	1943	Boston AL	2.90	14	Three Times			.600
15	**Kirk McCaskill**	**1989**	**California AL**	**2.93**					

The Top 15 Performances in Career Pitching Records

Rank	Games Pitched	Career	Games	Rank	Innings Pitched	Career	IP
1	Ferguson Jenkins	1965-1983	664	1	Ferguson Jenkins	1965-1983	4500.2
2	John Hiller	1965-1980	545	2	Reggie Cleveland	1969-1981	1809.0
3	Ron Taylor	1962-1972	491	**3**	**Kirk McCaskill**	**1985-1995**	**1677.1**
4	Claude Raymond	1959-1971	449	4	Russ Ford	1909-1915	1487.1
5	Reggie Cleveland	1969-1981	428	5	Dick Fowler	1941-1952	1303.0
6	**Kirk McCaskill**	**1985-1995**	**351**	6	John Hiller	1965-1980	1242.0
7	Dick Fowler	1941-1952	221	7	Phil Marchildon	1940-1950	1214.1
8	Ted Bowsfield	1958-1964	215	8	Ron Taylor	1962-1972	800.0
9	Steve Wilson	1988-1993	205	9	Bob Emslie	1883-1885	792.1
10	Russ Ford	1909-1915	199	10	Oscar Judd	1941-1948	771.1
11	Bob Hooper	1950-1955	194	11	Bill Magee	1897-1902	742.2
12	Phil Marchildon	1940-1950	185	12	Bill Hogg	1905-1908	730.0
13	Oscar Judd	1941-1948	161	13	Claude Raymond	1959-1971	721.0
14	Joe Krakauskas	1937-1946	149	14	Ted Bowsfield	1958-1964	662.1
15	**Paul Quantrill**	**1992-1995**	**144**	15	Bob Hooper	1950-1955	620.2

Rank	Games Won	Career	Wins	Rank	Games Lost	Career	Lost
1	Ferguson Jenkins	1965-1983	284	1	Ferguson Jenkins	1965-1983	226
2	Reggie Cleveland	1969-1981	105	2	Reggie Cleveland	1969-1981	106
3	**Kirk McCaskill**	**1985-1995**	**101**	**3**	**Kirk McCaskill**	**1985-1995**	**103**
4	Russ Ford	1909-1915	99	4	Dick Fowler	1941-1952	79
5	John Hiller	1965-1980	87	5	John Hiller	1965-1980	76
6	Phil Marchildon	1940-1950	68	6	Phil Marchildon	1940-1950	75
7	Dick Fowler	1941-1952	66	7	Russ Ford	1909-1915	71
8	Claude Raymond	1959-1971	46	8	Claude Raymond	1959-1971	53
9	Ron Taylor	1962-1972	45	9	Bill Magee	1897-1902	51
10	Bob Emslie	1883-1885	44	9	Oscar Judd	1941-1948	51
11	Bob Hooper	1950-1955	40	11	Bill Hogg	1905-1908	49
11	Oscar Judd	1941-1948	40	12	Bob Emslie	1883-1885	44
13	Bill Hogg	1905-1908	38	13	Ron Taylor	1962-1972	43
14	Ted Bowsfield	1958-1964	37	14	Bob Hooper	1950-1955	41
15	Two Players		31	15	Ted Bowsfield	1958-1964	39

The Top 15 Performances in Career Pitching Records

Rank	Strikeouts	Career	SO	Rank	Bases On Balls	Career	BB
1	Ferguson Jenkins	1965-1983	3192	1	Ferguson Jenkins	1965-1983	997
2	John Hiller	1965-1980	1036	2	Phil Marchildon	1940-1950	684
3	**Kirk McCaskill**	**1985-1995**	**975**	**3**	**Kirk McCaskill**	**1985-1995**	**634**
4	Reggie Cleveland	1969-1981	930	4	Dick Fowler	1941-1952	578
5	Russ Ford	1909-1915	710	5	Reggie Cleveland	1969-1981	543
6	Claude Raymond	1959-1971	497	6	John Hiller	1965-1980	535
7	Phil Marchildon	1940-1950	481	7	Oscar Judd	1941-1948	397
8	Ron Taylor	1962-1972	464	8	Russ Ford	1909-1915	376
9	Dick Fowler	1941-1952	382	9	Bill Magee	1897-1902	350
10	Bill Hogg	1905-1908	368	10	Bill Hogg	1905-1908	319
11	Bob Emslie	1883-1885	362	11	Bob Hooper	1950-1955	280
12	Joe Krakauskas	1937-1946	347	12	Ted Bowsfield	1958-1964	259
13	Ted Bowsfield	1958-1964	326	13	Claude Raymond	1959-1971	225
14	Rheal Cormier	1991-1995	325	14	Mike Kilkenny	1969-1973	224
15	Oscar Judd	1941-1948	304	15	Ron Taylor	1962-1972	209

Rank	Shutouts	Career	ShO	Rank	Games Saved	Career	Saves
1	Ferguson Jenkins	1965-1983	49	1	John Hiller	1965-1980	125
2	Russ Ford	1909-1915	15	2	Claude Raymond	1959-1971	83
3	Reggie Cleveland	1969-1981	12	3	Ron Taylor	1962-1972	72
4	**Kirk McCaskill**	**1985-1995**	**11**	4	Reggie Cleveland	1969-1981	25
4	Dick Fowler	1941-1952	11	4	Bob Hooper	1950-1955	25
6	Rube Vickers	1902-1909	7	6	Ron Piche	1960-1966	12
7	John Hiller	1965-1980	6	7	Bill Atkinson	1976-1979	11
7	Phil Marchildon	1940-1950	6	8	Russ Ford	1909-1915	9
7	Bill Hogg	1905-1908	6	9	Oscar Judd	1941-1948	7
10	Bill Mountjoy	1883-1885	5	9	Ferguson Jenkins	1965-1983	7
10	Bob Emslie	1883-1885	5	11	Steve Wilson	1988-1993	6
10	Bill Magee	1897-1902	5	11	Ted Bowsfield	1958-1964	6
13	Five Pitchers		4	11	Dick Lines	1966-1967	6
				14	Four Pitchers		5

The Top 15 Performances in Career Pitching Records

Rank	Runs Allowed	Career	Runs	Rank	Earned Runs	Career	ER
1	Ferguson Jenkins	1965-1983	1853	1	Ferguson Jenkins	1965-1983	1669
2	Reggie Cleveland	1969-1981	919	2	Reggie Cleveland	1969-1981	807
3	**Kirk McCaskill**	**1985-1995**	**835**	3	**Kirk McCaskill**	**1985-1995**	**751**
4	Dick Fowler	1941-1952	685	4	Dick Fowler	1941-1952	595
5	Phil Marchildon	1940-1950	605	5	Phil Marchildon	1940-1950	530
6	Russ Ford	1909-1915	602	6	Russ Ford	1909-1915	428
7	Bill Magee	1897-1902	522	7	Bill Magee	1897-1902	407
8	Bob Emslie	1883-1885	507	8	John Hiller	1965-1980	391
9	John Hiller	1965-1980	438	9	Ron Taylor	1962-1972	349
10	Oscar Judd	1941-1948	399	10	Oscar Judd	1941-1948	334
11	Bob Hooper	1950-1955	377	11	Bob Hooper	1950-1955	331
12	Harley Payne	1896-1899	371	12	Ted Bowsfield	1958-1964	320
13	Ron Taylor	1962-1972	370	13	Joe Krakauskas	1937-1946	294
14	Ted Bowsfield	1958-1964	369	14	Claude Raymond	1959-1971	293
15	Bill Hogg	1905-1908	354	15	Bob Emslie	1883-1885	281

Rank	Hits Allowed	Career	Hits	Rank	ERA (500+ IP)	Career	ERA
1	Ferguson Jenkins	1965-1983	4142	1	Russ Ford	1909-1915	2.59
2	Reggie Cleveland	1969-1981	1843	2	John Hiller	1965-1980	2.84
3	**Kirk McCaskill**	**1985-1995**	**1676**	3	Bill Hogg	1905-1908	3.06
4	Dick Fowler	1941-1952	1367	4	Bob Emslie	1883-1885	3.19
5	Russ Ford	1909-1915	1340	5	Bill Mountjoy	1883-1885	3.25
6	Phil Marchildon	1940-1950	1084	6	Ferguson Jenkins	1965-1983	3.34
7	John Hiller	1965-1980	1040	7	Claude Raymond	1959-1971	3.66
8	Bill Magee	1897-1902	837	8	Oscar Judd	1941-1948	3.90
9	Ron Taylor	1962-1972	794	9	Ron Taylor	1962-1972	3.93
10	Bob Emslie	1883-1885	775	10	Phil Marchildon	1940-1950	3.93
11	Oscar Judd	1941-1948	744	11	Reggie Cleveland	1969-1981	4.02
12	Claude Raymond	1959-1971	711	**12**	**Kirk McCaskill**	**1985-1995**	**4.03**
13	Ted Bowsfield	1958-1964	699	13	Harley Payne	1896-1899	4.04
14	Harley Payne	1896-1899	678	14	Dick Fowler	1941-1952	4.11
15	Bill Hogg	1905-1908	677	**15**	**Rheal Cormier**	**1991-1995**	**4.11**

The Top 15 Performances in Career Pitching Records

Rank	Games Started	Career	GS	Rank	Complete Games	Career	CG
1	Ferguson Jenkins	1965-1983	594	1	Ferguson Jenkins	1965-1983	267
2	**Kirk McCaskill**	**1985-1995**	**238**	2	Russ Ford	1909-1915	126
3	Reggie Cleveland	1969-1981	203	3	Bob Emslie	1883-1885	85
4	Russ Ford	1909-1915	170	4	Phil Marchildon	1940-1950	82
4	Dick Fowler	1941-1952	170	5	Dick Fowler	1941-1952	75
6	Phil Marchildon	1940-1950	162	6	Bill Magee	1897-1902	69
7	Oscar Judd	1941-1948	99	7	Harley Payne	1896-1899	57
8	Bob Emslie	1883-1885	90	7	Reggie Cleveland	1969-1981	57
9	Bill Hogg	1905-1908	89	9	Bill Mountjoy	1882-1885	56
10	Bill Magee	1897-1902	88	10	Bill Hogg	1905-1908	43
11	Ted Bowsfield	1958-1964	86	10	Oscar Judd	1941-1948	43
12	**Rheal Cormier**	**1991-1995**	**80**	12	Win Kellum	1901-1905	32
13	Harley Payne	1896-1899	72	13	Clarence Currie	1902-1903	31
14	Joe Krakauskas	1937-1946	63	**14**	**Kirk McCaskill**	**1985-1995**	**30**
15	Bob Steele	1916-1919	58	15	Rube Vickers	1902-1909	29

Rank	Games Finished	Career	GF	Rank	W-L Percentage	Career	PCT.
1	John Hiller	1965-1980	363	1	Russ Ford	1909-1915	.582
2	Ron Taylor	1962-1972	282	2	Bill Mountjoy	1883-1885	.564
3	Claude Raymond	1959-1971	270	3	Mike Kilkenny	1969-1973	.561
4	Reggie Cleveland	1969-1981	111	4	Ferguson Jenkins	1965-1983	.557
5	Bob Hooper	1950-1955	86	5	John Hiller	1965-1980	.534
6	Ken MacKenzie	1960-1965	57	**6**	**Rheal Cormier**	**1991-1995**	**.525**
7	Ron Piche	1960-1966	56	7	Bob Emslie	1883-1885	.500
8	Joe Krakauskas	1937-1946	54	8	Reggie Cleveland	1969-1981	.498
9	Ted Bowsfield	1958-1964	51	**9**	**Kirk McCaskill**	**1985-1995**	**.495**
10	Bill Atkinson	1976-1979	49	10	Bob Hooper	1950-1955	.494
11	Paul Calvert	1942-1951	47	11	Ted Bowsfield	1958-1964	.487
12	**Kirk McCaskill**	**1985-1995**	**42**	12	Phil Marchildon	1940-1950	.476
12	Steve Wilson	1988-1993	42	13	Claude Raymond	1959-1971	.465
14	Dick Lines	1966-1967	41	14	Rube Vickers	1902-1909	.460
15	Ferguson Jenkins	1965-1983	37	15	Dick Fowler	1941-1952	.455

The Top 6 Fielding Performances in a Season—First Base

	Games Played	Year	Team-League	G		Putouts	Year	Team-League	PO
1	Bill Phillips	1886	Brooklyn AA	141	1	Bill Phillips	1888	Kansas City AA	1476
2	Bill Phillips	1887	Brooklyn AA	132	2	Bill Phillips	1886	Brooklyn AA	1395
3	Bill Phillips	1888	Kansas City AA	129	3	Bill Phillips	1887	Brooklyn AA	1299
4	Bill Phillips	1884	Cleveland NL	111	4	Bill Phillips	1885	Brooklyn AA	1109
5	Tim Harkness	1963	New York NL	106	5	Bill Phillips	1884	Cleveland NL	1107
6	Bill Phillips	1885	Brooklyn AA	99	6	Bill Phillips	1883	Cleveland NL	953

	Assists	Year	Team-League	A		Double Plays	Year	Team-League	DP
1	Tim Harkness	1963	New York NL	112	1	Tim Harkness	1963	New York NL	73
2	Bill Phillips	1888	Kansas City AA	55	2	Bill Phillips	1888	Kansas City AA	66
2	Bill Phillips	1887	Brooklyn AA	46	3	Bill Phillips	1886	Brooklyn AA	65
4	Bill Phillips	1886	Brooklyn AA	33	4	Bill Phillips	1887	Brooklyn AA	62
5	**Larry Walker**	**1991**	**Montreal NL**	**30**	5	Bill Phillips	1884	Cleveland NL	59
5	Bill Phillips	1884	Cleveland NL	30	6	Bill Phillips	1882	Cleveland NL	55

The Top 6 Fielding Performances in a Season—First Base

	Total Chances	Year	Team-League	TC		Succ. Chances	Year	Team-League	SC
1	Bill Phillips	1888	Kansas City AA	1563	1	Bill Phillips	1888	Kansas City AA	1531
2	Bill Phillips	1886	Brooklyn AA	1460	2	Bill Phillips	1886	Brooklyn AA	1428
3	Bill Phillips	1887	Brooklyn AA	1369	3	Bill Phillips	1887	Brooklyn AA	1345
4	Bill Phillips	1884	Cleveland NL	1185	4	Bill Phillips	1884	Cleveland NL	1137
5	Bill Phillips	1885	Brooklyn AA	1165	5	Bill Phillips	1885	Brooklyn AA	1133
6	Tim Harkness	1963	New York NL	1024	6	Tim Harkness	1963	New York NL	1010

	Errors	Year	Team-League	E		Average	Year	Team-League	FA
1	Bill Phillips	1884	Cleveland NL	48	1	Tim Harkness	1963	New York NL	.986
2	Bill Phillips	1879	Cleveland NL	36	2	Bill Phillips	1887	Brooklyn AA	.982
3	Bill Phillips	1880	Cleveland NL	33	3	Bill Phillips	1888	Kansas City AA	.980
3	Bill Phillips	1883	Cleveland NL	33	4	Bill Phillips	1886	Brooklyn AA	.978
5	Three Times			32	5	Bill Phillips	1884	Cleveland NL	.959

The Top 6 Fielding Performances in a Season—Second Base

	Games Played	Year	Team-League	G		Putouts	Year	Team-League	PO
1	Dave McKay	1978	Toronto AL	140	1	Pop Smith	1885	Pittsburgh AA	372
2	Pop Smith	1890	Boston NL	134	2	Pop Smith	1890	Boston NL	324
3	John O'Brien	1895	Louisville NL	125	3	Dave McKay	1978	Toronto AL	310
4	John O'Brien	1896	Lou-Wash NL	122	4	Frank O'Rourke	1925	Detroit AL	309
5	Frank O'Rourke	1925	Detroit AL	118	4	John O'Brien	1899	Balt - Pitt NL	309
5	John O'Brien	1899	Balt-Pitt NL	118	6	John O'Brien	1895	Louisville NL	304

	Assists	Year	Team-League	A		Double Plays	Year	Team-League	DP
1	Dave McKay	1978	Toronto AL	408	1	Dave McKay	1978	Toronto AL	96
2	Pop Smith	1890	Boston NL	401	2	Frank O'Rourke	1925	Detroit AL	67
3	John O'Brien	1895	Louisville NL	396	3	John O'Brien	1895	Louisville NL	56
4	Pop Smith	1884	Columbus AA	394	4	Pop Smith	1884	Columbus AA	55
5	Pop Smith	1885	Pittsburgh AA	384	5	Pop Smith	1885	Pittsburgh AA	53
6	Frank O'Rourke	1925	Detroit AL	382	5	John O'Brien	1899	Balt - Pitt NL	53

The Top 6 Fielding Performances in a Season—Second Base

	Total Chances	Year	Team-League	TC		Succ. Chances	Year	Team-League	SC
1	Pop Smith	1885	Pittsburgh AA	820	1	Pop Smith	1885	Pittsburgh AA	756
2	Pop Smith	1884	Columbus AA	793	2	Pop Smith	1884	Columbus AA	718
3	John O'Brien	1895	Louisville NL	746	2	Dave McKay	1978	Toronto AL	718
4	Dave McKay	1978	Toronto AL	730	4	John O'Brien	1895	Louisville NL	700
5	John O'Brien	1899	Balt-Pitt NL	718	5	Frank O'Rourke	1925	Detroit AL	691
6	Frank O'Rourke	1925	Detroit AL	712	6	John O'Brien	1899	Balt-Pitt NL	684

	Errors	Year	Team-League	E		Average	Year	Team-League	FA
1	Pop Smith	1880	Cincinnati NL	89	1	Dave McKay	1978	Toronto AL	.984
2	Pop Smith	1884	Columbus AA	75	2	Frank O'Rourke	1925	Detroit AL	.971
3	Pop Smith	1885	Pittsburgh AA	64	3	John O'Brien	1899	Balt-Pitt NL	.953
4	Pop Smith	1883	Columbus AA	62	4	John O'Brien	1895	Louisville NL	.938
5	Pop Smith	1890	Boston NL	57	5	John O'Brien	1896	Lou-Wash NL	.938
6	Two Times			49	6	Pop Smith	1885	Pittsburgh AA	.922

The Top 6 Fielding Performances in a Season—Third Base

	Games Played	Year	Team-League	G		Putouts	Year	Team-League	PO
1	Pete Ward	1963	Chicago AL	154	1	Frank O'Rourke	1927	St. Louis AL	183
2	Frank O'Rourke	1929	St. Louis AL	151	2	Frank O'Rourke	1929	St. Louis AL	171
3	Pete Ward	1964	Chicago AL	138	3	Jimmy Knowles	1890	Rochester AA	162
4	Pete Ward	1965	Chicago AL	134	4	Pete Ward	1963	Chicago AL	156
5	Jimmy Knowles	1890	Rochester AA	123	5	Frank O'Rourke	1928	St. Louis AL	150
6	Frank O'Rourke	1927	St. Louis AL	121	6	Pete Ward	1964	Chicago AL	126

	Assists	Year	Team-League	A		Double Plays	Year	Team-League	DP
1	Pete Ward	1965	Chicago AL	319	1	Frank O'Rourke	1929	St. Louis AL	30
2	Pete Ward	1964	Chicago AL	309	2	Frank O'Rourke	1927	St. Louis AL	27
3	Jimmy Knowles	1890	Rochester AA	303	2	Pete Ward	1963	Chicago AL	27
4	Pete Ward	1963	Chicago AL	302	4	Pete Ward	1964	Chicago AL	24
5	Frank O'Rourke	1927	St. Louis AL	244	5	Pete Ward	1965	Chicago AL	22
6	Frank O'Rourke	1929	St. Louis AL	242	6	Jimmy Knowles	1890	Rochester AA	19

The Top 6 Fielding Performances in a Season—Third Base

	Total Chances	Year	Team-League	TC		Succ. Chances	Year	Team-League	SC
1	Jimmy Knowles	1890	Rochester AA	528	1	Jimmy Knowles	1890	Rochester AA	465
2	Pete Ward	1963	Chicago AL	496	2	Pete Ward	1963	Chicago AL	458
3	Pete Ward	1964	Chicago AL	454	3	Pete Ward	1964	Chicago AL	435
4	Frank O'Rourke	1927	St. Louis AL	447	4	Frank O'Rourke	1927	St. Louis AL	427
5	Frank O'Rourke	1929	St. Louis AL	438	5	Pete Ward	1965	Chicago AL	416
6	Pete Ward	1965	Chicago AL	437	6	Frank O'Rourke	1929	St. Louis AL	413

	Errors	Year	Team-League	E		Average	Year	Team-League	FA
1	John Irwin	1884	Boston UA	87	1	Pete Ward	1964	Chicago AL	.958
2	Jimmy Knowles	1890	Rochester AA	63	2	Frank O'Rourke	1927	St. Louis AL	.955
3	Arthur Irwin	1882	Worcester NL	45	3	Pete Ward	1965	Chicago AL	.952
4	Pete Ward	1963	Chicago AL	38	4	Frank O'Rourke	1929	St. Louis AL	.943
5	Jimmy Knowles	1886	Washington NL	34	5	Pete Ward	1963	Chicago AL	.923
6	John Irwin	1889	Washington NL	32	6	Jimmy Knowles	1890	Rochester AA	.881

The Top 6 Fielding Performances in a Season—Shortstop

	Games Played	Year	Team-League	G		Putouts	Year	Team-League	PO
1	Arthur Irwin	1888	Philadelphia NL	122	1	Frank O'Rourke	1921	Washington AL	272
1	Frank O'Rourke	1921	Washington AL	122	2	Pop Smith	1889	Pit-Bos NL	214
3	Pop Smith	1889	Pit-Bos NL	117	3	Arthur Irwin	1888	Philadelphia NL	204
4	Arthur Irwin	1889	Phil-Was NL	103	4	Arthur Irwin	1889	Phil-Was NL	190
5	Arthur Irwin	1884	Providence NL	102	5	Arthur Irwin	1887	Philadelphia NL	178
6	Two Times			100	6	Two Times			137

	Assists	Year	Team-League	A		Double Plays	Year	Team-League	DP
1	Frank O'Rourke	1921	Washington AL	378	1	Frank O'Rourke	1921	Washington AL	52
2	Arthur Irwin	1888	Philadelphia NL	374	2	Pop Smith	1889	Pit-Bos NL	44
3	Pop Smith	1889	Pit-Bos NL	357	2	Arthur Irwin	1890	Boston PL	44
4	Pop Smith	1886	Pittsburgh AA	356	4	Arthur Irwin	1889	Phil-Was NL	42
5	Arthur Irwin	1880	Worcester NL	339	5	Arthur Irwin	1888	Philadelphia NL	31
6	Arthur Irwin	1890	Boston PL	331	6	Arthur Irwin	1887	Philadelphia NL	30

The Top 6 Fielding Performances in a Season—Shortstop

	Total Chances	Year	Team-League	TC		Succ. Chances	Year	Team-League	SC
1	Frank O'Rourke	1921	Washington AL	705	1	Frank O'Rourke	1921	Washington AL	650
2	Arthur Irwin	1888	Philadelphia NL	642	2	Arthur Irwin	1888	Philadelphia NL	578
3	Pop Smith	1889	Pit-Bos NL	639	3	Pop Smith	1889	Pit-Bos NL	571
4	Arthur Irwin	1889	Phil-Was NL	580	4	Arthur Irwin	1889	Phil-Was NL	515
5	Pop Smith	1886	Pittsburgh AA	545	5	Pop Smith	1886	Pittsburgh AA	488
6	Arthur Irwin	1887	Philadelphia NL	537	6	Arthur Irwin	1887	Philadelphia NL	479

	Errors	Year	Team-League	E		Average	Year	Team-League	FA
1	Milt Whitehead	1884	St. Louis UA	87	1	Frank O'Rourke	1921	Washington AL	.922
2	Pop Smith	1889	Pitt - Bost NL	68	2	Arthur Irwin	1888	Philadelphia NL	.900
3	Arthur Irwin	1883	Providence NL	65	3	Pop Smith	1889	Pit-Bos NL	.894
3	Arthur Irwin	1889	Phil-Was NL	65	4	Arthur Irwin	1887	Philadelphia NL	.892
3	Arthur Irwin	1890	Boston PL	65	5	Arthur Irwin	1886	Philadelphia NL	.891
6	Arthur Irwin	1888	Philadelphia NL	64	6	Arthur Irwin	1889	Phil-Was NL	.890

The Top 15 Fielding Performances in a Season—Outfielders

	Games Played	Year	Team-League	G		Putouts	Year	Team-League	PO
1	Jack Graney	1916	Cleveland AL	154	1	Goody Rosen	1945	Brooklyn NL	392
2	Terry Puhl	1979	Houston NL	152	2	Terry Puhl	1978	Houston NL	386
3	Jeff Heath	1941	Cleveland AL	151	3	Terry Puhl	1979	Houston NL	352
4	Jack Graney	1913	Cleveland AL	148	4	Jeff Heath	1942	Cleveland AL	326
4	Terry Puhl	1978	Houston NL	148	5	Terry Puhl	1980	Houston NL	311
6	Jeff Heath	1942	Cleveland AL	146	6	Jack Graney	1916	Cleveland AL	309
6	Doc Miller	1911	Boston NL	146	7	Jeff Heath	1947	St. Louis AL	297
8	Jack Graney	1917	Cleveland AL	145	8	George Selkirk	1936	New York AL	290
9	Jack Graney	1911	Cleveland AL	142	9	Jack Graney	1919	Cleveland AL	288
10	Goody Rosen	1945	Brooklyn NL	141	10	Jack Graney	1919	Cleveland AL	281
11	Jeff Heath	1947	St. Louis AL	140	11	Tip O'Neill	1886	St. Louis AA	279
12	**Larry Walker**	1992	**Montreal NL**	**139**	12	Jack Graney	1913	Cleveland AL	275
13	Terry Puhl	1982	Houston NL	138	13	Jack Graney	1914	Cleveland AL	274
14	Tip O'Neill	1886	St. Louis AA	137	**14**	**Larry Walker**	**1993**	**Montreal NL**	**273**
14	Tip O'Neill	1890	Chicago PL	137	15	Two Times			269

The Top 15 Fielding Performances in a Season—Outfielders

	Assists	Year	Team-League	A		Double Plays	Year	Team-League	DP
1	Doc Miller	1911	Boston NL	26	1	George Selkirk	1940	New York AL	6
2	Jack Graney	1911	Cleveland AL	22	1	Jack Graney	1917	Cleveland AL	6
2	Jack Graney	1916	Cleveland AL	22	3	Jack Graney	1910	Cleveland AL	5
4	Doc Miller	1912	Bos-Phil NL	21	3	Jack Graney	1911	Cleveland AL	5
5	Jeff Heath	1941	Cleveland AL	20	3	Jack Graney	1912	Cleveland AL	5
6	Goody Rosen	1938	Brooklyn NL	19	3	Jack Graney	1913	Cleveland AL	5
6	Bill O'Hara	1909	New York NL	19	3	Jack Graney	1916	Cleveland AL	5
6	Bunk Congalton	1907	Clev-Bos AL	19	**3**	**Larry Walker**	**1990**	**Montreal NL**	**5**
9	Jack Graney	1915	Cleveland AL	17	3	Doc Miller	1912	Bos-Phil NL	5
10	**Larry Walker**	**1992**	**Montreal NL**	**16**	10	Seven Times			4
10	Jack Graney	1913	Cleveland AL	16					
12	Emil Frisk	1905	St. Louis AL	15					
12	Jack Graney	1914	Cleveland AL	15					
14	Four Times			14					

The Top 15 Fielding Performances in a Season—Outfielders

	Total Chances	Year	Team-League	TC		Succ. Chances	Year	Team-League	SC
1	Goody Rosen	1945	Brooklyn NL	402	1	Goody Rosen	1945	Brooklyn NL	399
2	Terry Puhl	1978	Houston NL	395	2	Terry Puhl	1978	Houston NL	392
3	Terry Puhl	1979	Houston NL	359	3	Terry Puhl	1979	Houston NL	359
4	Jeff Heath	1942	Cleveland AL	345	4	Jeff Heath	1942	Cleveland AL	338
4	Jack Graney	1916	Cleveland AL	345	5	Jack Graney	1916	Cleveland AL	331
6	Terry Puhl	1980	Houston NL	328	6	Terry Puhl	1980	Houston NL	325
7	Tip O'Neill	1886	St. Louis AA	315	7	Jeff Heath	1947	St. Louis AL	304
7	Jack Graney	1917	Cleveland AL	315	8	Jack Graney	1917	Cleveland AL	302
9	Jack Graney	1914	Cleveland AL	309	9	George Selkirk	1936	New York AL	300
10	George Selkirk	1936	New York AL	308	10	Jack Graney	1919	Cleveland AL	294
10	Jeff Heath	1947	St. Louis AL	308	11	Jack Graney	1913	Cleveland AL	291
12	Jack Graney	1919	Cleveland AL	306	12	Jack Graney	1914	Cleveland AL	289
13	Jack Graney	1911	Cleveland AL	302	**13**	**Larry Walker**	**1993**	**Montreal NL**	**286**
14	Jack Graney	1913	Cleveland AL	300	**14**	**Larry Walker**	**1992**	**Montreal NL**	**285**
15	Jeff Heath	1942	Cleveland AL	294	15	Goody Rosen	1938	Brooklyn NL	282

The Top 15 Fielding Performances in a Season—Outfielders

	Errors	Year	Team-League	E		Average	Year	Team-League	FA
1	Tip O'Neill	1887	St. Louis AA	30	1	Terry Puhl	1979	Houston NL	1.000
2	Tip O'Neill	1886	St. Louis AA	23	**2**	**Larry Walker**	**1992**	**Montreal NL**	**.993**
3	Jack Graney	1911	Cleveland AL	22	3	Goody Rosen	1938	Brooklyn NL	.993
4	Jack Graney	1914	Cleveland AL	20	4	Terry Puhl	1978	Houston NL	.992
5	Joe Knight	1890	Cincinnati NL	19	5	Terry Puhl	1983	Houston NL	.991
5	Bill O'Neill	1904	Bos-Was AL	19	6	Terry Puhl	1980	Houston NL	.991
5	Tip O'Neill	1889	St. Louis AA	19	7	Terry Puhl	1982	Houston NL	.989
5	Tip O'Neill	1890	Chicago PL	19	8	George Selkirk	1939	New York AL	.989
9	Tip O'Neill	1884	St. Louis AA	17	**9**	**Larry Walker**	**1995**	**Colorado NL**	**.988**
9	Tip O'Neill	1892	Cincinnati NL	17	10	Terry Puhl	1984	Houston NL	.986
11	Spud Johnson	1891	Cleveland NL	16	**11**	**Larry Walker**	**1990**	**Montreal NL**	**.985**
11	Tip O'Neill	1888	St. Louis AA	16	12	Jeff Heath	1942	Cleveland AL	.980
13	Fred Osborne	1890	Pittsburgh NL	15	13	Jeff Heath	1938	Cleveland AL	.974
13	Jeff Heath	1941	Cleveland AL	15	14	Bunk Congalton	1907	Cle-Bos AL	.971
13	Newt Randall	1907	Chi-Bos NL	15	15	Jack Graney	1913	Cleveland AL	.970

The Top 6 Fielding Performances in a Season—Catchers

	Games Played	Year	Team-League	G		Putouts	Year	Team-League	PO
1	George Gibson	1909	Pittsburgh NL	150	1	George Gibson	1909	Pittsburgh NL	655
2	George Gibson	1910	Pittsburgh NL	143	2	George Gibson	1910	Pittsburgh NL	633
3	George Gibson	1908	Pittsburgh NL	140	3	George Gibson	1908	Pittsburgh NL	607
4	Larry McLean	1910	Cincinnati NL	119	4	George Gibson	1915	Pittsburgh NL	551
5	George Gibson	1915	Pittsburgh NL	118	5	George Gibson	1907	Pittsburgh NL	499
6	Nig Clarke	1907	Cleveland AL	115	6	Larry McLean	1910	Cincinnati NL	485

	Assists	Year	Team-League	A		Double Plays	Year	Team-League	DP
1	George Gibson	1910	Pittsburgh NL	203	1	Frank Owens	1915	Baltimore FL	19
2	George Gibson	1909	Pittsburgh NL	192	2	Larry McLean	1910	Cincinnati NL	18
3	Larry McLean	1910	Cincinnati NL	158	3	Larry McLean	1909	Cincinnati NL	16
4	Frank Owens	1915	Baltimore FL	146	3	Larry McLean	1912	Cincinnati NL	16
5	George Gibson	1908	Pittsburgh NL	136	3	George Gibson	1911	Pittsburgh NL	16
6	George Gibson	1915	Pittsburgh NL	134	6	Nig Clarke	1907	Cleveland AL	15

The Top 6 Fielding Performances in a Season—Catchers

	Succ. Chances	Year	Team-League	SC		Passed Balls	Year	Team-League	PB
1	George Gibson	1909	Pittsburgh NL	847	1	John Humphries	1884	Wash (AA)-NY (NL)	65
2	George Gibson	1910	Pittsburgh NL	735	2	John Humphries	1883	New York NL	30
3	George Gibson	1908	Pittsburgh NL	743	3	Bill Phillips	1879	Cleveland AL	26
4	George Gibson	1915	Pittsburgh NL	685	4	Nig Clarke	1907	Cleveland AL	25
5	Larry McLean	1910	Cincinnati NL	643	5	Jim McKeever	1884	Boston UA	24
6	George Gibson	1907	Pittsburgh NL	624	6	Fred Wood	1884	Detroit NL	19

	Errors	Year	Team-League	E		Average	Year	Team-League	FA
1	John Humphries	1884	Wash (AA)-NY (NL)	51	1	George Gibson	1911	Pittsburgh NL	.990
2	Nig Clarke	1911	St. Louis AL	29	2	George Gibson	1910	Pittsburgh NL	.984
3	George Gibson	1915	Pittsburgh NL	25	3	Larry McLean	1910	Cincinnati NL	.983
4	Nig Clarke	1907	Cleveland AL	24	4	George Gibson	1909	Pittsburgh NL	.983
5	John Humphries	1883	New York NL	23	5	George Gibson	1912	Pittsburgh NL	.979
6	George Gibson	1908	Pittsburgh NL	21	6	Larry McLean	1909	Cincinnati NL	.978

The Top 15 Fielding Performances in a Season—Pitchers

	Games Played	Year	Team-League	G		Putouts	Year	Team-League	PO
1	John Hiller	1973	Detroit AL	65	1	Ferguson Jenkins	1971	Chicago NL	31
2	Ron Taylor	1963	St. Louis NL	63	2	Ferguson Jenkins	1978	Texas AL	29
3	Claude Raymond	1966	Houston NL	62	3	Ferguson Jenkins	1972	Chicago NL	28
4	Ferguson Jenkins	1966	Phi-Chi NL	61	4	Ferguson Jenkins	1975	Texas AL	27
5	Steve Wilson	1992	Los Angeles NL	60	4	Bob Emslie	1884	Baltimore AA	27
6	Claude Raymond	1959	Montreal NL	59	6	Ferguson Jenkins	1979	Texas AL	25
6	Ron Taylor	1969	New York NL	59	7	Ferguson Jenkins	1974	Texas AL	24
6	John Hiller	1974	Detroit AL	59	7	Ferguson Jenkins	1977	Boston AL	24
9	**Vince Horsman**	**1992**	**Oakland AL**	**58**	7	Ferguson Jenkins	1980	Texas AL	24
9	Ron Taylor	1968	New York NL	58	**7**	**Kirk McCaskill**	**1986**	**California AL**	**24**
11	Ron Taylor	1970	New York NL	57	**7**	**Kirk McCaskill**	**1992**	**Chicago AL**	**24**
11	Ron Taylor	1965	St.L-Hou NL	57	12	Bob Hooper	1952	Philadelphia AL	22
13	John Hiller	1976	Detroit AL	56	13	Ferguson Jenkins	1973	Chicago NL	21
14	Bill Atkinson	1977	Montreal NL	55	14	Ferguson Jenkins	1967	Chicago NL	20
14	**Kirk McCaskill**	**1995**	**Chicago AL**	**55**	15	Two Times			19

The Top 15 Fielding Performances in a Season—Pitchers

	Assists	Year	Team-League	A		Double Plays	Year	Team-League	DP
1	Russ Ford	1912	New York AL	88	1	Bob Hooper	1950	Philadelphia AL	10
2	Bob Emslie	1884	Baltimore AA	83	2	Russ Ford	1912	New York AL	6
2	Rube Vickers	1908	Philadelphia AL	83	2	Ferguson Jenkins	1973	Chicago NL	6
4	Harley Payne	1896	Brooklyn NL	76	3	Dick Fowler	1949	Philadelphia AL	5
5	Russ Ford	1910	New York AL	75	3	Phil Marchildon	1948	Philadelphia AL	5
6	Clarence Currie	1903	St.L-Chi NL	74	3	Bob Hooper	1952	Philadelphia AL	5
7	Russ Ford	1914	Buffalo FL	72	3	Ferguson Jenkins	1968	Chicago NL	5
8	Russ Ford	1911	New York AL	70	3	Ferguson Jenkins	1979	Texas AL	5
9	Harley Payne	1897	Brooklyn NL	68	**3**	**Kirk McCaskill**	**1989**	**California AL**	**5**
10	Bill Magee	1898	Louisville NL	65	10	Nine Times			4
11	Clarence Currie	1902	Cin-St.L NL	64					
11	Win Kellum	1904	Cincinnati NL	64					
11	Bill Mountjoy	1884	Cincinnati AA	64					
14	Russ Ford	1913	New York AL	56					
15	Ferguson Jenkins	1973	Chicago NL	53					

The Top 15 Fielding Performances in a Season—Pitchers

	Total Chances	Year	Team-League	TC		Succ. Chances	Year	Team-League	SC
1	Bob Emslie	1884	Baltimore AA	132	1	Bob Emslie	1884	Baltimore AA	110
2	Russ Ford	1912	New York AL	106	2	Russ Ford	1912	New York AL	101
3	Rube Vickers	1908	Philadelphia AL	100	3	Rube Vickers	1908	Philadelphia AL	93
4	Harley Payne	1896	Brooklyn NL	95	4	Harley Payne	1896	Brooklyn NL	88
5	Russ Ford	1911	New York AL	91	5	Russ Ford	1911	New York AL	86
5	Clarence Currie	1903	St.L-Chi NL	91	6	Clarence Currie	1903	St.L-Chi NL	83
7	Russ Ford	1910	New York AL	89	7	Russ Ford	1910	New York AL	82
8	Ferguson Jenkins	1971	Chicago NL	86	8	Russ Ford	1914	Buffalo FL	81
9	Harley Payne	1897	Brooklyn NL	84	9	Win Kellum	1904	Cincinnati NL	80
10	Bill Mountjoy	1884	Cincinnati AA	83	10	Harley Payne	1897	Brooklyn NL	79
11	Bill Magee	1898	Louisville NL	82	10	Ferguson Jenkins	1971	Chicago NL	79
12	Ferguson Jenkins	1972	Chicago NL	80	12	Ferguson Jenkins	1972	Chicago NL	78
13	Ferguson Jenkins	1973	Chicago NL	78	13	Bill Mountjoy	1884	Cincinnati AA	77
13	Ferguson Jenkins	1979	Texas AL	78	14	Bill Magee	1898	Louisville NL	76
15	Clarence Currie	1902	Cin-St.L NL	76	15	Ferguson Jenkins	1979	Texas AL	75

The Top 15 Fielding Performances in a Season—Pitchers

	Errors	Year	Team-League	E		Average	Year	Team-League	FA
1	Bob Emslie	1884	Baltimore AA	22	1	Oscar Judd	1946	Philadelphia AL	1.000
2	Bob Emslie	1883	Baltimore AA	12	1	Ferguson Jenkins	1968	Chicago NL	1.000
3	Pete Wood	1885	Buffalo NL	8	1	Paul Calvert	1979	Washington AL	1.000
3	Clarence Currie	1903	St.L-Chi NL	8	1	Russ Ford	1915	Buffalo FL	1.000
3	Bob Emslie	1885	Bal-Phi AA	8	1	Ferguson Jenkins	1976	Boston AL	1.000
3	Russ Ford	1913	New York AL	8	1	Ferguson Jenkins	1983	Chicago NL	1.000
7	Bill Magee	1897	Louisville NL	7	1	Reggie Cleveland	1980	Milwaukee AL	1.000
7	Bill Magee	1898	Lou-Phi NL	7	1	Ferguson Jenkins	1981	Texas AL	1.000
7	Harley Payne	1896	Brooklyn NL	7	1	John Hiller	1968	Detroit AL	1.000
7	Russ Ford	1910	New York AL	7	1	Oscar Judd	1945	Bos-Phi AL	1.000
7	Rube Vickers	1908	Philadelphia AL	7	1	Johnny Rutherford	1952	Brooklyn NL	1.000
7	Ferguson Jenkins	1971	Chicago NL	7	12	Russ Ford	1914	Buffalo FL	.988
13	Four Times			6	13	Ferguson Jenkins	1978	Texas AL	.985
					14	Dick Fowler	1949	Philadelphia AL	.984
					15	Bob Hooper	1952	Philadelphia AL	.982

The Top 6 Performances in Career Fielding Records—First Base

Rank	Games Played	Career	Games	Rank	Putouts	Career	PO
1	Bill Phillips	1879-1888	1032	1	Bill Phillips	1879-1888	10540
2	Tim Harkness	1961-1964	199	2	Tim Harkness	1961-1964	1276
3	Pete Ward	1962-1970	113	3	Jimmy Knowles	1884-1892	809
4	**Larry Walker**	**1989-1995**	**78**	4	Pete Ward	1962-1970	802
5	Jimmy Knowles	1884-1892	76	5	**Larry Walker**	**1989-1995**	**639**
6	Larry McLean	1903-1915	37	6	Larry McLean	1903-1915	314

Rank	Assists	Career	A	Rank	Double Plays	Career	DP
1	Bill Phillips	1879-1888	305	1	Bill Phillips	1879-1888	511
2	Tim Harkness	1961-1964	149	2	Tim Harkness	1961-1964	121
3	Pete Ward	1962-1970	57	3	Pete Ward	1962-1970	61
3	**Larry Walker**	**1989-1995**	**57**	4	**Larry Walker**	**1989-1995**	**50**
5	Jimmy Knowles	1884-1892	33	5	Jimmy Knowles	1884-1892	38
6	Frank Colman	1942-1947	16	6	Tom Burgess	1954-1962	27

Rank	Total Chances	Career	TC	Rank	Accepted	Career	SC
1	Bill Phillips	1879-1888	11169	1	Bill Phillips	1879-1888	10845
2	Tim Harkness	1961-1964	1441	2	Tim Harkness	1961-1964	1425
3	Jimmy Knowles	1884-1892	879	3	Pete Ward	1962-1970	859
4	Pete Ward	1962-1970	863	4	Jimmy Knowles	1884-1892	842
5	**Larry Walker**	**1989-1995**	**705**	5	**Larry Walker**	**1989-1995**	**696**
6	Larrry McLean	1903-1915	159	6	Larrry McLean	1903-1915	324

Rank	Errors	Career	E	Rank	Fielding Avg	Career	F.A.
1	Bill Phillips	1879-1888	324	1	Pete Ward	1962-1970	.995
2	Jimmy Knowles	1884-1892	37	2	Tim Harkness	1961-1964	.989
3	Tim Harkness	1961-1964	16	3	Bill Phillips	1879-1888	.971
4	Larrry McLean	1903-1915	11				
5	Dave Rowan	1911	10				
6	**Larry Walker**	**1989-1995**	**9**				

The Top 6 Performances in Career Fielding Records—Second Base

Rank	Games Played	Career	Games	Rank	Putouts	Career	PO
1	Pop Smith	1880-1891	711	1	Pop Smith	1880-1891	2012
2	John O'Brien	1891-1899	498	2	John O'Brien	1891-1899	1222
3	Dave McKay	1975-1982	385	3	Dave McKay	1975-1982	785
4	Frank O'Rourke	1912-1931	220	4	Frank O'Rourke	1912-1931	580
5	Sherry Robertson	1940-1952	109	5	Sam LaRoque	1888-1891	261
6	Sam LaRoque	1888-1891	90	6	Jimmy Knowles	1884-1892	245

Rank	Assists	Career	A	Rank	Double Plays	Career	DP
1	Pop Smith	1880-1891	2354	1	Pop Smith	1880-1891	303
2	John O'Brien	1891-1899	1516	2	Dave McKay	1975-1982	223
3	Dave McKay	1975-1982	1038	3	John O'Brien	1891-1899	218
4	Frank O'Rourke	1912-1931	719	4	Frank O'Rourke	1912-1931	138
5	Sherry Robertson	1940-1952	305	5	Sherry Robertson	1940-1952	59
6	Sam LaRoque	1888-1891	274	6	Sam LaRoque	1888-1891	39

Rank	Total Chances	Career	TC	Rank	Chances Acc	Career	SC
1	Pop Smith	1880-1891	4832	1	Pop Smith	1880-1891	4366
2	John O'Brien	1891-1899	2926	2	John O'Brien	1891-1899	2738
3	Dave McKay	1975-1982	1867	3	Dave McKay	1975-1982	1823
4	Frank O'Rourke	1912-1931	1341	4	Frank O'Rourke	1912-1931	1299
5	Sam LaRoque	1888-1891	584	5	Sherry Robertson	1940-1952	545
6	Sherry Robertson	1940-1952	573	6	Sam LaRoque	1888-1891	535

Rank	Erros	Career	E	Rank	Fielding Avg	Career	F.A.
1	Pop Smith	1880-1891	466	1	Dave McKay	1975-1982	.976
2	John O'Brien	1891-1899	188	2	Frank O'Rourke	1912-1931	.969
3	Jimmy Knowles	1884-1892	53	3	John O'Brien	1891-1899	.936
4	Sam LaRoque	1888-1891	49	4	Pop Smith	1880-1891	.904
4	Chub Collins	1884-1885	49				
6	Dave McKay	1975-1982	44				

The Top 6 Performances in Career Fielding Records—Third Base

Rank	Games Played	Career	Games	Rank	Putouts	Career	PO
1	Frank O'Rourke	1912-1931	598	1	Frank O'Rourke	1912-1931	798
2	Pete Ward	1962-1970	562	2	Pete Ward	1962-1970	470
3	John Irwin	1882-1891	258	3	John Irwin	1882-1891	311
4	Dave McKay	1975-1982	223	4	Jimmy Knowles	1884-1892	252
5	Jimmy Knowles	1884-1892	203	5	Dave McKay	1975-1982	182
6	Sherry Robertson	1940-1952	98	6	Two Players		87

Rank	Assists	Career	A	Rank	Double Plays	Career	DP
1	Pete Ward	1962-1970	1182	1	Frank O'Rourke	1912-1931	111
2	Frank O'Rourke	1912-1931	1101	2	Pete Ward	1962-1970	87
3	John Irwin	1882-1891	507	3	Dave McKay	1975-1982	41
4	Jimmy Knowles	1884-1892	469	4	John Irwin	1882-1891	36
5	Dave McKay	1975-1982	379	5	Jimmy Knowles	1884-1892	31
6	Sherry Robertson	1940-1952	164	6	Sherry Robertson	1940-1952	11

Rank	Total Chances	Career	TC	Rank	Accepted	Career	SC
1	Frank O'Rourke	1912-1931	2001	1	Frank O'Rourke	1912-1931	1899
2	Pete Ward	1962-1970	1749	2	Pete Ward	1962-1970	1652
3	John Irwin	1882-1891	987	3	John Irwin	1882-1891	818
4	Jimmy Knowles	1884-1892	837	4	Jimmy Knowles	1884-1892	721
5	Dave McKay	1975-1982	600	5	Dave McKay	1975-1982	561
6	Arthur Irwin	1880-1891	293	6	Sherry Robertson	1940-1952	251

Rank	Errors	Career	E	Rank	Fielding Avg	Career	F.A.
1	John Irwin	1882-1891	169	1	Frank O'Rourke	1912-1931	.949
2	Jimmy Knowles	1884-1892	116	2	Pete Ward	1962-1970	.945
3	Frank O'Rourke	1912-1931	102	3	Dave McKay	1975-1982	.935
4	Pete Ward	1962-1970	97	4	Jimmy Knowles	1884-1892	.861
5	Arthur Irwin	1880-1891	50	5	John Irwin	1882-1891	.829
6	Dave McKay	1975-1982	39				

The Top 6 Performances in Career Fielding Records—Shortstop

Rank	Games Played	Career	Games	Rank	Putouts	Career	PO
1	Arthur Irwin	1880-1894	947	1	Arthur Irwin	1880-1894	1301
2	Pop Smith	1880-1891	332	2	Frank O'Rourke	1912-1931	555
3	Frank O'Rourke	1912-1931	288	3	Pop Smith	1880-1891	520
4	Milt Whitehead	1884	95	4	Milt Whitehead	1884	85
5	Dave McKay	1975-1982	45	5	John Irwin	1882-1891	66
6	John Irwin	1882-1891	35	6	Dave McKay	1975-1982	61

Rank	Assists	Career	A	Rank	Double Plays	Career	DP
1	Arthur Irwin	1880-1894	3093	1	Arthur Irwin	1880-1894	293
2	Pop Smith	1880-1891	1100	2	Frank O'Rourke	1912-1931	112
3	Frank O'Rourke	1912-1931	852	3	Pop Smith	1880-1891	98
4	Milt Whitehead	1884	272	4	Milt Whitehead	1884	19
5	John Irwin	1882-1891	103	5	Dave McKay	1975-1982	13
6	Sam LaRoque	1888-1981	76	5	Sherry Robertson	1940-1952	13

Rank	Total Chances	Career	TC	Rank	Chances Acc	Career	SC
1	Arthur Irwin	1880-1894	4988	1	Arthur Irwin	1880-1894	4394
2	Pop Smith	1880-1891	1818	2	Pop Smith	1880-1891	1630
3	Frank O'Rourke	1912-1931	1520	3	Frank O'Rourke	1912-1931	1407
4	Milt Whitehead	1884	444	4	Milt Whitehead	1884	357
5	John Irwin	1882-1891	208	5	John Irwin	1882-1891	169
6	Sam LaRoque	1888-1981	160	6	Dave McKay	1975-1982	127

Rank	Errors	Career	E	Rank	Fielding Avg	Career	F.A.
1	Arthur Irwin	1880-1894	594	1	Frank O'Rourke	1912-1931	.926
2	Pop Smith	1880-1891	188	2	Pop Smith	1880-1891	.897
3	Frank O'Rourke	1912-1931	113	3	Arthur Irwin	1880-1894	.881
4	Milt Whitehead	1884	87				
5	Sam LaRoque	1888-1981	36				
6	John Irwin	1882-1891	29				

The Top 15 Performances in Career Fielding Records—Outfielder

Rank	Games Played	Career	Games	Rank	Putouts	Career	PO
1	Terry Puhl	1977-1991	1300	1	Jeff Heath	1936-1949	2705
2	Jeff Heath	1936-1949	1299	2	Terry Puhl	1977-1991	2576
3	Jack Graney	1908-1922	1282	3	Jack Graney	1908-1922	2488
4	Tip O'Neill	1883-1892	1024	4	Tip O'Neill	1883-1892	1794
5	George Selkirk	1934-1942	773	5	George Selkirk	1934-1942	1559
6	**Larry Walker**	**1989-1995**	**709**	**6**	**Larry Walker**	**1989-1995**	**1398**
7	Goody Rosen	1937-1946	472	7	Goody Rosen	1937-1946	1210
8	Doc Miller	1910-1914	425	8	Doc Miller	1910-1914	673
9	Bunk Congalton	1902-1907	300	9	Bunk Congalton	1902-1907	434
10	Spud Johnson	1889-1891	283	10	Sherry Robertson	1940-1952	339
11	Doug Frobel	1982-1987	202	11	Spud Johnson	1889-1891	338
12	Rob Ducey	1987-1994	201	12	Rob Ducey	1987-1994	300
13	Bill O'Neill	1904-1906	195	13	Doug Frobel	1982-1987	297
14	Pete Ward	1962-1970	185	14	Bill O'Neill	1904-1906	273
15	Sherry Robertson	1940-1952	163	15	Pete Ward	1962-1970	239

Rank	Assists	Career	A	Rank	Double Plays	Career	DP
1	Jack Graney	1908-1922	151	1	Jack Graney	1908-1922	34
2	Jeff Heath	1936-1949	85	2	Jeff Heath	1936-1949	21
3	Tip O'Neill	1883-1892	81	3	Terry Puhl	1977-1991	18
4	**Larry Walker**	**1989-1995**	**67**	3	George Selkirk	1934-1942	18
5	Doc Miller	1910-1914	58	5	Tip O'Neill	1883-1892	16
6	Terry Puhl	1977-1991	57	**6**	**Larry Walker**	**1989-1995**	**14**
7	George Selkirk	1934-1942	55	7	Doc Miller	1910-1914	13
8	Goody Rosen	1937-1946	42	8	Goody Rosen	1937-1946	6
9	Spud Johnson	1889-1891	34	9	Bunk Congalton	1902-1907	5
10	Bunk Congalton	1902-1907	33	10	Spud Johnson	1889-1891	4
11	Bill O'Neill	1904-1906	21	10	Doug Frobel	1982-1987	4
12	Bill O'Hara	1909-1910	20	10	Bill O'Hara	1909-1910	4
13	Emil Frisk	1899-1907	15	13	Six Players		2
14	Sherry Robertson	1940-1952	12				
15	Two Players		11				

The Top 15 Performances in Career Fielding Records—Outfielder

Rank	Total Chances	Career	TC	Rank	Accepted	Career	SC
1	Jeff Heath	1936-1949	2870	1	Jeff Heath	1936-1949	2790
2	Jack Graney	1908-1922	2769	2	Jack Graney	1908-1922	2639
3	Terry Puhl	1977-1991	2651	3	Terry Puhl	1977-1991	2633
4	Tip O'Neill	1883-1892	2044	4	Tip O'Neill	1883-1892	1875
5	George Selkirk	1934-1942	1652	5	George Selkirk	1934-1942	1614
6	**Larry Walker**	**1989-1995**	**1486**	**6**	**Larry Walker**	**1989-1995**	**1465**
7	Goody Rosen	1937-1946	1266	7	Goody Rosen	1937-1946	1252
8	Doc Miller	1910-1914	763	8	Doc Miller	1910-1914	731
9	Bunk Congalton	1902-1907	483	9	Bunk Congalton	1902-1907	467
10	Spud Johnson	1889-1891	414	10	Spud Johnson	1889-1891	372
11	Sherry Robertson	1940-1952	371	11	Sherry Robertson	1940-1952	351
12	Doug Frobel	1982-1987	322	12	Doug Frobel	1982-1987	308
13	Bill O'Neill	1904-1906	320	12	Rob Ducey	1987-1994	308
14	Rob Ducey	1987-1994	316	14	Bill O'Neill	1904-1906	294
15	Joe Knight	1884-1890	254	15	Pete Ward	1962-1970	248

Rank	Errors	Career	E	Rank	Fielding Avg	Career	F.A.
1	Tip O'Neill	1883-1892	169	1	Terry Puhl	1977-1991	.993
2	Jack Graney	1908-1922	130	2	Goody Rosen	1937-1946	.989
3	Jeff Heath	1936-1949	80	**3**	**Larry Walker**	**1989-1995**	**.986**
4	Spud Johnson	1889-1891	42	4	George Selkirk	1934-1942	.977
5	George Selkirk	1934-1942	38	5	Rob Ducey	1987-1994	.975
6	Doc Miller	1910-1914	32	6	Jeff Heath	1936-1949	.972
7	Bill O'Neill	1904-1906	26	7	Bunk Congalton	1902-1907	.967
8	**Larry Walker**	**1989-1995**	**21**	8	Doc Miller	1910-1914	.958
9	Sherry Robertson	1940-1952	20	9	Doug Frobel	1982-1987	.957
10	Joe Knight	1884-1890	19	10	Jack Graney	1908-1922	.953
11	Terry Puhl	1977-1991	18	11	Tip O'Neill	1883-1892	.917
12	Bunk Congalton	1902-1907	16	12	Spud Johnson	1889-1891	.899
13	Fred Osborne	1890-1890	15				
14	Three Players		14				

The Top 6 Performances in Career Fielding Records—Catcher

Rank	Games Played	Career	Games	Rank	Putouts	Career	PO
1	George Gibson	1905-1918	1194	1	George Gibson	1905-1918	5214
2	Larry McLean	1901-1915	761	2	Larry McLean	1901-1915	3032
3	Nig Clarke	1905-1920	462	3	Nig Clarke	1905-1920	1786
4	Frank Owens	1905-1915	215	4	Frank Owens	1905-1915	958
5	Tom Daly	1913-1921	144	5	Tom Daly	1913-1921	480
6	John Humphries	1883-1884	75	6	John Humphries	1883-1884	407

Rank	Assists	Career	A	Rank	Double Plays	Career	DP
1	George Gibson	1905-1918	1386	1	George Gibson	1905-1918	112
2	Larry McLean	1901-1915	905	2	Larry McLean	1901-1915	105
3	Nig Clarke	1905-1920	568	3	Nig Clarke	1905-1920	40
3	Frank Owens	1905-1915	276	4	Frank Owens	1905-1915	31
5	John Humphries	1883-1884	117	5	Tom Daly	1913-1921	17
6	Tom Daly	1913-1921	112	6	John Humphries	1883-1884	11

Rank	Chances Acc	Career	SC	Rank	Passed Balls	Career	PB
1	George Gibson	1905-1918	6600	1	George Gibson	1905-1918	101
2	Larry McLean	1901-1915	3937	2	John Humphries	1883-1884	96
3	Nig Clarke	1905-1920	2354	3	Nig Clarke	1905-1920	81
4	Frank Owens	1905-1915	1234	4	Larry McLean	1901-1915	61
5	Tom Daly	1913-1921	592	5	Bill Phillips	1879-1888	26
6	John Humphries	1883-1884	524	6	Jim McKeever	1884	24

Rank	Errors	Career	E	Rank	Fielding Avg	Career	F.A.
1	George Gibson	1905-1918	153	1	George Gibson	1905-1918	.977
2	Larry McLean	1901-1915	110	2	Larry McLean	1901-1915	.973
3	Nig Clarke	1905-1920	99	3	Frank Owens	1905-1915	.969
4	John Humphries	1883-1884	74	4	Nig Clarke	1905-1920	.960
4	Frank Owens	1905-1915	39				
6	Bill Phillips	1879-1888	18				

The Top 15 Performances in Career Fielding Records—Pitcher

Rank	Games Played	Career	Games	Rank	Putouts	Career	PO
1	Ferguson Jenkins	1965-1983	664	1	Ferguson Jenkins	1965-1983	363
2	John Hiller	1965-1980	545	**2**	**Kirk McCaskill**	**1985-1995**	**147**
3	Ron Taylor	1962-1972	491	3	Reggie Cleveland	1969-1981	121
4	Claude Raymond	1959-1971	449	4	Dick Fowler	1941-1952	83
5	Reggie Cleveland	1969-1981	428	5	Bob Hooper	1950-1955	64
6	**Kirk McCaskill**	**1985-1995**	**351**	6	Russ Ford	1909-1915	59
7	Dick Fowler	1941-1952	221	7	Phil Marchildon	1940-1950	52
8	Ted Bowsfield	1958-1964	215	8	Ted Bowsfield	1958-1964	49
9	Steve Wilson	1988-1993	205	8	Claude Raymond	1941-1952	49
10	Russ Ford	1909-1915	199	10	John Hiller	1937-1946	45
11	Bob Hooper	1950-1955	194	11	Bob Emslie	1883-1885	43
12	Phil Marchildon	1940-1950	185	12	Oscar Judd	1941-1948	38
13	Oscar Judd	1941-1948	161	13	Ron Taylor	1962-1972	37
14	Joe Krakauskas	1937-1946	149	**14**	**Mike Gardiner**	**1990-1995**	**35**
15	**Paul Quantrill**	**1992-1995**	**144**	15	Paul Calvert	1942-1951	29

Rank	Assists	Career	A	Rank	Double Plays	Career	DP
1	Ferguson Jenkins	1965-1983	660	1	Ferguson Jenkins	1965-1983	45
2	Russ Ford	1909-1915	403	2	Bob Hooper	1950-1955	20
3	**Kirk McCaskill**	**1985-1995**	**254**	2	Dick Fowler	1941-1952	20
4	Reggie Cleveland	1969-1981	227	**4**	**Kirk McCaskill**	**1985-1995**	**19**
5	Dick Fowler	1941-1952	201	5	Russ Ford	1909-1915	15
6	Oscar Judd	1941-1948	186	6	Reggie Cleveland	1969-1981	14
7	Bill Magee	1897-1902	184	7	Oscar Judd	1941-1948	12
8	Phil Marchildon	1940-1950	168	8	Phil Marchildon	1940-1950	11
9	Harley Payne	1896-1899	166	9	Ted Bowsfield	1958-1964	9
10	Bob Emslie	1883-1885	156	10	Claude Raymond	1959-1971	7
11	Bill Hogg	1905-1908	154	10	Bill Hogg	1905-1908	7
12	John Hiller	1965-1980	136	**12**	**Rheal Cormier**	**1991-1995**	**6**
13	Bob Hooper	1950-1955	132	**12**	**Paul Quantrill**	**1992-1995**	**6**
14	Ron Taylor	1962-1972	129	12	Ron Taylor	1962-1972	6
15	Rube Vickers	1902-1909	124	12	Clarence Currie	1902-1903	6

The Top 15 Performances in Career Fielding Records—Pitcher

Rank	Total Chances	Career	TC	Rank	Chances Acc	Career	SC
1	Ferguson Jenkins	1965-1983	1072	1	Ferguson Jenkins	1965-1983	1023
2	Russ Ford	1909-1915	489	2	Russ Ford	1909-1915	462
3	**Kirk McCaskill**	**1985-1995**	**422**	**3**	**Kirk McCaskill**	**1985-1995**	**401**
4	Reggie Cleveland	1969-1981	372	4	Reggie Cleveland	1969-1981	348
5	Dick Fowler	1941-1952	297	5	Dick Fowler	1941-1952	284
6	Bob Emslie	1883-1885	241	6	Oscar Judd	1941-1948	224
7	Bill Magee	1897-1902	235	7	Phil Marchildon	1940-1950	220
7	Phil Marchildon	1940-1950	235	8	Bill Magee	1897-1902	211
9	Oscar Judd	1941-1948	231	9	Bob Emslie	1883-1885	199
10	Harley Payne	1896-1899	203	10	Bob Hooper	1950-1955	196
11	Bob Hooper	1950-1955	202	11	Harley Payne	1896-1899	189
12	John Hiller	1965-1980	189	12	John Hiller	1965-1980	181
13	Bill Hogg	1905-1908	182	13	Bill Hogg	1905-1908	176
14	Ted Bowsfield	1958-1964	179	14	Ron Taylor	1962-1972	166
15	Claude Raymond	1959-1971	176	15	Ted Bowsfield	1958-1964	164

Rank	Errors	Career	E	Rank	Fielding Avg	Career	F.A.
1	Ferguson Jenkins	1965-1983	49	1	Ron Taylor	1962-1972	.982
2	Bob Emslie	1883-1885	42	2	Win Kellum	1901-1905	.977
3	Russ Ford	1909-1915	27	3	Bob Hooper	1950-1955	.970
4	Bill Magee	1897-1902	24	4	Oscar Judd	1941-1948	.970
4	Reggie Cleveland	1969-1981	24	5	Bill Hogg	1905-1908	.967
6	**Kirk McCaskill**	**1985-1995**	**21**	6	Paul Calvert	1942-1951	.963
7	Ted Bowsfield	1958-1964	15	7	John Hiller	1965-1980	.958
7	Phil Marchildon	1940-1950	15	8	Dick Fowler	1941-1952	.956
9	Harley Payne	1896-1899	14	9	Ferguson Jenkins	1965-1983	.954
9	Claude Raymond	1959-1971	14	**10**	**Rheal Cormier**	**1991-1995**	**.953**
11	Dick Fowler	1941-1952	13	**11**	**Kirk McCaskill**	**1985-1995**	**.950**
12	Clarence Currie	1902-1903	12	12	Russ Ford	1909-1915	.945
12	Bob Steele	1916-1919	12	13	Phil Marchildon	1940-1950	.936
14	Bill Mountjoy	1883-1885	11	14	Reggie Cleveland	1969-1981	.935
14	Pete Wood	1885-1889	11	15	Rube Vickers	1902-1909	.933

Player Register

(League leaders are shown in **boldface**)

GENERAL INFORMATION

Year - Major League season, **Team** - Major League team played for during that season, **Lg** - League - NL (National League) 1876-present, AL (American League) 1901-present, AA (American Association) 1882-1891, FL (Federal League) 1914-1915, UA (Union Association) 1884, PL (Players League) 1890

BATTING CATEGORIES

G - Games Played, **AB** - At-Bats, **H** - Base Hits, **2B** - Doubles, **3B** - Triples, **HR** - Home Runs, **TB** - Total Bases, **R** - Runs Scored, **RBI** - Runs Batted In, **TBB** - Total Bases on Balls, **IBB** - Intentional Bases on Balls (since 1955), **SO** - Strikeouts, **HBP** - Times Hit by Pitch (since 1884 in AA, since 1887 in NL and other leagues), **SH** - Sacrifice Hits (since 1894 with various rule changes), **SF** - Sacrifice Flies (since 1954), **SB** - Stolen Bases (some years before 1890 were not recorded), **CS** - Caught Stealing (records are inconsistently recorded since 1912, complete since 1951), **SB%** - Stolen Base Percentage, **GDP** - Grounded into Double Plays (since 1933 in NL, since 1939 in AL), **Avg** - Batting Average, **OBP** - On-Base Percentage, **SLG** - Slugging Percentage

PITCHING CATEGORIES

G - Games Pitched, **GS** - Games Started, **CG** - Complete Games, **GF** - Games Finished, **IP** - Innings Pitched, **BFP** - Batters Facing Pitcher, **H** - Hits allowed, **R** - Runs allowed, **ER** - Earned Runs allowed, **HR** - Home Runs allowed, **SH** - Sacrifice Hits allowed (since 1894 with various rule changes), **SF** - Sacrifice Flies allowed (since 1954), **HB** - Hit Batsmen, **TBB** - Bases on Balls, **IBB** - Intentional Bases on Balls (since 1955), **SO** - Strikeouts, **WP** - Wild Pitches, **Bk** - Balks, **W** - Games Won, **L** - Games Lost, **Pct** - Winning Percentage, **ShO** - Shutouts, **Sv** - Saves, **ERA** - Earned Run Average

FIELDING CATEGORIES

G - Games Played at that Position, **TC** - Total Chances, **PO** - Putouts, **A** - Assists, **E** - Errors, **DP** - Double Plays, **PB** - Passed Balls (only for catchers), **Pct** - Fielding Percentage, **Range** - Range Factor (Successful Chances divided by Games Played, not shown for pitchers, catchers and first basemen)

All categories which were unknown or not recorded at the time are left blank in the register section.

Minor league records are provided for only the most recent players (since 1985).

Batting records for pitchers exclude seasons with the Designated Hitter.

Bob Alexander

Robert Somerville Alexander
Pitches: Right **Bats:** Right

Height: 6'2" **Weight:** 205
Born on August 7, 1922 in Vancouver, British Columbia
Died on April 7, 1993 in Oceanside, California

				HOW MUCH HE PITCHED				WHAT HE GAVE UP										THE RESULTS					
Year Team	Lg	G	GS	CG	GF	IP	BFP	H	R	ER	HR	SH	SF	HB	TBB	IBB	SO	WP	Bk	W	L	Pct.	ShO	Sv	ERA
1955 Baltimore	AL	4	0	0	2	4	22	8	6	6	0	0	1	1	2	0	1	1	0	1	0	1.000	0	0	13.50
1957 Cleveland	AL	5	0	0	3	7	35	10	7	7	0	0	1	1	5	2	1	1	0	0	1	.000	0	0	9.00
2 ML YEARS		9	0	0	5	11	57	18	13	13	0	0	2	2	7	2	2	2	0	1	1	.500	0	0	10.64

					BATTING														BASERUNNING				PERCENTAGES		
Year Team	Lg	G	AB	H	2B	3B	HR	(Hm	Rd)	TB	R	RBI	TBB	IBB	SO	HBP	SH	SF	SB	CS	SB%	GDP	Avg	OBP	SLG
1955 Baltimore	AL	4	0	0	0	0	0	(0	0)	0	0	0	0	0	0	0	0	0	0	0	.00	0	.000	.000	.000
1957 Cleveland	AL	5	1	0	0	0	0	(0	0)	0	0	0	0	0	0	1	0	0	0	0	.00	0	.000	.000	.000
2 ML YEARS		9	1	0	0	0	0	(0	0)	0	0	0	0	0	0	1	0	0	0	0	.00	0	.000	.000	.000

			FIELDING AS PITCHER								
Year Team	Lg	G	TC	PO	A	E	DP	PB	Pct.	Range
1955 Baltimore	AL	4	0	0	0	0	0	--	.000	---
1957 Cleveland	AL	5	0	0	0	0	0	--	.000	---
2 ML YEARS		9	0	0	0	0	0	--	.000	---

Wiman Andrus

William Wiman Andrus
Bats: Unknown **Throws:** Right

Height: Unknown **Weight:** Unknown
Born on October 14, 1858 in Orono, Ontario
Died on June 17, 1935 in Miles City, Montana

					BATTING														BASERUNNING				PERCENTAGES		
Year Team	Lg	G	AB	H	2B	3B	HR	(Hm	Rd)	TB	R	RBI	TBB	IBB	SO	HBP	SH	SF	SB	CS	SB%	GDP	Avg	OBP	SLG
1885 Providence	NL	1	4	0	0	0	0	--	--	0	0	0	0		1								.000	.000	.000

			FIELDING AS THIRD BASEMAN								
Year Team	Lg	G	TC	PO	A	E	DP	PB	Pct.	Range
1885 Providence	NL	1	5	2	3	0	0	--	1.000	5.00

Jimmy Archer

James Patrick Archer
Bats: Right **Throws:** Right

Height: 5'10" **Weight:** 168
Born on May 13, 1883 in Dublin, Ireland
Died on March 29, 1958 in Milwaukee, Wisconsin

					BATTING														BASERUNNING				PERCENTAGES		
Year Team	Lg	G	AB	H	2B	3B	HR	(Hm	Rd)	TB	R	RBI	TBB	IBB	SO	HBP	SH	SF	SB	CS	SB%	GDP	Avg	OBP	SLG
1904 Pittsburg	NL	7	20	3	0	0	0	--	--	3	1	1	0			0	0		0				.150	.150	.150
1907 Detroit	AL	18	42	5	0	0	0	--	--	5	6	0	4			0	2		0				.119	.196	.119
1909 Chicago	NL	80	261	60	9	2	1	--	--	76	31	30	12			1	12		5				.230	.266	.291
1910 Chicago	NL	98	313	81	17	6	2	--	--	116	36	41	14		49	1	16		6				.259	.293	.371
1911 Chicago	NL	116	387	98	18	5	4	--	--	138	41	41	18		43	1	13		5				.253	.288	.357
1912 Chicago	NL	120	385	109	20	2	5	--	--	148	35	58	22		36	5	14		7				.283	.330	.384
1913 Chicago	NL	111	368	98	14	7	2	--	--	132	38	44	19		27	5	11		4				.266	.311	.359
1914 Chicago	NL	79	248	64	9	2	0	--	--	77	17	19	9		9	0	5		1				.258	.284	.310
1915 Chicago	NL	97	309	75	11	5	1	--	--	99	21	27	11		38	2	9		5	6	.45		.243	.273	.320
1916 Chicago	NL	77	205	45	6	2	1	--	--	58	11	30	12		24	2	9		3				.220	.269	.283
1917 Chicago	NL	2	2	0	0	0	0	--	--	0	0	0	0		1	0	0		0				.000	.000	.000
1918 3 ML Teams		42	106	22	2	3	0	--	--	30	10	5	3		14	2	2		0				.208	.243	.283
1918 Pittsburg	NL	24	58	9	1	2	0	--	--	14	4	3	1		6	2	2		0				.155	.197	.241
Brooklyn	NL	9	22	6	0	1	0	--	--	8	3	0	1		5	0	0		0				.273	.304	.364
Cincinnati	NL	9	26	7	1	0	0	--	--	8	3	2	1		3	0	0		0				.269	.296	.308
12 ML YEARS		847	2646	660	106	34	16	--	--	882	247	296	124		19	93			36				.249	.288	.333

World Series Batting

					BATTING														BASERUNNING				PERCENTAGES		
Year Team	Lg	G	AB	H	2B	3B	HR	(Hm	Rd)	TB	R	RBI	TBB	IBB	SO	HBP	SH	SF	SB	CS	SB%	GDP	Avg	OBP	SLG
1907 Detroit	AL	1	3	0	0	0	0	(0	0)	0	0	0	0	0	1	0	0		0	0	.00	0	.000	.000	.000
1910 Chicago	NL	3	11	2	1	0	0	(0	0)	3	1	0	0	0	3	0	0		0	0	.00	0	.182	.182	.273
2 ML YEARS		4	14	2	1	0	0	(0	0)	3	1	0	0	0	4	0	0		0	0	.00	0	.143	.143	.214

FIELDING AS CATCHER

Year Team	Lg	G	TC	PO	A	E	DP	PB	Pct.	Range
1904 Pittsburgh	NL	7	37	25	9	3	0	1	.919	---
1907 Detroit	AL	17	80	62	16	2	0	1	.975	---
1909 Chicago	NL	80	526	408	97	21	7	5	.960	---
1910 Chicago	NL	49	329	239	80	10	6	2	.970	---
1911 Chicago	NL	102	614	476	124	14	11	5	.977	---
1912 Chicago	NL	118	676	504	**149**	**23**	15	9	.966	---
1913 Chicago	NL	103	612	455	138	19	6	7	.969	---
1914 Chicago	NL	76	485	367	105	13	8	**16**	.973	---
1915 Chicago	NL	88	556	419	124	13	11	**14**	.977	---
1916 Chicago	NL	61	327	236	84	7	5	4	.979	---
1918 3 ML Teams		35	157	102	53	2	7	6	.987	---
1918 Pittsburgh	NL	21	94	63	30	1	4	0	.989	---
Brooklyn	NL	7	31	17	13	1	0	3	.968	---
Cincinnati	NL	7	32	22	10	0	3	3	1.000	---
11 ML YEARS		736	4399	3293	979	127	76	70	.971	---

FIELDING AS FIRST BASEMAN

Year Team	Lg	G	TC	PO	A	E	DP	PB	Pct.	Range
1910 Chicago	NL	40	408	381	17	10	25	--	.975	---
1911 Chicago	NL	10	89	84	4	1	6	--	.989	---
1913 Chicago	NL	8	65	58	5	2	4	--	.969	---
1918 2 ML Teams		2	17	15	1	1	1	--	.941	---
1918 Pittsburgh	NL	1	4	4	0	0	0	--	1.000	---
Cincinnati	NL	1	13	11	1	1	1	--	.923	---
4 ML YEARS		60	579	538	27	14	36	--	.976	---

FIELDING AS SECOND BASEMAN

Year Team	Lg	G	TC	PO	A	E	DP	PB	Pct.	Range
1907 Detroit	AL	1	7	2	4	1	0	--	.857	6.00
1911 Chicago	NL	1	0	0	0	0	0	--	.000	.00
2 ML YEARS		2	7	2	4	1	0	--	.857	3.00

FIELDING AS THIRD BASEMAN

Year Team	Lg	G	TC	PO	A	E	DP	PB	Pct.	Range
1916 Chicago	NL	1	0	0	0	0	0	--	.000	.00

FIELDING AS OUTFIELDER

Year Team	Lg	G	TC	PO	A	E	DP	PB	Pct.	Range
1904 Pittsburgh	NL	1	0	0	0	0	0	--	.000	.00

World Series Fielding

FIELDING AS CATCHER

Year Team	Lg	G	TC	PO	A	E	DP	PB	Pct.	Range
1907 Detroit	AL	1	5	4	1	0	0	0	1.000	---
1910 Chicago	NL	2	22	18	4	0	1	0	1.000	---
2 ML YEARS		3	27	22	5	0	1	0	1.000	---

FIELDING AS FIRST BASEMAN

Year Team	Lg	G	TC	PO	A	E	DP	PB	Pct.	Range
1910 Chicago	NL	1	9	9	0	0	1	--	1.000	---

Bill Atkinson

William Cecil Glenn Atkinson
Pitches: Right **Bats:** Left
Height: 5'7" **Weight:** 165
Born on October 4, 1954 in Chatham, Ontario

	HOW MUCH HE PITCHED						WHAT HE GAVE UP												THE RESULTS					
Year Team	Lg	G	GS	CG	GF	IP	BFP	H	R	ER	HR	SH	SF	HB	TBB	IBB	SO	WP	Bk	W	L	Pct.	ShO	Sv	ERA
1976 Montreal	NL	4	0	0	0	5	18	3	0	0	0	0	0	0	1	1	4	2	0	0	0	.000	0	0	0.00
1977 Montreal	NL	55	0	0	30	83.1	346	72	33	31	12	5	4	0	29	11	56	5	0	7	2	.778	0	7	3.35
1978 Montreal	NL	29	0	0	14	45.1	204	45	23	22	5	4	3	1	28	4	32	0	0	2	2	.500	0	3	4.37
1979 Montreal	NL	10	0	0	5	13.2	57	9	4	3	0	0	0	0	4	1	7	0	0	2	0	1.000	0	1	1.98
4 ML YEARS		98	0	0	49	147.1	625	129	60	56	17	9	7	1	62	17	99	7	0	11	4	.733	0	11	3.42

	BATTING															BASERUNNING				PERCENTAGES		
Year Team	Lg	G	AB	H	2B	3B	HR	(Hm | Rd)	TB	R	RBI	TBB	IBB	SO	HBP	SH	SF	SB	CS	SB%	GDP	Avg	OBP	SLG
1976 Montreal	NL	4	0	0	0	0	0	(0 | 0)	0	0	0	0	0	0	0	0	0	0	0	.00	0	.000	.000	.000
1977 Montreal	NL	56	5	1	0	0	0	(0 | 0)	1	0	0	0	0	1	0	1	0	0	0	.00	0	.200	.200	.200
1978 Montreal	NL	29	4	2	0	0	0	(0 | 0)	2	0	1	0	0	0	0	0	0	0	0	.00	0	.500	.500	.500
1979 Montreal	NL	10	1	0	0	0	0	(0 | 0)	0	0	0	0	0	0	0	0	0	0	0	.00	0	.000	.000	.000
4 ML YEARS		99	10	3	0	0	0	(0 | 0)	3	0	1	0	0	1	0	1	0	0	0	.00	0	.300	.300	.300

FIELDING AS PITCHER

Year Team	Lg	G	TC	PO	A	E	DP	PB	Pct.	Range
1976 Montreal	NL	4	1	0	1	0	0	--	1.000	---
1977 Montreal	NL	55	25	6	18	1	0	--	.960	---
1978 Montreal	NL	29	13	2	9	2	1	--	.846	---
1979 Montreal	NL	10	1	1	0	0	0	--	1.000	---
4 ML YEARS		98	40	9	28	3	1	--	.925	---

Ed Bahr

Edson Garfield Bahr

Height: 6'1" **Weight:** 172

Pitches: Right **Bats:** Right

Born on October 16, 1919 in Rouleau, Saskatchewan

HOW MUCH HE PITCHED / WHAT HE GAVE UP / THE RESULTS

Year Team	Lg	G	GS	CG	GF	IP	BFP	H	R	ER	HR	SH	SF	HB	TBB	IBB	SO	WP	Bk	W	L	Pct.	ShO	Sv	ERA
1946 Pittsburgh	NL	27	14	7	7	136.2	577	128	57	40	8	16		5	52		44	2	0	8	6	.571	0	0	2.63
1947 Pittsburgh	NL	19	11	1	4	82.1	360	82	45	42	6	2		3	43		25	0	0	3	5	.375	0	0	4.59
2 ML YEARS		46	25	8	11	219	937	210	102	82	14	18		8	95		69	2	0	11	11	.500	0	0	3.37

BATTING / BASERUNNING / PERCENTAGES

Year Team	Lg	G	AB	H	2B	3B	HR	(Hm	Rd)	TB	R	RBI	TBB	IBB	SO	HBP	SH	SF	SB	CS	SB%	GDP	Avg	OBP	SLG
1946 Pittsburgh	NL	29	45	8	0	1	0	--	--	10	2	5	0		10	0	1		1			0	.178	.178	.222
1947 Pittsburgh	NL	21	23	2	0	0	0	--	--	2	0	0	0		8	0	3		0			2	.087	.087	.087
2 ML YEARS		50	68	10	0	1	0	--	--	12	2	5	0		18	0	4		1			2	.147	.147	.176

FIELDING AS PITCHER

Year Team	Lg	G	TC	PO	A	E	DP	PB	Pct.	Range
1946 Pittsburgh	NL	27	41	8	28	5	2	--	.878	---
1947 Pittsburgh	NL	19	15	2	12	1	1	--	.933	---
2 ML YEARS		46	56	10	40	6	3	--	.893	---

John Balaz

John Lawrence Balaz

Height: 6'3" **Weight:** 180

Bats: Right **Throws:** Right

Born on November 24, 1950 in Toronto, Ontario

BATTING / BASERUNNING / PERCENTAGES

Year Team	Lg	G	AB	H	2B	3B	HR	(Hm	Rd)	TB	R	RBI	TBB	IBB	SO	HBP	SH	SF	SB	CS	SB%	GDP	Avg	OBP	SLG
1974 California	AL	14	42	10	0	0	1	(0	1)	13	4	5	2	0	10	1	1	0	0	0	.00	0	.238	.289	.310
1975 California	AL	45	120	29	8	1	1	(1	0)	42	10	10	5	0	25	0	1	1	0	0	.00	1	.242	.270	.350
2 ML YEARS		59	162	39	8	1	2	(1	1)	55	14	15	7	0	35	1	2	1	0	0	.00	1	.241	.275	.340

FIELDING AS OUTFIELDER

Year Team	Lg	G	TC	PO	A	E	DP	PB	Pct.	Range
1974 California	AL	12	17	17	0	0	0	--	1.000	1.42
1975 California	AL	27	43	40	3	0	1	--	1.000	1.59
2 ML YEARS		39	60	57	3	0	1	--	1.000	1.54

Vince Barton

Vincent David Barton

Height: 6'0" **Weight:** 180

Bats: Left **Throws:** Right

Born on February 1, 1908 in Edmonton, Alberta

Died on September 13, 1973 in Toronto, Ontario

BATTING / BASERUNNING / PERCENTAGES

Year Team	Lg	G	AB	H	2B	3B	HR	(Hm	Rd)	TB	R	RBI	TBB	IBB	SO	HBP	SH	SF	SB	CS	SB%	GDP	Avg	OBP	SLG
1931 Chicago	NL	66	239	57	10	1	13	--	--	108	45	50	21		40	9	1		1				.238	.323	.452
1932 Chicago	NL	36	134	30	2	3	3	--	--	47	19	15	8		22	1	1		0				.224	.273	.351
2 ML YEARS		102	373	87	12	4	16	--	--	155	64	65	29		62	10	2		1				.233	.306	.416

FIELDING AS OUTFIELDER

Year Team	Lg	G	TC	PO	A	E	DP	PB	Pct.	Range
1931 Chicago	NL	61	140	133	2	5	0	--	.964	2.21
1932 Chicago	NL	34	67	64	3	0	1	--	1.000	1.97
2 ML YEARS		95	207	197	5	5	1	--	.976	2.13

Reno Bertoia

Reno Peter Bertoia

Height: 5'11" **Weight:** 185

Bats: Right **Throws:** Right

Born on January 8, 1935 in St. Vito Udine, Italy

BATTING / BASERUNNING / PERCENTAGES

Year Team	Lg	G	AB	H	2B	3B	HR	(Hm	Rd)	TB	R	RBI	TBB	IBB	SO	HBP	SH	SF	SB	CS	SB%	GDP	Avg	OBP	SLG
1953 Detroit	AL	1	1	0	0	0	0	(0	0)	0	0	0	0	0	0	0	0	0	0	0	.00	0	.000	.000	.000

157

Year Team	Lg	G	AB	H	2B	3B	HR	Hm	Rd	TB	R	RBI	TBB	IBB	SO	HBP	SH	SF	SB	CS	SB%	GDP	Avg	OBP	SLG
1954 Detroit	AL	54	37	6	2	0	1	(1	0)	11	13	2	5		9	0	0	0	1	0	1.00	0	.162	.262	.297
1955 Detroit	AL	38	68	14	2	1	1	(0	1)	21	13	10	5	1	11	0	1	2	0	0	.00	1	.206	.253	.309
1956 Detroit	AL	22	66	12	2	0	1	(0	1)	17	7	5	6	0	12	1	0	0	0	0	.00	4	.182	.260	.258
1957 Detroit	AL	97	295	81	16	2	4	(2	2)	113	28	28	19	2	43	4	5	1	2	3	.40	7	.275	.326	.383
1958 Detroit	AL	86	240	56	6	0	6	(4	2)	80	28	27	20	2	35	2	4	7	5	2	.71	4	.233	.290	.333
1959 Washington	AL	90	308	73	10	0	8	(5	3)	107	33	29	29	3	48	1	0	3	2	5	.29	10	.237	.302	.347
1960 Washington	AL	121	460	122	17	7	4	(3	1)	165	44	45	26	2	58	8	13	4	3	5	.38	11	.265	.313	.359
1961 3 ML Teams	AL	98	270	61	5	0	2	(1	1)	72	35	25	32	1	35	0	8	6	3	0	1.00	9	.226	.302	.267
1962 Detroit	AL	5	0	0	0	0	0	(0	0)	0	3	0	0	0	0	0	0	0	0	0	.00	0	.000	.000	.000
1961 Minnesota	AL	35	104	22	2	0	1	(0	1)	27	17	8	20	1	12	0	2	2	0	0	.00	3	.212	.333	.260
Kansas City	AL	39	120	29	2	0	0	(0	0)	31	12	13	9	0	15	0	4	4	1	0	1.00	6	.242	.286	.258
Detroit	AL	24	46	10	1	0	1	(1	0)	14	6	4	3	0	8	0	2	0	2	0	1.00	0	.217	.265	.304
10 ML YEARS		612	1745	425	60	10	27	(16	11)	586	204	171	142		251	16	31		16	15	.52	46	.244	.306	.336

FIELDING AS SECOND BASEMAN

Year Team	Lg	G	TC	PO	A	E	DP	PB	Pct.	Range
1953 Detroit	AL	1	2	1	0	1	0	--	.500	1.00
1954 Detroit	AL	15	64	26	36	2	6	--	.969	4.13
1955 Detroit	AL	6	30	7	22	1	4	--	.967	4.83
1956 Detroit	AL	18	110	51	57	2	18	--	.982	6.00
1957 Detroit	AL	2	3	2	1	0	0	--	1.000	1.50
1959 Washington	AL	71	347	139	198	10	40	--	.971	4.75
1960 Washington	AL	21	47	26	20	1	8	--	.979	2.19
1961 2 ML Teams		13	39	19	20	0	8	--	1.000	3.00
1962 Detroit	AL	1	1	0	1	0	0	--	1.000	1.00
1961 Kansas City	AL	6	25	12	13	0	5	--	1.000	4.17
Detroit	AL	7	14	7	7	0	3	--	1.000	2.00
9 ML YEARS		148	643	271	355	17	84	--	.974	4.23

FIELDING AS THIRD BASEMAN

Year Team	Lg	G	TC	PO	A	E	DP	PB	Pct.	Range
1954 Detroit	AL	8	3	1	2	0	0	--	1.000	.38
1955 Detroit	AL	14	39	12	24	3	4	--	.923	2.57
1956 Detroit	AL	2	7	3	4	0	1	--	1.000	3.50
1957 Detroit	AL	83	211	76	125	10	8	--	.953	2.42
1958 Detroit	AL	68	220	70	139	11	13	--	.950	3.07
1959 Washington	AL	5	14	6	8	0	1	--	1.000	2.80
1960 Washington	AL	112	334	94	227	13	19	--	.961	2.87
1961 3 ML Teams		74	222	59	146	17	11	--	.923	2.77
1962 Detroit	AL	1	1	0	1	0	0	--	1.000	1.00
1961 Minnesota	AL	32	90	22	59	9	3	--	.900	2.53
Kansas City	AL	29	103	27	70	6	6	--	.942	3.34
Detroit	AL	13	29	10	17	2	2	--	.931	2.08
9 ML YEARS		367	1051	321	676	54	57	--	.949	2.72

FIELDING AS SHORTSTOP

Year Team	Lg	G	TC	PO	A	E	DP	PB	Pct.	Range
1954 Detroit	AL	3	4	0	3	1	1	--	.750	1.00
1955 Detroit	AL	5	10	4	6	0	1	--	1.000	2.00
1957 Detroit	AL	7	3	1	2	0	8	--	1.000	.43
1958 Detroit	AL	5	6	2	3	1	0	--	.833	1.00
1959 Washington	AL	1	1	0	1	0	0	--	1.000	1.00
1961 Detroit	AL	1	0	0	0	0	0	--	.000	.00
1962 Detroit	AL	1	0	0	0	0	0	--	.000	.00
7 ML YEARS		23	24	7	15	2	1	--	.917	.96

FIELDING AS OUTFIELDER

Year Team	Lg	G	TC	PO	A	E	DP	PB	Pct.	Range
1958 Detroit	AL	1	0	0	0	0	0	--	.000	.00

Hank Biasatti

Henry Arcado Biasatti
Bats: Left   **Throws:** Left

Height: 5'11"   **Weight:** 175
Born on January 14, 1922 in Beano, Italy

		BATTING																	BASERUNNING				PERCENTAGES		
Year Team	Lg	G	AB	H	2B	3B	HR	Hm	Rd	TB	R	RBI	TBB	IBB	SO	HBP	SH	SF	SB	CS	SB%	GDP	Avg	OBP	SLG
1949 Philadelphia	AL	21	24	2	2	0	0	--	--	4	6	2	8		5	0	1		0	0	.00	0	.083	.313	.167

FIELDING AS FIRST BASEMAN

Year Team	Lg	G	TC	PO	A	E	DP	PB	Pct.	Range
1949 Philadelphia	AL	8	47	44	2	1	4	--	.979	---

Denis Boucher

Denis Boucher
Pitches: Left **Bats:** Right

Height: 6'1" **Weight:** 195
Born on March 7, 1968 in Montreal, Quebec

HOW MUCH HE PITCHED / WHAT HE GAVE UP / THE RESULTS

Year	Team	Lg	G	GS	CG	GF	IP	BFP	H	R	ER	HR	SH	SF	HB	TBB	IBB	SO	WP	Bk	W	L	Pct.	ShO	Sv	ERA
1988	Myrtle Bch	A	33	32	1	0	196.2	809	161	81	62	11	7	6	8	63	1	169	15	21	13	12	.520	0	0	2.84
1989	Dunedin	A	33	28	1	1	164.2	675	142	80	56	6	3	8	6	58	2	117	13	8	10	10	.500	1	0	3.06
1990	Dunedin	A	9	9	2	0	60	226	45	8	5	1	0	0	2	8	0	62	4	0	7	0	1.000	2	0	0.75
	Syracuse	AAA	17	17	2	0	107.2	449	100	51	46	7	4	4	2	37	2	80	6	0	8	5	.615	1	0	3.85
1991	Syracuse	AAA	8	8	1	0	56.2	241	57	24	20	5	4	1	3	19	1	28	2	0	2	1	.667	0	0	3.18
	Colo. Sprng	AAA	3	3	0	0	14.1	59	14	8	8	1	0	1	0	2	0	9	0	0	1	0	1.000	0	0	5.02
1992	Colo. Sprng	AAA	20	18	6	1	124	497	119	50	48	4	3	4	2	30	1	40	7	2	11	4	.733	0	0	3.48
1993	Las Vegas	AAA	24	7	1	2	70	331	101	59	50	12	4	1	6	27	3	46	4	1	4	7	.364	0	1	6.43
	Ottawa	AAA	11	6	0	1	43	169	36	13	13	0	2	0	1	11	0	22	3	0	6	0	1.000	0	0	2.72
1994	Ottawa	AAA	18	18	0	0	114	480	110	52	47	10	3	3	2	37	1	49	1	1	7	6	.538	0	0	3.71
1995	Ottawa	AAA	14	11	0	1	55.1	254	65	39	35	1	3	3	0	31	0	22	4	0	2	3	.400	0	0	5.69
1991	2 ML Teams		12	12	0	0	58	270	74	41	39	12	3	1	2	24	1	29	1	4	1	7	.125	0	0	6.05
1992	Cleveland	AL	8	7	0	0	41	184	48	29	29	9	1	3	1	20	0	17	1	0	2	2	.500	0	0	6.37
1993	Montreal	NL	5	5	0	0	28.1	111	24	7	6	1	0	3	0	3	1	14	0	2	3	1	.750	0	0	1.91
1994	Montreal	NL	10	2	0	3	18.2	84	24	16	14	6	2	1	0	7	0	17	1	0	0	1	.000	0	0	6.75
1991	Toronto	AL	7	7	0	0	35.1	162	39	20	18	6	3	1	2	16	1	16	0	4	0	3	.000	0	0	4.58
	Cleveland	AL	5	5	0	0	22.2	108	35	21	21	6	0	0	0	8	0	13	1	0	1	4	.200	0	0	8.34
	4 ML YEARS		35	26	0	3	146	649	170	93	88	28	6	8	3	54	2	77	3	6	6	11	.353	0	0	5.42

BATTING / BASERUNNING / PERCENTAGES

Year	Team	Lg	G	AB	H	2B	3B	HR	(Hm	Rd)	TB	R	RBI	TBB	IBB	SO	HBP	SH	SF	SB	CS	SB%	GDP	Avg	OBP	SLG
1993	Montreal	NL	5	6	1	1	0	0	(0	0)	2	0	0	0	0	3	0	2	0	0	0	.00	0	.167	.167	.333
1994	Montreal	NL	10	3	1	1	0	0	(0	0)	2	1	0	0	0	1	0	1	0	0	0	.00	0	.333	.333	.667
	2 ML YEARS		15	9	2	2	0	0	(0	0)	4	1	0	0	0	4	0	3	0	0	0	.00	0	.222	.222	.444

FIELDING AS PITCHER

Year	Team	Lg	G	TC	PO	A	E	DP	PB	Pct.	Range
1991	2 ML Teams		12	17	2	13	2	2	--	.882	---
1992	Cleveland	AL	8	6	3	3	0	0	--	1.000	---
1993	Montreal	NL	5	5	1	4	0	0	--	1.000	---
1994	Montreal	NL	10	4	1	3	0	0	--	1.000	---
1991	Toronto	AL	7	11	2	8	1	1	--	.909	---
	Cleveland	AL	5	6	0	5	1	1	--	.833	---
	4 ML YEARS		35	32	7	23	2	2	--	.938	---

Ted Bowsfield

Edward Oliver Bowsfield
Pitches: Left **Bats:** Right

Height: 6'1" **Weight:** 190
Born on January 10, 1935 in Vernon, British Columbia

HOW MUCH HE PITCHED / WHAT HE GAVE UP / THE RESULTS

Year	Team	Lg	G	GS	CG	GF	IP	BFP	H	R	ER	HR	SH	SF	HB	TBB	IBB	SO	WP	Bk	W	L	Pct.	ShO	Sv	ERA
1958	Boston	AL	16	10	2	3	65.2	290	58	32	28	3	3	1	1	36	1	38	1	0	4	2	.667	0	0	3.84
1959	Boston	AL	5	2	0	1	9	50	16	15	15	2	0	0	0	9	0	4	0	0	0	1	.000	0	0	15.00
1960	2 ML Teams		28	8	1	9	61.2	276	67	42	35	2	3	3	1	33	1	32	2	0	4	6	.400	1	2	5.11
1961	Los Angeles	AL	41	21	4	6	157	683	154	75	65	18	8	8	1	63	3	88	3	0	11	8	.579	1	0	3.73
1962	Los Angeles	AL	34	25	1	4	139	610	154	82	68	12	6	6	2	40	0	52	3	0	9	8	.529	0	1	4.40
1963	Kansas City	AL	41	11	2	14	111.1	488	115	60	55	14	7	3	3	47	5	67	2	0	5	7	.417	1	3	4.45
1964	Kansas City	AL	50	9	2	14	118.2	523	135	63	54	12	10	4	4	31	4	45	3	1	4	7	.364	1	4	4.10
1960	Boston	AL	17	2	0	6	21	94	20	12	12	1	1	2	1	13	0	18	2	0	1	2	.333	0	2	5.14
	Cleveland	AL	11	6	1	3	40.2	182	47	30	23	1	2	1	0	20	1	14	0	0	3	4	.429	1	0	5.09
	7 ML YEARS		215	86	12	51	662.1	2920	699	369	320	63	37	25	12	259	14	326	14	1	37	39	.487	4	6	4.35

BATTING / BASERUNNING / PERCENTAGES

Year	Team	Lg	G	AB	H	2B	3B	HR	(Hm	Rd)	TB	R	RBI	TBB	IBB	SO	HBP	SH	SF	SB	CS	SB%	GDP	Avg	OBP	SLG
1958	Boston	AL	17	26	4	0	0	0	(0	0)	4	2	1	0	0	9	0	0	0	0	0	.00	0	.154	.154	.154
1959	Boston	AL	5	1	0	0	0	0	(0	0)	0	0	0	0	0	1	0	0	0	0	0	.00	0	.000	.000	.000
1960	2 ML Teams		28	14	2	0	0	0	(0	0)	2	2	2	1	0	4	0	3	0	0	0	.00	0	.143	.200	.143
1961	Los Angeles	AL	46	51	7	1	1	0	(0	0)	10	5	2	2	0	19	0	2	0	0	0	.00	1	.137	.170	.196
1962	Los Angeles	AL	44	37	6	1	0	0	(0	0)	7	7	1	6	0	15	0	4	0	0	0	.00	0	.162	.279	.189
1963	Kansas City	AL	43	23	1	1	0	0	(0	0)	2	2	3	0	0	9	0	2	0	0	0	.00	0	.043	.154	.087
1964	Kansas City	AL	52	21	2	0	0	0	(0	0)	2	1	0	2	0	9	0	2	0	0	0	.00	0	.095	.174	.095
1960	Boston	AL	17	4	1	0	0	0	(0	0)	1	1	2	0	0	1	0	2	0	0	0	.00	0	.250	.250	.250
	Cleveland	AL	11	10	1	0	0	0	(0	0)	1	1	0	1	0	3	0	1	0	0	0	.00	0	.100	.182	.100
	7 ML YEARS		235	173	22	3	1	0	(0	0)	27	19	8	14	0	66	0	13	0	0	0	.00	1	.127	.193	.156

FIELDING AS PITCHER										
Year Team	Lg	G	TC	PO	A	E	DP	PB	Pct.	Range
1958 Boston	AL	16	22	5	16	1	1	--	.955	---
1959 Boston	AL	5	1	1	0	0	0	--	1.000	---
1960 2 ML Teams		28	22	6	15	1	3	--	.955	---
1961 Los Angeles	AL	41	35	4	26	5	1	--	.857	---
1962 Los Angeles	AL	34	30	12	13	5	0	--	.833	---
1963 Kansas City	AL	41	38	12	25	1	2	--	.974	---
1964 Kansas City	AL	50	31	9	20	2	2	--	.935	---
1960 Boston	AL	17	9	2	7	0	1	--	1.000	---
Cleveland	AL	11	13	4	8	1	2	--	.923	---
7 ML YEARS		215	179	49	115	15	9	--	.916	---

Tom Burgess

Thomas Roland Burgess (Tim)
Bats: Left **Throws:** Left
Height: 6'0" **Weight:** 180
Born on September 1, 1927 in London, Ontario

BATTING																	BASERUNNING				PERCENTAGES		
Year Team	Lg	G	AB	H	2B	3B	HR	(Hm | Rd)	TB	R	RBI	TBB	IBB	SO	HBP	SH	SF	SB	CS	SB%	GDP	Avg	OBP	SLG
1954 St. Louis	NL	17	21	1	1	0	0	(0 | 0)	2	2	1	3		9	0	0	0	0	0	.00	0	.048	.167	.095
1962 Los Angeles	AL	87	143	28	7	1	2	(1 | 1)	43	17	13	36	8	20	0	2	2	2	0	1.00	1	.196	.354	.301
2 ML YEARS		104	164	29	8	1	2	(1 | 1)	45	19	14	39		29	0	2	2	2	0	1.00	1	.177	.332	.274

FIELDING AS FIRST BASEMAN										
Year Team	Lg	G	TC	PO	A	E	DP	PB	Pct.	Range
1962 Los Angeles	AL	35	299	283	15	1	27	--	.997	---

FIELDING AS OUTFIELDER										
Year Team	Lg	G	TC	PO	A	E	DP	PB	Pct.	Range
1954 St. Louis	NL	4	4	3	0	1	0	--	.750	.75
1962 Los Angeles	AL	2	3	3	0	0	0	--	1.000	1.50
2 ML YEARS		6	7	6	0	1	0	--	.857	1.00

Sheldon Burnside

Sheldon John Burnside
Pitches: Left **Bats:** Right
Height: 6'5" **Weight:** 200
Born on December 22, 1954 in South Bend, Indiana

HOW MUCH HE PITCHED								WHAT HE GAVE UP											THE RESULTS					
Year Team	Lg	G	GS	CG	GF	IP	BFP	H	R	ER	HR	SH	SF	HB	TBB	IBB	SO	WP	Bk	W	L	Pct.	ShO	Sv	ERA
1978 Detroit	AL	2	0	0	1	4	18	4	4	4	0	0	0	0	2	0	3	0	0	0	0	.000	0	0	9.00
1979 Detroit	AL	10	0	0	2	21.1	96	28	16	15	2	2	1	1	8	2	13	0	0	1	1	.500	0	0	6.33
1980 Cincinnati	NL	7	0	0	3	4.2	19	6	1	1	1	0	1	0	1	0	2	0	0	1	0	1.000	0	0	1.93
3 ML YEARS		19	0	0	6	30	133	38	21	20	3	2	1	1	11	2	18	0	0	2	1	.667	0	0	6.00

BATTING																	BASERUNNING				PERCENTAGES		
Year Team	Lg	G	AB	H	2B	3B	HR	(Hm | Rd)	TB	R	RBI	TBB	IBB	SO	HBP	SH	SF	SB	CS	SB%	GDP	Avg	OBP	SLG
1978 Detroit	AL	2	0	0	0	0	0	(0 | 0)	0	0	0	0	0	0	0	0	0	0	0	.00	0	.000	.000	.000
1980 Cincinnati	NL	7	1	0	0	0	0	(0 | 0)	0	0	0	1	0	0	0	0	0	0	0	.00	0	.000	.000	.000
2 ML YEARS		9	1	0	0	0	0	(0 | 0)	0	0	0	1	0	0	0	0	0	0	0	.00	0	.000	.000	.000

FIELDING AS PITCHER										
Year Team	Lg	G	TC	PO	A	E	DP	PB	Pct.	Range
1978 Detroit	AL	2	0	0	0	0	0	--	.000	---
1979 Detroit	AL	10	4	0	4	0	1	--	1.000	---
1980 Cincinnati	NL	7	4	0	4	0	0	--	1.000	---
3 ML YEARS		19	8	0	8	0	1	--	1.000	---

Rob Butler

Robert Frank J. Butler
Bats: Left **Throws:** Left
Height: 5'11" **Weight:** 185
Born on April 10, 1970 in Toronto, Ontario

BATTING																	BASERUNNING				PERCENTAGES		
Year Team	Lg	G	AB	H	2B	3B	HR	(Hm	Rd)	TB	R	RBI	TBB	IBB	SO	HBP	SH	SF	SB	CS	SB%	GDP	Avg	OBP	SLG
1991 St. Cathrns	A	76	311	105	16	5	7	--	--	152	71	45	20	5	21	2	6	3	31	15	.67	2	.338	.378	.489
1992 Dunedin	A	92	391	140	13	7	4	--	--	179	67	41	22	2	36	2	2	1	19	14	.58	7	.358	.394	.458
1993 Syracuse	AAA	55	208	59	11	2	1	--	--	77	30	14	15	2	29	3	3	2	7	5	.58	6	.284	.338	.370
1994 Syracuse	AAA	25	95	25	6	1	1	--	--	36	16	11	8	1	12	1	0	2	2	0	1.00	1	.263	.321	.379
1995 Scranton-Wb	AAA	92	327	98	16	4	3	--	--	131	46	35	24	2	39	6	4	4	5	8	.38	14	.300	.355	.401
1993 Toronto	AL	17	48	13	4	0	0	(0	0)	17	8	2	7	0	12	1	0	0	2	2	.50	0	.271	.375	.354
1994 Toronto	AL	41	74	13	0	1	0	(0	0)	15	13	5	7	0	8	1	4	2	0	1	.00	3	.176	.250	.203
2 ML YEARS		58	122	26	4	1	0	(0	0)	32	21	7	14	0	20	2	4	2	2	3	.40	3	.213	.300	.262

World Series Batting

Year	Team	Lg	G	AB	H	2B	3B	HR	(Hm	Rd)	TB	R	RBI	TBB	IBB	SO	HBP	SH	SF	SB	CS	SB%	GDP	Avg	OBP	SLG
1993	Toronto	AL	2	2	1	0	0	0	(0	0)	1	1	0	0	0	0	0	0	0	0	0	.00	0	.500	.500	.500

FIELDING AS OUTFIELDER

Year	Team	Lg	G	TC	PO	A	E	DP	PB	Pct.	Range
1993	Toronto	AL	16	33	32	0	1	0	--	.970	2.00
1994	Toronto	AL	31	44	43	0	1	0	--	.977	1.39
	2 ML YEARS		47	77	75	0	2	0	--	.974	1.60

Ralph Buxton

Ralph Stanley Buxton (Buck)
Pitches: Right **Bats:** Right

Height: 5'11" **Weight:** 163
Born on June 7, 1911 in Weyburn, Saskatchewan
Died on January 6, 1988 in San Leandro, California

HOW MUCH HE PITCHED / WHAT HE GAVE UP / THE RESULTS

Year	Team	Lg	G	GS	CG	GF	IP	BFP	H	R	ER	HR	SH	SF	HB	TBB	IBB	SO	WP	Bk	W	L	Pct.	ShO	Sv	ERA
1938	Philadelphia	AL	5	0	0	3	9.1	43	12	7	5	1	1		0	5		9	0	0	0	1	.000	0	0	4.82
1949	New York	AL	14	0	0	7	26.2	113	22	13	12	3	1		0	16		14	0	0	0	1	.000	0	2	4.05
	2 ML YEARS		19	0	0	10	36	156	34	20	17	4	2		0	21		23	0	0	0	2	.000	0	2	4.25

BATTING / BASERUNNING / PERCENTAGES

Year	Team	Lg	G	AB	H	2B	3B	HR	(Hm	Rd)	TB	R	RBI	TBB	IBB	SO	HBP	SH	SF	SB	CS	SB%	GDP	Avg	OBP	SLG
1938	Philadelphia	AL	5	1	0	0	0	0	--	--	0	0	0	0		1	0	0		0	0	.00		.000	.000	.000
1949	New York	AL	14	3	0	0	0	0	--	--	0	0	0	0		2	0	0		0	0	.00	0	.000	.000	.000
	2 ML YEARS		19	4	0	0	0	0	--	--	0	0	0	0		3	0	0		0	0	.00	0	.000	.000	.000

FIELDING AS PITCHER

Year	Team	Lg	G	TC	PO	A	E	DP	PB	Pct.	Range
1938	Philadelphia	AL	5	1	0	1	0	0	--	1.000	---
1949	New York	AL	14	5	2	3	0	0	--	1.000	---
	2 ML YEARS		19	6	2	4	0	0	--	1.000	---

Paul Calvert

Paul Leo Emile Calvert
Pitches: Right **Bats:** Right

Height: 6'0" **Weight:** 175
Born on October 6, 1917 in Montreal, Quebec

HOW MUCH HE PITCHED / WHAT HE GAVE UP / THE RESULTS

Year	Team	Lg	G	GS	CG	GF	IP	BFP	H	R	ER	HR	SH	SF	HB	TBB	IBB	SO	WP	Bk	W	L	Pct.	ShO	Sv	ERA
1942	Cleveland	AL	1	0	0	1	2	7	0	0	0	0	0		0	2		2	0	0	0	0	.000	0	0	0.00
1943	Cleveland	AL	5	0	0	2	8.1	37	6	4	4	0	0		1	6		2	0	0	0	0	.000	0	0	4.32
1944	Cleveland	AL	35	4	0	15	77	353	89	48	39	4	7		0	38		31	3	0	1	3	.250	0	0	4.56
1945	Cleveland	AL	1	0	0	0	1.1	8	3	2	2	0	0		0	1		1	0	0	0	0	.000	0	0	13.50
1949	Washington	AL	34	23	5	9	160.2	735	175	111	97	11	20		2	86		52	8	0	6	17	.261	0	1	5.43
1950	Detroit	AL	32	0	0	19	51.1	250	71	42	36	7	4		2	25		14	3	0	2	2	.500	0	4	6.31
1951	Detroit	AL	1	0	0	1	1	4	1	0	0	0	0		0	0		0	0	0	0	0	.000	0	0	0.00
	7 ML YEARS		109	27	5	47	301.2	1394	345	207	178	22	31		5	158		102	14	0	9	22	.290	0	5	5.31

BATTING / BASERUNNING / PERCENTAGES

Year	Team	Lg	G	AB	H	2B	3B	HR	(Hm	Rd)	TB	R	RBI	TBB	IBB	SO	HBP	SH	SF	SB	CS	SB%	GDP	Avg	OBP	SLG
1942	Cleveland	AL	1	0	0	0	0	0	--	--	0	0	0	0		0	0	0		0	0	.00		.000	.000	.000
1943	Cleveland	AL	5	1	0	0	0	0	--	--	0	0	0	0		0	0	0		0	0	.00	0	.000	.000	.000
1944	Cleveland	AL	35	15	4	0	1	0	--	--	6	0	1	0		3	0	1		0	0	.00	0	.267	.267	.400
1945	Cleveland	AL	1	0	0	0	0	0	--	--	0	0	0	0		0	0	0		0	0	.00	0	.000	.000	.000
1949	Washington	AL	35	51	7	0	0	0	--	--	7	6	1	3		9	0	4		0	0	.00	1	.137	.185	.137
1950	Detroit	AL	32	7	0	0	0	0	(0	0)	0	2	1	1		0	1	0		0	0	.00	1	.000	.222	.000
1951	Detroit	AL	1	0	0	0	0	0	(0	0)	0	0	0	0		0	0	0		0	0	.00	0	.000	.000	.000
	7 ML YEARS		110	74	11	0	1	0	--	--	13	8	3	4		12	1	5		0	0	.00	2	.149	.203	.176

FIELDING AS PITCHER

Year	Team	Lg	G	TC	PO	A	E	DP	PB	Pct.	Range
1942	Cleveland	AL	1	0	0	0	0	0	--	.000	---
1943	Cleveland	AL	5	2	0	2	0	0	--	1.000	---
1944	Cleveland	AL	35	33	9	21	3	2	--	.909	---
1945	Cleveland	AL	1	0	0	0	0	0	--	.000	---
1949	Washington	AL	34	55	15	40	0	2	--	1.000	---
1950	Detroit	AL	32	18	5	12	1	0	--	.944	---
1951	Detroit	AL	1	1	0	1	0	0	--	1.000	---
	7 ML YEARS		109	109	29	76	4	4	--	.963	---

161

Jack Cameron

John S. Cameron (Happy Jack)
Bats: Unknown **Throws:** Unknown

Height: Unknown **Weight:** Unknown
Born in September, 1884 in Nova Scotia
Died on August 17, 1951 in Boston, Massachusetts

									BATTING										BASERUNNING				PERCENTAGES		
Year Team	Lg	G	AB	H	2B	3B	HR	(Hm	Rd)	TB	R	RBI	TBB	IBB	SO	HBP	SH	SF	SB	CS	SB%	GDP	Avg	OBP	SLG
1906 Boston	NL	18	61	11	0	0	0	--	--	11	3	4	2			0	0		0				.180	.206	.180

					HOW MUCH HE PITCHED						WHAT HE GAVE UP										THE RESULTS				
Year Team	Lg	G	GS	CG	GF	IP	BFP	H	R	ER	HR	SH	SF	HB	TBB	IBB	SO	WP	Bk	W	L	Pct.	ShO	Sv	ERA
1906 Boston	NL	2	1	0	1	6	26	4	0	0	0	1		0	6		2	0	0	0	0	.000	0	0	0.00

			FIELDING AS PITCHER								
Year Team	Lg	G	TC	PO	A	E	DP	PB	Pct.	Range
1906 Boston	NL	2	2	0	2	0	0	--	1.000	---

			FIELDING AS OUTFIELDER								
Year Team	Lg	G	TC	PO	A	E	DP	PB	Pct.	Range
1906 Boston	NL	16	27	20	3	4	1	--	.852	1.44

Bob Casey

Orrin Robinson Casey
Bats: Unknown **Throws:** Unknown

Height: 5'11" **Weight:** 190
Born on January 26, 1859 in Adolphustown, Ontario
Died on November 28, 1936 in Syracuse, New York

									BATTING										BASERUNNING			PERCENTAGES		
Year Team	Lg	G	AB	H	2B	3B	HR	(Hm	Rd)	TB	R	RBI	TBB	IBB	SO	HBP	SH	SF	SB	CS	SB%	GDP	Avg	OBP	SLG
1882 Detroit	NL	9	39	9	2	1	1	--	--	16	5	7	0		15								.231	.231	.410

			FIELDING AS SECOND BASEMAN								
Year Team	Lg	G	TC	PO	A	E	DP	PB	Pct.	Range
1882 Detroit	NL	1	2	0	0	2	0	--	.000	.00

			FIELDING AS THIRD BASEMAN								
Year Team	Lg	G	TC	PO	A	E	DP	PB	Pct.	Range
1882 Detroit	NL	8	30	10	10	10	0	--	.667	2.50

Nig Clarke

Jay Justin Clarke
Bats: Left **Throws:** Right

Height: 5'8" **Weight:** 165
Born on December 15, 1882 in Amherstburg, Ontario
Died on June 15, 1949 in River Rouge, Michigan

									BATTING										BASERUNNING				PERCENTAGES		
Year Team	Lg	G	AB	H	2B	3B	HR	(Hm	Rd)	TB	R	RBI	TBB	IBB	SO	HBP	SH	SF	SB	CS	SB%	GDP	Avg	OBP	SLG
1905 2 ML Teams		45	130	27	6	1	1	--	--	38	12	10	11			1	2		0				.208	.275	.292
1906 Cleveland	AL	57	179	64	12	4	1	--	--	87	22	21	13			1	2		3				.358	.404	.486
1907 Cleveland	AL	120	390	105	19	6	3	--	--	145	44	33	35			2	3		3				.269	.333	.372
1908 Cleveland	AL	97	290	70	8	6	1	--	--	93	34	27	30			1	7		6				.241	.315	.321
1909 Cleveland	AL	55	164	45	4	2	0	--	--	53	15	14	9			0	5		1				.274	.312	.323
1910 Cleveland	AL	21	58	9	2	0	0	--	--	11	4	2	8			0	3		0				.155	.258	.190
1911 St. Louis	AL	82	256	55	10	1	0	--	--	67	22	18	26			0	7		2				.215	.287	.262
1919 Philadelphia	NL	26	62	15	3	0	0	--	--	18	4	2	4	5		1	1		1				.242	.299	.290
1920 Pittsburgh	NL	3	7	0	0	0	0	--	--	0	0	0	2	4		0	0		0	0	.00		.000	.222	.000
1905 Cleveland	AL	42	123	24	6	1	0	--	--	32	11	9	11			0	1		0				.195	.261	.260
Detroit	AL	3	7	3	0	0	1	--	--	8	1	1	0			1	1		0				.429	.500	.857
9 ML YEARS		506	1536	390	64	20	6	--	--	512	157	127	138			6	30		16				.254	.318	.333

			FIELDING AS CATCHER								
Year Team	Lg	G	TC	PO	A	E	DP	PB	Pct.	Range
1905 2 ML Teams		44	227	178	41	8	3	13	.965	---
1906 Cleveland	AL	54	274	211	58	5	4	2	.982	---
1907 Cleveland	AL	115	613	470	119	24	9	25	.961	---
1908 Cleveland	AL	90	449	327	108	14	6	12	.969	---
1909 Cleveland	AL	44	270	192	65	13	2	13	.952	---
1910 Cleveland	AL	17	117	82	32	3	0	1	.974	---
1911 St. Louis	AL	73	391	251	111	29	15	12	.926	---
1919 Philadelphia	NL	22	96	63	30	3	1	3	.969	---
1920 Pittsburgh	NL	2	16	12	4	0	0	0	1.000	---
1905 Cleveland	AL	42	213	166	39	8	3	12	.962	---
Detroit	AL	2	14	12	2	0	0	1	1.000	---
9 ML YEARS		461	2453	1786	568	99	40	81	.960	---

162

FIELDING AS FIRST BASEMAN										
Year Team	Lg	G	TC	PO	A	E	DP	PB	Pct.	Range
1911 St. Louis	AL	4	41	37	1	3	2	--	.927	---

Reggie Cleveland

Reginald Leslie Cleveland
Pitches: Right **Bats:** Right

Height: 6'1" **Weight:** 195
Born on May 23, 1948 in Swift Current, Saskatchewan

		HOW MUCH HE PITCHED						WHAT HE GAVE UP										THE RESULTS					
Year Team	Lg	G	GS	CG	GF	IP	BFP	H	R	ER	HR	SH	SF	HB	TBB	IBB	SO	WP	Bk	W	L	Pct.	ShO	Sv	ERA
1969 St. Louis	NL	1	1	0	0	4	20	7	4	4	0	0	0	0	1	0	3	0	0	0	0	.000	0	0	9.00
1970 St. Louis	NL	16	1	0	5	26	129	31	27	22	3	4	3	0	18	6	22	2	0	0	4	.000	0	0	7.62
1971 St. Louis	NL	34	34	10	0	222	953	238	107	99	20	9	7	6	53	12	148	3	1	12	12	.500	2	0	4.01
1972 St. Louis	NL	33	33	11	0	230.2	971	229	120	101	21	10	7	5	60	12	153	3	2	14	15	.483	3	0	3.94
1973 St. Louis	NL	32	32	6	0	224	939	211	88	75	13	12	6	4	61	12	122	3	0	14	10	.583	3	0	3.01
1974 Boston	AL	41	27	10	10	221.1	960	234	121	106	25	11	8	9	69	5	103	6	1	12	14	.462	0	0	4.31
1975 Boston	AL	31	20	3	6	170.2	724	173	90	84	19	4	8	3	52	1	78	9	0	13	9	.591	1	0	4.43
1976 Boston	AL	41	14	3	10	170	719	159	73	58	3	5	3	4	61	4	76	6	0	10	9	.526	0	2	3.07
1977 Boston	AL	36	27	9	2	190.1	809	211	97	90	20	4	7	4	43	2	85	3	0	11	8	.579	1	2	4.26
1978 2 ML Teams		54	0	0	41	76	318	66	34	26	5	7	6	3	23	6	46	1	1	5	8	.385	0	12	3.08
1979 Milwaukee	AL	29	1	0	11	55	258	77	44	41	9	4	7	0	23	4	22	2	1	1	5	.167	0	4	6.71
1980 Milwaukee	AL	45	13	5	16	154.1	657	150	73	64	9	4	9	5	49	2	54	5	0	11	9	.550	2	4	3.73
1981 Milwaukee	AL	35	0	0	10	64.2	274	57	41	37	5	4	1	1	30	2	18	6	0	2	3	.400	0	1	5.15
1978 Boston	AL	1	0	0	0	0.1	3	1	1	0	0	0	0	0	0	0	0	0	0	0	1	.000	0	0	0.00
Texas	AL	53	0	0	41	75.2	315	65	33	26	5	7	6	3	23	6	46	1	1	5	7	.417	0	12	3.09
13 ML YEARS		428	203	57	111	1809	7731	1843	919	807	152	78	72	44	543	68	930	49	6	105	106	.498	12	25	4.01

League Championship Pitching

		HOW MUCH HE PITCHED						WHAT HE GAVE UP										THE RESULTS					
Year Team	Lg	G	GS	CG	GF	IP	BFP	H	R	ER	HR	SH	SF	HB	TBB	IBB	SO	WP	Bk	W	L	Pct.	ShO	Sv	ERA
1975 Boston	AL	1	1	0	0	5	21	7	3	3	1	0	0	0	1	0	2	0	0	0	0	.000	0	0	5.40

World Series Pitching

		HOW MUCH HE PITCHED						WHAT HE GAVE UP										THE RESULTS					
Year Team	Lg	G	GS	CG	GF	IP	BFP	H	R	ER	HR	SH	SF	HB	TBB	IBB	SO	WP	Bk	W	L	Pct.	ShO	Sv	ERA
1975 Boston	AL	3	1	0	1	6.2	26	7	5	5	2	0	0	0	3	0	5	0	0	0	1	.000	0	0	6.75

		BATTING															BASERUNNING				PERCENTAGES		
Year Team	Lg	G	AB	H	2B	3B	HR	(Hm | Rd)	TB	R	RBI	TBB	IBB	SO	HBP	SH	SF	SB	CS	SB%	GDP	Avg	OBP	SLG
1969 St. Louis	NL	1	1	0	0	0	0	(0 | 0)	0	0	0	0	0	0	0	1	0	0	0	.00	0	.000	.000	.000
1970 St. Louis	NL	16	4	1	0	0	0	(0 | 0)	1	0	0	0	0	2	0	0	0	0	0	.00	0	.250	.250	.250
1971 St. Louis	NL	34	82	14	2	0	0	(0 | 0)	16	5	7	1	0	16	0	4	1	0	0	.00	1	.171	.179	.195
1972 St. Louis	NL	33	71	17	0	0	0	(0 | 0)	17	3	7	1	0	13	1	11	0	0	0	.00	3	.239	.260	.239
1973 St. Louis	NL	32	74	17	4	0	0	(0 | 0)	21	5	3	4	0	19	0	9	0	0	0	.00	2	.230	.269	.284
5 ML YEARS		116	232	49	6	0	0	(0 | 0)	55	13	17	6	0	50	1	25	1	0	0	.00	6	.211	.233	.237

League Championship Batting

		BATTING															BASERUNNING				PERCENTAGES		
Year Team	Lg	G	AB	H	2B	3B	HR	(Hm | Rd)	TB	R	RBI	TBB	IBB	SO	HBP	SH	SF	SB	CS	SB%	GDP	Avg	OBP	SLG
1975 Boston	AL	1	0	0	0	0	0	(0 | 0)	0	0	0	0	0	0	0	0	0	0	0	.00	0	.000	.000	.000

World Series Batting

		BATTING															BASERUNNING				PERCENTAGES		
Year Team	Lg	G	AB	H	2B	3B	HR	(Hm | Rd)	TB	R	RBI	TBB	IBB	SO	HBP	SH	SF	SB	CS	SB%	GDP	Avg	OBP	SLG
1975 Boston	AL	3	2	0	0	0	0	(0 | 0)	0	0	0	0	0	2	0	0	0	0	0	.00	0	.000	.000	.000

FIELDING AS PITCHER										
Year Team	Lg	G	TC	PO	A	E	DP	PB	Pct.	Range
1969 St. Louis	NL	1	0	0	0	0	0	--	.000	---
1970 St. Louis	NL	16	3	1	1	1	0	--	.667	---
1971 St. Louis	NL	34	46	15	30	1	1	--	.978	---
1972 St. Louis	NL	33	46	17	25	4	0	--	.913	---
1973 St. Louis	NL	32	38	11	24	3	2	--	.921	---
1974 Boston	AL	41	52	12	38	2	0	--	.962	---
1975 Boston	AL	31	39	12	25	2	1	--	.949	---
1976 Boston	AL	41	39	10	25	4	4	--	.897	---
1977 Boston	AL	36	41	18	20	3	3	--	.927	---
1978 2 ML Teams		54	17	3	13	1	0	--	.941	---
1979 Milwaukee	AL	29	9	2	5	2	1	--	.778	---

Year	Team	Lg	G	TC	PO	A	E	DP	PB	Pct.	Range
1980	Milwaukee	AL	45	33	17	16	0	1	--	1.000	---
1981	Milwaukee	AL	35	9	3	5	1	1	--	.889	---
1978	Boston	AL	1	0	0	0	0	0	--	.000	---
	Texas	AL	53	17	3	13	1	0	--	.941	---
13	ML YEARS		428	372	121	227	24	14	--	.935	---

League Championship Fielding

FIELDING AS PITCHER

Year	Team	Lg	G	TC	PO	A	E	DP	PB	Pct.	Range
1975	Boston	AL	1	1	0	1	0	0	--	1.000	---

World Series Fielding

FIELDING AS PITCHER

Year	Team	Lg	G	TC	PO	A	E	DP	PB	Pct.	Range
1975	Boston	AL	3	0	0	0	0	0	--	.000	---

Jim Cockman

James Cockman
Bats: Right **Throws:** Right

Height: 5'6" **Weight:** 145
Born on April 26, 1873 in Guelph, Ontario
Died on September 28, 1947 in Guelph, Ontario

						BATTING												BASERUNNING				PERCENTAGES		
Year	Team	Lg	G	AB	H	2B	3B	HR	(Hm	Rd)	TB	R	RBI	TBB	IBB	SO	HBP	SH	SF	SB	CS	SB%	GDP	Avg	OBP	SLG
1905	New York	AL	13	38	4	0	0	0	--	--	4	5	2	4			0	0		2				.105	.190	.105

FIELDING AS THIRD BASEMAN

Year	Team	Lg	G	TC	PO	A	E	DP	PB	Pct.	Range
1905	New York	AL	13	32	10	18	4	0	--	.875	2.15

Chub Collins

Charles Augustine Collins
Bats: Both **Throws:** Unknown

Height: 6'0" **Weight:** 165
Born on October 12, 1857 in Dundas, Ontario
Died on May 20, 1914 in Dundas, Ontario

						BATTING												BASERUNNING				PERCENTAGES		
Year	Team	Lg	G	AB	H	2B	3B	HR	(Hm	Rd)	TB	R	RBI	TBB	IBB	SO	HBP	SH	SF	SB	CS	SB%	GDP	Avg	OBP	SLG
1884	2 ML Teams		83	307	61	9	1	0	--	--	72	42		23										.199	.255	.235
1885	Detroit	NL	14	55	10	0	2	0	--	--	14	8	6	0		11								.182	.182	.255
1884	Buffalo	NL	45	169	30	6	0	0	--	--	36	24	20	14		36								.178	.240	.213
	Indianapolis	AA	38	138	31	3	1	0	--	--	36	18		9			0							.225	.272	.261
2	ML YEARS		97	362	71	9	3	0	--	--	86	50		23			0	0						.196	.244	.238

FIELDING AS SECOND BASEMAN

Year	Team	Lg	G	TC	PO	A	E	DP	PB	Pct.	Range
1884	2 ML Teams		80	496	205	242	49	25	--	.901	5.59
1884	Buffalo	NL	42	268	108	137	23	15	--	.914	5.83
	Indianapolis	AA	38	228	97	105	26	10	--	.886	5.32

FIELDING AS SHORTSTOP

Year	Team	Lg	G	TC	PO	A	E	DP	PB	Pct.	Range
1884	Buffalo	NL	3	10	0	6	4	1	--	.600	2.00
1885	Detroit	NL	14	53	7	35	11	3	--	.792	3.00
2	ML YEARS		17	63	7	41	15	4	--	.762	2.82

Frank Colman

Frank Lloyd Colman
Bats: Left **Throws:** Left

Height: 5'11" **Weight:** 186
Born on March 2, 1918 in London, Ontario
Died on February 19, 1983 in London, Ontario

						BATTING												BASERUNNING				PERCENTAGES		
Year	Team	Lg	G	AB	H	2B	3B	HR	(Hm	Rd)	TB	R	RBI	TBB	IBB	SO	HBP	SH	SF	SB	CS	SB%	GDP	Avg	OBP	SLG
1942	Pittsburgh	NL	10	37	5	0	0	1	--	--	8	2	2	2		2	0	1		0			0	.135	.179	.216
1943	Pittsburgh	NL	32	59	16	2	2	0	--	--	22	9	4	8		7	0	1		0			0	.271	.358	.373
1944	Pittsburgh	NL	99	226	61	9	5	6	--	--	98	30	53	25		27	1	0		0			5	.270	.345	.434
1945	Pittsburgh	NL	77	153	32	11	1	4	--	--	57	18	30	9		16	0	0		0			4	.209	.253	.373
1946	2 ML Teams		31	68	13	3	0	2	--	--	22	5	11	3		8	1	0		0			0	.191	.236	.324
1947	New York	AL	22	28	3	0	0	2	--	--	9	2	6	2		6	0	0		0	0	.00	0	.107	.167	.321
1946	Pittsburgh	NL	26	53	9	3	0	1	--	--	15	3	6	2		7	1	0		0			0	.170	.214	.283
	New York	AL	5	15	4	0	0	1	--	--	7	2	5	1		1	0	0		0	0	.00	0	.267	.313	.467
6	ML YEARS		271	571	130	25	8	15	--	--	216	66	106	49		66	2	2		0			9	.228	.291	.378

FIELDING AS FIRST BASEMAN

Year	Team	Lg	G	TC	PO	A	E	DP	PB	Pct.	Range
1944	Pittsburgh	NL	6	7	7	0	0	0	--	1.000	---
1945	Pittsburgh	NL	22	141	126	14	1	10	--	.993	---
1946	Pittsburgh	NL	2	19	16	2	1	2	--	.947	---
	3 ML YEARS		30	167	149	16	2	12	--	.988	---

FIELDING AS OUTFIELDER

Year	Team	Lg	G	TC	PO	A	E	DP	PB	Pct.	Range
1942	Pittsburgh	NL	8	16	14	2	0	0	--	1.000	2.00
1943	Pittsburgh	NL	11	27	27	0	0	0	--	1.000	2.45
1944	Pittsburgh	NL	53	110	102	4	4	0	--	.964	2.00
1945	Pittsburgh	NL	12	17	17	0	0	0	--	1.000	1.42
1946	2 ML Teams		13	25	24	1	0	0	--	1.000	1.92
1947	New York	AL	6	8	7	1	0	0	--	1.000	1.33
1946	Pittsburgh	NL	8	16	15	1	0	0	--	1.000	2.00
	New York	AL	5	9	9	0	0	0	--	1.000	1.80
	6 ML YEARS		103	203	191	8	4	0	--	.980	1.93

Bunk Congalton

William Millar Congalton
Bats: Left **Throws:** Left

Height: 5'11" **Weight:** 190
Born on January 24, 1875 in Guelph, Ontario
Died on August 16, 1937 in Cleveland, Ohio

						BATTING																BASERUNNING				PERCENTAGES		
Year	Team	Lg	G	AB	H	2B	3B	HR	(Hm	Rd)	TB	R	RBI	TBB	IBB	SO	HBP	SH	SF		SB	CS	SB%	GDP	Avg	OBP	SLG
1902	Chicago	NL	45	179	40	3	0	1	--	--	46	14	24	7			0	4			3				.223	.253	.257
1905	Cleveland	AL	12	47	17	0	0	0	--	--	17	4	5	2			0	0			3				.362	.388	.362
1906	Cleveland	AL	117	419	134	13	5	3	--	--	166	51	50	24			3	24			12				.320	.361	.396
1907	2 ML Teams		136	518	146	11	8	2	--	--	179	46	49	24			3	13			13				.282	.317	.346
1907	Cleveland	AL	9	22	4	0	0	0	--	--	4	2	2	4			0	0			0				.182	.308	.182
	Boston	AL	127	496	142	11	8	2	--	--	175	44	47	20			3	13			13				.286	.318	.353
	4 ML YEARS		310	1163	337	27	13	6	--	--	408	115	128	57			6	41			31				.290	.326	.351

FIELDING AS OUTFIELDER

Year	Team	Lg	G	TC	PO	A	E	DP	PB	Pct.	Range
1902	Chicago	NL	45	78	71	6	1	1	--	.987	1.71
1905	Cleveland	AL	12	13	10	2	1	0	--	.923	1.00
1906	Cleveland	AL	114	188	174	6	8	0	--	.957	1.58
1907	2 ML Teams		129	204	179	19	6	4	--	.971	1.53
1907	Cleveland	AL	6	11	10	1	0	0	--	1.000	1.83
	Boston	AL	123	193	169	18	6	4	--	.969	1.52
	4 ML YEARS		300	483	434	33	16	5	--	.967	1.56

Earl Cook

Earl Davis Cook
Pitches: Right **Bats:** Right

Height: 6'0" **Weight:** 195
Born on December 10, 1908 in Stouffville, Ontario

			HOW MUCH HE PITCHED					WHAT HE GAVE UP										THE RESULTS					
Year	Team	Lg	G	GS	CG	GF	IP	BFP	H	R	ER	HR	SH	SF	HB	TBB	IBB	SO	WP	Bk	W	L	Pct.	ShO	Sv	ERA
1941	Detroit	AL	1	0	0	1	2	10	4	1	1	0	0			0		1	0	0	0	0	.000	0	0	4.50

						BATTING															BASERUNNING				PERCENTAGES		
Year	Team	Lg	G	AB	H	2B	3B	HR	(Hm	Rd)	TB	R	RBI	TBB	IBB	SO	HBP	SH	SF	SB	CS	SB%	GDP	Avg	OBP	SLG
1941	Detroit	AL	1	0	0	0	0	0	--	--	0	0	0	0	0	0	0	0	0	0	0	.00	0	.000	.000	.000

FIELDING AS PITCHER

Year	Team	Lg	G	TC	PO	A	E	DP	PB	Pct.	Range
1941	Detroit	AL	1	0	0	0	0	0	--	.000	

Rheal Cormier

Rheal Paul Cormier
Attended Rhode Island CC
Pitches: Left **Bats:** Left

Height: 5'10" **Weight:** 185
Born on April 23, 1967 in Moncton, New Brunswick

			HOW MUCH HE PITCHED					WHAT HE GAVE UP										THE RESULTS					
Year	Team	Lg	G	GS	CG	GF	IP	BFP	H	R	ER	HR	SH	SF	HB	TBB	IBB	SO	WP	Bk	W	L	Pct.	ShO	Sv	ERA
1989	St. Pete	A	26	26	4	0	169.2	669	141	63	42	9	6	3	0	33	2	122	4	7	12	7	.632	2	0	2.23
1990	Arkansas	AA	22	21	3	1	121.1	530	133	81	68	9	6	2	5	30	2	102	5	1	5	12	.294	1	0	5.04
	Louisville	AAA	4	4	0	0	24	92	18	8	6	1	0	0	0	3	0	9	4	0	1	1	.500	0	0	2.25

Year Team	Lg	G	GS	CG	GF	IP	BFP	H	R	ER	HR	SH	SF	HB	TBB	IBB	SO	WP	Bk	W	L	Pct.	ShO	Sv	ERA
1991 Louisville	AAA	21	21	3	0	127.2	543	140	64	60	5	10	6	6	31	1	74	6	1	7	9	.438	3	0	4.23
1992 Louisville	AAA	1	1	0	0	4	20	8	4	3	0	0	0	0	0	0	1	0	0	0	1	.000	0	0	6.75
1994 Arkansas	AA	2	2	0	0	9.1	35	9	2	2	0	0	0	0	0	0	11	0	0	1	0	1.000	0	0	1.93
Louisville	AAA	3	3	1	0	22	95	21	11	11	3	0	0	3	8	1	13	2	0	1	2	.333	0	0	4.50
1991 St. Louis	NL	11	10	2	1	67.2	281	74	35	31	5	1	3	2	8	1	38	2	1	4	5	.444	0	0	4.12
1992 St. Louis	NL	31	30	3	1	186	772	194	83	76	15	11	3	5	33	2	117	4	2	10	10	.500	0	0	3.68
1993 St. Louis	NL	38	21	1	4	145.1	619	163	80	70	18	10	4	4	27	3	75	6	0	7	6	.538	0	0	4.33
1994 St. Louis	NL	7	7	0	0	39.2	169	40	24	24	6	1	2	3	7	0	26	2	0	3	2	.600	0	0	5.45
1995 Boston	AL	48	12	0	3	115	488	131	60	52	12	6	2	3	31	2	69	4	0	7	5	.583	0	0	4.07
5 ML YEARS		135	80	6	9	553.2	2329	602	282	253	56	29	14	17	106	8	325	18	3	31	28	.525	0	0	4.11

Division Playoffs Pitching

		HOW MUCH HE PITCHED						WHAT HE GAVE UP												THE RESULTS					
Year Team	Lg	G	GS	CG	GF	IP	BFP	H	R	ER	HR	SH	SF	HB	TBB	IBB	SO	WP	Bk	W	L	Pct.	ShO	Sv	ERA
1995 Boston	AL	2	0	0	0	0.2	6	2	1	1	0	0	0	1	1	0	2	0	0	0	0	.000	0	0	13.50

		BATTING																	BASERUNNING				PERCENTAGES		
Year Team	Lg	G	AB	H	2B	3B	HR	(Hm	Rd)	TB	R	RBI	TBB	IBB	SO	HBP	SH	SF	SB	CS	SB%	GDP	Avg	OBP	SLG
1991 St. Louis	NL	11	21	5	0	0	0	(0	0)	5	2	1	0	0	5	0	1	0	0	0	.00	0	.238	.238	.238
1992 St. Louis	NL	31	59	6	2	0	0	(0	0)	8	3	2	0	0	13	0	10	0	0	0	.00	0	.102	.102	.136
1993 St. Louis	NL	38	47	11	2	0	0	(0	0)	13	5	4	0	0	11	0	6	0	0	0	.00	0	.234	.234	.277
1994 St. Louis	NL	7	14	4	0	0	0	(0	0)	4	2	1	1	0	2	1	0	0	0	0	.00	0	.286	.375	.286
4 ML YEARS		87	141	26	4	0	0	(0	0)	30	12	8	1	0	31	1	17	0	0	0	.00	1	.184	.196	.213

Division Playoffs Batting

		BATTING																	BASERUNNING				PERCENTAGES		
Year Team	Lg	G	AB	H	2B	3B	HR	(Hm	Rd)	TB	R	RBI	TBB	IBB	SO	HBP	SH	SF	SB	CS	SB%	GDP	Avg	OBP	SLG
1995 Boston	AL	2	0	0	0	0	0	(0	0)	0	0	0	0	0	0	0	0	0	0	0	.00	0	.000	.000	.000

		FIELDING AS PITCHER								
Year Team	Lg	G	TC	PO	A	E	DP	PB	Pct.	Range
1991 St. Louis	NL	11	11	3	8	0	0	--	1.000	---
1992 St. Louis	NL	31	43	9	34	0	2	--	1.000	---
1993 St. Louis	NL	38	38	8	27	3	2	--	.921	---
1994 St. Louis	NL	7	5	1	3	1	0	--	.800	---
1995 Boston	AL	48	30	7	21	2	2	--	.933	---
5 ML YEARS		135	127	28	93	6	6	--	.953	---

Division Playoffs Fielding

		FIELDING AS PITCHER								
Year Team	Lg	G	TC	PO	A	E	DP	PB	Pct.	Range
1995 Boston	AL	2	0	0	0	0	0	--	.000	---

Barry Cort

Barry Lee Cort
Pitches: Right **Bats:** Right

Height: 6'5" **Weight:** 210
Born on April 15, 1956 in Toronto, Ontario

		HOW MUCH HE PITCHED						WHAT HE GAVE UP												THE RESULTS					
Year Team	Lg	G	GS	CG	GF	IP	BFP	H	R	ER	HR	SH	SF	HB	TBB	IBB	SO	WP	Bk	W	L	Pct.	ShO	Sv	ERA
1977 Milwaukee	AL	7	3	1	1	24.1	102	25	9	9	1	2	1	1	9	1	17	1	0	1	1	.500	0	0	3.33

		FIELDING AS PITCHER								
Year Team	Lg	G	TC	PO	A	E	DP	PB	Pct.	Range
1977 Milwaukee	AL	7	5	1	4	0	0	--	1.000	---

Pete Craig

Peter Joel Craig
Pitches: Right **Bats:** Left

Height: 6'5" **Weight:** 220
Born on July 10, 1940 in LaSalle, Ontario

		HOW MUCH HE PITCHED						WHAT HE GAVE UP												THE RESULTS					
Year Team	Lg	G	GS	CG	GF	IP	BFP	H	R	ER	HR	SH	SF	HB	TBB	IBB	SO	WP	Bk	W	L	Pct.	ShO	Sv	ERA
1964 Washington	AL	2	1	0	0	1.2	16	8	9	9	1	0	1	0	4	1	0	0	0	0	1	.000	0	0	48.60
1965 Washington	AL	3	3	0	0	14.1	67	18	15	13	1	1	2	0	8	1	2	1	0	0	3	.000	0	0	8.16
1966 Washington	AL	1	0	0	0	2	10	2	2	1	0	0	1	0	1	1	1	0	0	0	0	.000	0	0	4.50
3 ML YEARS		6	4	0	0	18	93	28	26	23	2	2	2	0	13	3	3	1	0	0	3	.000	0	0	11.50

		BATTING																	BASERUNNING				PERCENTAGES		
Year Team	Lg	G	AB	H	2B	3B	HR	(Hm	Rd)	TB	R	RBI	TBB	IBB	SO	HBP	SH	SF	SB	CS	SB%	GDP	Avg	OBP	SLG
1964 Washington	AL	2	0	0	0	0	0	(0	0)	0	0	0	0	0	0	0	0	0	0	0	.00	0	.000	.000	.000
1965 Washington	AL	3	3	2	0	0	0	(0	0)	2	1	0	0	0	0	0	0	0	0	0	.00	0	.667	.750	.667

1966 Washington	AL	1	0	0	0	0	0	(0	0)	0	0	0	0	0	0	0	0	.00	0	.000	.000	.000
3 ML YEARS		6	3	2	0	0	0	(0	0)	2	1	0	1	0	0	0	0	.00	0	.667	.750	.667

FIELDING AS PITCHER

Year Team	Lg	G	TC	PO	A	E	DP	PB	Pct.	Range
1964 Washington	AL	2	0	0	0	0	0	--	.000	---
1965 Washington	AL	3	9	6	3	0	0	--	1.000	---
1966 Washington	AL	1	1	0	0	1	0	--	.000	---
3 ML YEARS		6	10	6	3	1	0	--	.900	---

Ken Crosby

Kenneth Stewart Crosby

Height: 6'2" **Weight:** 179

Pitches: Right **Bats:** Right

Born on December 15, 1947 in New Denver, British Columbia

HOW MUCH HE PITCHED / WHAT HE GAVE UP / THE RESULTS

Year Team	Lg	G	GS	CG	GF	IP	BFP	H	R	ER	HR	SH	SF	HB	TBB	IBB	SO	WP	Bk	W	L	Pct.	ShO	Sv	ERA
1975 Chicago	NL	9	0	0	6	8.1	42	10	3	3	0	1	0	0	7	0	6	0	1	1	0	1.000	0	0	3.24
1976 Chicago	NL	7	1	0	1	12	64	20	16	16	3	3	0	0	8	0	5	0	0	0	0	.000	0	0	12.00
2 ML YEARS		16	1	0	7	20.1	106	30	19	19	3	4	0	0	15	0	11	0	1	1	0	1.000	0	0	8.41

BATTING / BASERUNNING / PERCENTAGES

Year Team	Lg	G	AB	H	2B	3B	HR	(Hm	Rd)	TB	R	RBI	TBB	IBB	SO	HBP	SH	SF	SB	CS	SB%	GDP	Avg	OBP	SLG
1975 Chicago	NL	9	0	0	0	0	0	(0	0)	0	1	0	1	0	0	0	0	0	0	0	.00	0	.000	1.000	.000
1976 Chicago	NL	7	2	1	0	0	0	(0	0)	1	0	0	0	0	0	0	0	0	0	0	.00	0	.500	.500	.500
2 ML YEARS		16	2	1	0	0	0	(0	0)	1	1	0	1	0	0	0	0	0	0	0	.00	0	.500	.667	.500

FIELDING AS PITCHER

Year Team	Lg	G	TC	PO	A	E	DP	PB	Pct.	Range
1975 Chicago	NL	9	3	0	3	0	0	--	1.000	---
1976 Chicago	NL	7	3	1	2	0	0	--	1.000	---
2 ML YEARS		16	6	1	5	0	0	--	1.000	---

Clarence Currie

Clarence Franklin Currie

Height: Unknown **Weight:** Unknown

Pitches: Right **Bats:** Right

Born on December 30, 1878 in Glencoe, Ontario

Died on July 15, 1941 in Little Chute, Wisconsin

HOW MUCH HE PITCHED / WHAT HE GAVE UP / THE RESULTS

Year Team	Lg	G	GS	CG	GF	IP	BFP	H	R	ER	HR	SH	SF	HB	TBB	IBB	SO	WP	Bk	W	L	Pct.	ShO	Sv	ERA
1902 2 ML Teams		25	19	16	4	190	774	195	91	63	1	13		8	52		50	3	0	10	9	.526	3	0	2.98
1903 2 ML Teams		28	19	15	8	180.2	779	190	118	77	8	17		3	69		61	4	0	5	14	.263	1	2	3.84
1902 Cincinnati	NL	10	7	6	2	65.1	269	70	37	27	1	0		2	17		20	0	0	3	4	.429	1	0	3.72
St. Louis	NL	15	12	10	2	124.2	505	125	54	36	0	13		6	35		30	3	0	7	5	.583	2	0	2.60
1903 St. Louis	NL	22	16	13	5	148	623	155	93	66	7	11		0	60		52	4	0	4	12	.250	1	1	4.01
Chicago	NL	6	3	2	3	32.2	156	35	25	11	1	6		3	9		9	0	0	1	2	.333	0	1	3.03
2 ML YEARS		53	38	31	12	370.2	1553	385	209	140	9	30		11	121		111	7	0	15	23	.395	4	2	3.40

BATTING / BASERUNNING / PERCENTAGES

Year Team	Lg	G	AB	H	2B	3B	HR	(Hm	Rd)	TB	R	RBI	TBB	IBB	SO	HBP	SH	SF	SB	CS	SB%	GDP	Avg	OBP	SLG
1902 2 ML Teams		26	70	11	2	0	0	--	--	13	3	5	2			1	2		1				.157	.192	.186
1903 2 ML Teams		28	59	9	0	1	0	--	--	11	2	4	4			0	2						.153	.206	.186
1902 Cincinnati	NL	10	24	2	0	0	0	--	--	2	0	2	1			0	1						.083	.120	.083
St. Louis	NL	16	46	9	2	0	0	--	--	11	3	3	1			1	1		1				.196	.229	.239
1903 St. Louis	NL	22	47	4	0	1	0	--	--	6	1	1	3			0	2						.085	.140	.128
Chicago	NL	6	12	5	0	0	0	--	--	5	1	3	1			0	0						.417	.462	.417
2 ML YEARS		54	129	20	2	1	0	--	--	24	5	9	6			1	4		1				.155	.199	.186

FIELDING AS PITCHER

Year Team	Lg	G	TC	PO	A	E	DP	PB	Pct.	Range
1902 2 ML Teams		25	76	4	64	4	3	--	.947	---
1903 2 ML Teams		28	91	9	74	8	3	--	.912	---
1902 Cincinnati	NL	10	23	3	20	0	1	--	1.000	---
St. Louis	NL	15	53	5	44	4	2	--	.925	---
1903 St. Louis	NL	22	72	6	60	6	3	--	.917	---
Chicago	NL	6	19	3	14	2	0	--	.895	---
2 ML YEARS		53	167	17	138	12	6	--	.928	---

Tom Daly

Thomas Daniel Daly
Bats: Right **Throws:** Right

Height: 5'11" **Weight:** 171
Born on December 12, 1891 in St. John, New Brunswick
Died on November 7, 1946 in Medford, Massachusetts

BATTING / BASERUNNING / PERCENTAGES

Year Team	Lg	G	AB	H	2B	3B	HR	(Hm	Rd)	TB	R	RBI	TBB	IBB	SO	HBP	SH	SF	SB	CS	SB%	GDP	Avg	OBP	SLG
1913 Chicago	AL	1	3	0	0	0	0	--	--	0	0	0	0		0	0	0	0	0				.000	.000	.000
1914 Chicago	AL	61	133	31	2	0	0	--	--	33	13	8	7		13	0	2		3	4	.43		.233	.271	.248
1915 Chicago	AL	29	47	9	1	0	0	--	--	10	5	3	5		9	0	1		0	0	.00		.191	.269	.213
1916 Cleveland	AL	31	73	16	1	0	0	--	--	19	3	8	1		2	0	1		0				.219	.230	.260
1918 Chicago	NL	1	1	0	0	0	0	--	--	0	0	0	0		0	0	0		0				.000	.000	.000
1919 Chicago	NL	25	50	11	0	1	0	--	--	13	4	1	2		5	0	1		0				.220	.250	.260
1920 Chicago	NL	44	90	28	6	0	0	--	--	34	12	13	2		6	1	1		1	1	.50		.311	.333	.378
1921 Chicago	NL	51	143	34	7	1	0	--	--	43	12	22	8		8	0	2		1	2	.33		.238	.278	.301
8 ML YEARS		243	540	129	17	3	0	--	--	152	49	55	25		43	1	8		5				.239	.274	.281

FIELDING AS CATCHER

Year Team	Lg	G	TC	PO	A	E	DP	PB	Pct.	Range
1913 Chicago	AL	1	7	6	1	0	1	0	1.000	---
1914 Chicago	AL	4	15	13	2	0	1	0	1.000	---
1915 Chicago	AL	19	71	59	9	3	0	2	.958	---
1916 Cleveland	AL	25	112	86	24	2	3	1	.982	---
1918 Chicago	NL	1	3	2	0	1	0	0	.667	---
1919 Chicago	NL	18	68	55	10	3	2	1	.956	---
1920 Chicago	NL	29	108	88	18	2	0	1	.981	---
1921 Chicago	NL	47	225	171	48	6	10	2	.973	---
8 ML YEARS		144	609	480	112	17	17	7	.972	

FIELDING AS FIRST BASEMAN

Year Team	Lg	G	TC	PO	A	E	DP	PB	Pct.	Range
1914 Chicago	AL	2	27	25	1	1	2	--	.963	---
1915 Chicago	AL	1	2	2	0	0	0	--	1.000	---
2 ML YEARS		3	29	27	1	1	2	--	.966	

FIELDING AS THIRD BASEMAN

Year Team	Lg	G	TC	PO	A	E	DP	PB	Pct.	Range
1914 Chicago	AL	5	6	3	2	1	0	--	.833	1.00

FIELDING AS OUTFIELDER

Year Team	Lg	G	TC	PO	A	E	DP	PB	Pct.	Range
1914 Chicago	AL	23	22	19	1	2	0	--	.909	.87
1916 Cleveland	AL	1	0	0	0	0	0	--	.000	.00
2 ML YEARS		24	22	19	1	2	0	--	.909	.83

Ray Daviault

Raymond Joseph Robert Daviault
Pitches: Right **Bats:** Right

Height: 6'1" **Weight:** 170
Born on May 27, 1934 in Montreal, Quebec

HOW MUCH HE PITCHED / WHAT HE GAVE UP / THE RESULTS

Year Team	Lg	G	GS	CG	GF	IP	BFP	H	R	ER	HR	SH	SF	HB	TBB	IBB	SO	WP	Bk	W	L	Pct.	ShO	Sv	ERA
1962 New York	NL	36	3	0	14	81	377	92	64	56	14	2	4	4	48	1	51	6	1	1	5	.167	0	0	6.22

BATTING / BASERUNNING / PERCENTAGES

Year Team	Lg	G	AB	H	2B	3B	HR	(Hm	Rd)	TB	R	RBI	TBB	IBB	SO	HBP	SH	SF	SB	CS	SB%	GDP	Avg	OBP	SLG
1962 New York	NL	36	15	1	0	0	0	(0	0)	1	0	0	1	0	8	0	0	0	0	0	.00	0	.067	.125	.067

FIELDING AS PITCHER

Year Team	Lg	G	TC	PO	A	E	DP	PB	Pct.	Range
1962 New York	NL	36	15	9	6	0	0	--	1.000	---

Shorty Dee

Maurice Leo Dee
Bats: Right **Throws:** Right

Height: 5'6" **Weight:** 155
Born on October 4, 1889 in Halifax, Nova Scotia
Died on August 12, 1971 in Jamaica Plains, Massachusetts

BATTING / BASERUNNING / PERCENTAGES

Year Team	Lg	G	AB	H	2B	3B	HR	(Hm	Rd)	TB	R	RBI	TBB	IBB	SO	HBP	SH	SF	SB	CS	SB%	GDP	Avg	OBP	SLG
1915 St. Louis	AL	1	3	0	0	0	0	--	--	0	1	0	1		0	0	0		0	1	.00		.000	.250	.000

FIELDING AS SHORTSTOP										
Year Team	Lg	G	TC	PO	A	E	DP	PB	Pct.	Range
1915 St. Louis	AL	1	4	1	1	2	0	--	.500	2.00

Fred Demarais

Frederick Demarais Demarais
Pitches: Right **Bats:** Unknown

Height: 5'9" **Weight:** 168
Born on November 1, 1866 in Quebec
Died on March 6, 1919 in Stamford, Connecticut

		HOW MUCH HE PITCHED						WHAT HE GAVE UP										THE RESULTS					
Year Team	Lg	G	GS	CG	GF	IP	BFP	H	R	ER	HR	SH	SF	HB	TBB	IBB	SO	WP	Bk	W	L	Pct.	ShO	Sv	ERA
1890 Chicago	NL	1	0	0	1	2	10	1	0	0	0			0	1		1	2	0	0	0	.000	0	0	0.00

		BATTING																BASERUNNING				PERCENTAGES		
Year Team	Lg	G	AB	H	2B	3B	HR	(Hm	Rd)	TB	R	RBI	TBB	IBB	SO	HBP	SH	SF	SB	CS	SB%	GDP	Avg	OBP	SLG
1890 Chicago	NL	1	2	0	0	0	0	--	--	0	0	0	0		1	0			0				.000	.000	.000

FIELDING AS PITCHER										
Year Team	Lg	G	TC	PO	A	E	DP	PB	Pct.	Range
1890 Chicago	NL	1	1	0	1	0	0	--	1.000	---

Jerry Dorsey

Michael Jeremiah Dorsey
Pitches: Unknown **Bats:** Unknown

Height: Unknown **Weight:** Unknown
Born in 1854 in Canada
Died on November 3, 1938 in Auburn, New York

		HOW MUCH HE PITCHED						WHAT HE GAVE UP										THE RESULTS					
Year Team	Lg	G	GS	CG	GF	IP	BFP	H	R	ER	HR	SH	SF	HB	TBB	IBB	SO	WP	Bk	W	L	Pct.	ShO	Sv	ERA
1884 Baltimore	UA	1	1	0	0	4	22	7	8	4	1				0		3	1	0	0	1	.000	0	0	9.00

		BATTING																BASERUNNING				PERCENTAGES		
Year Team	Lg	G	AB	H	2B	3B	HR	(Hm	Rd)	TB	R	RBI	TBB	IBB	SO	HBP	SH	SF	SB	CS	SB%	GDP	Avg	OBP	SLG
1884 Baltimore	UA	1	3	0	0	0	0	--	--	0	0	0	0			0							.000	.000	.000

FIELDING AS PITCHER										
Year Team	Lg	G	TC	PO	A	E	DP	PB	Pct.	Range
1884 Baltimore	UA	1	1	0	1	0	0	--	1.000	---

FIELDING AS OUTFIELDER										
Year Team	Lg	G	TC	PO	A	E	DP	PB	Pct.	Range
1884 Baltimore	UA	1	0	0	0	0	0	--	.000	.00

John Doyle

John Aloysius Doyle
Bats: Unknown **Throws:** Unknown

Height: Unknown **Weight:** Unknown
Born in 1858 in Nova Scotia
Died on December 24, 1915 in Providence, Rhode Island

		BATTING																BASERUNNING				PERCENTAGES		
Year Team	Lg	G	AB	H	2B	3B	HR	(Hm	Rd)	TB	R	RBI	TBB	IBB	SO	HBP	SH	SF	SB	CS	SB%	GDP	Avg	OBP	SLG
1882 St. Louis	AA	3	11	2	0	0	0	--	--	2	0	0	0										.182	.182	.182

		HOW MUCH HE PITCHED						WHAT HE GAVE UP										THE RESULTS					
Year Team	Lg	G	GS	CG	GF	IP	BFP	H	R	ER	HR	SH	SF	HB	TBB	IBB	SO	WP	Bk	W	L	Pct.	ShO	Sv	ERA
1882 St. Louis	AA	3	3	3	0	24	125	41	33	7	0				3		5	2	0	0	3	.000	0	0	2.63

FIELDING AS PITCHER										
Year Team	Lg	G	TC	PO	A	E	DP	PB	Pct.	Range
1882 St. Louis	AA	3	6	1	5	0	0	--	1.000	---

Rob Ducey

Robert Thomas Ducey
Attended Seminole CC
Bats: Left **Throws:** Right

Height: 6'2" **Weight:** 175
Born on May 24, 1965 in Toronto, Ontario

		BATTING																BASERUNNING				PERCENTAGES		
Year Team	Lg	G	AB	H	2B	3B	HR	(Hm	Rd)	TB	R	RBI	TBB	IBB	SO	HBP	SH	SF	SB	CS	SB%	GDP	Avg	OBP	SLG
1984 Medicne Hat	R	63	235	71	10	3	12	--	--	123	49	49	41	0	61	1	1	1	13	6	.68	4	.302	.406	.523
1985 Florence	A	134	529	133	22	2	13	--	--	198	78	86	49	2	103	1	3	7	12	4	.75	3	.251	.312	.374
1986 Ventura	A	47	178	60	11	3	12	--	--	113	36	38	21	2	24	1	1	2	17	5	.77	3	.337	.406	.635

169

Year Team	Lg	G	AB	H	2B	3B	HR	(Hm Rd)	TB	R	RBI	TBB	IBB	SO	HBP	SH	SF	SB	CS	SB%	GDP	Avg	OBP	SLG
Knoxville	AA	88	344	106	22	3	11	-- --	167	49	58	29	3	59	0	0	4	7	7	.50	2	.308	.358	.485
1987 Syracuse	AAA	100	359	102	14	10	10	-- --	166	62	60	61	5	88	3	0	5	7	7	.50	6	.284	.388	.462
1988 Syracuse	AAA	90	317	81	14	4	7	-- --	124	40	42	43	0	81	3	2	4	7	6	.54	3	.256	.346	.391
1989 Syracuse	AAA	10	29	3	0	1	0	-- --	5	0	3	10	0	13	0	0	1	0	0	.00	0	.103	.325	.172
1990 Syracuse	AAA	127	438	117	32	7	7	-- --	184	53	47	60	6	87	4	1	1	13	9	.59	10	.267	.360	.420
1991 Syracuse	AAA	72	266	78	10	3	8	-- --	118	53	40	51	4	58	0	4	2	5	7	.42	1	.293	.404	.444
1993 Okla. City	AAA	105	389	118	17	10	17	-- --	206	68	56	46	2	97	1	0	4	17	9	.65	5	.303	.375	.530
1994 Okla. City	AAA	115	403	108	27	9	17	-- --	204	69	65	75	1	91	5	0	3	9	5	.64	3	.268	.387	.506
1987 Toronto	AL	34	48	9	1	0	1	(1 0)	13	12	6	8	0	10	0	0	1	2	0	1.00	0	.188	.298	.271
1988 Toronto	AL	27	54	17	4	1	0	(0 0)	23	15	6	5	0	7	0	2	2	1	0	1.00	1	.315	.361	.426
1989 Toronto	AL	41	76	16	4	0	0	(0 0)	20	5	7	9	1	25	0	1	0	1	1	.67	2	.211	.294	.263
1990 Toronto	AL	19	53	16	5	0	0	(0 0)	21	7	7	7	0	15	1	0	1	1	1	.50	0	.302	.387	.396
1991 Toronto	AL	39	68	16	2	2	1	(0 1)	25	8	4	6	0	26	0	1	0	2	0	1.00	1	.235	.297	.368
1992 2 ML Teams		54	80	15	4	0	0	(0 0)	19	7	2	5	0	22	0	0	1	2	4	.33	1	.188	.233	.238
1993 Texas	AL	27	85	24	6	3	2	(2 0)	42	15	9	10	2	17	0	2	2	2	3	.40	1	.282	.351	.494
1994 Texas	AL	11	29	5	1	0	0	(0 0)	6	1	1	2	0	1	0	0	0	0	0	.00	1	.172	.226	.207
1992 Toronto	AL	23	21	1	1	0	0	(0 0)	2	3	0	0	0	10	0	0	0	0	1	.00	0	.048	.048	.095
California	AL	31	59	14	3	0	0	(0 0)	17	4	2	5	0	12	0	0	1	2	3	.40	1	.237	.292	.288
8 ML YEARS		252	493	118	27	6	4	(3 1)	169	70	42	52	3	123	1	6	7	12	9	.57	7	.239	.309	.343

League Championship Batting

		BATTING																BASERUNNING				PERCENTAGES		
Year Team	Lg	G	AB	H	2B	3B	HR	(Hm Rd)	TB	R	RBI	TBB	IBB	SO	HBP	SH	SF	SB	CS	SB%	GDP	Avg	OBP	SLG
1991 Toronto	AL	1	1	0	0	0	0	(0 0)	0	0	0	0	0	0	0	0	0	0	0	.00	0	.000	.000	.000

FIELDING AS OUTFIELDER

Year Team	Lg	G	TC	PO	A	E	DP	PB	Pct.	Range
1987 Toronto	AL	28	31	31	0	0	0	--	1.000	1.11
1988 Toronto	AL	26	36	35	1	0	0	--	1.000	1.38
1989 Toronto	AL	35	59	56	3	0	2	--	1.000	1.69
1990 Toronto	AL	19	37	37	0	0	0	--	1.000	1.95
1991 Toronto	AL	24	37	32	1	4	0	--	.892	1.38
1992 2 ML Teams		33	47	43	2	2	0	--	.957	1.36
1993 Texas	AL	26	52	51	1	0	0	--	1.000	2.00
1994 Texas	AL	10	17	15	0	2	0	--	.882	1.50
1992 Toronto	AL	13	11	11	0	0	0	--	1.000	.85
California	AL	20	36	32	2	2	0	--	.944	1.70
8 ML YEARS		201	316	300	8	8	2	--	.975	1.53

League Championship Fielding

FIELDING AS OUTFIELDER

Year Team	Lg	G	TC	PO	A	E	DP	PB	Pct.	Range
1991 Toronto	AL	1	0	0	0	0	0	--	.000	.00

Gus Dugas

Augustin Joseph Dugas

Height: 5'9" **Weight:** 165

Bats: Left **Throws:** Left

Born on March 24, 1907 in St. Jean de Matha, Quebec

		BATTING																BASERUNNING				PERCENTAGES		
Year Team	Lg	G	AB	H	2B	3B	HR	(Hm Rd)	TB	R	RBI	TBB	IBB	SO	HBP	SH	SF	SB	CS	SB%	GDP	Avg	OBP	SLG
1930 Pittsburgh	NL	9	31	9	2	0	0	-- --	11	8	1	7		4	0	1		0				.290	.421	.355
1932 Pittsburgh	NL	55	97	23	3	3	3	-- --	41	13	12	7		11	0	0		0				.237	.288	.423
1933 Philadelphia	NL	37	71	12	3	0	0	-- --	15	4	9	1		9	0	2		0			2	.169	.181	.211
1934 Washington	AL	24	19	1	1	0	0	-- --	2	2	1	3		3	0	0		0	0	.00		.053	.182	.105
4 ML YEARS		125	218	45	9	3	3	-- --	69	27	23	18		27	0	3		0				.206	.267	.317

FIELDING AS FIRST BASEMAN

Year Team	Lg	G	TC	PO	A	E	DP	PB	Pct.	Range
1933 Philadelphia	NL	11	122	112	8	2	7	--	.984	---

FIELDING AS OUTFIELDER

Year Team	Lg	G	TC	PO	A	E	DP	PB	Pct.	Range
1930 Pittsburgh	NL	9	22	18	1	3	0	--	.864	2.11
1932 Pittsburgh	NL	20	42	40	0	2	0	--	.952	2.00
1933 Philadelphia	NL	1	1	1	0	0	0	--	1.000	1.00
1934 Washington	AL	2	3	3	0	0	0	--	1.000	1.50
4 ML YEARS		32	68	62	1	5	0	--	.926	1.97

Steve Dunn

Stephen B. Dunn
Bats: Unknown **Throws:** Unknown

Height: 5'10" **Weight:** 173
Born on December 21, 1858 in London, Ontario
Died on May 5, 1933 in London, Ontario

					BATTING															BASERUNNING				PERCENTAGES		
Year Team	Lg	G	AB	H	2B	3B	HR	(Hm	Rd)	TB	R	RBI	TBB	IBB	SO	HBP	SH	SF		SB	CS	SB%	GDP	Avg	OBP	SLG
1884 St. Paul	UA	9	32	8	2	0	0	--	--	10	2		0											.250	.250	.313

				FIELDING AS FIRST BASEMAN								
Year Team	Lg	G	TC	PO	A	E	DP	PB	Pct.	Range
1884 St. Paul	UA	9	71	64	5	2	2	--	.972	

				FIELDING AS THIRD BASEMAN								
Year Team	Lg	G	TC	PO	A	E	DP	PB	Pct.	Range
1884 St. Paul	UA	1	5	3	0	2	1	--	.600	3.00

Bob Emslie

Robert Daniel Emslie
Pitches: Right **Bats:** Right

Height: 5'11" **Weight:** Unknown
Born on January 27, 1859 in Guelph, Ontario
Died on April 26, 1943 in St. Thomas, Ontario

		HOW MUCH HE PITCHED						WHAT HE GAVE UP											THE RESULTS					
Year Team	Lg	G	GS	CG	GF	IP	BFP	H	R	ER	HR	SH	SF	HB	TBB	IBB	SO	WP	Bk	W	L	Pct.	ShO	Sv	ERA
1883 Baltimore	AA	24	23	21	1	201.1	876	188	149	71	3				41		62	12	0	9	13	.409	1	0	3.17
1884 Baltimore	AA	50	50	50	0	455.1	1971	419	241	139	5			14	88		264	43	0	32	17	.653	4	0	2.75
1885 2 ML Teams		17	17	14	0	135.2	607	168	117	71	1			5	36		36	15		3	14	.176	0	0	4.71
1885 Baltimore	AA	13	13	11	0	107	474	131	87	51	0			5	30		27	12		3	10	.231	0	0	4.29
Philadelphia	AA	4	4	3	0	28.2	133	37	30	20	1			0	6		9	3		0	4	.000	0	0	6.28
3 ML YEARS		91	90	85	1	792.1	3454	775	507	281	9				165		362	70		44	44	.500	5	0	3.19

					BATTING															BASERUNNING				PERCENTAGES		
Year Team	Lg	G	AB	H	2B	3B	HR	(Hm	Rd)	TB	R	RBI	TBB	IBB	SO	HBP	SH	SF		SB	CS	SB%	GDP	Avg	OBP	SLG
1883 Baltimore	AA	27	97	16	1	2	0	--	--	21	14		6											.165	.214	.216
1884 Baltimore	AA	51	195	37	6	3	0	--	--	49	21		2			0								.190	.198	.251
1885 2 ML Teams		17	63	13	1	1	0	--	--	16	7		0											.206	.206	.254
1885 Baltimore	AA	13	51	12	1	1	0	--	--	15	6		0			0								.235	.235	.294
Philadelphia	AA	4	12	1	0	0	0	--	--	1	1		0			0								.083	.083	.083
3 ML YEARS		95	355	66	8	6	0	--	--	86	42		8			0	0							.186	.204	.242

				FIELDING AS PITCHER								
Year Team	Lg	G	TC	PO	A	E	DP	PB	Pct.	Range
1883 Baltimore	AA	24	72	10	50	12	1	--	.833	---
1884 Baltimore	AA	50	132	27	83	22	0	--	.833	---
1885 2 ML Teams		17	37	6	23	8	0	--	.784	---
1885 Baltimore	AA	13	25	5	14	6	0	--	.760	---
Philadelphia	AA	4	12	1	9	2	0	--	.833	---
3 ML YEARS		91	241	43	156	42	1	--	.826	---

				FIELDING AS OUTFIELDER								
Year Team	Lg	G	TC	PO	A	E	DP	PB	Pct.	Range
1883 Baltimore	AA	5	9	7	0	2	0	--	.778	1.40
1884 Baltimore	AA	1	2	1	1	0	0	--	1.000	2.00
1885 2 ML Teams		3	1	0	0	1	0	--	.000	.00
1885 Baltimore	AA	2	1	0	0	1	0	--	.000	.00
Philadelphia	AA	1	0	0	0	0	0	--	.000	.00
3 ML YEARS		9	12	8	1	3	0	--	.750	1.00

Joe Erautt

Joseph Michael Erautt (Stubby)
Bats: Right **Throws:** Right

Height: 5'9" **Weight:** 175
Born on September 1, 1921 in Vibank, Saskatchewan
Died on October 6, 1976 in Portland, Oregon

					BATTING															BASERUNNING				PERCENTAGES		
Year Team	Lg	G	AB	H	2B	3B	HR	(Hm	Rd)	TB	R	RBI	TBB	IBB	SO	HBP	SH	SF		SB	CS	SB%	GDP	Avg	OBP	SLG
1950 Chicago	AL	16	18	4	0	0	0	(0	0)	4	0	1	1		3	0	0			0	0	.00	0	.222	.263	.222
1951 Chicago	AL	16	25	4	1	0	0	(0	0)	5	3	0	3		2	1	0			0	0	.00	3	.160	.276	.200
2 ML YEARS		32	43	8	1	0	0	(0	0)	9	3	1	4		5	1	0			0	0	.00	3	.186	.271	.209

				FIELDING AS CATCHER								
Year Team	Lg	G	TC	PO	A	E	DP	PB	Pct.	Range
1950 Chicago	AL	5	14	12	2	0	0	0	1.000	---
1951 Chicago	AL	12	44	37	6	1	1	0	.977	---
2 ML YEARS		17	58	49	8	1	1	0	.983	---

Harry Fisher

Harry Devereaux Fisher
Pitches: Right **Bats:** Left

Height: 6'0" **Weight:** 180
Born on January 3, 1926 in Newbury, Ontario
Died on September 20, 1981 in Waterloo, Ontario

				HOW MUCH HE PITCHED				WHAT HE GAVE UP										THE RESULTS					
Year Team	Lg	G	GS	CG	GF	IP	BFP	H	R	ER	HR	SH	SF	HB	TBB	IBB	SO	WP	Bk	W	L	Pct.	ShO	Sv	ERA
1952 Pittsburgh	NL	8	3	0	4	18.1	83	17	14	14	4	4		2	13		5	1	0	1	2	.333	0	0	6.87

				BATTING														BASERUNNING			PERCENTAGES		
Year Team	Lg	G	AB	H	2B	3B	HR	(Hm | Rd)	TB	R	RBI	TBB	IBB	SO	HBP	SH	SF	SB	CS	SB%	GDP	Avg	OBP	SLG
1951 Pittsburgh	NL	3	3	0	0	0	0	(0 | 0)	0	0	0	0		0	0	0		0	0	.00	0	.000	.000	.000
1952 Pittsburgh	NL	15	15	5	1	0	0	(0 | 0)	6	0	1	0		3	0	0		0	0	.00	1	.333	.333	.400
2 ML YEARS		18	18	5	1	0	0	(0 | 0)	6	0	1	0		3	0	0		0	0	.00	1	.278	.278	.333

		FIELDING AS PITCHER									
Year Team	Lg	G	TC	PO	A	E	DP	PB	Pct.	Range
1952 Pittsburgh	NL	8	2	1	1	0	0	--	1.000	---

Gene Ford

Eugene Wyman Ford
Pitches: Right **Bats:** Right

Height: 6'0" **Weight:** 170
Born on April 16, 1881 in Milton, Nova Scotia
Died on August 23, 1973 in Dunedin, Florida

				HOW MUCH HE PITCHED				WHAT HE GAVE UP										THE RESULTS					
Year Team	Lg	G	GS	CG	GF	IP	BFP	H	R	ER	HR	SH	SF	HB	TBB	IBB	SO	WP	Bk	W	L	Pct.	ShO	Sv	ERA
1905 Detroit	AL	7	1	1	6	35	175	51	30	22	0	6		2	14		20	1	0	0	1	.000	0	0	5.66

				BATTING														BASERUNNING			PERCENTAGES		
Year Team	Lg	G	AB	H	2B	3B	HR	(Hm	Rd)	TB	R	RBI	TBB	IBB	SO	HBP	SH	SF	SB	CS	SB%	GDP	Avg	OBP	SLG
1905 Detroit	AL	7	10	0	0	0	0	--	--	0	0	0	2		0	1			0				.000	.167	.000

		FIELDING AS PITCHER									
Year Team	Lg	G	TC	PO	A	E	DP	PB	Pct.	Range
1905 Detroit	AL	7	16	1	12	3	0	--	.813	---

Russ Ford

Russell William Ford
Pitches: Right **Bats:** Right

Height: 5'11" **Weight:** 175
Born on April 25, 1883 in Brandon, Manitoba
Died on January 24, 1960 in Rockingham, North Carolina

				HOW MUCH HE PITCHED				WHAT HE GAVE UP										THE RESULTS					
Year Team	Lg	G	GS	CG	GF	IP	BFP	H	R	ER	HR	SH	SF	HB	TBB	IBB	SO	WP	Bk	W	L	Pct.	ShO	Sv	ERA
1909 New York	AL	1	0	0	1	3	20	4	4	3	0	1		3	4		2	0	0	0	0	.000	0	0	9.00
1910 New York	AL	36	33	29	3	299.2	1141	194	69	55	4	29		8	70	209	5	1	26	6	.813	8	1	1.65
1911 New York	AL	37	33	26	4	281.1	1172	251	119	71	3	35		4	76	158	5	0	22	11	.667	1	0	2.27
1912 New York	AL	36	35	30	1	291.2	1265	317	165	115	10	47		5	79	112	3	2	13	21	.382	0	0	3.55
1913 New York	AL	33	28	15	5	237	967	244	108	70	9	17		4	58	72	4	0	12	18	.400	1	2	2.66
1914 Buffalo	FL	35	26	19	9	247.1	948	190	63	50	11	11		7	41	123	0	0	21	6	.778	5	6	1.82
1915 Buffalo	FL	21	15	7	5	127.1	559	140	74	64	7	17		3	48	34	3	0	5	9	.357	0	0	4.52
7 ML YEARS		199	170	126	28	1487.1	6072	1340	602	428	44	155		34	376	710	20	3	99	71	.582	15	9	2.59

				BATTING														BASERUNNING			PERCENTAGES		
Year Team	Lg	G	AB	H	2B	3B	HR	(Hm	Rd)	TB	R	RBI	TBB	IBB	SO	HBP	SH	SF	SB	CS	SB%	GDP	Avg	OBP	SLG
1909 New York	AL	1	1	0	0	0	0	--	--	0	0	0	0			0	0		0				.000	.000	.000
1910 New York	AL	36	96	20	1	5	0	--	--	31	8	7	9		1	6			1				.208	.283	.323
1911 New York	AL	37	102	20	2	1	0	--	--	24	10	8	3		0	4			2				.196	.219	.235
1912 New York	AL	40	112	32	8	0	1	--	--	43	15	8	6		0	7			2				.286	.322	.384
1913 New York	AL	35	74	12	1	1	0	--	--	15	5	3	7		29	1	2		5				.162	.244	.203
1914 Buffalo	FL	35	78	10	1	0	0	--	--	11	10	7	8		28	0	4		3				.128	.209	.141
1915 Buffalo	FL	22	43	12	4	1	0	--	--	18	7	4	1		9	0	3		1				.279	.295	.419
7 ML YEARS		206	506	106	17	8	1	--	--	142	55	37	34		2	26			14				.209	.262	.281

		FIELDING AS PITCHER									
Year Team	Lg	G	TC	PO	A	E	DP	PB	Pct.	Range
1909 New York	AL	1	4	1	2	1	1	--	.750	---
1910 New York	AL	36	89	7	75	7	4	--	.921	---
1911 New York	AL	37	91	16	70	5	0	--	.945	---
1912 New York	AL	36	106	13	88	5	6	--	.953	---
1913 New York	AL	33	75	11	56	8	1	--	.893	---

Year Team	Lg	G	TC/G	PO	A	E	DP	PB	Pct.	Range
1914 Buffalo	FL	35	82	9	72	1	2	--	.988	---
1915 Buffalo	FL	21	42	2	40	0	1	--	1.000	---
7 ML YEARS		199	489	59	403	27	15	--	.945	---

FIELDING AS SECOND BASEMAN

Year Team	Lg	G	TC	PO	A	E	DP	PB	Pct.	Range
1912 New York	AL	2	12	2	8	2	0	--	.833	5.00

FIELDING AS OUTFIELDER

Year Team	Lg	G	TC	PO	A	E	DP	PB	Pct.	Range
1912 New York	AL	2	4	3	1	0	0	--	1.000	2.00

Dick Fowler

Richard John Fowler
Pitches: Right **Bats:** Right

Height: 6'4" **Weight:** 215
Born on March 30, 1921 in Toronto, Ontario
Died on May 22, 1972 in Oneonta, New York

		HOW MUCH HE PITCHED						WHAT HE GAVE UP									THE RESULTS					
Year Team	Lg	G	GS	CG	GF	IP	BFP	H	R	ER	HR	SH	SF	HB	TBB	IBB	SO	WP	Bk	W	L	Pct.	ShO	Sv	ERA
1941 Philadelphia	AL	4	3	1	1	24	101	26	11	9	4	3		0	8		8	0	0	1	2	.333	0	0	3.38
1942 Philadelphia	AL	31	17	4	13	140	605	159	90	77	13	6		0	45		38	3	0	6	11	.353	0	1	4.95
1945 Philadelphia	AL	7	3	2	3	37.1	167	41	21	20	1	4		0	18		21	2	0	1	2	.333	1	0	4.82
1946 Philadelphia	AL	32	28	14	3	205.2	900	213	101	75	16	13		2	75		89	2	0	9	16	.360	1	0	3.28
1947 Philadelphia	AL	36	31	16	2	227.1	943	210	77	71	12	10		3	85		75	0	0	12	11	.522	3	0	2.81
1948 Philadelphia	AL	29	26	16	2	204.2	879	221	93	86	17	13		4	76		50	0	1	15	8	.652	2	2	3.78
1949 Philadelphia	AL	31	28	15	3	213.2	929	210	108	89	14	12		2	115		43	2	0	15	11	.577	4	1	3.75
1950 Philadelphia	AL	11	9	2	1	66.2	315	75	52	48	7	6		3	56		15	1	0	1	5	.167	0	0	6.48
1951 Philadelphia	AL	22	22	4	0	125	568	141	89	78	11	10		1	72		29	0	0	5	11	.313	0	0	5.62
1952 Philadelphia	AL	18	3	1	8	58.2	273	71	43	42	4	6		4	28		14	2	0	1	2	.333	0	0	6.44
10 ML YEARS		221	170	75	36	1303	5680	1367	685	595	99	83		19	578		382	12	1	66	79	.455	11	4	4.11

		BATTING															BASERUNNING				PERCENTAGES		
Year Team	Lg	G	AB	H	2B	3B	HR	(Hm | Rd)	TB	R	RBI	TBB	IBB	SO	HBP	SH	SF	SB	CS	SB%	GDP	Avg	OBP	SLG
1941 Philadelphia	AL	4	9	0	0	0	0	--	--	0	0	0	0		3	0	0		0	0	.00	0	.000	.000	.000
1942 Philadelphia	AL	32	50	8	0	0	0	--	--	8	1	2	0		10	1	1		0	0	.00	0	.160	.176	.160
1945 Philadelphia	AL	11	18	8	2	1	0	--	--	12	3	2	0		0	0	0		0	0	.00	1	.444	.444	.667
1946 Philadelphia	AL	32	71	13	1	0	0	--	--	14	1	3	0		9	0	2		0	0	.00	1	.183	.183	.197
1947 Philadelphia	AL	36	82	14	1	0	0	--	--	15	3	2	0		17	0	4		0	0	.00	3	.171	.171	.183
1948 Philadelphia	AL	29	82	14	1	0	1	--	--	18	5	8	3		10	0	4		0	0	.00	2	.171	.200	.220
1949 Philadelphia	AL	31	77	18	2	0	0	--	--	20	5	11	7		10	0	2		0	1	.00	3	.234	.298	.260
1950 Philadelphia	AL	11	26	5	0	0	0	(0 | 0)	5	2	2	0		1	0	0		0	0	.00	3	.192	.192	.192
1951 Philadelphia	AL	22	42	8	3	0	0	(0 | 0)	11	2	2	4		6	0	1		0	0	.00	3	.190	.261	.262
1952 Philadelphia	AL	18	15	0	0	0	0	(0 | 0)	0	0	0	1		3	0	0		0	1	.00	1	.000	.063	.000
10 ML YEARS		226	472	88	10	1	1	--	--	103	22	32	15		69	1	14		0	2	.00	15	.186	.213	.218

FIELDING AS PITCHER

Year Team	Lg	G	TC	PO	A	E	DP	PB	Pct.	Range
1941 Philadelphia	AL	4	4	0	4	0	1	--	1.000	---
1942 Philadelphia	AL	31	29	8	18	3	2	--	.897	---
1945 Philadelphia	AL	7	5	1	4	0	0	--	1.000	---
1946 Philadelphia	AL	32	45	13	29	3	2	--	.933	---
1947 Philadelphia	AL	36	45	14	29	2	1	--	.956	---
1948 Philadelphia	AL	29	41	10	30	1	4	--	.976	---
1949 Philadelphia	AL	31	62	15	46	1	5	--	.984	---
1950 Philadelphia	AL	11	18	6	11	1	2	--	.944	---
1951 Philadelphia	AL	22	29	11	16	2	3	--	.931	---
1952 Philadelphia	AL	18	19	5	14	0	0	--	1.000	---
10 ML YEARS		221	297	83	201	13	20	--	.956	---

Emil Frisk

John Emil Frisk
Bats: Left **Throws:** Right

Height: 6'1" **Weight:** 190
Born on October 15, 1874 in Ignace, Ontario
Died on January 27, 1922 in Seattle, Washington

		BATTING															BASERUNNING				PERCENTAGES		
Year Team	Lg	G	AB	H	2B	3B	HR	(Hm | Rd)	TB	R	RBI	TBB	IBB	SO	HBP	SH	SF	SB	CS	SB%	GDP	Avg	OBP	SLG
1899 Cincinnati	NL	9	25	7	1	0	0	--	--	8	5	2	2			1	0		0				.280	.357	.320
1901 Detroit	AL	20	48	15	3	0	1	--	--	21	10	7	3			1	0		0				.313	.365	.438
1905 St. Louis	AL	127	429	112	11	6	3	--	--	144	58	36	42			11	11		7				.261	.342	.336
1907 St. Louis	AL	4	4	1	0	0	0	--	--	1	0	0	1			0	0		0				.250	.400	.250
4 ML YEARS		160	506	135	15	6	4	--	--	174	73	45	48			13	11		7				.267	.346	.344

			HOW MUCH HE PITCHED						WHAT HE GAVE UP										THE RESULTS					
Year Team	Lg	G	GS	CG	GF	IP	BFP	H	R	ER	HR	SH	SF	HB	TBB	IBB	SO	WP	Bk	W	L	Pct.	ShO	Sv	ERA
1899 Cincinnati	NL	9	9	9	0	68.1	311	81	52	30	1	1		6	17		17	4	0	3	6	.333	0	0	3.95
1901 Detroit	AL	11	7	6	3	74.2	349	94	60	36	1	9		2	26		22	1	0	5	4	.556	0	0	4.34
2 ML YEARS		20	16	15	3	143	660	175	112	66	2	10		8	43		39	5	0	8	10	.444	0	0	4.15

		FIELDING AS PITCHER								
Year Team	Lg	G	TC	PO	A	E	DP	PB	Pct.	Range
1899 Cincinnati	NL	9	20	4	15	1	0	--	.950	---
1901 Detroit	AL	11	47	4	36	7	0	--	.851	---
2 ML YEARS		20	67	8	51	8	0	--	.881	---

		FIELDING AS OUTFIELDER								
Year Team	Lg	G	TC	PO	A	E	DP	PB	Pct.	Range
1901 Detroit	AL	2	4	3	0	1	0	--	.750	1.50
1905 St. Louis	AL	115	143	117	15	11	2	--	.923	1.15
2 ML YEARS		117	147	120	15	12	2	--	.918	1.15

Doug Frobel

Douglas Steven Frobel
Bats: Left **Throws:** Right

Height: 6'4" **Weight:** 196
Born on June 6, 1959 in Ottawa, Ontario

		BATTING																BASERUNNING				PERCENTAGES		
Year Team	Lg	G	AB	H	2B	3B	HR	(Hm	Rd)	TB	R	RBI	TBB	IBB	SO	HBP	SH	SF	SB	CS	SB%	GDP	Avg	OBP	SLG
1982 Pittsburgh	NL	16	34	7	2	0	2	(2	0)	15	5	3	1	0	11	0	0	0	1	1	.50	0	.206	.229	.441
1983 Pittsburgh	NL	32	60	17	4	1	3	(3	0)	32	10	11	4	0	17	0	0	0	1	1	.50	2	.283	.328	.533
1984 Pittsburgh	NL	126	276	56	9	3	12	(6	6)	107	33	28	24	2	84	2	3	1	7	5	.58	7	.203	.271	.388
1985 2 ML Teams		65	132	25	6	0	1	(0	1)	34	17	11	21	5	30	0	3	0	4	3	.57	4	.189	.301	.258
1987 Cleveland	AL	29	40	4	0	0	2	(2	0)	10	5	5	5	1	13	0	0	1	0	0	.00	1	.100	.196	.250
1985 Pittsburgh	NL	53	109	22	5	0	0	(0	0)	27	14	7	19	5	24	0	2	0	4	3	.57	2	.202	.320	.248
Montreal	NL	12	23	3	1	0	1	(0	1)	7	3	4	2	0	6	0	1	0	0	0	.00	2	.130	.200	.304
5 ML YEARS		268	542	109	21	4	20	(13	7)	198	70	58	55	8	155	2	6	2	13	10	.57	14	.201	.276	.365

		FIELDING AS OUTFIELDER								
Year Team	Lg	G	TC	PO	A	E	DP	PB	Pct.	Range
1982 Pittsburgh	NL	12	18	18	0	0	0	--	1.000	1.50
1983 Pittsburgh	NL	24	28	27	0	1	0	--	.964	1.13
1984 Pittsburgh	NL	112	206	188	9	9	3	--	.956	1.76
1985 2 ML Teams		42	64	58	2	4	1	--	.938	1.43
1987 Cleveland	AL	12	6	6	0	0	0	--	1.000	.50
1985 Pittsburgh	NL	36	51	46	2	3	1	--	.941	1.33
Montreal	NL	6	13	12	0	1	0	--	.923	2.00
5 ML YEARS		202	322	297	11	14	4	--	.957	1.52

Mike Gardiner

Michael James Gardiner
Attended Indiana St.
Pitches: Right **Bats:** Both

Height: 6'0" **Weight:** 185
Born on October 19, 1965 in Sarnia, Ontario

			HOW MUCH HE PITCHED						WHAT HE GAVE UP										THE RESULTS					
Year Team	Lg	G	GS	CG	GF	IP	BFP	H	R	ER	HR	SH	SF	HB	TBB	IBB	SO	WP	Bk	W	L	Pct.	ShO	Sv	ERA
1987 Bellingham	A	2	1	0	0	10	35	6	0	0	0	0	0	0	1	0	11	0	0	2	0	1.000	0	0	0.00
Wausau	A	13	13	2	0	81	368	91	54	47	9	2	5	3	33	2	80	3	1	3	5	.375	1	0	5.22
1988 Wausau	A	11	6	0	4	31.1	132	31	16	11	1	0	0	1	13	0	24	1	1	2	1	.667	0	1	3.16
1989 Wausau	A	15	1	0	11	30.1	120	21	5	2	0	2	0	1	11	0	48	0	0	4	0	1.000	0	7	0.59
Williamsprt	AA	30	3	1	14	63.1	274	54	25	20	6	1	3	1	32	6	60	4	1	4	6	.400	0	2	2.84
1990 Williamsprt	AA	26	26	5	0	179.2	697	136	47	38	8	4	3	1	29	1	149	4	1	12	8	.600	1	0	1.90
1991 Pawtucket	AAA	8	8	2	0	57.2	220	59	16	15	2	3	2	1	11	0	42	0	0	7	1	.875	1	0	2.34
1992 Pawtucket	AAA	5	5	2	0	32.2	138	32	14	12	3	0	0	0	9	0	37	0	0	1	3	.250	0	0	3.31
1993 Ottawa	AAA	5	5	0	0	25	101	17	8	6	2	1	2	0	9	0	25	1	0	1	1	.500	0	0	2.16
Toledo	AAA	4	0	0	2	5	22	6	3	3	0	0	0	0	2	0	10	0	0	0	1	.000	0	1	5.40
1995 Toledo	AAA	11	0	0	4	16.1	77	9	8	8	2	1	1	0	13	0	10	1	0	0	1	.000	0	0	4.41
1990 Seattle	AL	5	3	0	1	12.2	66	22	17	15	1	0	1	2	5	0	6	0	0	0	2	.000	0	0	10.66
1991 Boston	AL	22	22	0	0	130	562	140	79	70	18	1	3	0	47	2	91	1	0	9	10	.474	0	0	4.85
1992 Boston	AL	28	18	0	3	130.2	566	126	78	69	12	3	5	2	58	2	79	8	0	4	10	.286	0	0	4.75
1993 2 ML Teams		34	2	0	4	49.1	224	52	33	27	3	2	3	1	26	3	25	2	0	2	3	.400	0	0	4.93
1994 Detroit	AL	38	1	0	14	58.2	254	53	35	27	10	2	2	0	23	5	31	1	0	2	2	.500	0	5	4.14
1995 Detroit	AL	9	0	0	1	12.1	66	27	20	20	5	3	2	0	2	1	7	1	0	0	0	.000	0	0	14.59
1993 Montreal	NL	24	2	0	3	38	173	40	28	22	3	1	3	1	19	2	21	0	0	2	3	.400	0	0	5.21
Detroit	AL	10	0	0	1	11.1	51	12	5	5	0	1	0	0	7	1	4	2	0	0	0	.000	0	0	3.97
6 ML YEARS		136	46	0	23	393.2	1738	420	262	228	49	11	16	5	161	13	239	13	0	17	27	.386	0	5	5.21

			BATTING																BASERUNNING				PERCENTAGES		
Year Team	Lg	G	AB	H	2B	3B	HR	(Hm	Rd)	TB	R	RBI	TBB	IBB	SO	HBP	SH	SF	SB	CS	SB%	GDP	Avg	OBP	SLG
1993 Montreal	NL	24	4	0	0	0	0	(0	0)	0	0	0	0	1	0	3	0	0	0	0	0	.00	0	.000	.200	.000

	FIELDING AS PITCHER									
Year Team	Lg	G	TC	PO	A	E	DP	PB	Pct.	Range
1990 Seattle	AL	5	3	1	2	0	0	--	1.000	---
1991 Boston	AL	22	26	12	13	1	2	--	.962	---
1992 Boston	AL	28	29	13	15	1	2	--	.966	---
1993 2 ML Teams		34	8	1	7	0	0	--	1.000	---
1994 Detroit	AL	38	8	6	2	0	0	--	1.000	---
1995 Detroit	AL	9	3	2	1	0	0	--	1.000	---
1993 Montreal	NL	24	6	1	5	0	0	--	1.000	---
Detroit	AL	10	2	0	2	0	0	--	1.000	---
6 ML YEARS		136	77	35	40	2	4	--	.974	

Alex Gardner

Alexander Gardner
Bats: Unknown **Throws:** Unknown

Height: Unknown **Weight:** Unknown
Born on April 28, 1861 in Toronto, Ontario
Died on June 18, 1926 in Danvers, Massachusetts

			BATTING																BASERUNNING				PERCENTAGES		
Year Team	Lg	G	AB	H	2B	3B	HR	(Hm	Rd)	TB	R	RBI	TBB	IBB	SO	HBP	SH	SF	SB	CS	SB%	GDP	Avg	OBP	SLG
1884 Washington	AA	1	3	0	0	0	0	--	--	0	0	0	0			0								.000	.000	.000

	FIELDING AS CATCHER									
Year Team	Lg	G	TC	PO	A	E	DP	PB	Pct.	Range
1884 Washington	AA	1	15	6	3	6	0	6	.600	---

George Gibson

George C. Gibson (Moon)
Bats: Right **Throws:** Right

Height: 5'11" **Weight:** 190
Born on July 22, 1880 in London, Ontario
Died on January 25, 1967 in London, Ontario

			BATTING																BASERUNNING				PERCENTAGES		
Year Team	Lg	G	AB	H	2B	3B	HR	(Hm	Rd)	TB	R	RBI	TBB	IBB	SO	HBP	SH	SF	SB	CS	SB%	GDP	Avg	OBP	SLG
1905 Pittsburgh	NL	46	135	24	2	2	2	--	--	36	14	14	15			2	4		2				.178	.270	.267
1906 Pittsburgh	NL	81	259	46	6	1	0	--	--	54	8	20	16			0	7		1				.178	.225	.208
1907 Pittsburgh	NL	113	382	84	8	7	3	--	--	115	28	35	18			3	10		2				.220	.261	.301
1908 Pittsburgh	NL	143	486	111	19	4	2	--	--	144	37	45	19			2	10		4				.228	.260	.296
1909 Pittsburgh	NL	150	510	135	25	9	2	--	--	184	42	52	44			2	15		9				.265	.326	.361
1910 Pittsburgh	NL	143	482	125	22	6	3	--	--	168	53	44	47	31		6	9		7				.259	.333	.349
1911 Pittsburgh	NL	100	311	65	12	2	0	--	--	81	32	19	29	16		2	5		3				.209	.281	.260
1912 Pittsburgh	NL	95	300	72	14	3	2	--	--	98	23	35	20	16		1	10		0				.240	.290	.327
1913 Pittsburgh	NL	48	118	33	4	2	0	--	--	41	6	12	10	8		1	7		2				.280	.341	.347
1914 Pittsburgh	NL	102	274	78	9	5	0	--	--	97	19	30	27	27		5	7		4	2	.67		.285	.359	.354
1915 Pittsburgh	NL	120	351	88	15	6	1	--	--	118	28	30	31	25		1	13		5	2	.71		.251	.313	.336
1916 Pittsburgh	NL	33	84	17	2	2	0	--	--	23	4	4	3	7		1	3		0				.202	.239	.274
1917 New York	NL	35	82	14	3	0	0	--	--	17	1	5	7	2		0	2		1				.171	.236	.207
1918 New York	NL	4	2	1	1	0	0	--	--	2	0	0	0	0		0	0		0				.500	.500	1.000
14 ML YEARS		1213	3776	893	142	49	15	--	--	1178	295	345	286			26	102		40				.236	.295	.312

World Series Batting

			BATTING																BASERUNNING				PERCENTAGES		
Year Team	Lg	G	AB	H	2B	3B	HR	(Hm	Rd)	TB	R	RBI	TBB	IBB	SO	HBP	SH	SF	SB	CS	SB%	GDP	Avg	OBP	SLG
1909 Pittsburgh	NL	7	25	6	2	0	0	(0	0)	8	2	2	1	0	1	0	4		2	1	.67	1	.240	.269	.320

	FIELDING AS CATCHER									
Year Team	Lg	G	TC	PO	A	E	DP	PB	Pct.	Range
1905 Pittsburgh	NL	44	263	200	54	9	4	8	.966	---
1906 Pittsburgh	NL	81	422	336	73	13	10	13	.969	---
1907 Pittsburgh	NL	109	642	499	125	18	12	14	.972	---
1908 Pittsburgh	NL	140	764	607	136	21	10	4	.973	---
1909 Pittsburgh	NL	150	862	655	192	15	9	10	.983	---
1910 Pittsburgh	NL	143	850	633	203	14	8	8	.984	---
1911 Pittsburgh	NL	98	581	452	117	12	16	10	.979	---
1912 Pittsburgh	NL	94	591	484	101	6	11	12	.990	---
1913 Pittsburgh	NL	48	219	182	34	3	4	0	.986	---

1914	Pittsburgh	NL	101	497	358	126	13	8	10	.974	---
1915	Pittsburgh	NL	118	710	551	134	**25**	14	8	.965	---
1916	Pittsburgh	NL	29	181	140	39	2	2	3	.989	---
1917	New York	NL	35	145	116	27	2	4	1	.986	---
1918	New York	NL	4	2	1	1	0	0	0	1.000	---
	14 ML YEARS		1194	6729	5214	1362	153	112	101	.977	---

FIELDING AS FIRST BASEMAN

Year	Team	Lg	G	TC	PO	A	E	DP	PB	Pct.	Range
1907	Pittsburgh	NL	1	2	2	0	0	0	--	1.000	---

World Series Fielding

FIELDING AS CATCHER

Year	Team	Lg	G	TC	PO	A	E	DP	PB	Pct.	Range
1909	Pittsburgh	NL	7	37	28	9	0	0	0	1.000	---

Jim Gillespie

James Wheatfield Gillespie
Bats: Left   **Throws:** Right

Height: Unknown   **Weight:** Unknown
Born in September, 1858 in Canada
Died on September 5, 1921 in North Tonawanda, New York

BATTING / BASERUNNING / PERCENTAGES

Year	Team	Lg	G	AB	H	2B	3B	HR	(Hm	Rd)	TB	R	RBI	TBB	IBB	SO	HBP	SH	SF	SB	CS	SB%	GDP	Avg	OBP	SLG
1890	Buffalo	PL	1	3	0	0	0	0	--	--	0	0	0	0	0	2	0			0				.000	.000	.000

FIELDING AS OUTFIELDER

Year	Team	Lg	G	TC	PO	A	E	DP	PB	Pct.	Range
1890	Buffalo	PL	1	4	0	1	3	0	--	.250	1.00

Roland Gladu

Roland Edouard Gladu
Bats: Left   **Throws:** Right

Height: 5'8"   **Weight:** 185
Born on May 10, 1911 in Montreal, Quebec
Died on July 26, 1994 in Montreal, Quebec

BATTING / BASERUNNING / PERCENTAGES

Year	Team	Lg	G	AB	H	2B	3B	HR	(Hm	Rd)	TB	R	RBI	TBB	IBB	SO	HBP	SH	SF	SB	CS	SB%	GDP	Avg	OBP	SLG
1944	Boston	NL	21	66	16	2	1	1	--	--	23	5	7	3		8	0	1		0			2	.242	.275	.348

FIELDING AS THIRD BASEMAN

Year	Team	Lg	G	TC	PO	A	E	DP	PB	Pct.	Range
1944	Boston	NL	15	46	20	21	5	6	--	.891	2.73

FIELDING AS OUTFIELDER

Year	Team	Lg	G	TC	PO	A	E	DP	PB	Pct.	Range
1944	Boston	NL	3	1	1	0	0	0	--	1.000	.33

Glen Gorbous

Glen Edward Gorbous
Bats: Left   **Throws:** Right

Height: 6'2"   **Weight:** 175
Born on July 8, 1930 in Drumheller, Alberta
Died on June 12, 1990 in Calgary, Alberta

BATTING / BASERUNNING / PERCENTAGES

Year	Team	Lg	G	AB	H	2B	3B	HR	(Hm	Rd)	TB	R	RBI	TBB	IBB	SO	HBP	SH	SF	SB	CS	SB%	GDP	Avg	OBP	SLG
1955	2 ML Teams		99	242	59	12	1	4	(2	2)	85	27	27	24	3	18	0	2	1	0	3	.00	6	.244	.311	.351
1956	Philadelphia	NL	15	33	6	0	0	0	(0	0)	6	1	1	0	0	1	0	0	0	0	0	.00	0	.182	.182	.182
1957	Philadelphia	NL	3	2	1	1	0	0	(0	0)	2	1	1	0	0	0	0	0	0	0	0	.00	0	.500	.667	1.000
1955	Cincinnati	NL	8	18	6	3	0	0	(0	0)	9	2	4	3	0	1	0	0	0	0	0	.00	0	.333	.429	.500
	Philadelphia	NL	91	224	53	9	1	4	(2	2)	76	25	23	21	3	17	0	2	1	0	3	.00	6	.237	.301	.339
	3 ML YEARS		117	277	66	13	1	4	(2	2)	93	29	29	25	3	19	0	2	1	0	3	.00	6	.238	.300	.336

FIELDING AS OUTFIELDER

Year	Team	Lg	G	TC	PO	A	E	DP	PB	Pct.	Range
1955	2 ML Teams		62	139	125	10	4	2	--	.971	2.18
1956	Philadelphia	NL	8	8	8	0	0	0	--	1.000	1.00
1955	Cincinnati	NL	5	14	12	0	2	0	--	.857	2.40
	Philadelphia	NL	57	125	113	10	2	2	--	.984	2.16
	2 ML YEARS		70	147	133	10	4	2	--	.973	2.04

Note: In 1957, Gorbous established record by throwing a ball 445 feet, 10 inches on the fly.

Jack Graney

John Gladstone Graney
Bats: Left   **Throws:** Left

Height: 5'9"   **Weight:** 180
Born on June 10, 1886 in St. Thomas, Ontario
Died on April 20, 1978 in Louisiana, Missouri

												BATTING									BASERUNNING				PERCENTAGES		
Year Team	Lg	G	AB	H	2B	3B	HR	(Hm	Rd)	TB	R	RBI	TBB	IBB	SO	HBP	SH	SF	SB	CS	SB%	GDP	Avg	OBP	SLG
1908 Cleveland	AL	2	0	0	0	0	0	--	--	0	0	0	0				0	0	0					.000	.000	.000
1910 Cleveland	AL	116	454	107	13	9	1	--	--	141	62	31	37				0	8		18				.236	.293	.311
1911 Cleveland	AL	146	527	142	25	5	1	--	--	180	84	45	66				11	16		21				.269	.363	.342
1912 Cleveland	AL	78	264	64	13	2	0	--	--	81	44	20	50				2	5		9				.242	.367	.307
1913 Cleveland	AL	148	517	138	18	12	3	--	--	189	56	68	48		55		5	13		27				.267	.335	.366
1914 Cleveland	AL	130	460	122	17	10	1	--	--	162	63	39	67		46		3	6		20	18	.53		.265	.362	.352
1915 Cleveland	AL	116	404	105	20	7	1	--	--	142	42	56	59		29		2	11		12	15	.44		.260	.357	.351
1916 Cleveland	AL	155	589	142	41	14	5	--	--	226	106	54	102		72		2	9		10				.241	.355	.384
1917 Cleveland	AL	146	535	122	29	7	3	--	--	174	87	35	94		49		4	15		16				.228	.348	.325
1918 Cleveland	AL	70	177	42	7	4	0	--	--	57	27	9	28		13		3	3		3				.237	.351	.322
1919 Cleveland	AL	128	461	108	22	8	1	--	--	149	79	30	105		39		3	16		7				.234	.380	.323
1920 Cleveland	AL	62	152	45	11	1	0	--	--	58	31	13	27		21		3	9		4	2	.67		.296	.412	.382
1921 Cleveland	AL	68	107	32	3	0	2	--	--	41	19	18	20		9		1	5		1	1	.50		.299	.414	.383
1922 Cleveland	AL	37	58	9	0	0	0	--	--	9	6	2	9		12		1	3		0	0	.00		.155	.279	.155
14 ML YEARS		1402	4705	1178	219	79	18	--	--	1609	706	420	712				40	119		148				.250	.354	.342

World Series Batting

												BATTING									BASERUNNING				PERCENTAGES		
Year Team	Lg	G	AB	H	2B	3B	HR	(Hm	Rd)	TB	R	RBI	TBB	IBB	SO	HBP	SH	SF	SB	CS	SB%	GDP	Avg	OBP	SLG
1920 Cleveland	AL	3	3	0	0	0	0	(0	0)	0	0	0	0	0	2	0	0	0	0	0	.00	0	.000	.000	.000

				HOW MUCH HE PITCHED				WHAT HE GAVE UP										THE RESULTS					
Year Team	Lg	G	GS	CG	GF	IP	BFP	H	R	ER	HR	SH	SF	HB	TBB	IBB	SO	WP	Bk	W	L	Pct.	ShO	Sv	ERA
1908 Cleveland	AL	2	0	0	1	3.1	16	6	2	2	0	0		0	1		0	0	0	0	0	.000	0	0	5.40

FIELDING AS PITCHER

Year Team	Lg	G	TC	PO	A	E	DP	PB	Pct.	Range
1908 Cleveland	AL	2	0	0	0	0	0	--	.000	---

FIELDING AS OUTFIELDER

Year Team	Lg	G	TC	PO	A	E	DP	PB	Pct.	Range
1910 Cleveland	AL	114	235	209	14	12	5	--	.949	1.96
1911 Cleveland	AL	142	302	258	22	22	5	--	.927	1.97
1912 Cleveland	AL	75	166	148	11	7	5	--	.958	2.12
1913 Cleveland	AL	148	300	275	16	9	5	--	.970	1.97
1914 Cleveland	AL	127	309	274	15	20	0	--	.935	2.28
1915 Cleveland	AL	115	251	227	17	7	1	--	.972	2.12
1916 Cleveland	AL	154	345	309	22	14	5	--	.959	2.15
1917 Cleveland	AL	145	315	288	14	13	6	--	.959	2.08
1918 Cleveland	AL	45	81	77	2	2	0	--	.975	1.76
1919 Cleveland	AL	125	306	281	13	12	2	--	.961	2.35
1920 Cleveland	AL	47	85	76	4	5	0	--	.941	1.70
1921 Cleveland	AL	32	45	42	0	3	0	--	.933	1.31
1922 Cleveland	AL	13	29	24	1	4	0	--	.862	1.92
13 ML YEARS		1282	2769	2488	151	130	34	--	.953	2.06

World Series Fielding

FIELDING AS OUTFIELDER

Year Team	Lg	G	TC	PO	A	E	DP	PB	Pct.	Range
1920 Cleveland	AL	2	0	0	0	0	0	--	.000	.00

Best known as first player-turned-broadcaster.

Vern Handrahan

James Vernon Handrahan
Pitches: Right   **Bats:** Left

Height: 6'2"   **Weight:** 185
Born on November 27, 1938 in Charlottetown, Prince Edward Island

				HOW MUCH HE PITCHED				WHAT HE GAVE UP										THE RESULTS					
Year Team	Lg	G	GS	CG	GF	IP	BFP	H	R	ER	HR	SH	SF	HB	TBB	IBB	SO	WP	Bk	W	L	Pct.	ShO	Sv	ERA
1964 Kansas City	AL	18	1	0	7	35.2	161	33	24	24	9	2	1	2	25	0	18	3	0	0	1	.000	0	0	6.06
1966 Kansas City	AL	16	1	0	5	25.1	106	20	12	12	5	1	1	1	15	1	18	3	0	0	1	.000	0	1	4.26
2 ML YEARS		34	2	0	12	61	267	53	36	36	14	3	2	3	40	1	36	6	0	0	2	.000	0	1	5.31

			BATTING																BASERUNNING			PERCENTAGES		
Year Team	Lg	G	AB	H	2B	3B	HR	(Hm	Rd)	TB	R	RBI	TBB	IBB	SO	HBP	SH	SF	SB	CS	SB%	GDP	Avg	OBP	SLG
1964 Kansas City	AL	18	9	2	0	0	0	(0	0)	2	1	0	0	0	3	0	0	0	0	0	.00	0	.222	.222	.222
1966 Kansas City	AL	16	3	0	0	0	0	(0	0)	0	0	0	0	0	2	0	0	0	0	0	.00	0	.000	.000	.000
2 ML YEARS		34	12	2	0	0	0	(0	0)	2	1	0	0	0	5	0	0	0	0	0	.00	0	.167	.167	.167

		FIELDING AS PITCHER								
Year Team	Lg	G	TC	PO	A	E	DP	PB	Pct.	Range
1964 Kansas City	AL	18	7	1	6	0	1	--	1.000	---
1966 Kansas City	AL	16	6	2	4	0	1	--	1.000	---
2 ML YEARS		34	13	3	10	0	2	--	1.000	---

Pat Hannifin

Patrick James Hannifin
Bats: Unknown **Throws:** Left

Height: Unknown **Weight:** Unknown
Born in 1868 in Nova Scotia
Died on November 5, 1908 in Springfield, Massachusetts

			BATTING																BASERUNNING			PERCENTAGES		
Year Team	Lg	G	AB	H	2B	3B	HR	(Hm	Rd)	TB	R	RBI	TBB	IBB	SO	HBP	SH	SF	SB	CS	SB%	GDP	Avg	OBP	SLG
1897 Brooklyn	NL	10	20	5	0	0	0	--	--	5	4	2	1		3	2			4				.250	.375	.250

		FIELDING AS SECOND BASEMAN								
Year Team	Lg	G	TC	PO	A	E	DP	PB	Pct.	Range
1897 Brooklyn	NL	2	7	5	1	1	0	--	.857	3.00

		FIELDING AS OUTFIELDER								
Year Team	Lg	G	TC	PO	A	E	DP	PB	Pct.	Range
1897 Brooklyn	NL	3	15	11	2	2	1	--	.867	4.33

Alex Hardy

David Alexander Hardy (Dooney)
Pitches: Left **Bats:** Left

Height: Unknown **Weight:** Unknown
Born on September 29, 1877 in Toronto, Ontario
Died on April 22, 1940 in Toronto, Ontario

		HOW MUCH HE PITCHED						WHAT HE GAVE UP											THE RESULTS					
Year Team	Lg	G	GS	CG	GF	IP	BFP	H	R	ER	HR	SH	SF	HB	TBB	IBB	SO	WP	Bk	W	L	Pct.	ShO	Sv	ERA
1902 Chicago	NL	4	4	4	0	35	137	29	19	14	0	0		0	12		12	1	0	2	2	.500	1	0	3.60
1903 Chicago	NL	3	3	1	0	12.2	65	21	10	9	0	1		1	7		4	0	0	1	1	.500	0	0	6.39
2 ML YEARS		7	7	5	0	47.2	202	50	29	23	0	1		1	19		16	1	0	3	3	.500	1	0	4.34

			BATTING																BASERUNNING			PERCENTAGES		
Year Team	Lg	G	AB	H	2B	3B	HR	(Hm	Rd)	TB	R	RBI	TBB	IBB	SO	HBP	SH	SF	SB	CS	SB%	GDP	Avg	OBP	SLG
1902 Chicago	NL	4	14	3	1	0	0	--	--	4	3	4	1		0	0			0				.214	.267	.286
1903 Chicago	NL	3	6	1	0	0	0	--	--	1	0	1	1		1	0			0				.167	.375	.167
2 ML YEARS		7	20	4	1	0	0	--	--	5	3	5	2		1	0			0				.200	.304	.250

		FIELDING AS PITCHER								
Year Team	Lg	G	TC	PO	A	E	DP	PB	Pct.	Range
1902 Chicago	NL	4	8	1	6	1	0	--	.875	---
1903 Chicago	NL	3	6	0	6	0	0	--	1.000	---
2 ML YEARS		7	14	1	12	1	0	--	.929	---

Tim Harkness

Thomas William Harkness
Bats: Left **Throws:** Left

Height: 6'2" **Weight:** 182
Born on December 23, 1937 in Lachine, Quebec

			BATTING																BASERUNNING			PERCENTAGES		
Year Team	Lg	G	AB	H	2B	3B	HR	(Hm	Rd)	TB	R	RBI	TBB	IBB	SO	HBP	SH	SF	SB	CS	SB%	GDP	Avg	OBP	SLG
1961 Los Angeles	NL	5	8	4	2	0	0	(0	0)	6	4	0	3	0	1	0	0	0	1	0	1.00	0	.500	.636	.750
1962 Los Angeles	NL	92	62	16	2	0	2	(0	2)	24	9	7	10	1	20	1	0	0	1	0	1.00	0	.258	.370	.387
1963 New York	NL	123	375	79	12	3	10	(6	4)	127	35	41	36	5	79	7	0	2	4	3	.57	5	.211	.290	.339
1964 New York	NL	39	117	33	2	1	2	(1	1)	43	11	13	9	1	18	1	0	1	1	1	.50	5	.282	.336	.368
4 ML YEARS		259	562	132	18	4	14	(7	7)	200	59	61	58	7	118	9	0	3	7	4	.64	10	.235	.315	.356

		FIELDING AS FIRST BASEMAN								
Year Team	Lg	G	TC	PO	A	E	DP	PB	Pct.	Range
1961 Los Angeles	NL	2	12	11	1	0	2	--	1.000	---
1962 Los Angeles	NL	59	124	116	8	0	14	--	1.000	---
1963 New York	NL	106	1024	898	112	14	73	--	.986	---
1964 New York	NL	32	281	251	28	2	32	--	.993	---
4 ML YEARS		199	1441	1276	149	16	121	--	.989	---

Bill Harris

William Thomas Harris
Pitches: Right **Bats:** Left

Height: 5'8" **Weight:** 187
Born on December 3, 1931 in Duguayville, New Brunswick

HOW MUCH HE PITCHED / WHAT HE GAVE UP / THE RESULTS

Year Team	Lg	G	GS	CG	GF	IP	BFP	H	R	ER	HR	SH	SF	HB	TBB	IBB	SO	WP	Bk	W	L	Pct.	ShO	Sv	ERA
1957 Brooklyn	NL	1	1	0	0	7	30	9	3	3	1	1	0	0	1	0	3	0	0	0	1	.000	0	0	3.86
1959 Los Angeles	NL	1	0	0	0	1.2	8	0	0	0	0	0	0	0	3	1	0	0	0	0	0	.000	0	0	0.00
2 ML YEARS		2	1	0	0	8.2	38	9	3	3	1	1	0	0	4	1	3	0	0	0	1	.000	0	0	3.12

BATTING / BASERUNNING / PERCENTAGES

Year Team	Lg	G	AB	H	2B	3B	HR	(Hm	Rd)	TB	R	RBI	TBB	IBB	SO	HBP	SH	SF	SB	CS	SB%	GDP	Avg	OBP	SLG
1957 Brooklyn	NL	1	2	1	0	0	0	(0	0)	1	0	0	0	0	1	0	0	0	0	0	.00	0	.500	.500	.500
1959 Los Angeles	NL	1	0	0	0	0	0	(0	0)	0	0	0	0	0	0	0	0	0	0	0	.00	0	.000	.000	.000
2 ML YEARS		2	2	1	0	0	0	(0	0)	1	0	0	0	0	1	0	0	0	0	0	.00	0	.500	.500	.500

FIELDING AS PITCHER

Year Team	Lg	G	TC	PO	A	E	DP	PB	Pct.	Range
1957 Brooklyn	NL	1	2	0	2	0	0	--	1.000	---
1959 Los Angeles	NL	1	1	0	1	0	0	--	1.000	---
2 ML YEARS		2	3	0	3	0	0	--	1.000	---

Tom Harrison

Thomas James Harrison
Pitches: Right **Bats:** Right

Height: 6'3" **Weight:** 200
Born on January 18, 1945 in Trail, British Columbia

HOW MUCH HE PITCHED / WHAT HE GAVE UP / THE RESULTS

Year Team	Lg	G	GS	CG	GF	IP	BFP	H	R	ER	HR	SH	SF	HB	TBB	IBB	SO	WP	Bk	W	L	Pct.	ShO	Sv	ERA
1965 Kansas City	AL	1	0	0	0	0.2	4	2	1	1	0	0	0	0	1	0	0	0	0	0	0	.000	0	0	13.50

BATTING / BASERUNNING / PERCENTAGES

Year Team	Lg	G	AB	H	2B	3B	HR	(Hm	Rd)	TB	R	RBI	TBB	IBB	SO	HBP	SH	SF	SB	CS	SB%	GDP	Avg	OBP	SLG
1965 Kansas City	AL	2	0	0	0	0	0	(0	0)	0	0	0	0	0	0	0	0	0	0	0	.00	0	.000	.000	.000

FIELDING AS PITCHER

Year Team	Lg	G	TC	PO	A	E	DP	PB	Pct.	Range
1965 Kansas City	AL	1	0	0	0	0	0	--	.000	---

Jeff Heath

John Geoffrey Heath
Bats: Left **Throws:** Right

Height: 5'11" **Weight:** 200
Born on April 1, 1915 in Fort William, Ontario
Died on December 9, 1975 in Seattle, Washington

BATTING / BASERUNNING / PERCENTAGES

Year Team	Lg	G	AB	H	2B	3B	HR	(Hm	Rd)	TB	R	RBI	TBB	IBB	SO	HBP	SH	SF	SB	CS	SB%	GDP	Avg	OBP	SLG
1936 Cleveland	AL	12	41	14	3	3	1	--	--	26	6	8	3		4	0	0		1	0	1.00		.341	.386	.634
1937 Cleveland	AL	20	61	14	1	4	0	--	--	23	8	8	0		9	0	0		0	1	.00		.230	.230	.377
1938 Cleveland	AL	126	502	172	31	18	21	--	--	302	104	112	33		55	0	3		3	1	.75		.343	.383	.602
1939 Cleveland	AL	121	431	126	31	7	14	--	--	213	64	69	41		64	0	0		8	4	.67	7	.292	.354	.494
1940 Cleveland	AL	100	356	78	16	3	14	--	--	142	55	50	40		62	0	0		5	3	.63	2	.219	.298	.399
1941 Cleveland	AL	151	585	199	32	20	24	--	--	343	89	123	50		69	4	4		18	12	.60	5	.340	.396	.586
1942 Cleveland	AL	147	568	158	37	13	10	--	--	251	82	76	62		66	1	3		9	9	.50	10	.278	.350	.442
1943 Cleveland	AL	118	424	116	22	6	18	--	--	204	58	79	63		58	1	0		5	8	.38	4	.274	.369	.481
1944 Cleveland	AL	60	151	50	5	2	5	--	--	74	20	33	18		12	0	1		0	1	.00	2	.331	.402	.490
1945 Cleveland	AL	102	370	113	16	7	15	--	--	188	60	61	56		39	1	2		3	1	.75	6	.305	.398	.508
1946 2 ML Teams		134	482	134	32	7	16	--	--	228	69	84	73		73	1	2		0	6	.00	3	.278	.374	.473
1947 St. Louis	AL	141	491	123	20	7	27	--	--	238	81	85	88		87	1	2		2	1	.67	14	.251	.366	.485
1948 Boston	NL	115	364	116	26	5	20	--	--	212	64	76	51		46	1	3		2			4	.319	.404	.582
1949 Boston	NL	36	111	34	7	0	9	--	--	68	17	23	15		26	0	2		0			2	.306	.389	.613
1946 Washington	AL	48	166	47	12	3	4	--	--	77	23	27	36		36	0	1		0	4	.00	1	.283	.411	.464
St. Louis	AL	86	316	87	20	4	12	--	--	151	46	57	37		37	1	1		0	2	.00	2	.275	.353	.478
14 ML YEARS		1383	4937	1447	279	102	194	--	--	2512	777	887	593		670	10	20		56				.293	.370	.509

All-Star Game Batting

Year Team	Lg	G	AB	H	2B	3B	HR	(Hm	Rd)	TB	R	RBI	TBB	IBB	SO	HBP	SH	SF	SB	CS	SB%	GDP	Avg	OBP	SLG
1941 Cleveland	AL	1	2	0	0	0	0	(0	0)	0	0	0	1	0	1	0	0	0	0	0	.00	0	.000	.333	.000
1943 Cleveland	AL	1	1	0	0	0	0	(0	0)	0	0	0	0	0	0	0	0	0	0	0	.00	0	.000	.000	.000
2 ML YEARS		2	3	0	0	0	0	(0	0)	0	0	0	1	0	1	0	0	0	0	0	.00	0	.000	.250	.000

FIELDING AS OUTFIELDER										
Year Team	Lg	G	TC	PO	A	E	DP	PB	Pct.	Range
1936 Cleveland	AL	12	11	10	1	0	0	--	1.000	.92
1937 Cleveland	AL	14	27	27	0	0	0	--	1.000	1.93
1938 Cleveland	AL	122	266	254	5	7	2	--	.974	2.12
1939 Cleveland	AL	108	280	263	7	10	2	--	.964	2.50
1940 Cleveland	AL	90	209	197	6	6	1	--	.971	2.26
1941 Cleveland	AL	151	294	259	20	15	1	--	.949	1.85
1942 Cleveland	AL	146	345	326	12	7	3	--	.980	2.32
1943 Cleveland	AL	111	277	264	4	9	1	--	.968	2.41
1944 Cleveland	AL	37	84	76	4	4	2	--	.952	2.16
1945 Cleveland	AL	101	223	214	3	6	1	--	.973	2.15
1946 2 ML Teams		130	256	239	8	9	1	--	.965	1.90
1947 St. Louis	AL	140	308	297	7	4	4	--	.987	2.17
1948 Boston	NL	106	231	223	6	2	2	--	**.991**	2.16
1949 Boston	NL	31	59	56	2	1	1	--	.983	1.87
1946 Washington	AL	47	98	92	3	3	0	--	.969	2.02
St. Louis	AL	83	158	147	5	6	1	--	.962	1.83
14 ML YEARS		1299	2870	2705	85	80	21	--	.972	2.15

All-Star Game Fielding

FIELDING AS OUTFIELDER										
Year Team	Lg	G	TC	PO	A	E	DP	PB	Pct.	Range
1941 Cleveland	AL	1	2	1	0	1	0	--	.500	1.00

Career Interruption: 1948—Broke leg sliding in last week of season.

John Hiller

John Frederick Hiller
Pitches: Left **Bats:** Right

Height: 6'1" **Weight:** 185
Born on April 8, 1943 in Toronto, Ontario

HOW MUCH HE PITCHED							WHAT HE GAVE UP											THE RESULTS					
Year Team	Lg	G	GS	CG	GF	IP	BFP	H	R	ER	HR	SH	SF	HB	TBB	IBB	SO	WP	Bk	W	L	Pct.	ShO	Sv	ERA
1965 Detroit	AL	5	0	0	2	6	23	5	0	0	0	0	0	0	1	0	4	0	0	0	0	.000	0	1	0.00
1966 Detroit	AL	1	0	0	1	2	10	2	2	2	0	0	1	0	2	0	1	0	0	0	0	.000	0	0	9.00
1967 Detroit	AL	23	6	2	11	65	256	57	20	19	4	1	1	0	9	0	49	0	0	4	3	.571	2	3	2.63
1968 Detroit	AL	39	12	4	13	128	518	92	37	34	9	6	1	0	51	4	78	2	0	9	6	.600	1	2	2.39
1969 Detroit	AL	40	8	1	13	99.1	431	97	50	44	13	6	3	1	44	2	74	3	0	4	4	.500	1	4	3.99
1970 Detroit	AL	47	5	1	18	104	432	82	39	35	12	2	7	2	46	4	89	3	0	6	6	.500	1	3	3.03
1972 Detroit	AL	24	3	1	8	44.1	186	39	13	10	4	2	0	3	13	2	26	2	0	1	2	.333	0	3	2.03
1973 Detroit	AL	65	0	0	60	125.1	498	89	21	20	7	6	4	0	39	7	124	1	0	10	5	.667	0	38	1.44
1974 Detroit	AL	59	0	0	52	150	633	127	51	44	10	11	7	3	62	**19**	134	7	0	17	14	.548	0	13	2.64
1975 Detroit	AL	36	0	0	34	70.2	295	52	20	17	6	2	3	0	36	4	87	1	0	2	3	.400	0	14	2.17
1976 Detroit	AL	56	1	1	46	121	510	93	37	32	7	9	8	2	67	9	117	6	0	12	8	.600	1	13	2.38
1977 Detroit	AL	45	8	3	27	124	539	120	59	49	15	7	5	1	61	8	115	6	0	8	14	.364	0	7	3.56
1978 Detroit	AL	51	0	0	46	92.1	363	64	27	24	6	5	6	0	35	4	74	3	0	9	4	.692	0	15	2.34
1979 Detroit	AL	43	0	0	30	79.1	372	83	47	46	14	11	3	0	55	7	46	4	0	4	7	.364	0	9	5.22
1980 Detroit	AL	11	0	0	2	30.2	140	55	15	15	3	1	2	0	14	1	18	1	1	1	0	1.000	0	0	4.40
15 ML YEARS		545	43	13	363	1242	5206	1040	438	391	110	69	51	12	535	71	1036	39	1	87	76	.534	6	125	2.83

League Championship Pitching

HOW MUCH HE PITCHED							WHAT HE GAVE UP											THE RESULTS					
Year Team	Lg	G	GS	CG	GF	IP	BFP	H	R	ER	HR	SH	SF	HB	TBB	IBB	SO	WP	Bk	W	L	Pct.	ShO	Sv	ERA
1972 Detroit	AL	3	0	0	3	3.1	12	1	0	0	0	0	0	0	1	0	1	0	0	1	0	1.000	0	0	0.00

World Series Pitching

HOW MUCH HE PITCHED							WHAT HE GAVE UP											THE RESULTS					
Year Team	Lg	G	GS	CG	GF	IP	BFP	H	R	ER	HR	SH	SF	HB	TBB	IBB	SO	WP	Bk	W	L	Pct.	ShO	Sv	ERA
1968 Detroit	AL	2	0	0	1	2	16	6	4	3	0	0	0	0	3	0	1	0	0	0	0	.000	0	0	13.50

BATTING																		BASERUNNING				PERCENTAGES		
Year Team	Lg	G	AB	H	2B	3B	HR	(Hm	Rd)	TB	R	RBI	TBB	IBB	SO	HBP	SH	SF	SB	CS	SB%	GDP	Avg	OBP	SLG
1965 Detroit	AL	5	0	0	0	0	0	(0	0)	0	0	0	0	0	0	0	0	0	0	0	.00	0	.000	.000	.000
1966 Detroit	AL	1	0	0	0	0	0	(0	0)	0	0	0	0	0	0	0	0	0	0	0	.00	0	.000	.000	.000
1967 Detroit	AL	23	15	2	0	0	0	(0	0)	2	0	2	1	0	5	0	1	0	0	0	.00	0	.133	.188	.133
1968 Detroit	AL	39	37	3	0	0	0	(0	0)	3	1	2	0	0	14	0	0	1	0	0	.00	0	.081	.081	.081
1969 Detroit	AL	41	21	6	1	0	0	(0	0)	7	1	0	1	0	3	0	2	0	0	0	.00	0	.286	.318	.333
1970 Detroit	AL	47	23	0	0	0	0	(0	0)	0	0	0	1	0	9	0	1	0	0	0	.00	0	.000	.042	.000
1972 Detroit	AL	24	4	0	0	0	0	(0	0)	0	0	0	0	0	3	0	0	0	0	0	.00	0	.000	.000	.000

Year Team	Lg	G	AB	H	2B	3B	HR	(Hm	Rd)	TB	R	RBI	TBB	IBB	SO	HBP	SH	SF	SB	CS	SB%	GDP	Avg	OBP	SLG
1976 Detroit	AL	56	1	0	0	0	0	(0	0)	0	0	0	0	0	0	0	0	0	0	0	.00	0	.000	.000	.000
8 ML YEARS		236	101	11	1	0	0	(0	0)	12	2	4	3	0	34	0	4	0	0	0	.00	1	.109	.135	.119

League Championship Batting

							BATTING												BASERUNNING			PERCENTAGES		
Year Team	Lg	G	AB	H	2B	3B	HR	(Hm	Rd)	TB	R	RBI	TBB	IBB	SO	HBP	SH	SF	SB	CS	SB%	GDP	Avg	OBP	SLG
1972 Detroit	AL	3	0	0	0	0	0	(0	0)	0	0	0	0	0	0	0	0	0	0	0	.00	0	.000	.000	.000

World Series Batting

							BATTING												BASERUNNING			PERCENTAGES		
Year Team	Lg	G	AB	H	2B	3B	HR	(Hm	Rd)	TB	R	RBI	TBB	IBB	SO	HBP	SH	SF	SB	CS	SB%	GDP	Avg	OBP	SLG
1968 Detroit	AL	2	0	0	0	0	0	(0	0)	0	0	0	0	0	0	0	0	0	0	0	.00	0	.000	.000	.000

FIELDING AS PITCHER

Year Team	Lg	G	TC	PO	A	E	DP	PB	Pct.	Range
1965 Detroit	AL	5	0	0	0	0	0	--	.000	---
1966 Detroit	AL	1	0	0	0	0	0	--	.000	---
1967 Detroit	AL	23	14	4	9	1	0	--	.929	---
1968 Detroit	AL	39	27	12	15	0	1	--	1.000	---
1969 Detroit	AL	40	14	2	11	1	0	--	.929	---
1970 Detroit	AL	47	13	3	10	0	0	--	1.000	---
1972 Detroit	AL	24	10	1	9	0	2	--	1.000	---
1973 Detroit	AL	65	25	8	16	1	1	--	.960	---
1974 Detroit	AL	59	14	2	11	1	0	--	.929	---
1975 Detroit	AL	36	9	1	8	0	0	--	1.000	---
1976 Detroit	AL	56	16	2	13	1	0	--	.938	---
1977 Detroit	AL	45	17	4	11	2	1	--	.882	---
1978 Detroit	AL	51	10	1	9	0	0	--	1.000	---
1979 Detroit	AL	43	14	4	10	0	0	--	1.000	---
1980 Detroit	AL	11	6	1	4	1	0	--	.833	---
15 ML YEARS		545	189	45	136	8	5	--	.958	---

League Championship Fielding

FIELDING AS PITCHER

Year Team	Lg	G	TC	PO	A	E	DP	PB	Pct.	Range
1972 Detroit	AL	3	1	1	0	0	0	--	1.000	---

World Series Fielding

FIELDING AS PITCHER

Year Team	Lg	G	TC	PO	A	E	DP	PB	Pct.	Range
1968 Detroit	AL	2	0	0	0	0	0	--	.000	---

Career Interruption: 1971—Suffered near-fatal heart attack.

Paul Hodgson

Paul Joseph Denis Hodgson
Bats: Right **Throws:** Right
Height: 6'2" **Weight:** 190
Born on April 14, 1960 in Montreal, Quebec

							BATTING												BASERUNNING			PERCENTAGES		
Year Team	Lg	G	AB	H	2B	3B	HR	(Hm	Rd)	TB	R	RBI	TBB	IBB	SO	HBP	SH	SF	SB	CS	SB%	GDP	Avg	OBP	SLG
1980 Toronto	AL	20	41	9	0	1	1	(0	1)	14	5	5	3	0	12	0	2	0	0	1	.00	2	.220	.273	.341

FIELDING AS OUTFIELDER

Year Team	Lg	G	TC	PO	A	E	DP	PB	Pct.	Range
1980 Toronto	AL	11	20	19	1	0	0	--	1.000	1.82

Bill Hogg

William Johnston Hogg
Pitches: Right **Bats:** Right
Height: 6'0" **Weight:** 200
Born on September 11, 1881 in Canada
Died on December 8, 1909 in New Orleans, Louisiana

			HOW MUCH HE PITCHED						WHAT HE GAVE UP									THE RESULTS					
Year Team	Lg	G	GS	CG	GF	IP	BFP	H	R	ER	HR	SH	SF	HB	TBB	IBB	SO	WP	Bk	W	L	Pct.	ShO	Sv	ERA
1905 New York	AL	39	22	9	13	205	892	178	104	73	1	27		13	101		125	14	1	9	13	.409	3	1	3.20
1906 New York	AL	28	25	15	3	206	855	171	77	67	5	24		12	72		107	6	0	14	13	.519	3	0	2.93
1907 New York	AL	25	21	13	3	166.2	742	173	84	57	3	20		6	83		64	7	0	11	8	.579	0	0	3.08
1908 New York	AL	24	21	7	3	152.1	683	155	89	51	4	25		4	63		72	6	0	4	15	.211	0	0	3.01
4 ML YEARS		116	89	44	22	730	3172	677	354	248	13	96		35	319		368	33	1	38	49	.437	6	1	3.06

Year Team	Lg	G	AB	H	2B	3B	HR	(Hm	Rd)	TB	R	RBI	TBB	IBB	SO	HBP	SH	SF	SB	CS	SB%	GDP	Avg	OBP	SLG
1905 New York	AL	39	67	4	0	0	0	--	--	4	3	1	5			0	1		0				.060	.125	.060
1906 New York	AL	28	72	9	1	0	0	--	--	10	8	3	1			0	5		1				.125	.137	.139
1907 New York	AL	27	64	11	1	0	1	--	--	15	5	4	3			0	0		0				.172	.209	.234
1908 New York	AL	24	43	4	0	0	0	--	--	4	1	3	1			0	1		0				.093	.114	.093
4 ML YEARS		118	246	28	2	0	1	--	--	33	17	11	10			0	7		1				.114	.148	.134

FIELDING AS PITCHER

Year Team	Lg	G	TC	PO	A	E	DP	PB	Pct.	Range
1905 New York	AL	39	42	5	35	2	3	--	.952	---
1906 New York	AL	28	41	5	35	1	4	--	.976	---
1907 New York	AL	25	56	7	47	2	0	--	.964	---
1908 New York	AL	24	43	5	37	1	0	--	.977	---
4 ML YEARS		116	182	22	154	6	7	--	.967	---

Bob Hooper

Robert Nelson Hooper
Pitches: Right **Bats:** Right

Height: 5'11" **Weight:** 195
Born on May 30, 1922 in Leamington, Ontario
Died on March 17, 1980 in Brunswick, New Jersey

Year Team	Lg	G	GS	CG	GF	IP	BFP	H	R	ER	HR	SH	SF	HB	TBB	IBB	SO	WP	Bk	W	L	Pct.	ShO	Sv	ERA
1950 Philadelphia	AL	45	20	3	22	170.1	763	181	108	95	15	6		1	91		58	4	1	15	10	.600	0	5	5.02
1951 Philadelphia	AL	38	23	9	8	189	790	192	98	92	13	7		3	61		64	4	0	12	10	.545	0	4	4.38
1952 Philadelphia	AL	43	14	4	21	144.1	649	158	100	83	13	11		4	68		40	2	1	8	15	.348	0	6	5.18
1953 Cleveland	AL	43	0	0	26	69.1	288	50	37	31	4	5		2	38		16	2	0	5	4	.556	0	7	4.02
1954 Cleveland	AL	17	0	0	8	34.2	155	39	22	19	3	1	2	1	16		12	0	0	0	0	.000	0	2	4.93
1955 Cincinnati	NL	8	0	0	1	13	65	20	12	11	2	3	0	0	6	0	6	0	0	0	2	.000	0	0	7.62
6 ML YEARS		194	57	16	86	620.2	2710	640	377	331	50	33		11	280		196	12	2	40	41	.494	0	25	4.80

Year Team	Lg	G	AB	H	2B	3B	HR	(Hm	Rd)	TB	R	RBI	TBB	IBB	SO	HBP	SH	SF	SB	CS	SB%	GDP	Avg	OBP	SLG
1950 Philadelphia	AL	45	56	7	2	0	1	(1	0)	12	4	8	0		21	2	4		0	0	.00	2	.125	.155	.214
1951 Philadelphia	AL	38	72	15	3	0	1	(0	1)	21	8	8	1		19	0	2		0	0	.00	1	.208	.219	.292
1952 Philadelphia	AL	43	41	8	1	0	2	(2	0)	15	3	3	1		10	0	3		0	0	.00	1	.195	.214	.366
1953 Cleveland	AL	43	12	1	0	0	0	(0	0)	1	0	0	1		0	0	0		0	0	.00	0	.083	.154	.083
1954 Cleveland	AL	17	5	0	0	0	0	(0	0)	0	0	0	0		1	0	0	0	0	0	.00	0	.000	.000	.000
1955 Cincinnati	NL	8	1	0	0	0	0	(0	0)	0	0	0	0	0	0	0	0	0	0	0	.00	0	.000	.000	.000
6 ML YEARS		194	187	31	6	0	4	(3	1)	49	15	19	3		51	2	9		0	0	.00	4	.166	.188	.262

FIELDING AS PITCHER

Year Team	Lg	G	TC	PO	A	E	DP	PB	Pct.	Range
1950 Philadelphia	AL	45	58	19	37	2	10	--	.966	---
1951 Philadelphia	AL	38	58	18	37	3	3	--	.948	---
1952 Philadelphia	AL	43	55	22	32	1	5	--	.982	---
1953 Cleveland	AL	43	19	3	16	0	2	--	1.000	---
1954 Cleveland	AL	17	8	2	6	0	0	--	1.000	---
1955 Cincinnati	NL	8	4	0	4	0	0	--	1.000	---
6 ML YEARS		194	202	64	132	6	20	--	.970	---

Vince Horsman

Vincent Stanley Joseph Horsman
Pitches: Left **Bats:** Right

Height: 6'2" **Weight:** 175
Born on March 9, 1967 in Halifax, Nova Scotia

Year Team	Lg	G	GS	CG	GF	IP	BFP	H	R	ER	HR	SH	SF	HB	TBB	IBB	SO	WP	Bk	W	L	Pct.	ShO	Sv	ERA
1985 Medicne Hat	R	18	1	0	2	40.1	0	56	31	28	1	0	0	0	23	3	30	1	0	0	3	.000	0	1	6.25
1986 Florence	A	29	9	1	10	90.2	419	93	56	41	8	1	6	1	49	0	64	5	4	4	3	.571	1	1	4.07
1987 Myrtle Bch	A	30	28	0	1	149	621	144	74	55	20	6	5	2	37	2	109	5	2	7	7	.500	0	0	3.32
1988 Knoxville	AA	20	6	1	6	58.1	260	57	34	30	5	4	4	3	28	3	40	4	1	3	2	.600	0	0	4.63
Dunedin	A	14	2	0	3	39.2	159	28	7	6	1	1	1	1	13	2	34	4	1	3	1	.750	0	1	1.36
1989 Dunedin	A	35	1	0	23	79	330	72	24	22	3	5	1	1	27	3	60	3	4	5	6	.455	0	8	2.51
Knoxville	AA	4	0	0	3	5	19	3	1	1	0	0	0	0	2	1	3	0	0	0	0	.000	0	1	1.80
1990 Dunedin	A	28	0	0	14	50	209	53	21	18	0	2	2	1	15	2	41	2	0	4	7	.364	0	1	3.24
Knoxville	AA	8	0	0	2	11.2	51	11	7	6	1	1	0	0	5	2	10	1	0	2	1	.667	0	1	4.63
1991 Knoxville	AA	42	2	0	17	80.2	335	80	23	21	2	3	1	0	19	5	80	3	1	4	1	.800	0	3	2.34
1993 Tacoma	AAA	26	0	0	10	33.2	149	37	25	16	11	1	2	0	9	2	23	1	1	1	2	.333	0	3	4.28
1994 Tacoma	AAA	7	0	0	2	7	26	5	2	2	1	1	0	0	1	0	6	0	0	1	0	1.000	0	0	2.57

Year	Team	Lg	G	GS	CG	GF	IP	BFP	H	R	ER	HR	SH	SF	HB	TBB	IBB	SO	WP	Bk	W	L	Pct.	ShO	Sv	ERA
1995	Salt Lake	AAA	16	0	0	7	13	64	23	15	15	3	0	0	0	4	2	10	1	0	1	0	1.000	0	0	10.38
1991	Toronto	AL	4	0	0	2	4	16	2	0	0	0	1	0	0	3	1	2	0	0	0	0	.000	0	0	0.00
1992	Oakland	AL	58	0	0	9	43.1	180	39	13	12	3	3	1	0	21	4	18	1	0	2	1	.667	0	1	2.49
1993	Oakland	AL	40	0	0	5	25	116	25	15	15	2	0	0	3	15	1	17	1	0	2	0	1.000	0	0	5.40
1994	Oakland	AL	33	0	0	6	29.1	127	29	17	16	2	3	3	1	11	2	20	1	1	0	1	.000	0	0	4.91
1995	Minnesota	AL	6	0	0	3	9	43	12	8	7	2	2	1	0	4	1	4	0	0	0	0	.000	0	0	7.00
	5 ML YEARS		141	0	0	25	110.2	482	107	53	50	9	9	5	4	54	9	61	3	1	4	2	.667	0	1	4.07

BATTING

Year	Team	Lg	G	AB	H	2B	3B	HR	(Hm	Rd)	TB	R	RBI	TBB	IBB	SO	HBP	SH	SF	SB	CS	SB%	GDP	Avg	OBP	SLG
1993	Oakland	AL	2	0	0	0	0	0	(0	0)	0	0	0	0	0	0	0	0	0	0	0	.00	0	.000	.000	.000
1995	Minnesota	AL	1	0	0	0	0	0	(0	0)	0	0	0	0	0	0	0	0	0	0	0	.00	0	.000	.000	.000
	2 ML YEARS		3	0	0	0	0	0	(0	0)	0	0	0	0	0	0	0	0	0	0	0	.00	0	.000	.000	.000

FIELDING AS PITCHER

Year	Team	Lg	G	TC	PO	A	E	DP	PB	Pct.	Range
1991	Toronto	AL	4	0	0	0	0	0	--	.000	---
1992	Oakland	AL	58	6	1	5	0	0	--	1.000	---
1993	Oakland	AL	40	2	0	2	0	0	--	1.000	---
1994	Oakland	AL	33	8	2	6	0	0	--	1.000	---
1995	Minnesota	AL	6	4	1	3	0	0	--	1.000	---
	5 ML YEARS		141	20	4	16	0	0	--	1.000	---

Peter Hoy

Peter Alexander Hoy
Attended Le Moyne
Pitches: Right **Bats:** Left

Height: 6'7" **Weight:** 220
Born on June 29, 1966 in Brockville, Ontario

HOW MUCH HE PITCHED / WHAT HE GAVE UP / THE RESULTS

Year	Team	Lg	G	GS	CG	GF	IP	BFP	H	R	ER	HR	SH	SF	HB	TBB	IBB	SO	WP	Bk	W	L	Pct.	ShO	Sv	ERA
1989	Elmira	A	26	12	3	6	118	486	109	52	37	6	6	2	4	37	1	73	3	4	6	10	.375	0	1	2.82
1990	Winter Havn	A	52	3	0	30	108.2	460	110	54	43	3	10	5	3	30	1	48	5	5	2	10	.167	0	7	3.56
1991	New Britain	AA	47	0	0	40	68	269	47	20	11	2	9	1	0	22	8	39	1	2	4	4	.500	0	15	1.46
	Pawtucket	AAA	15	0	0	13	22.2	93	18	8	6	2	2	0	0	10	1	12	2	0	1	2	.333	0	5	2.38
1992	Pawtucket	AAA	45	0	0	22	73.1	317	83	41	39	9	3	3	3	25	5	38	5	3	3	2	.600	0	5	4.79
1993	Ft. Laud	A	4	0	0	4	4.1	14	2	0	0	0	0	0	0	0	0	4	0	0	0	0	.000	0	1	0.00
	New Britain	AA	51	0	0	21	79.2	359	86	38	34	3	7	2	5	41	6	37	3	1	9	4	.692	0	0	3.84
1994	Regina	IND	16	0	0	5	27	116	21	11	9	1	0	0	0	9	0	13	3	0	1	1	.500	0	1	3.00
1995	Glens Falls	IND	30	0	0	13	47.1	195	41	18	11	2	1	1	1	15	4	18	5	0	2	2	.500	0	4	2.09
1992	Boston	AL	5	0	0	2	3.2	19	8	3	3	0	0	0	0	2	1	2	0	0	0	0	.000	0	0	7.36

FIELDING AS PITCHER

Year	Team	Lg	G	TC	PO	A	E	DP	PB	Pct.	Range
1992	Boston	AL	5	1	0	1	0	1	--	1.000	---

John Humphries

John Henry Humphries
Bats: Left **Throws:** Left

Height: 6'0" **Weight:** 185
Born on November 12, 1861 in North Gower, Ontario
Died on November 29, 1933 in Salinas, California

BATTING

Year	Team	Lg	G	AB	H	2B	3B	HR	(Hm	Rd)	TB	R	RBI	TBB	IBB	SO	HBP	SH	SF	SB	CS	SB%	GDP	Avg	OBP	SLG
1883	New York	NL	29	107	12	1	0	0	--	--	13	5	4	1		22								.112	.120	.121
1884	2 ML Teams		69	257	40	2	0	0	--	--	42	29		18										.156	.211	.163
1884	Washington	AA	49	193	34	2	0	0	--	--	36	23		9			1							.176	.217	.187
	New York	NL	20	64	6	0	0	0	--	--	6	6	2	9		19								.094	.205	.094
	2 ML YEARS		98	364	52	3	0	0	--	--	55	34		19			0	0						.143	.185	.151

FIELDING AS CATCHER

Year	Team	Lg	G	TC	PO	A	E	DP	PB	Pct.	Range
1883	New York	NL	20	124	71	30	23	3	31	.815	---
1884	2 ML Teams		55	474	336	87	51	8	65	.892	---
1884	Washington	AA	35	281	198	52	31	6	44	.890	---
	New York	NL	20	193	138	35	20	2	21	.896	---
	2 ML YEARS		75	598	407	117	74	11	96	.876	---

FIELDING AS FIRST BASEMAN

Year	Team	Lg	G	TC	PO	A	E	DP	PB	Pct.	Range
1884	Washington	AA	4	36	33	1	2	0	--	.944	---

FIELDING AS OUTFIELDER

Year	Team	Lg	G	TC	PO	A	E	DP	PB	Pct.	Range
1883	New York	NL	12	17	13	1	3	0	--	.824	1.17
1884	Washington	AA	12	36	25	0	11	0	--	.694	2.08
	2 ML YEARS		24	53	38	1	14	0	--	.736	1.63

Bill Hunter

William Robert Hunter
Bats: Unknown **Throws:** Unknown

Height: 5'7" **Weight:** 160
Born Unknown in St. Thomas, Ontario

					BATTING														BASERUNNING				PERCENTAGES		
Year Team	Lg	G	AB	H	2B	3B	HR	(Hm	Rd)	TB	R	RBI	TBB	IBB	SO	HBP	SH	SF	SB	CS	SB%	GDP	Avg	OBP	SLG
1884 Louisville	AA	2	7	1	0	0	0	--	--	1	1		0		0								.143	.143	.143

			FIELDING AS CATCHER								
Year Team	Lg	G	TC	PO	A	E	DP	PB	Pct.	Range
1884 Louisville	AA	2	9	5	1	3	0	2	.667	---

Jim Hyndman

James William Hyndman
Bats: Unknown **Throws:** Unknown

Height: Unknown **Weight:** Unknown
Born in July, 1865 in Ontario

					BATTING														BASERUNNING				PERCENTAGES		
Year Team	Lg	G	AB	H	2B	3B	HR	(Hm	Rd)	TB	R	RBI	TBB	IBB	SO	HBP	SH	SF	SB	CS	SB%	GDP	Avg	OBP	SLG
1886 Philadelphia	AA	1	4	0	0	0	0	--	--	0	0		0		0				0				.000	.000	.000

			HOW MUCH HE PITCHED					WHAT HE GAVE UP									THE RESULTS					
Year Team	Lg	G	GS	CG	GF	IP	BFP	H	R	ER	HR	SH	SF	HB	TBB	IBB	SO	WP	Bk	W	L	Pct.	ShO	Sv	ERA
1886 Philadelphia	AA	1	1	0	0	2	17	5	10	6	1				5		1	0	0	0	1	.000	0	0	27.00

			FIELDING AS PITCHER								
Year Team	Lg	G	TC	PO	A	E	DP	PB	Pct.	Range
1886 Philadelphia	AA	1	3	1	1	1	0	--	.667	---

			FIELDING AS OUTFIELDER								
Year Team	Lg	G	TC	PO	A	E	DP	PB	Pct.	Range
1886 Philadelphia	AA	1	2	2	0	0	0	--	1.000	2.00

Arthur Irwin

Arthur Albert Irwin (Doc, Sandy, Cut Rate)
Bats: Left **Throws:** Right

Height: 5'8" **Weight:** 158
Born on February 14, 1858 in Toronto, Ontario
Died on July 16, 1921 in , Atlantic Ocean

					BATTING														BASERUNNING				PERCENTAGES		
Year Team	Lg	G	AB	H	2B	3B	HR	(Hm	Rd)	TB	R	RBI	TBB	IBB	SO	HBP	SH	SF	SB	CS	SB%	GDP	Avg	OBP	SLG
1880 Worcester	NL	85	352	91	19	4	1	--	--	121	53	35	11		27								.259	.281	.344
1881 Worcester	NL	50	206	55	8	2	0	--	--	67	27	24	7		4								.267	.291	.325
1882 Worcester	NL	84	333	73	12	4	0	--	--	93	30	30	14		34								.219	.251	.279
1883 Providence	NL	98	406	116	22	7	0	--	--	152	67	44	12		38								.286	.306	.374
1884 Providence	NL	102	404	97	14	3	2	--	--	123	73	44	28		52								.240	.289	.304
1885 Providence	NL	59	218	39	2	1	0	--	--	43	16	14	14		29								.179	.228	.197
1886 Philadelphia	NL	101	373	87	6	6	0	--	--	105	51	34	35		39				24				.233	.299	.282
1887 Philadelphia	NL	100	374	95	14	8	2	--	--	131	65	56	48	3	26				19				.254	.344	.350
1888 Philadelphia	NL	125	448	98	12	4	0	--	--	118	51	28	33	3	56				19				.219	.277	.263
1889 2 ML Teams		103	386	89	15	5	0	--	--	114	58	42	48	1	43				15				.231	.317	.295
1890 Boston	PL	96	354	92	17	1	0	--	--	111	60	45	57		29	1			16				.260	.364	.314
1891 Boston	AA	6	17	2	0	0	0	--	--	2	1	0	2		1	2			0				.118	.286	.118
1894 Philadelphia	NL	1	0	0	0	0	0	--	--	0	0	0	0	0	0				0				.000	.000	.000
1889 Philadelphia	NL	18	73	16	5	0	0	--	--	21	9	10	6		6	0			6				.219	.278	.288
Washington	NL	85	313	73	10	5	0	--	--	93	49	32	42	1	37	1			9				.233	.326	.297
13 ML YEARS		1010	3871	934	141	45	5	--	--	1180	552	396	309		378	10	0						.241	.299	.305

World Series Batting

					BATTING														BASERUNNING				PERCENTAGES		
Year Team	Lg	G	AB	H	2B	3B	HR	(Hm	Rd)	TB	R	RBI	TBB	IBB	SO	HBP	SH	SF	SB	CS	SB%	GDP	Avg	OBP	SLG
1884 Providence	NL	3	9	2	0	1	0	(0	0)	4	2		0	0	2								.222	.222	.444

			HOW MUCH HE PITCHED					WHAT HE GAVE UP									THE RESULTS					
Year Team	Lg	G	GS	CG	GF	IP	BFP	H	R	ER	HR	SH	SF	HB	TBB	IBB	SO	WP	Bk	W	L	Pct.	ShO	Sv	ERA
1884 Providence	NL	1	0	0	1	3	15	5	2	1	0				1		0	0	0	0	0	.000	0	0	3.00
1889 Washington	NL	1	0	0	1	1		1	1	0	0				0		0	0	0	0	0	.000	0	0	0.00
2 ML YEARS		2	0	0	1	4		6	3	1	0				1		0	0	0	0	0	.000	0	0	2.25

FIELDING AS PITCHER

Year	Team	Lg	G	TC	PO	A	E	DP	PB	Pct.	Range
1884	Providence	NL	1	1	0	1	0	0	--	1.000	---
1889	Washington	NL	1	0	0	0	0	0	--	.000	---
	2 ML YEARS		2	1	0	1	0	0	--	1.000	---

FIELDING AS CATCHER

Year	Team	Lg	G	TC	PO	A	E	DP	PB	Pct.	Range
1880	Worcester	NL	1	0	0	0	0	0	0	.000	---

FIELDING AS SECOND BASEMAN

Year	Team	Lg	G	TC	PO	A	E	DP	PB	Pct.	Range
1883	Providence	NL	4	16	7	8	1	0	--	.938	3.75
1885	Providence	NL	1	3	0	1	2	0	--	.333	1.00
1888	Philadelphia	NL	3	14	5	9	0	2	--	1.000	4.67
1889	Washington	NL	1	2	2	0	0	0	--	1.000	2.00
	4 ML YEARS		9	35	14	18	3	2	--	.914	3.56

FIELDING AS THIRD BASEMAN

Year	Team	Lg	G	TC	PO	A	E	DP	PB	Pct.	Range
1880	Worcester	NL	3	11	3	6	2	0	--	.818	3.00
1882	Worcester	NL	51	276	84	147	45	8	--	.837	4.53
1885	Providence	NL	1	3	0	2	1	0	--	.667	2.00
1886	Philadelphia	NL	1	3	0	1	2	0	--	.333	1.00
	4 ML YEARS		56	293	87	156	50	8	--	.829	4.34

FIELDING AS SHORTSTOP

Year	Team	Lg	G	TC	PO	A	E	DP	PB	Pct.	Range
1880	Worcester	NL	82	485	95	339	51	27	--	.895	5.29
1881	Worcester	NL	50	241	50	155	36	11	--	.851	4.10
1882	Worcester	NL	33	197	41	123	33	16	--	.832	4.97
1883	Providence	NL	94	451	93	293	65	29	--	.856	4.11
1884	Providence	NL	102	461	99	307	55	20	--	.881	3.98
1885	Providence	NL	58	319	70	209	40	17	--	.875	4.81
1886	Philadelphia	NL	100	515	137	322	56	21	--	.891	4.59
1887	Philadelphia	NL	100	537	178	301	58	30	--	.892	4.79
1888	Philadelphia	NL	122	642	204	374	64	31	--	.900	4.74
1889	2 ML Teams		103	580	190	325	65	42	--	.888	5.00
1890	Boston	PL	96	533	137	331	65	44	--	.878	4.88
1891	Boston	AA	6	27	7	14	6	5	--	.778	3.50
1894	Philadelphia	NL	1	0	0	0	0	0	--	.000	.00
1889	Philadelphia	NL	18	84	25	46	13	6	--	.845	3.94
	Washington	NL	85	496	165	279	52	36	--	.895	5.22
	13 ML YEARS		947	4988	1301	3093	594	293	--	.881	4.64

World Series Fielding

FIELDING AS SHORTSTOP

Year	Team	Lg	G	TC	PO	A	E	DP	PB	Pct.	Range
1884	Providence	NL	3	14	2	8	4	2	--	.714	3.33

John Irwin

John Irwin
Bats: Left **Throws:** Right

Height: 5'10" **Weight:** 168
Born on July 21, 1861 in Toronto, Ontario
Died on February 28, 1934 in Boston, Massachusetts

BATTING / BASERUNNING / PERCENTAGES

Year	Team	Lg	G	AB	H	2B	3B	HR	(Hm	Rd)	TB	R	RBI	TBB	IBB	SO	HBP	SH	SF	SB	CS	SB%	GDP	Avg	OBP	SLG
1882	Worcester	NL	1	4	0	0	0	0	--	--	0	0	0	0		2								.000	.000	.000
1884	Boston	UA	105	432	101	22	6	1	--	--	138	81		15										.234	.260	.319
1886	Philadelphia	AA	3	13	3	1	0	0	--	--	4	4		0			0			0				.231	.231	.308
1887	Washington	NL	8	31	11	2	0	2	--	--	19	6	3	3		6	1			6				.355	.429	.613
1888	Washington	NL	37	126	28	5	2	0	--	--	37	14	8	5		18	2			15				.222	.263	.294
1889	Washington	NL	58	228	66	11	4	0	--	--	85	42	25	25		14	4			10				.289	.370	.373
1890	Buffalo	PL	77	308	72	11	4	0	--	--	91	62	34	43		19	4			18				.234	.335	.295
1891	2 ML Teams		33	127	31	3	3	0	--	--	40	13	22	11		15	1			7				.244	.309	.315
1891	Boston	AA	19	72	16	2	2	0	--	--	22	6	15	6		9	0			6				.222	.282	.306
	Louisville	AA	14	55	15	1	1	0	--	--	18	7	7	5		6	1			1				.273	.344	.327
	8 ML YEARS		322	1269	312	55	19	3	--	--	414	222		102			12	0							.246	.308	.326

FIELDING AS FIRST BASEMAN

Year	Team	Lg	G	TC	PO	A	E	DP	PB	Pct.	Range
1882	Worcester	NL	1	11	7	0	4	1	--	.636	---
1890	Buffalo	PL	12	115	103	11	1	13	--	.991	---
	2 ML YEARS		13	126	110	11	5	14	--	.960	---

FIELDING AS SECOND BASEMAN										
Year Team	Lg	G	TC	PO	A	E	DP	PB	Pct.	Range
1890 Buffalo	PL	1	9	2	5	2	1	--	.778	7.00

FIELDING AS THIRD BASEMAN										
Year Team	Lg	G	TC	PO	A	E	DP	PB	Pct.	Range
1884 Boston	UA	105	395	117	191	87	7	--	.780	2.93
1886 Philadelphia	AA	1	4	0	4	0	0	--	1.000	4.00
1887 Washington	NL	4	13	4	7	2	0	--	.846	2.75
1888 Washington	NL	10	29	12	10	7	1	--	.759	2.20
1889 Washington	NL	58	243	82	129	32	14	--	.868	3.64
1890 Buffalo	PL	64	247	79	139	29	13	--	.883	3.41
1891 2 ML Teams		16	56	17	27	12	1	--	.786	2.75
1891 Boston	AA	2	12	4	5	3	0	--	.750	4.50
Louisville	AA	14	44	13	22	9	1	--	.795	2.50
7 ML YEARS		258	987	311	507	169	36	--	.829	3.17

FIELDING AS SHORTSTOP										
Year Team	Lg	G	TC	PO	A	E	DP	PB	Pct.	Range
1886 Philadelphia	AA	2	7	2	3	2	0	--	.714	2.50
1887 Washington	NL	5	24	9	12	3	1	--	.875	4.20
1888 Washington	NL	27	164	54	87	23	5	--	.860	5.22
1891 Boston	AA	1	3	1	1	1	0	--	.667	2.00
4 ML YEARS		35	198	66	103	29	6	--	.854	4.83

FIELDING AS OUTFIELDER										
Year Team	Lg	G	TC	PO	A	E	DP	PB	Pct.	Range
1891 Boston	AA	17	34	25	5	4	0	--	.882	1.76

Fergie Jenkins

Ferguson Arthur Jenkins

Height: 6'5" **Weight:** 205

Pitches: Right **Bats:** Right

Born on December 13, 1943 in Chatham, Ontario

	HOW MUCH HE PITCHED						WHAT HE GAVE UP											THE RESULTS				
Year Team	Lg	G	GS	CG	GF	IP	BFP	H	R	ER	HR	SH	SF	HB	TBB	IBB	SO	WP	Bk	W	L	Pct.	ShO	Sv	ERA
1965 Philadelphia	NL	7	0	0	6	12.1	46	7	3	3	2	0	0	0	2	0	10	0	0	2	1	.667	0	1	2.19
1966 2 ML Teams		61	12	2	22	184.1	752	150	77	68	24	10	4	3	52	12	150	1	1	6	8	.429	1	5	3.32
1967 Chicago	NL	38	38	20	0	289.1	1156	230	101	90	30	7	3	4	83	6	236	2	0	20	13	.606	3	0	2.80
1968 Chicago	NL	40	40	20	0	308	1231	255	96	90	26	11	4	3	65	7	260	6	1	20	15	.571	3	0	2.63
1969 Chicago	NL	43	42	23	1	311.1	1275	284	122	111	27	17	7	8	71	15	273	7	1	21	15	.583	7	1	3.21
1970 Chicago	NL	40	39	24	1	313	1265	265	128	118	30	6	7	7	60	6	274	9	0	22	16	.579	3	0	3.39
1971 Chicago	NL	39	39	30	0	325	1299	304	114	100	29	11	10	5	37	6	263	3	4	24	13	.649	3	0	2.77
1972 Chicago	NL	36	36	23	0	289.1	1176	253	111	103	32	17	9	7	62	7	184	3	1	20	12	.625	5	0	3.20
1973 Chicago	NL	38	38	7	0	271	1119	267	133	117	35	17	11	4	57	10	170	1	0	14	16	.467	2	0	3.89
1974 Texas	AL	41	41	29	0	328.1	1305	286	117	103	27	9	12	8	45	3	225	4	2	25	12	.676	6	0	2.82
1975 Texas	AL	37	37	22	0	270	1119	261	130	118	37	9	4	9	56	7	157	3	0	17	18	.486	4	0	3.93
1976 Boston	AL	30	29	12	1	209	857	201	85	76	20	5	10	5	43	6	142	3	1	12	11	.522	2	0	3.27
1977 Boston	AL	28	28	11	0	193	790	190	91	79	30	10	4	0	36	2	105	2	0	10	10	.500	1	0	3.68
1978 Texas	AL	34	30	16	3	249	990	228	92	84	21	10	6	3	41	2	157	2	1	18	8	.692	4	0	3.04
1979 Texas	AL	37	37	10	0	259	1089	252	127	117	40	10	9	3	81	6	164	4	0	16	14	.533	3	0	4.07
1980 Texas	AL	29	29	12	0	198	827	190	90	83	22	5	5	4	52	8	129	5	0	12	12	.500	0	0	3.77
1981 Texas	AL	19	16	1	2	106	467	122	55	53	14	5	1	0	40	4	63	2	0	5	8	.385	0	0	4.50
1982 Chicago	NL	34	34	4	0	217.1	932	221	92	76	19	10	13	5	68	2	134	3	3	14	15	.483	1	0	3.15
1983 Chicago	NL	33	29	1	1	167.1	705	176	89	80	19	7	5	6	46	5	96	2	3	6	9	.400	1	0	4.30
1966 Philadelphia	NL	1	0	0	0	2.1	12	3	2	1	0	0	0	0	1	1	2	0	0	0	0	.000	0	0	3.86
Chicago	NL	60	12	2	22	182	740	147	75	67	24	10	4	3	51	11	148	1	1	6	8	.429	1	5	3.31
19 ML YEARS		664	594	267	37	4500.2	18400	4142	1853	1669	484	176	124	84	997	116	3192	62	18	284	226	.557	49	7	3.34

All-Star Game Pitching

	HOW MUCH HE PITCHED						WHAT HE GAVE UP											THE RESULTS				
Year Team	Lg	G	GS	CG	GF	IP	BFP	H	R	ER	HR	SH	SF	HB	TBB	IBB	SO	WP	Bk	W	L	Pct.	ShO	Sv	ERA
1967 Chicago	NL	1	0	0	0	3	11	3	1	1	1	0	0	0	0	0	6	0	0	0	0	.000	0	0	3.00
1971 Cleveland	AL	1	0	0	0	1	5	3	2	2	1	0	0	0	0	0	0	0	0	0	0	.000	0	0	18.00
2 ML YEARS		2	0	0	0	4	16	6	3	3	2	0	0	0	0	0	6	0	0	0	0	.000	0	0	6.75

	BATTING																BASERUNNING			PERCENTAGES		
Year Team	Lg	G	AB	H	2B	3B	HR	(Hm | Rd)	TB	R	RBI	TBB	IBB	SO	HBP	SH	SF	SB	CS	SB%	GDP	Avg	OBP	SLG
1965 Philadelphia	NL	7	1	0	0	0	0	(0 | 0)	0	0	0	0	0	1	0	0	0	0	0	.00	0	.000	.000	.000
1966 2 ML Teams		61	51	7	0	1	1	(1 | 0)	12	6	2	3	0	25	0	3	0	0	0	.00	0	.137	.185	.235
1967 Chicago	NL	39	93	14	3	1	0	(0 | 0)	19	5	10	6	0	35	0	8	1	0	0	.00	1	.151	.200	.204
1968 Chicago	NL	40	100	16	4	0	1	(0 | 1)	23	4	10	6	0	41	0	6	0	0	1	.00	0	.160	.208	.230

186

1969 Chicago	NL	43	108	15	2	1	1	(0	1)	22	6	9	6	0	42	0	4	1	0	0	.00	3	.139	.183	.204
1970 Chicago	NL	40	113	14	2	0	3	(1	2)	25	4	11	1	0	36	0	10	2	0	0	.00	1	.124	.129	.221
1971 Chicago	NL	39	115	28	7	1	6	(6	0)	55	13	20	7	0	40	0	8	2	0	0	.00	2	.243	.282	.478
1972 Chicago	NL	36	109	20	1	1	1	(1	0)	26	8	8	5	0	34	0	3	0	0	0	.00	1	.183	.219	.239
1973 Chicago	NL	38	84	10	4	0	0	(0	0)	14	2	4	6	0	40	0	7	0	0	0	.00	1	.119	.178	.167
1974 Texas	AL	41	2	1	0	0	0	(0	0)	1	1	0	0	0	1	0	0	0	0	0	.00	0	.500	.500	.500
1982 Chicago	NL	34	67	10	2	0	0	(0	0)	12	2	6	0	0	23	0	12	1	0	0	.00	0	.149	.147	.179
1983 Chicago	NL	33	53	13	2	1	0	(0	0)	17	3	5	1	0	8	0	5	0	0	0	.00	0	.245	.259	.321
1966 Philadelphia	NL	1	0	0	0	0	0	(0	0)	0	0	0	0	0	0	0	0	0	0	0	.00	0	.000	.000	.000
Chicago	NL	60	51	7	0	1	1	(1	0)	12	6	2	3	0	25	0	3	0	0	0	.00	0	.137	.185	.235
12 ML YEARS		451	896	148	27	6	13	(9	4)	226	54	85	41	0	326	0	66	7	0	1	.00	9	.165	.200	.252

All-Star Game Batting

BATTING																			BASERUNNING				PERCENTAGES		
Year Team	Lg	G	AB	H	2B	3B	HR	(Hm	Rd)	TB	R	RBI	TBB	IBB	SO	HBP	SH	SF	SB	CS	SB%	GDP	Avg	OBP	SLG
1967 Chicago	NL	1	1	0	0	0	0	(0	0)	0	0	0	0	0	0	0	0	0	0	0	.00	0	.000	.000	.000
1971 Chicago	NL	1	0	0	0	0	0	(0	0)	0	0	0	0	0	0	0	0	0	0	0	.00	0	.000	.000	.000
2 ML YEARS		2	1	0	0	0	0	(0	0)	0	0	0	0	0	0	0	0	0	0	0	.00	0	.000	.000	.000

FIELDING AS PITCHER										
Year Team	Lg	G	TC	PO	A	E	DP	PB	Pct.	Range
1965 Philadelphia	NL	7	1	0	1	0	0	--	1.000	---
1966 2 ML Teams		61	33	11	19	3	0	--	.909	---
1967 Chicago	NL	38	71	20	49	2	4	--	.972	---
1968 Chicago	NL	40	55	14	41	0	**5**	--	1.000	---
1969 Chicago	NL	43	65	14	47	4	3	--	.938	---
1970 Chicago	NL	40	57	14	39	4	1	--	.930	---
1971 Chicago	NL	39	86	**31**	48	7	1	--	.919	---
1972 Chicago	NL	36	80	**28**	50	2	2	--	.975	---
1973 Chicago	NL	38	78	21	53	4	6	--	.949	---
1974 Texas	AL	41	69	24	41	4	3	--	.942	---
1975 Texas	AL	37	71	27	39	5	1	--	.930	---
1976 Boston	AL	30	36	13	23	0	3	--	1.000	---
1977 Boston	AL	28	58	24	30	4	1	--	.931	---
1978 Texas	AL	34	67	**29**	37	1	4	--	.985	---
1979 Texas	AL	37	78	25	50	3	5	--	.962	---
1980 Texas	AL	29	49	24	23	2	3	--	.959	---
1981 Texas	AL	19	32	10	22	0	3	--	1.000	---
1982 Chicago	NL	34	52	18	30	4	0	--	.923	---
1983 Chicago	NL	33	34	16	18	0	0	--	1.000	---
1966 Philadelphia	NL	1	0	0	0	0	0	--	.000	---
Chicago	NL	60	33	11	19	3	0	--	.909	---
19 ML YEARS		664	1072	363	660	49	45	--	.954	---

All-Star Game Fielding

FIELDING AS PITCHER										
Year Team	Lg	G	TC	PO	A	E	DP	PB	Pct.	Range
1967 Chicago	NL	1	0	0	0	0	0	--	.000	---
1971 Chicago	NL	1	0	0	0	0	0	--	.000	---
2 ML YEARS		2	0	0	0	0	0	--	.000	---

Elected to the Hall of Fame in 1991. Cy Young Award in 1971.

Abbie Johnson

Albert J. Johnson

Height: 5'9" **Weight:** 165

Bats: Unknown **Throws:** Unknown

Born on July 26, 1872 in London, Ontario

BATTING																			BASERUNNING				PERCENTAGES		
Year Team	Lg	G	AB	H	2B	3B	HR	(Hm	Rd)	TB	R	RBI	TBB	IBB	SO	HBP	SH	SF	SB	CS	SB%	GDP	Avg	OBP	SLG
1896 Louisville	NL	25	87	20	2	1	0	--	--	24	10	14	4		6	0	2		0				.230	.264	.276
1897 Louisville	NL	48	161	39	6	1	0	--	--	47	16	23	13			1	1		2				.242	.303	.292
2 ML YEARS		73	248	59	8	2	0	--	--	71	26	37	17			1	3		2				.238	.289	.286

			FIELDING AS SECOND BASEMAN								
Year Team	Lg	G	TC	PO	A	E	DP	PB	Pct.	Range
1896 Louisville	NL	25	126	57	61	8	9	--	.937	4.72
1897 Louisville	NL	33	182	68	92	22	8	--	.879	4.85
2 ML YEARS		58	308	125	153	30	17	--	.903	4.79

			FIELDING AS SHORTSTOP								
Year Team	Lg	G	TC	PO	A	E	DP	PB	Pct.	Range
1897 Louisville	NL	12	60	28	27	5	7	--	.917	4.58

Spud Johnson

John Ralph Johnson
Bats: Left **Throws:** Left

Height: 5'9" **Weight:** 175
Born in 1860 in Canada

					BATTING													BASERUNNING				PERCENTAGES		
Year Team	Lg	G	AB	H	2B	3B	HR	(Hm | Rd)	TB	R	RBI	TBB	IBB	SO	HBP	SH	SF	SB	CS	SB%	GDP	Avg	OBP	SLG
1889 Columbus	AA	116	459	130	14	10	2	--	--	170	91	79	39		47	12			34				.283	.355	.370
1890 Columbus	AA	135	538	186	23	18	1	--	--	248	106		48			10			43				.346	.409	.461
1891 Cleveland	NL	80	327	84	8	3	1	--	--	101	49	46	22		23	8			16				.257	.319	.309
3 ML YEARS		331	1324	400	45	31	4	--	--	519	246		109			30	0		93				.302	.368	.392

			FIELDING AS FIRST BASEMAN								
Year Team	Lg	G	TC	PO	A	E	DP	PB	Pct.	Range
1889 Columbus	AA	2	18	16	0	2	0	--	.889	---
1891 Cleveland	NL	1	12	11	0	1	0	--	.917	---
2 ML YEARS		3	30	27	0	3	0	--	.900	---

			FIELDING AS THIRD BASEMAN								
Year Team	Lg	G	TC	PO	A	E	DP	PB	Pct.	Range
1889 Columbus	AA	44	164	62	75	27	8	--	.835	3.11

			FIELDING AS SHORTSTOP								
Year Team	Lg	G	TC	PO	A	E	DP	PB	Pct.	Range
1889 Columbus	AA	1	3	3	0	0	0	--	1.000	3.00

			FIELDING AS OUTFIELDER								
Year Team	Lg	G	TC	PO	A	E	DP	PB	Pct.	Range
1889 Columbus	AA	69	99	75	12	12	2	--	.879	1.26
1890 Columbus	AA	135	190	164	12	14	1	--	.926	1.30
1891 Cleveland	NL	79	125	99	10	16	1	--	.872	1.38
3 ML YEARS		283	414	338	34	42	4	--	.899	1.31

Bill Jones

William Dennis Jones (Midget)
Bats: Left **Throws:** Right

Height: 5'6" **Weight:** 157
Born on April 8, 1887 in Hartland, New Brunswick
Died on October 10, 1946 in Boston, Massachusetts

					BATTING													BASERUNNING				PERCENTAGES		
Year Team	Lg	G	AB	H	2B	3B	HR	(Hm | Rd)	TB	R	RBI	TBB	IBB	SO	HBP	SH	SF	SB	CS	SB%	GDP	Avg	OBP	SLG
1911 Boston	NL	24	51	11	2	1	0	--	--	15	6	3	15		7	0	1		1				.216	.394	.294
1912 Boston	NL	3	2	1	0	0	0	--	--	1	0	2	0		1	0	0		0				.500	.500	.500
2 ML YEARS		27	53	12	2	1	0	--	--	16	6	5	15		8	0	1		1				.226	.397	.302

			FIELDING AS OUTFIELDER								
Year Team	Lg	G	TC	PO	A	E	DP	PB	Pct.	Range
1911 Boston	NL	18	45	36	3	6	0	--	.867	2.17

Mike Jones

Michael Jones
Pitches: Left **Bats:** Left

Height: 6'0" **Weight:** 168
Born on July 6, 1865 in Hamilton, Ontario
Died on March 24, 1894 in Hamilton, Ontario

			HOW MUCH HE PITCHED					WHAT HE GAVE UP											THE RESULTS					
Year Team	Lg	G	GS	CG	GF	IP	BFP	H	R	ER	HR	SH	SF	HB	TBB	IBB	SO	WP	Bk	W	L	Pct.	ShO	Sv	ERA
1890 Louisville	AA	3	3	2	0	22	97	21	12	8	2			0	9		6	0	0	2	0	1.000	0	0	3.27

					BATTING													BASERUNNING				PERCENTAGES		
Year Team	Lg	G	AB	H	2B	3B	HR	(Hm | Rd)	TB	R	RBI	TBB	IBB	SO	HBP	SH	SF	SB	CS	SB%	GDP	Avg	OBP	SLG
1890 Louisville	AA	3	9	4	0	0	0	--	--	4	1		2		0				0				.444	.545	.444

188

			FIELDING AS PITCHER								
Year Team	Lg	G	TC	PO	A	E	DP	PB	Pct.	Range	
1890 Louisville	AA	3	8	2	4	2	0	--	.750	---	

Oscar Judd

Thomas William Oscar Judd (Ossie) **Height:** 6'0" **Weight:** 180

Pitches: Left **Bats:** Left **Born** on February 14, 1908 in London, Ontario

		HOW MUCH HE PITCHED					WHAT HE GAVE UP										THE RESULTS				
Year Team	Lg	G	GS	CG	GF	IP	BFP	H	R	ER	HR	SH	SF	HB	TBB	IBB	SO	WP	Bk	W	L	Pct.	ShO	Sv	ERA
1941 Boston	AL	7	0	0	4	12.1	60	15	12	12	1	0		0	10		5	2	0	0	0	.000	0	1	8.76
1942 Boston	AL	31	19	11	7	150.1	664	135	72	65	3	7		2	90		70	7	0	8	10	.444	0	2	3.89
1943 Boston	AL	23	20	8	2	155.1	653	131	58	50	2	12		3	69		53	7	0	11	6	.647	1	0	2.90
1944 Boston	AL	9	6	1	2	30	132	30	16	12	1	2		0	15		9	0	1	1	1	.500	0	0	3.60
1945 2 ML Teams		25	10	3	9	89	399	90	55	41	5	10		1	43		41	7	0	5	5	.500	1	2	4.15
1946 Philadelphia	NL	30	24	12	3	173.1	760	169	86	68	6	18		1	90		65	4	0	11	12	.478	1	2	3.53
1947 Philadelphia	NL	32	19	8	4	146.2	639	155	86	75	6	11		3	69		54	8	0	4	15	.211	1	0	4.60
1948 Philadelphia	NL	4	1	0	1	14	73	19	14	11	1	2		0	11		7	0	0	0	2	.000	0	0	7.07
1945 Boston	AL	2	1	0	0	6.1	34	10	8	6	1	1		0	3		5	0	0	0	1	.000	0	0	8.53
Philadelphia	NL	23	9	3	9	82.2	365	80	47	35	4	9		1	40		36	7	0	5	4	.556	1	2	3.81
8 ML YEARS		161	99	43	32	771	3380	744	399	334	25	62		10	397		304	35	1	40	51	.440	4	7	3.90

		BATTING																BASERUNNING				PERCENTAGES		
Year Team	Lg	G	AB	H	2B	3B	HR	(Hm	Rd)	TB	R	RBI	TBB	IBB	SO	HBP	SH	SF	SB	CS	SB%	GDP	Avg	OBP	SLG
1941 Boston	AL	10	4	2	1	0	0	--	--	3	2	2	3	0	0	0			0	0	.00	0	.500	.714	.750
1942 Boston	AL	36	67	18	2	1	2	--	--	28	10	4	3		7	0	3		0	0	.00	0	.269	.300	.418
1943 Boston	AL	27	54	14	1	1	0	--	--	17	2	0	5		4	0	3		0	0	.00	0	.259	.322	.315
1944 Boston	AL	10	11	2	0	0	0	--	--	2	4	1	3		0	0	0		0	0	.00	0	.182	.357	.182
1945 2 ML Teams		29	32	9	2	0	0	--	--	11	4	2	4		4	0	1		0			1	.281	.361	.344
1946 Philadelphia	NL	46	79	25	2	1	1	--	--	32	7	8	4		4	0	4		0			1	.316	.349	.405
1947 Philadelphia	NL	44	64	12	2	2	0	--	--	18	6	2	4		16	1	0		0				.188	.246	.281
1948 Philadelphia	NL	4	6	1	1	0	0	--	--	2	1	0	1		2	0	0		0			0	.167	.286	.333
1945 Boston	AL	2	2	1	0	0	0	--	--	1	0	0	0		0	0	0		0	0	.00	0	.500	.500	.500
Philadelphia	NL	27	30	8	2	0	0	--	--	10	4	2	4		4	0	1		0			1	.267	.353	.333
8 ML YEARS		206	317	83	11	5	3	--	--	113	36	19	27		37	1	11		0			2	.262	.322	.356

				FIELDING AS PITCHER							
Year Team	Lg	G	TC	PO	A	E	DP	PB	Pct.	Range	
1941 Boston	AL	7	5	0	4	1	0	--	.800	---	
1942 Boston	AL	31	36	6	29	1	1	--	.972	---	
1943 Boston	AL	23	53	9	41	3	4	--	.943	---	
1944 Boston	AL	9	5	1	4	0	0	--	1.000	---	
1945 2 ML Teams		25	27	4	23	0	0	--	1.000	---	
1946 Philadelphia	NL	30	60	10	50	0	4	--	1.000	---	
1947 Philadelphia	NL	32	41	7	33	1	3	--	.976	---	
1948 Philadelphia	NL	4	4	1	2	1	0	--	.750	---	
1945 Boston	AL	2	2	0	2	0	0	--	1.000	---	
Philadelphia	NL	23	25	4	21	0	0	--	1.000	---	
8 ML YEARS		161	231	38	186	7	12	--	.970	---	

Win Kellum

Winford Ansley Kellum **Height:** 5'10" **Weight:** 190

Pitches: Left **Bats:** Both **Born** on April 11, 1876 in Waterford, Ontario

Died on August 10, 1951 in Big Rapids, Michigan

		HOW MUCH HE PITCHED					WHAT HE GAVE UP										THE RESULTS				
Year Team	Lg	G	GS	CG	GF	IP	BFP	H	R	ER	HR	SH	SF	HB	TBB	IBB	SO	WP	Bk	W	L	Pct.	ShO	Sv	ERA
1901 Boston	AL	6	6	5	0	48	210	61	42	34	3	4		3	7		8	2	0	2	3	.400	0	0	6.38
1904 Cincinnati	NL	31	24	22	7	224.2	916	206	98	65	1	16		10	46		70	2	2	15	10	.600	1	2	2.60
1905 St. Louis	NL	11	7	5	4	74	297	70	30	24	1	11		1	10		19	1	0	3	3	.500	1	0	2.92
3 ML YEARS		48	37	32	11	346.2	1423	337	170	123	5	31		14	63		97	5	2	20	16	.556	2	2	3.19

BATTING

Year	Team	Lg	G	AB	H	2B	3B	HR	(Hm	Rd)	TB	R	RBI	TBB	IBB	SO	HBP	SH	SF	SB	CS	SB%	GDP	Avg	OBP	SLG
1901	Boston	AL	6	18	3	0	0	0	--	--	3	2	0	1				0	0	0					.167	.211	.167
1904	Cincinnati	NL	36	82	13	3	2	0	--	--	20	13	8	11				3	3	2					.159	.281	.244
1905	St. Louis	NL	11	25	5	0	0	0	--	--	5	2	3	3				0	1	0					.200	.286	.200
	3 ML YEARS		53	125	21	3	2	0	--	--	28	17	11	15				3	4	2					.168	.273	.224

FIELDING AS PITCHER

Year	Team	Lg	G	TC	PO	A	E	DP	PB	Pct.	Range
1901	Boston	AL	6	20	2	18	0	0	--	1.000	---
1904	Cincinnati	NL	31	82	16	64	2	1	--	.976	---
1905	St. Louis	NL	11	31	2	28	1	0	--	.968	---
	3 ML YEARS		48	133	20	110	3	1	--	.977	---

FIELDING AS OUTFIELDER

Year	Team	Lg	G	TC	PO	A	E	DP	PB	Pct.	Range
1904	Cincinnati	NL	5	5	5	0	0	0	--	1.000	1.00

Mel Kerr

John Melville Kerr
Bats: Left   **Throws:** Left

Height: 5'11" **Weight:** 155
Born on May 22, 1903 in Souris, Manitoba
Died on August 9, 1980 in Vero Beach, Florida

BATTING

Year	Team	Lg	G	AB	H	2B	3B	HR	(Hm	Rd)	TB	R	RBI	TBB	IBB	SO	HBP	SH	SF	SB	CS	SB%	GDP	Avg	OBP	SLG
1925	Chicago	NL	1	0	0	0	0	0	--	--	0	1	0	0	0	0	0	0	0	0	0	.00		.000	.000	.000

Mike Kilkenny

Michael David Kilkenny
Pitches: Left   **Bats:** Right

Height: 6'3" **Weight:** 175
Born on April 11, 1945 in Bradford, Ontario

HOW MUCH HE PITCHED / WHAT HE GAVE UP / THE RESULTS

Year	Team	Lg	G	GS	CG	GF	IP	BFP	H	R	ER	HR	SH	SF	HB	TBB	IBB	SO	WP	Bk	W	L	Pct.	ShO	Sv	ERA
1969	Detroit	AL	39	15	6	11	128.1	544	99	54	48	13	6	2	4	63	1	97	1	1	8	6	.571	4	2	3.37
1970	Detroit	AL	36	21	3	5	129	588	141	77	74	10	9	2	2	70	0	105	3	1	7	6	.538	0	0	5.16
1971	Detroit	AL	30	11	2	5	86.1	387	83	52	48	8	4	1	2	44	3	47	4	0	4	5	.444	0	0	5.00
1972	4 ML Teams		29	7	1	10	64.1	285	59	28	27	7	0	1	0	42	4	49	4	0	4	1	.800	0	1	3.78
1973	Cleveland	AL	5	0	0	1	2	17	5	5	5	1	0	0	1	5	0	3	0	0	0	0	.000	0	0	22.50
1972	Detroit	AL	1	0	0	1	1	4	1	1	1	1	0	0	0	0	0	0	0	0	0	0	.000	0	0	9.00
	Oakland	AL	1	0	0	0	1	3	0	0	0	0	0	0	0	0	0	0	0	0	0	0	.000	0	0	0.00
	Cleveland	AL	22	7	1	6	58	255	51	23	22	5	0	1	0	39	4	44	3	0	4	1	.800	0	0	3.41
	San Diego	NL	5	0	0	3	4.1	23	7	4	4	1	0	0	0	3	0	5	1	0	0	0	.000	0	0	8.31
	5 ML YEARS		139	54	12	32	410	1821	387	216	202	39	19	6	9	224	8	301	12	2	23	18	.561	4	4	4.43

BATTING

Year	Team	Lg	G	AB	H	2B	3B	HR	(Hm	Rd)	TB	R	RBI	TBB	IBB	SO	HBP	SH	SF	SB	CS	SB%	GDP	Avg	OBP	SLG
1969	Detroit	AL	39	37	2	0	0	0	(0	0)	2	1	4	2	0	21	0	3	0	0	0	.00	0	.054	.103	.054
1970	Detroit	AL	37	39	3	0	0	0	(0	0)	3	0	1	0	0	19	0	4	1	0	0	.00	0	.077	.075	.077
1971	Detroit	AL	30	24	2	0	0	0	(0	0)	2	0	0	0	0	14	0	1	0	0	0	.00	0	.083	.083	.083
1972	4 ML Teams		29	14	1	0	0	0	(0	0)	1	0	0	0	0	10	0	2	0	0	0	.00	0	.071	.071	.071
1972	Detroit	AL	1	0	0	0	0	0	(0	0)	0	0	0	0	0	0	0	0	0	0	0	.00	0	.000	.000	.000
	Oakland	AL	1	0	0	0	0	0	(0	0)	0	0	0	0	0	0	0	0	0	0	0	.00	0	.000	.000	.000
	Cleveland	AL	22	14	1	0	0	0	(0	0)	1	0	0	0	0	10	0	2	0	0	0	.00	0	.071	.071	.071
	San Diego	NL	5	0	0	0	0	0	(0	0)	0	0	0	0	0	0	0	0	0	0	0	.00	0	.000	.000	.000
	4 ML YEARS		135	114	8	0	0	0	(0	0)	8	1	5	2	0	64	0	10	1	0	0	.00	0	.070	.085	.070

FIELDING AS PITCHER

Year	Team	Lg	G	TC	PO	A	E	DP	PB	Pct.	Range
1969	Detroit	AL	39	25	5	19	1	0	--	.960	---
1970	Detroit	AL	36	27	6	20	1	1	--	.963	---
1971	Detroit	AL	30	20	4	14	2	0	--	.900	---
1972	4 ML Teams		29	15	4	11	0	2	--	1.000	---
1973	Cleveland	AL	5	1	0	1	0	0	--	1.000	---
1972	Detroit	AL	1	0	0	0	0	0	--	.000	---
	Oakland	AL	1	0	0	0	0	0	--	.000	---
	Cleveland	AL	22	14	4	10	0	2	--	1.000	---
	San Diego	NL	5	1	0	1	0	0	--	1.000	---
	5 ML YEARS		139	88	19	65	4	3	--	.955	---

Joe Knight

Joseph William Knight (Quiet Joe)
Bats: Left **Throws:** Left

Height: 5'11" **Weight:** 185
Born on September 28, 1859 in Port Stanley, Ontario
Died on October 16, 1938 in Lynhurst, Ontario

BATTING / BASERUNNING / PERCENTAGES

Year Team	Lg	G	AB	H	2B	3B	HR	(Hm	Rd)	TB	R	RBI	TBB	IBB	SO	HBP	SH	SF	SB	CS	SB%	GDP	Avg	OBP	SLG
1884 Philadelphia	NL	6	24	6	3	0	0	--	--	9	2	2	0		2								.250	.250	.375
1890 Cincinnati	NL	127	481	150	26	8	4	--	--	204	67	67	38		31	4			17				.312	.367	.424
2 ML YEARS		133	505	156	29	8	4	--	--	213	69	69	38		33	4	0						.309	.362	.422

HOW MUCH HE PITCHED / WHAT HE GAVE UP / THE RESULTS

Year Team	Lg	G	GS	CG	GF	IP	BFP	H	R	ER	HR	SH	SF	HB	TBB	IBB	SO	WP	Bk	W	L	Pct.	ShO	Sv	ERA
1884 Philadelphia	NL	6	6	6	0	51	246	66	53	31	2				21		8	2	0	2	4	.333	0	0	5.47

FIELDING AS PITCHER

Year Team	Lg	G	TC	PO	A	E	DP	PB	Pct.	Range
1884 Philadelphia	NL	6	19	3	12	4	0	--	.789	---

FIELDING AS OUTFIELDER

Year Team	Lg	G	TC	PO	A	E	DP	PB	Pct.	Range
1890 Cincinnati	NL	127	254	224	11	19	0	--	.925	1.85

Jimmy Knowles

James Knowles (Darby)
Bats: Unknown **Throws:** Unknown

Height: 5'9" **Weight:** 160
Born in 1859 in Toronto, Ontario
Died on February 11, 1912 in Jersey City, New Jersey

BATTING / BASERUNNING / PERCENTAGES

Year Team	Lg	G	AB	H	2B	3B	HR	(Hm	Rd)	TB	R	RBI	TBB	IBB	SO	HBP	SH	SF	SB	CS	SB%	GDP	Avg	OBP	SLG
1884 2 ML Teams		87	335	78	10	8	1	--	--	107	38		8			3							.233	.257	.319
1886 Washington	NL	115	443	94	16	11	3	--	--	141	43	35	15		73				20				.212	.238	.318
1887 New York	AA	16	60	15	1	1	0	--	--	18	12		1			0			6				.250	.262	.300
1890 Rochester	AA	123	491	138	12	8	5	--	--	181	83		59			1			55				.281	.359	.369
1892 New York	NL	16	59	9	1	0	0	--	--	10	9	7	6	8		0			2				.153	.231	.169
1884 Pittsburgh	AA	46	182	42	5	7	0	--	--	61	19		5			2							.231	.259	.335
Brooklyn	AA	41	153	36	5	1	1	--	--	46	19		3			1							.235	.255	.301
5 ML YEARS		357	1388	334	40	28	9	--	--	457	185		89			4	0						.241	.288	.329

FIELDING AS FIRST BASEMAN

Year Team	Lg	G	TC	PO	A	E	DP	PB	Pct.	Range
1884 2 ML Teams		76	879	809	33	37	38	--	.958	---
1884 Pittsburgh	AA	46	535	499	15	21	20	--	.961	---
Brooklyn	AA	30	344	310	18	16	18	--	.953	---

FIELDING AS SECOND BASEMAN

Year Team	Lg	G	TC	PO	A	E	DP	PB	Pct.	Range
1886 Washington	NL	62	467	196	224	47	32	--	.899	6.77
1887 New York	AA	16	91	49	36	6	4	--	.934	5.31
2 ML YEARS		78	558	245	260	53	36	--	.905	6.47

FIELDING AS THIRD BASEMAN

Year Team	Lg	G	TC	PO	A	E	DP	PB	Pct.	Range
1884 Brooklyn	AA	11	35	9	18	8	0	--	.771	2.45
1886 Washington	NL	53	224	68	122	34	10	--	.848	3.58
1887 New York	AA	1	2	0	1	1	0	--	.500	1.00
1890 Rochester	AA	123	528	162	303	63	19	--	.881	3.78
1892 New York	NL	15	48	13	25	10	2	--	.792	2.53
5 ML YEARS		203	837	252	469	116	31	--	.861	3.55

FIELDING AS SHORTSTOP

Year Team	Lg	G	TC	PO	A	E	DP	PB	Pct.	Range
1892 New York	NL	1	2	1	1	0	0	--	1.000	2.00

George Korince

George Eugene Korince (Moose)
Pitches: Right **Bats:** Right

Height: 6'3" **Weight:** 210
Born on January 10, 1946 in Ottawa, Ontario

HOW MUCH HE PITCHED / WHAT HE GAVE UP / THE RESULTS

Year Team	Lg	G	GS	CG	GF	IP	BFP	H	R	ER	HR	SH	SF	HB	TBB	IBB	SO	WP	Bk	W	L	Pct.	ShO	Sv	ERA
1966 Detroit	AL	2	0	0	2	3	15	1	0	0	0	0	0	1	3	0	2	0	0	0	0	.000	0	0	0.00
1967 Detroit	AL	9	0	0	2	14	64	10	8	8	1	2	2	0	11	1	11	0	0	1	0	1.000	0	0	5.14
2 ML YEARS		11	0	0	4	17	79	11	8	8	1	2	2	1	14	1	13	0	0	1	0	1.000	0	0	4.24

							BATTING													BASERUNNING				PERCENTAGES		
Year Team	Lg	G	AB	H	2B	3B	HR	(Hm	Rd)	TB	R	RBI	TBB	IBB	SO	HBP	SH	SF		SB	CS	SB%	GDP	Avg	OBP	SLG
1966 Detroit	AL	2	0	0	0	0	0	(0	0)	0	0	0	0	0	0	0	0	0		0	0	.00	0	.000	.000	.000
1967 Detroit	AL	9	1	0	0	0	0	(0	0)	0	0	0	0	0	1	0	0	0		0	0	.00	0	.000	.000	.000
2 ML YEARS		11	1	0	0	0	0	(0	0)	0	0	0	0	0	1	0	0	0		0	0	.00	0	.000	.000	.000

				FIELDING AS PITCHER							
Year Team	Lg	G	TC	PO	A	E	DP	PB	Pct.	Range	
1966 Detroit	AL	2	0	0	0	0	0	--	.000	---	
1967 Detroit	AL	9	3	1	2	0	0	--	1.000	---	
2 ML YEARS		11	3	1	2	0	0	--	1.000	---	

Joe Krakauskas

Joseph Victor Lawrence Krakauskas

Pitches: Left **Bats:** Left

Height: 6'1" **Weight:** 203

Born on March 28, 1915 in Montreal, Quebec

Died on July 8, 1960 in Hamilton, Ontario

				HOW MUCH HE PITCHED						WHAT HE GAVE UP										THE RESULTS					
Year Team	Lg	G	GS	CG	GF	IP	BFP	H	R	ER	HR	SH	SF	HB	TBB	IBB	SO	WP	Bk	W	L	Pct.	ShO	Sv	ERA
1937 Washington	AL	5	4	3	1	40	168	33	14	12	0	0		0	22		18	0	0	4	1	.800	0	0	2.70
1938 Washington	AL	29	10	5	11	121.1	551	99	61	42	4	11		3	88		104	4	0	7	5	.583	1	0	3.12
1939 Washington	AL	39	29	12	8	217.1	966	230	125	111	13	17		1	114		110	5	1	11	17	.393	0	1	4.60
1940 Washington	AL	32	10	2	16	109	527	137	90	78	7	10		0	73		68	7	0	1	6	.143	0	2	6.44
1941 Cleveland	AL	12	5	0	5	41.2	189	39	25	19	3	1		0	29		25	1	0	1	2	.333	0	0	4.10
1942 Cleveland	AL	3	0	0	2	7	32	7	3	3	1	1		0	4		2	1	0	0	0	.000	0	0	3.86
1946 Cleveland	AL	29	5	0	11	47.1	221	60	31	29	2	5		0	25		20	1	0	2	5	.286	0	1	5.51
7 ML YEARS		149	63	22	54	583.2	2654	605	349	294	30	45		4	355		347	19	1	26	36	.419	1	4	4.53

							BATTING													BASERUNNING				PERCENTAGES		
Year Team	Lg	G	AB	H	2B	3B	HR	(Hm	Rd)	TB	R	RBI	TBB	IBB	SO	HBP	SH	SF		SB	CS	SB%	GDP	Avg	OBP	SLG
1937 Washington	AL	5	16	2	0	1	0	--	--	4	2	1	1		7	0	0			0	0	.00		.125	.176	.250
1938 Washington	AL	29	33	6	2	0	0	--	--	8	7	1	4		12	0	3			0	0	.00		.182	.270	.242
1939 Washington	AL	39	77	16	3	1	0	--	--	21	6	8	8		24	0	3			0	0	.00	3	.208	.282	.273
1940 Washington	AL	32	32	8	2	0	0	--	--	10	3	1	0		10	0	0			0	0	.00	3	.250	.250	.313
1941 Cleveland	AL	12	13	1	0	0	0	--	--	1	0	0	0		5	0	0			0	0	.00	0	.077	.077	.077
1942 Cleveland	AL	3	2	0	0	0	0	--	--	0	0	0	0		0	0	0			0	0	.00		.000	.000	.000
1946 Cleveland	AL	29	10	0	0	0	0	--	--	0	0	0	0		4	0	0			0	0	.00		.000	.000	.000
7 ML YEARS		149	183	33	7	2	0	--	--	44	18	11	13		62	0	6			0	0	.00		.180	.235	.240

				FIELDING AS PITCHER							
Year Team	Lg	G	TC	PO	A	E	DP	PB	Pct.	Range	
1937 Washington	AL	5	8	1	4	3	0	--	.625	---	
1938 Washington	AL	29	20	3	16	1	0	--	.950	---	
1939 Washington	AL	39	35	6	26	3	2	--	.914	---	
1940 Washington	AL	32	28	2	24	2	3	--	.929	---	
1941 Cleveland	AL	12	13	2	11	0	0	--	1.000	---	
1942 Cleveland	AL	3	4	0	4	0	0	--	1.000	---	
1946 Cleveland	AL	29	15	2	12	1	0	--	.933	---	
7 ML YEARS		149	123	16	97	10	5	--	.919	---	

Andy Kyle

Andrew Ewing Kyle

Bats: Left **Throws:** Left

Height: 5'8" **Weight:** 160

Born on October 29, 1889 in Toronto, Ontario

Died on September 6, 1971 in Toronto, Ontario

							BATTING													BASERUNNING				PERCENTAGES		
Year Team	Lg	G	AB	H	2B	3B	HR	(Hm	Rd)	TB	R	RBI	TBB	IBB	SO	HBP	SH	SF		SB	CS	SB%	GDP	Avg	OBP	SLG
1912 Cincinnati	NL	9	21	7	1	0	0	--	--	8	3	4	4		2	0	1			0				.333	.440	.381

				FIELDING AS OUTFIELDER							
Year Team	Lg	G	TC	PO	A	E	DP	PB	Pct.	Range	
1912 Cincinnati	NL	7	16	15	1	0	0	--	1.000	2.29	

Ty LaForest

Byron Joseph LaForest
Bats: Right **Throws:** Right

Height: 5'9" **Weight:** 165
Born on April 18, 1917 in Edmundston, New Brunswick
Died on May 5, 1947 in Arlington, Massachusetts

								BATTING											BASERUNNING				PERCENTAGES		
Year Team	Lg	G	AB	H	2B	3B	HR	(Hm Rd)	TB	R	RBI	TBB	IBB	SO	HBP	SH	SF	SB	CS	SB%	GDP	Avg	OBP	SLG
1945 Boston	AL	52	204	51	7	4	2	-- --	72	25	16	10		35	0	6		4	4	.50	7	.250	.285	.353

FIELDING AS THIRD BASEMAN

Year Team	Lg	G	TC	PO	A	E	DP	PB	Pct.	Range
1945 Boston	AL	45	147	45	97	5	11	--	.966	3.16

FIELDING AS OUTFIELDER

Year Team	Lg	G	TC	PO	A	E	DP	PB	Pct.	Range
1945 Boston	AL	5	6	6	0	0	0	--	1.000	1.20

Fred Lake

Frederick Lovett Lake
Bats: Right **Throws:** Right

Height: 5'10" **Weight:** 170
Born on October 16, 1866 in Nova Scotia
Died on November 24, 1931 in Boston, Massachusetts

								BATTING											BASERUNNING				PERCENTAGES		
Year Team	Lg	G	AB	H	2B	3B	HR	(Hm Rd)	TB	R	RBI	TBB	IBB	SO	HBP	SH	SF	SB	CS	SB%	GDP	Avg	OBP	SLG
1891 Boston	NL	5	7	1	0	0	0	-- --	1	1	0	2		4	0			0				.143	.333	.143
1894 Louisville	NL	16	42	12	2	0	1	-- --	17	8	10	11		6	4	0		2				.286	.474	.405
1897 Boston	NL	19	62	15	4	0	0	-- --	19	2	5	1		0	2			2				.242	.254	.306
1898 Pittsburgh	NL	5	13	1	0	0	0	-- --	1	1	1	2		0	1			0				.077	.200	.077
1910 Boston	NL	3	1	0	0	0	0	-- --	0	0	0	1	0	0	0			0				.000	.500	.000
5 ML YEARS		48	125	29	6	0	1	-- --	38	12	16	17		4	3			4				.232	.342	.304

World Series (Temple Cup) Batting

								BATTING											BASERUNNING				PERCENTAGES		
Year Team	Lg	G	AB	H	2B	3B	HR	(Hm Rd)	TB	R	RBI	TBB	IBB	SO	HBP	SH	SF	SB	CS	SB%	GDP	Avg	OBP	SLG
1897 Boston	NL	1	4	0	0	0	0	(0 0)	0	0	0	0	0	1	0	0		0	0	.00		.000	.000	.000

FIELDING AS CATCHER

Year Team	Lg	G	TC	PO	A	E	DP	PB	Pct.	Range
1891 Boston	NL	4	4	3	1	0	0	1	1.000	---
1894 Louisville	NL	5	30	20	5	5	1	0	.833	---
1897 Boston	NL	18	66	49	15	2	0	4	.970	---
3 ML YEARS		27	100	72	21	7	1	5	.930	---

FIELDING AS FIRST BASEMAN

Year Team	Lg	G	TC	PO	A	E	DP	PB	Pct.	Range
1898 Pittsburgh	NL	3	34	33	1	0	3	--	1.000	---

FIELDING AS SECOND BASEMAN

Year Team	Lg	G	TC	PO	A	E	DP	PB	Pct.	Range
1894 Louisville	NL	6	22	10	9	3	4	--	.864	3.17

FIELDING AS SHORTSTOP

Year Team	Lg	G	TC	PO	A	E	DP	PB	Pct.	Range
1894 Louisville	NL	5	16	6	7	3	0	--	.813	2.60

FIELDING AS OUTFIELDER

Year Team	Lg	G	TC	PO	A	E	DP	PB	Pct.	Range
1891 Boston	NL	1	1	0	1	0	0	--	1.000	1.00

World Series (Temple Cup) Fielding

FIELDING AS CATCHER

Year Team	Lg	G	TC	PO	A	E	DP	PB	Pct.	Range
1897 Boston	NL	1	3	1	1	1	0	0	.667	---

Larry Landreth

Larry Robert Landreth
Pitches: Right **Bats:** Right

Height: 6'1" **Weight:** 175
Born on March 11, 1955 in Stratford, Ontario

		HOW MUCH HE PITCHED						WHAT HE GAVE UP												THE RESULTS					
Year Team	Lg	G	GS	CG	GF	IP	BFP	H	R	ER	HR	SH	SF	HB	TBB	IBB	SO	WP	Bk	W	L	Pct.	ShO	Sv	ERA
1976 Montreal	NL	3	3	0	0	11	53	13	8	5	1	0	1	0	10	0	7	0	1	1	2	.333	0	0	4.09
1977 Montreal	NL	4	1	0	0	9.1	51	16	11	10	0	0	1	0	8	1	5	1	0	0	2	.000	0	0	9.64
2 ML YEARS		7	4	0	0	20.1	104	29	19	15	1	0	2	0	18	1	12	1	1	1	4	.200	0	0	6.64

						BATTING														BASERUNNING				PERCENTAGES		
Year Team	Lg	G	AB	H	2B	3B	HR	(Hm	Rd)	TB	R	RBI	TBB	IBB	SO	HBP	SH	SF	SB	CS	SB%	GDP	Avg	OBP	SLG
1976 Montreal	NL	3	3	0	0	0	0	(0	0)	0	0	0	0	0	2	0	0	0	0	0	.00	0	.000	.000	.000
1977 Montreal	NL	4	2	0	0	0	0	(0	0)	0	0	0	0	0	1	0	0	0	0	0	.00	0	.000	.000	.000
2 ML YEARS		7	5	0	0	0	0	(0	0)	0	0	0	0	0	3	0	0	0	0	0	.00	0	.000	.000	.000

FIELDING AS PITCHER

Year Team	Lg	G	TC	PO	A	E	DP	PB	Pct.	Range
1976 Montreal	NL	3	1	0	1	0	0	--	1.000	---
1977 Montreal	NL	4	0	0	0	0	0	--	.000	---
2 ML YEARS		7	1	0	1	0	0	--	1.000	---

Sam LaRoque

Samuel H.J. LaRoque **Height:** 5'11" **Weight:** 190
Bats: Unknown **Throws:** Right **Born** on February 26, 1864 in St. Mathias, Quebec

						BATTING														BASERUNNING				PERCENTAGES		
Year Team	Lg	G	AB	H	2B	3B	HR	(Hm	Rd)	TB	R	RBI	TBB	IBB	SO	HBP	SH	SF	SB	CS	SB%	GDP	Avg	OBP	SLG
1888 Detroit	NL	2	9	4	0	0	0	--	--	4	1	2	1		1	0			0				.444	.500	.444
1890 Pittsburgh	NL	111	434	105	20	4	1	--	--	136	59	40	35		29	12			27				.242	.316	.313
1891 2 ML Teams		11	39	11	2	1	1	--	--	18	6	8	5		9	2			1				.282	.391	.462
1891 Pittsburgh	NL	1	4	0	0	0	0	--	--	0	0	0	0		1	0			0				.000	.000	.000
Louisville	AA	10	35	11	2	1	1	--	--	18	6	8	5		8	2			1				.314	.429	.514
3 ML YEARS		124	482	120	22	5	2	--	--	158	66	50	41		39	14	0		28				.249	.326	.328

FIELDING AS FIRST BASEMAN

Year Team	Lg	G	TC	PO	A	E	DP	PB	Pct.	Range
1890 Pittsburgh	NL	2	17	15	1	1	1	--	.941	---
1891 Louisville	AA	1	2	2	0	0	0	--	1.000	---
2 ML YEARS		3	19	17	1	1	1	--	.947	---

FIELDING AS SECOND BASEMAN

Year Team	Lg	G	TC	PO	A	E	DP	PB	Pct.	Range
1888 Detroit	NL	2	19	7	8	4	3	--	.789	7.50
1890 Pittsburgh	NL	78	509	227	244	38	32	--	.925	6.04
1891 Louisville	AA	10	56	27	22	7	4	--	.875	4.90
3 ML YEARS		90	584	261	274	49	39	--	.916	5.94

FIELDING AS THIRD BASEMAN

Year Team	Lg	G	TC	PO	A	E	DP	PB	Pct.	Range
1891 Pittsburgh	NL	1	7	2	3	2	0	--	.714	5.00

FIELDING AS SHORTSTOP

Year Team	Lg	G	TC	PO	A	E	DP	PB	Pct.	Range
1890 Pittsburgh	NL	31	160	48	76	36	2	--	.775	4.00

FIELDING AS OUTFIELDER

Year Team	Lg	G	TC	PO	A	E	DP	PB	Pct.	Range
1890 Pittsburgh	NL	1	3	2	0	1	0	--	.667	2.00

Ron Law

Ronald David Law **Height:** 6'2" **Weight:** 165
Pitches: Right **Bats:** Right **Born** on March 14, 1946 in Hamilton, Ontario

		HOW MUCH HE PITCHED						WHAT HE GAVE UP										THE RESULTS					
Year Team	Lg	G	GS	CG	GF	IP	BFP	H	R	ER	HR	SH	SF	HB	TBB	IBB	SO	WP	Bk	W	L	Pct.	ShO	Sv	ERA
1969 Cleveland	AL	35	1	0	14	52.1	254	68	34	29	2	6	3	2	34	5	29	4	0	3	4	.429	0	1	4.99

						BATTING														BASERUNNING				PERCENTAGES		
Year Team	Lg	G	AB	H	2B	3B	HR	(Hm	Rd)	TB	R	RBI	TBB	IBB	SO	HBP	SH	SF	SB	CS	SB%	GDP	Avg	OBP	SLG
1969 Cleveland	AL	35	7	1	0	0	0	(0	0)	1	0	0	0	0	1	0	0	0	0	0	.00	1	.143	.143	.143

FIELDING AS PITCHER

Year Team	Lg	G	TC	PO	A	E	DP	PB	Pct.	Range
1969 Cleveland	AL	35	14	4	9	1	1	--	.929	---

Jim Lawrence

James Ross Lawrence
Bats: Left **Throws:** Right

Height: 6'1" **Weight:** 185
Born on February 12, 1939 in Hamilton, Ontario

BATTING | | | BASERUNNING | PERCENTAGES

Year Team	Lg	G	AB	H	2B	3B	HR	(Hm	Rd)	TB	R	RBI	TBB	IBB	SO	HBP	SH	SF	SB	CS	SB%	GDP	Avg	OBP	SLG
1963 Cleveland	AL	2	0	0	0	0	0	(0	0)	0	0	0	0	0	0	0	0	0	0	0	.00	0	.000	.000	.000

FIELDING AS CATCHER

Year Team	Lg	G	TC	PO	A	E	DP	PB	Pct.	Range
1963 Cleveland	AL	2	4	3	0	1	0	0	.750	---

Pete LePine

Louis Joseph LePine
Bats: Left **Throws:** Left

Height: 5'10" **Weight:** 142
Born on September 5, 1876 in Montreal, Quebec
Died on December 3, 1949 in Woonsocket, Rhode Island

BATTING | | | BASERUNNING | PERCENTAGES

Year Team	Lg	G	AB	H	2B	3B	HR	(Hm	Rd)	TB	R	RBI	TBB	IBB	SO	HBP	SH	SF	SB	CS	SB%	GDP	Avg	OBP	SLG
1902 Detroit	AL	30	96	20	3	2	1	--	--	30	8	19	8			1	3		1				.208	.276	.313

FIELDING AS FIRST BASEMAN

Year Team	Lg	G	TC	PO	A	E	DP	PB	Pct.	Range
1902 Detroit	AL	8	69	59	7	3	5	--	.957	---

FIELDING AS OUTFIELDER

Year Team	Lg	G	TC	PO	A	E	DP	PB	Pct.	Range
1902 Detroit	AL	19	20	18	2	0	1	--	1.000	1.05

Dick Lines

Richard George Lines
Pitches: Left **Bats:** Right

Height: 6'1" **Weight:** 175
Born on August 17, 1938 in Montreal, Quebec

HOW MUCH HE PITCHED | | | WHAT HE GAVE UP | | | THE RESULTS

Year Team	Lg	G	GS	CG	GF	IP	BFP	H	R	ER	HR	SH	SF	HB	TBB	IBB	SO	WP	Bk	W	L	Pct.	ShO	Sv	ERA
1966 Washington	AL	53	0	0	20	83	326	63	23	21	4	4	1	1	24	7	49	2	0	5	2	.714	0	2	2.28
1967 Washington	AL	54	0	0	21	85.2	370	83	43	32	6	3	4	0	24	6	54	4	0	2	5	.286	0	4	3.36
2 ML YEARS		107	0	0	41	168.2	696	146	66	53	10	7	5	1	48	13	103	6	0	7	7	.500	0	6	2.83

BATTING | | | BASERUNNING | PERCENTAGES

Year Team	Lg	G	AB	H	2B	3B	HR	(Hm	Rd)	TB	R	RBI	TBB	IBB	SO	HBP	SH	SF	SB	CS	SB%	GDP	Avg	OBP	SLG
1966 Washington	AL	53	10	0	0	0	0	(0	0)	0	0	0	0	0	6	0	2	0	0	0	.00	0	.000	.000	.000
1967 Washington	AL	54	9	1	0	0	0	(0	0)	1	2	0	3	0	3	0	0	0	0	0	.00	0	.111	.333	.111
2 ML YEARS		107	19	1	0	0	0	(0	0)	1	2	0	3	0	9	0	2	0	0	0	.00	0	.053	.182	.053

FIELDING AS PITCHER

Year Team	Lg	G	TC	PO	A	E	DP	PB	Pct.	Range
1966 Washington	AL	53	28	4	23	1	3	--	.964	---
1967 Washington	AL	54	24	5	16	3	2	--	.875	---
2 ML YEARS		107	52	9	39	4	5	--	.923	---

Rick Lisi

Ricardo Patrick Emilio Lisi
Bats: Right **Throws:** Right

Height: 6'0" **Weight:** 175
Born on March 17, 1956 in Halifax, Nova Scotia

BATTING | | | BASERUNNING | PERCENTAGES

Year Team	Lg	G	AB	H	2B	3B	HR	(Hm	Rd)	TB	R	RBI	TBB	IBB	SO	HBP	SH	SF	SB	CS	SB%	GDP	Avg	OBP	SLG
1981 Texas	AL	9	16	5	0	0	0	(0	0)	5	6	1	4	0	0	0	0	0	0	1	.00	0	.313	.450	.313

FIELDING AS OUTFIELDER

Year Team	Lg	G	TC	PO	A	E	DP	PB	Pct.	Range
1981 Texas	AL	8	9	9	0	0	0	--	1.000	1.13

Red Long

Nelson Long
Pitches: Right **Bats:** Right

Height: 6'1" **Weight:** 190
Born on September 28, 1876 in Burlington, Ontario
Died on August 11, 1929 in Hamilton, Ontario

				HOW MUCH HE PITCHED				WHAT HE GAVE UP										THE RESULTS				
Year Team	Lg	G	GS	CG	GF	IP	BFP	H	R	ER	HR	SH	SF	HB	TBB	IBB	SO	WP	Bk	W	L	Pct.	ShO	Sv	ERA
1902 Boston	NL	1	1	1	0	8	33	4	2	1	0	0		1	3		5	0	0	0	0	.000	0	0	1.13

					BATTING													BASERUNNING				PERCENTAGES		
Year Team	Lg	G	AB	H	2B	3B	HR	(Hm	Rd)	TB	R	RBI	TBB	IBB	SO	HBP	SH	SF	SB	CS	SB%	GDP	Avg	OBP	SLG
1902 Boston	NL	1	3	0	0	0	0	--	--	0	0	0	0		0	0			0				.000	.000	.000

			FIELDING AS PITCHER							
Year Team	Lg	G	TC	PO	A	E	DP	PB	Pct.	Range
1902 Boston	NL	1	1	1	0	0	0	--	1.000	---

Pat Lyons

Patrick Jerry Lyons
Bats: Unknown **Throws:** Right

Height: Unknown **Weight:** Unknown
Born in March, 1860 in Canada
Died on January 20, 1914 in Springfield, Ohio

					BATTING													BASERUNNING				PERCENTAGES		
Year Team	Lg	G	AB	H	2B	3B	HR	(Hm	Rd)	TB	R	RBI	TBB	IBB	SO	HBP	SH	SF	SB	CS	SB%	GDP	Avg	OBP	SLG
1890 Cleveland	NL	11	38	2	1	0	0	--	--	3	2	1	4		4	0			0				.053	.143	.079

			FIELDING AS SECOND BASEMAN							
Year Team	Lg	G	TC	PO	A	E	DP	PB	Pct.	Range
1890 Cleveland	NL	11	62	24	28	10	2	--	.839	4.73

Eric MacKenzie

Eric Hugh MacKenzie
Bats: Left **Throws:** Right

Height: 6'0" **Weight:** 185
Born on August 29, 1932 in Glendon, Alberta

					BATTING													BASERUNNING				PERCENTAGES		
Year Team	Lg	G	AB	H	2B	3B	HR	(Hm	Rd)	TB	R	RBI	TBB	IBB	SO	HBP	SH	SF	SB	CS	SB%	GDP	Avg	OBP	SLG
1955 Kansas City	AL	1	1	0	0	0	0	(0	0)	0	0	0	0	0	0	0	0	0	0	0	.00	0	.000	.000	.000

			FIELDING AS CATCHER							
Year Team	Lg	G	TC	PO	A	E	DP	PB	Pct.	Range
1955 Kansas City	AL	1	0	0	0	0	0	0	.000	---

Ken MacKenzie

Kenneth Purvis MacKenzie
Pitches: Left **Bats:** Right

Height: 6'0" **Weight:** 185
Born on March 10, 1934 in Gore Bay, Ontario

				HOW MUCH HE PITCHED				WHAT HE GAVE UP										THE RESULTS				
Year Team	Lg	G	GS	CG	GF	IP	BFP	H	R	ER	HR	SH	SF	HB	TBB	IBB	SO	WP	Bk	W	L	Pct.	ShO	Sv	ERA
1960 Milwaukee	NL	9	0	0	6	8.1	37	9	7	6	2	1	1	0	3	2	9	0	0	0	1	.000	0	0	6.48
1961 Milwaukee	NL	5	0	0	1	7	31	8	5	4	1	1	0	1	2	0	5	0	0	0	1	.000	0	0	5.14
1962 New York	NL	42	1	0	16	80	355	87	47	44	10	4	3	3	34	3	51	0	0	5	4	.556	0	1	4.95
1963 2 ML Teams		42	0	0	21	66.1	291	72	41	36	12	1	1	2	15	3	48	0	0	3	1	.750	0	3	4.88
1964 San Francisco	NL	10	0	0	3	9	41	9	7	5	1	2	2	0	3	0	3	0	0	0	0	.000	0	1	5.00
1965 Houston	NL	21	0	0	10	37	161	46	22	16	7	1	0	0	6	0	26	1	0	0	3	.000	0	0	3.89
1963 New York	NL	34	0	0	17	57.2	252	63	35	32	11	1	1	2	12	2	41	0	0	3	1	.750	0	3	4.99
St. Louis	NL	8	0	0	4	8.2	39	9	6	4	1	0	0	0	3	1	7	0	0	0	0	.000	0	0	4.15
6 ML YEARS		129	1	0	57	207.2	916	231	129	111	33	10	7	6	63	8	142	1	0	8	10	.444	0	5	4.81

					BATTING													BASERUNNING				PERCENTAGES		
Year Team	Lg	G	AB	H	2B	3B	HR	(Hm	Rd)	TB	R	RBI	TBB	IBB	SO	HBP	SH	SF	SB	CS	SB%	GDP	Avg	OBP	SLG
1960 Milwaukee	NL	9	1	0	0	0	0	(0	0)	0	0	0	1	0	0	0	0	0	0	0	.00	0	.000	.000	.000
1961 Milwaukee	NL	5	2	0	0	0	0	(0	0)	0	1	0	0	0	0	0	0	0	0	0	.00	0	.000	.000	.000
1962 New York	NL	42	12	1	0	0	0	(0	0)	1	0	1	0	0	6	0	1	0	0	0	.00	0	.083	.083	.083
1963 2 ML Teams		42	10	0	0	0	0	(0	0)	0	0	0	0	0	5	0	0	0	0	0	.00	0	.000	.000	.000
1964 San Francisco	NL	10	0	0	0	0	0	(0	0)	0	0	0	0	0	0	0	0	0	0	0	.00	0	.000	.000	.000
1965 Houston	NL	21	11	3	0	0	0	(0	0)	3	0	0	0	0	5	0	0	0	0	0	.00	0	.273	.273	.273
1963 New York	NL	34	10	0	0	0	0	(0	0)	0	0	0	0	0	5	0	0	0	0	0	.00	0	.000	.000	.000
St. Louis	NL	8	0	0	0	0	0	(0	0)	0	0	0	0	0	0	0	0	0	0	0	.00	0	.000	.000	.000
6 ML YEARS		129	36	4	0	0	0	(0	0)	4	1	1	0	0	17	0	1	0	0	0	.00	0	.111	.111	.111

Year	Team	Lg	G	TC	PO	A	E	DP	PB	Pct.	Range
FIELDING AS PITCHER											
1960	Milwaukee	NL	9	1	1	0	0	0	--	1.000	---
1961	Milwaukee	NL	5	3	0	3	0	0	--	1.000	---
1962	New York	NL	42	21	3	16	2	3	--	.905	---
1963	2 ML Teams		42	11	3	6	2	0	--	.818	---
1964	San Francisco	NL	10	4	1	3	0	0	--	1.000	---
1965	Houston	NL	21	6	0	6	0	1	--	1.000	---
1963	New York	NL	34	10	3	6	1	0	--	.900	---
	St. Louis	NL	8	1	0	0	1	0	--	.000	---
	6 ML YEARS		129	46	8	34	4	4	--	.913	---

Bill Magee

William J. Magee

Pitches: Right   **Bats:** Right

Height: 5'10"   **Weight:** 154
Born in 1875 in Canada

			HOW MUCH HE PITCHED						**WHAT HE GAVE UP**											**THE RESULTS**					
Year	Team	Lg	G	GS	CG	GF	IP	BFP	H	R	ER	HR	SH	SF	HB	TBB	IBB	SO	WP	Bk	W	L	Pct.	ShO	Sv	ERA
1897	Louisville	NL	22	16	13	6	155.1	754	186	136	93	6	5		11	99		44	6	0	4	12	.250	1	0	5.39
1898	Louisville	NL	38	33	29	5	295.1	1293	294	163	133	8	26		19	129		55	3	1	16	15	.516	1	0	4.05
1899	3 ML Teams		29	26	17	3	183	869	227	153	125	4	9		23	88		28	6	1	7	16	.304	1	0	6.15
1901	2 ML Teams		7	6	4	1	50.1	233	64	40	32	4	8		4	15		17	2	0	0	4	.000	0	0	5.72
1902	2 ML Teams		10	7	6	3	58.2	247	66	30	24	1	1		3	19		17	1	0	2	4	.333	0	0	3.68
1899	Louisville	NL	12	10	6	2	71	335	91	58	41	1	3		9	28		13	2	0	3	7	.300	1	0	5.20
	Philadelphia	NL	9	9	7	0	70	328	82	50	44	0	6		7	32		4	3	1	3	5	.375	0	0	5.66
	Washington	NL	8	7	4	1	42	206	54	45	40	3	0		7	28		11	1	0	1	4	.200	0	0	8.57
1901	St. Louis	NL	1	1	0	0	8	35	8	4	4	0	0		0	4		3	1	0	0	0	.000	0	0	4.50
	New York	NL	6	5	4	1	42.1	198	56	36	28	4	8		4	11		14	1	0	0	4	.000	0	0	5.95
1902	New York	NL	2	1	0	1	5	21	5	2	2	0	0		0	1		2	0	0	0	0	.000	0	0	3.60
	Philadelphia	NL	8	6	6	2	53.2	226	61	28	22	1	1		3	18		15	1	0	2	4	.333	0	0	3.69
	5 ML YEARS		106	88	69	18	742.2	3396	837	522	407	23	49		60	350		161	18	2	29	51	.363	5	0	4.93

			BATTING																		**BASERUNNING**				**PERCENTAGES**		
Year	Team	Lg	G	AB	H	2B	3B	HR	(Hm	Rd)	TB	R	RBI	TBB	IBB	SO	HBP	SH	SF	SB	CS	SB%	GDP	Avg	OBP	SLG
1897	Louisville	NL	22	62	13	1	0	0	--	--	14	4	9	4			0	1		0				.210	.258	.226
1898	Louisville	NL	38	111	14	1	0	0	--	--	15	10	5	2			1	1		2				.126	.149	.135
1899	3 ML Teams		29	73	13	2	1	0	--	--	17	2	9	2			0	4		0				.178	.200	.233
1901	2 ML Teams		7	18	4	0	1	0	--	--	6	1	2	1			0	0		0				.222	.263	.333
1902	2 ML Teams		10	20	4	0	0	0	--	--	4	2	2	0			0	0		0				.200	.200	.200
1899	Louisville	NL	12	27	3	1	1	0	--	--	6	1	5	0			0	2		0				.111	.111	.222
	Philadelphia	NL	9	31	5	0	0	0	--	--	5	0	2	1			0	1		0				.161	.188	.161
	Washington	NL	8	15	5	1	0	0	--	--	6	1	2	1			0	1		0				.333	.375	.400
1901	St. Louis	NL	1	4	2	0	1	0	--	--	4	1	0	0			0	0		0				.500	.500	1.000
	New York	NL	6	14	2	0	0	0	--	--	2	0	2	1			0	0		0				.143	.200	.143
1902	New York	NL	2	1	0	0	0	0	--	--	0	0	0	0			0	0		0				.000	.000	.000
	Philadelphia	NL	8	19	4	0	0	0	--	--	4	2	2	0			0	0		0				.211	.211	.211
	5 ML YEARS		106	284	48	4	2	0	--	--	56	19	27	9			1	6		2				.169	.197	.197

Year	Team	Lg	G	TC	PO	A	E	DP	PB	Pct.	Range
FIELDING AS PITCHER											
1897	Louisville	NL	22	53	4	42	7	1	--	.868	---
1898	Louisville	NL	38	82	11	65	6	3	--	.927	---
1899	3 ML Teams		29	66	8	51	7	0	--	.894	---
1901	2 ML Teams		7	14	4	10	0	0	--	1.000	---
1902	2 ML Teams		10	20	0	16	4	1	--	.800	---
1899	Louisville	NL	12	29	5	22	2	0	--	.931	---
	Philadelphia	NL	9	22	1	16	5	0	--	.773	---
	Washington	NL	8	15	2	13	0	0	--	1.000	---
1901	St. Louis	NL	1	1	1	0	0	0	--	1.000	---
	New York	NL	6	13	3	10	0	0	--	1.000	---
1902	New York	NL	2	1	0	1	0	0	--	1.000	---
	Philadelphia	NL	8	19	0	15	4	1	--	.789	---
	5 ML YEARS		106	235	27	184	24	5	--	.898	---

197

Georges Maranda

Georges Henri Maranda
Pitches: Right **Bats:** Right

Height: 6'2" **Weight:** 195
Born on January 15, 1932 in Levis, Quebec

HOW MUCH HE PITCHED / WHAT HE GAVE UP / THE RESULTS

Year	Team	Lg	G	GS	CG	GF	IP	BFP	H	R	ER	HR	SH	SF	HB	TBB	IBB	SO	WP	Bk	W	L	Pct.	ShO	Sv	ERA
1960	San Francisco	NL	17	4	0	4	50.2	230	50	32	26	6	2	1	0	30	7	28	1	0	1	4	.200	0	0	4.62
1962	Minnesota	AL	32	4	0	8	72.2	318	69	43	36	11	3	2	4	35	3	36	5	0	1	3	.250	0	0	4.46
	2 ML YEARS		49	8	0	12	123.1	548	119	75	62	17	5	3	4	65	10	64	6	0	2	7	.222	0	0	4.52

BATTING / BASERUNNING / PERCENTAGES

Year	Team	Lg	G	AB	H	2B	3B	HR	(Hm	Rd)	TB	R	RBI	TBB	IBB	SO	HBP	SH	SF	SB	CS	SB%	GDP	Avg	OBP	SLG
1960	San Francisco	NL	17	12	2	0	0	0	(0	0)	2	0	0	0	0	6	0	0	0	0	0	.00	0	.167	.167	.167
1962	Minnesota	AL	32	16	4	2	0	0	(0	0)	6	0	1	1	0	6	0	0	1	0	0	.00	1	.250	.294	.375
	2 ML YEARS		49	28	6	2	0	0	(0	0)	8	0	1	1	0	12	0	0	1	0	0	.00	1	.214	.241	.286

FIELDING AS PITCHER

Year	Team	Lg	G	TC	PO	A	E	DP	PB	Pct.	Range
1960	San Francisco	NL	17	23	5	17	1	1	--	.957	---
1962	Minnesota	AL	32	20	3	16	1	2	--	.950	---
	2 ML YEARS		49	43	8	33	2	3	--	.953	---

Phil Marchildon

Philip Joseph Marchildon
Pitches: Right **Bats:** Right

Height: 5'10" **Weight:** 170
Born on October 25, 1913 in Penetanguishene, Ontario

HOW MUCH HE PITCHED / WHAT HE GAVE UP / THE RESULTS

Year	Team	Lg	G	GS	CG	GF	IP	BFP	H	R	ER	HR	SH	SF	HB	TBB	IBB	SO	WP	Bk	W	L	Pct.	ShO	Sv	ERA
1940	Philadelphia	AL	2	2	1	0	10	51	12	9	8	1	1			8		4	2	0	0	2	.000	0	0	7.20
1941	Philadelphia	AL	30	27	14	1	204.1	898	188	94	81	15	10		3	118		74	12	3	10	15	.400	1	0	3.57
1942	Philadelphia	AL	38	31	18	7	244	1081	215	126	114	14	22		4	140		110	13	0	17	14	.548	1	1	4.20
1945	Philadelphia	AL	3	2	0	0	9	41	5	5	4	0	2		0	11		2	1	0	0	1	.000	0	0	4.00
1946	Philadelphia	AL	36	29	16	6	226.2	963	197	104	88	14	14		4	114		95	7	2	13	16	.448	1	1	3.49
1947	Philadelphia	AL	35	35	21	0	276.2	1172	228	110	99	15	8		7	141		128	1	0	19	9	.679	2	0	3.22
1948	Philadelphia	AL	33	30	12	3	226.1	1007	214	134	114	19	19		4	131		66	7	0	9	15	.375	1	0	4.53
1949	Philadelphia	AL	7	6	0	1	16	89	24	23	21	3	2		1	19		2	2	0	0	3	.000	0	0	11.81
1950	Boston	AL	1	0	0	0	1.1	7	1	1	1	0	0		0	2		0	0	0	0	0	.000	0	0	6.75
	9 ML YEARS		185	162	82	18	1214.1	5309	1084	605	530	81	78		23	684		481	45	5	68	75	.476	6	2	3.93

BATTING / BASERUNNING / PERCENTAGES

Year	Team	Lg	G	AB	H	2B	3B	HR	(Hm	Rd)	TB	R	RBI	TBB	IBB	SO	HBP	SH	SF	SB	CS	SB%	GDP	Avg	OBP	SLG
1940	Philadelphia	AL	2	2	0	0	0	0	--	--	0	0	0	0		1	0	1		0	0	.00	0	.000	.000	.000
1941	Philadelphia	AL	30	66	11	0	1	0	--	--	13	4	5	7		17	0	8		0	0	.00	1	.167	.247	.197
1942	Philadelphia	AL	38	84	20	2	0	0	--	--	22	3	7	4		13	0	5		0	1	.00	2	.238	.273	.262
1945	Philadelphia	AL	3	2	1	1	0	0	--	--	2	0	0	0		0	0	0		0	0	.00	0	.500	.500	1.000
1946	Philadelphia	AL	36	75	5	1	0	0	--	--	6	3	3	2		21	0	7		0	0	.00	0	.067	.091	.080
1947	Philadelphia	AL	35	98	15	3	0	1	--	--	21	8	9	4		25	1	12		0	0	.00	2	.153	.194	.214
1948	Philadelphia	AL	33	72	5	0	0	0	--	--	5	3	2	10		30	0	3		0	0	.00	2	.069	.183	.069
1949	Philadelphia	AL	7	6	1	0	0	0	--	--	1	0	0	0		3	0	0		0	0	.00	0	.167	.167	.167
1950	Boston	AL	1	0	0	0	0	0	(0	0)	0	0	0	0		0	0	0		0	0	.00	0	.000	.000	.000
	9 ML YEARS		185	405	58	7	1	1	--	--	70	21	26	27		110	1	36		0	1	.00	7	.143	.199	.173

FIELDING AS PITCHER

Year	Team	Lg	G	TC	PO	A	E	DP	PB	Pct.	Range
1940	Philadelphia	AL	2	3	0	3	0	0	--	1.000	---
1941	Philadelphia	AL	30	34	11	22	1	1	--	.971	---
1942	Philadelphia	AL	38	50	13	35	2	3	--	.960	---
1945	Philadelphia	AL	3	3	1	2	0	0	--	1.000	---
1946	Philadelphia	AL	36	46	9	33	4	0	--	.913	---
1947	Philadelphia	AL	35	44	7	34	3	2	--	.932	---
1948	Philadelphia	AL	33	50	10	36	4	5	--	.920	---
1949	Philadelphia	AL	7	5	1	3	1	0	--	.800	---
1950	Boston	AL	1	0	0	0	0	0	--	.000	---
	9 ML YEARS		185	235	52	168	15	11	--	.936	---

Note: Marchildon spent nine months in a German POW camp in WWII.

Matt Maysey

Matthew Samuel Maysey
Pitches: Right **Bats:** Right

Height: 6'4" **Weight:** 225
Born on January 8, 1967 in Hamilton, Ontario

HOW MUCH HE PITCHED / WHAT HE GAVE UP / THE RESULTS

Year Team	Lg	G	GS	CG	GF	IP	BFP	H	R	ER	HR	SH	SF	HB	TBB	IBB	SO	WP	Bk	W	L	Pct.	ShO	Sv	ERA
1985 Spokane	A	7	4	0	2	29	0	27	18	15	3	0	0	1	16	0	18	5	0	0	3	.000	0	0	4.66
1986 Charleston	A	18	5	0	11	43	196	43	28	24	5	3	0	3	24	2	39	5	2	3	2	.600	0	1	5.02
1987 Charlstn-Sc	A	41	18	5	21	150.1	623	112	71	53	13	8	7	5	59	4	143	13	3	14	11	.560	0	7	3.17
1988 Wichita	AA	28	28	4	0	187	789	180	88	77	15	7	6	5	68	1	120	18	5	9	9	.500	0	0	3.71
1989 Las Vegas	AAA	28	28	4	0	176.1	773	173	94	80	19	3	1	2	84	3	96	12	3	8	12	.400	1	0	4.08
1990 Las Vegas	AAA	26	25	1	1	137.2	634	155	97	86	10	6	5	5	88	5	72	12	1	6	10	.375	0	0	5.62
1991 Harrisburg	AA	15	15	2	0	104.2	419	90	26	22	3	2	3	2	28	0	86	8	0	6	5	.545	2	0	1.89
Indianapols	AAA	12	12	0	0	63	272	60	45	36	7	0	1	2	33	2	45	6	0	3	6	.333	0	0	5.14
1992 Indianapols	AAA	35	1	0	14	67	286	63	32	32	9	4	2	0	28	5	38	2	1	5	3	.625	0	5	4.30
1993 New Orleans	AAA	29	5	0	6	52.1	215	48	25	24	8	1	2	0	14	1	40	2	1	0	3	.000	0	2	4.13
1994 Buffalo	AAA	10	0	0	1	15	57	11	7	7	0	2	1	1	2	0	9	2	0	2	0	1.000	0	0	4.20
1995 Calgary	AAA	44	12	0	4	103	468	122	67	63	9	2	3	7	44	3	71	7	0	8	7	.533	0	1	5.50
1992 Montreal	NL	2	0	0	1	2.1	12	4	1	1	1	0	0	1	0	0	1	0	0	0	0	.000	0	0	3.86
1993 Milwaukee	AL	23	0	0	12	22	105	28	14	14	4	2	2	1	13	1	10	4	0	1	2	.333	0	1	5.73
2 ML YEARS		25	0	0	13	24.1	117	32	15	15	5	2	2	2	13	1	11	4	0	1	2	.333	0	1	5.55

BATTING / BASERUNNING / PERCENTAGES

Year Team	Lg	G	AB	H	2B	3B	HR	(Hm	Rd)	TB	R	RBI	TBB	IBB	SO	HBP	SH	SF	SB	CS	SB%	GDP	Avg	OBP	SLG
1992 Montreal	NL	2	0	0	0	0	0	(0	0)	0	0	0	0	0	0	0	0	0	0	0	.00	0	.000	.000	.000
1993 Milwaukee	AL	23	1	1	0	0	0	(0	0)	1	0	0	0	0	0	0	0	0	0	0	.00	0	1.000	1.000	1.000
2 ML YEARS		25	1	1	0	0	0	(0	0)	1	0	0	0	0	0	0	0	0	0	0	.00	0	1.000	1.000	1.000

FIELDING AS PITCHER

Year Team	Lg	G	TC	PO	A	E	DP	PB	Pct.	Range
1992 Montreal	NL	2	0	0	0	0	0	--	.000	---
1993 Milwaukee	AL	23	5	1	2	2	0	--	.600	---
2 ML YEARS		25	5	1	2	2	0	--	.600	---

Ralph McCabe

Ralph Herbert McCabe
Pitches: Right **Bats:** Right

Height: 6'4" **Weight:** 195
Born on October 21, 1918 in Napanee, Ontario
Died on May 3, 1974 in Windsor, Ontario

HOW MUCH HE PITCHED / WHAT HE GAVE UP / THE RESULTS

Year Team	Lg	G	GS	CG	GF	IP	BFP	H	R	ER	HR	SH	SF	HB	TBB	IBB	SO	WP	Bk	W	L	Pct.	ShO	Sv	ERA
1946 Cleveland	AL	1	1	0	0	4	19	5	5	5	3	0		1	2		3	0	0	0	1	.000	0	0	11.25

BATTING / BASERUNNING / PERCENTAGES

Year Team	Lg	G	AB	H	2B	3B	HR	(Hm	Rd)	TB	R	RBI	TBB	IBB	SO	HBP	SH	SF	SB	CS	SB%	GDP	Avg	OBP	SLG
1946 Cleveland	AL	1	1	0	0	0	0	--	--	0	0	0	0	0	0	0	0	0	0	0	.00	0	.000	.000	.000

FIELDING AS PITCHER

Year Team	Lg	G	TC	PO	A	E	DP	PB	Pct.	Range
1946 Cleveland	AL	1	1	1	0	0	0	--	1.000	---

Kirk McCaskill

Kirk Edward McCaskill
Attended Vermont
Pitches: Right **Bats:** Right

Height: 6'1" **Weight:** 190
Born on April 9, 1961 in Kapuskasing, Ontario

HOW MUCH HE PITCHED / WHAT HE GAVE UP / THE RESULTS

Year Team	Lg	G	GS	CG	GF	IP	BFP	H	R	ER	HR	SH	SF	HB	TBB	IBB	SO	WP	Bk	W	L	Pct.	ShO	Sv	ERA
1984 Edmonton	AAA	24	22	2	0	143	0	162	104	91	19	0	0	1	74	1	75	1	2	7	11	.389	0	0	5.73
1985 Edmonton	AAA	3	3	0	0	17.2	0	17	7	4	1	0	0	0	6	0	18	0	0	1	1	.500	0	0	2.04
1987 Palm Spring	A	2	2	0	0	10	35	4	1	0	0	0	0	0	3	0	7	0	0	2	0	1.000	0	0	0.00
Edmonton	AAA	1	1	0	0	6	24	3	2	2	0	0	1	0	4	0	4	0	0	1	0	1.000	0	0	3.00
1993 South Bend	A	1	1	0	0	6	25	3	2	1	0	0	0	0	3	0	5	0	0	1	0	1.000	0	0	1.50
1985 California	AL	30	29	6	0	189.2	807	189	105	99	23	2	5	4	64	1	102	5	0	12	12	.500	1	0	4.70
1986 California	AL	34	33	10	1	246.1	1013	207	98	92	19	6	5	5	92	1	202	10	2	17	10	.630	2	0	3.36
1987 California	AL	14	13	1	0	74.2	334	84	52	47	14	3	1	2	34	0	56	1	0	4	6	.400	1	0	5.67
1988 California	AL	23	23	4	0	146.1	635	155	78	70	9	1	6	1	61	3	98	13	2	8	6	.571	2	0	4.31
1989 California	AL	32	32	6	0	212	864	202	73	69	16	3	4	3	59	1	107	7	2	15	10	.600	4	0	2.93
1990 California	AL	29	29	2	0	174.1	738	161	77	63	9	3	1	2	72	1	78	6	1	12	11	.522	1	0	3.25

Year Team	Lg	G	GS	CG	GF	IP	BFP	H	R	ER	HR	SH	SF	HB	TBB	IBB	SO	WP	Bk	W	L	Pct.	ShO	Sv	ERA
1991 California	AL	30	30	1	0	177.2	762	193	93	84	19	6	6	3	66	1	71	6	0	10	**19**	.345	0	0	4.26
1992 Chicago	AL	34	34	0	0	209	911	193	116	97	11	7	7	6	95	5	109	6	2	12	13	.480	0	0	4.18
1993 Chicago	AL	30	14	0	6	113.2	502	144	71	66	12	2	3	1	36	6	65	6	0	4	8	.333	0	2	5.23
1994 Chicago	AL	40	0	0	18	52.2	228	51	22	20	6	1	3	0	22	4	37	1	0	1	4	.200	0	3	3.42
1995 Chicago	AL	55	1	0	17	81	365	97	50	44	10	3	3	5	33	4	50	10	0	6	4	.600	0	2	4.89
11 ML YEARS		351	238	30	42	1677.1	7159	1676	835	751	148	37	44	32	634	27	975	71	9	101	103	.495	11	7	4.03

League Championship Pitching

		HOW MUCH HE PITCHED						WHAT HE GAVE UP												THE RESULTS					
Year Team	Lg	G	GS	CG	GF	IP	BFP	H	R	ER	HR	SH	SF	HB	TBB	IBB	SO	WP	Bk	W	L	Pct.	ShO	Sv	ERA
1986 California	AL	2	2	0	0	9.1	48	16	13	8	0	1	0	0	5	0	7	0	0	0	2	.000	0	0	7.71
1993 Chicago	AL	39	12	4	13	3.2	16	3	3	0	0	0	0	0	1	0	3	0	0	0	0	.000	1	2	0.00
2 ML YEARS		41	14	4	13	13	64	19	16	8	0	1	0	0	6	0	10	0	0	0	2	.000	1	2	5.54

FIELDING AS PITCHER										
Year Team	Lg	G	TC	PO	A	E	DP	PB	Pct.	Range
1985 California	AL	30	41	11	27	3	1	--	.927	---
1986 California	AL	34	51	24	26	1	0	--	.980	---
1987 California	AL	14	21	8	12	1	1	--	.952	---
1988 California	AL	23	33	12	18	3	2	--	.909	---
1989 California	AL	32	61	16	42	3	5	--	.951	---
1990 California	AL	29	51	19	29	3	2	--	.941	---
1991 California	AL	30	43	17	25	1	4	--	.977	---
1992 Chicago	AL	34	57	24	31	2	0	--	.965	---
1993 Chicago	AL	30	32	7	23	2	4	--	.938	---
1994 Chicago	AL	40	12	4	8	0	0	--	1.000	---
1995 Chicago	AL	55	20	5	13	2	0	--	.900	---
11 ML YEARS		351	422	147	254	21	19	--	.950	---

League Championship Fielding

FIELDING AS PITCHER										
Year Team	Lg	G	TC	PO	A	E	DP	PB	Pct.	Range
1986 California	AL	2	1	1	0	0	1	--	1.000	---
1993 Chicago	AL	3	2	0	2	0	0	--	1.000	---
2 ML YEARS		5	3	1	2	0	1	--	1.000	---

Art McGovern

Arthur John McGovern

Height: 5'10" **Weight:** 160

Bats: Right **Throws:** Right

Born on February 27, 1882 in St. John, New Brunswick

Died on November 14, 1915 in Thornton, Rhode Island

		BATTING																	BASERUNNING				PERCENTAGES		
Year Team	Lg	G	AB	H	2B	3B	HR	(Hm	Rd)	TB	R	RBI	TBB	IBB	SO	HBP	SH	SF	SB	CS	SB%	GDP	Avg	OBP	SLG
1905 Boston	AL	15	44	5	1	0	0	--	--	6	1	1	4			1	1		0				.114	.204	.136

FIELDING AS CATCHER										
Year Team	Lg	G	TC	PO	A	E	DP	PB	Pct.	Range
1905 Boston	AL	15	82	67	11	4	1	3	.951	---

Dave McKay

David Lawrence McKay

Height: 6'1" **Weight:** 195

Attended Creighton

Born on March 14, 1950 in Vancouver, British Columbia

Bats: Both **Throws:** Right

		BATTING																	BASERUNNING				PERCENTAGES		
Year Team	Lg	G	AB	H	2B	3B	HR	(Hm	Rd)	TB	R	RBI	TBB	IBB	SO	HBP	SH	SF	SB	CS	SB%	GDP	Avg	OBP	SLG
1975 Minnesota	AL	33	125	32	4	1	2	(1	1)	44	8	16	6	0	14	1	1	2	1	1	.50	4	.256	.291	.352
1976 Minnesota	AL	45	138	28	2	0	0	(0	0)	30	8	8	9	0	27	4	4	0	1	2	.33	6	.203	.272	.217
1977 Toronto	AL	95	274	54	4	3	3	(2	1)	73	18	22	7	0	51	2	9	1	2	1	.67	9	.197	.222	.266
1978 Toronto	AL	145	504	120	20	8	7	(4	3)	177	59	45	20	2	91	1	10	2	4	4	.50	17	.238	.268	.351
1979 Toronto	AL	47	156	34	9	0	0	(0	0)	43	19	12	7	0	19	1	5	0	1	1	.50	5	.218	.256	.276
1980 Oakland	AL	123	295	72	16	1	1	(0	1)	93	29	29	10	0	57	6	11	0	1	1	.50	4	.244	.283	.315
1981 Oakland	AL	79	224	59	11	1	4	(1	3)	84	25	21	16	0	43	2	3	4	4	1	.80	4	.263	.313	.375
1982 Oakland	AL	78	212	42	4	1	4	(1	3)	60	25	17	11	0	35	0	0	3	6	1	.86	0	.198	.235	.283
8 ML YEARS		645	1928	441	70	15	21	(9	12)	604	191	170	86	2	337	17	43	12	20	12	.63	49	.229	.266	.313

Division Playoffs Batting

		BATTING																BASERUNNING				PERCENTAGES		
Year Team	Lg	G	AB	H	2B	3B	HR	(Hm | Rd)	TB	R	RBI	TBB	IBB	SO	HBP	SH	SF	SB	CS	SB%	GDP	Avg	OBP	SLG
1981 Oakland	AL	3	11	3	0	0	1	--	--	6	1	1	1	0	1	0	0	0	0	0	.00	0	.273	.333	.545

League Championship Batting

		BATTING																BASERUNNING				PERCENTAGES		
Year Team	Lg	G	AB	H	2B	3B	HR	(Hm	Rd)	TB	R	RBI	TBB	IBB	SO	HBP	SH	SF	SB	CS	SB%	GDP	Avg	OBP	SLG
1981 Oakland	AL	3	11	3	0	0	0	(0	0)	3	0	1	0	0	2	0	0	0	0	0	.00	0	.273	.273	.273

FIELDING AS SECOND BASEMAN

Year Team	Lg	G	TC	PO	A	E	DP	PB	Pct.	Range
1977 Toronto	AL	40	188	75	107	6	21	--	.968	4.55
1978 Toronto	AL	140	730	310	408	12	96	--	.984	5.13
1979 Toronto	AL	46	274	119	148	7	37	--	.974	5.80
1980 Oakland	AL	62	256	99	151	6	24	--	.977	4.03
1981 Oakland	AL	38	197	83	108	6	23	--	.970	5.03
1982 Oakland	AL	59	222	99	116	7	22	--	.968	3.64
6 ML YEARS		385	1867	785	1038	44	223	--	.976	4.74

FIELDING AS THIRD BASEMAN

Year Team	Lg	G	TC	PO	A	E	DP	PB	Pct.	Range
1975 Minnesota	AL	33	117	38	70	9	12	--	.923	3.27
1976 Minnesota	AL	41	112	25	77	10	13	--	.911	2.49
1977 Toronto	AL	32	102	32	65	5	7	--	.951	3.03
1978 Toronto	AL	2	5	0	5	0	0	--	1.000	2.50
1979 Toronto	AL	2	2	0	2	0	0	--	1.000	1.00
1980 Oakland	AL	54	109	39	66	4	5	--	.963	1.94
1981 Oakland	AL	43	95	29	59	7	3	--	.926	2.05
1982 Oakland	AL	16	58	19	35	4	1	--	.931	3.38
8 ML YEARS		223	600	182	379	39	41	--	.935	2.52

FIELDING AS SHORTSTOP

Year Team	Lg	G	TC	PO	A	E	DP	PB	Pct.	Range
1976 Minnesota	AL	2	2	2	0	0	0	--	1.000	1.00
1977 Toronto	AL	20	70	34	33	3	8	--	.957	3.35
1978 Toronto	AL	3	1	0	1	0	0	--	1.000	.33
1980 Oakland	AL	10	42	17	25	0	4	--	1.000	4.20
1981 Oakland	AL	7	11	6	5	0	0	--	1.000	1.57
1982 Oakland	AL	3	4	2	2	0	1	--	1.000	1.33
6 ML YEARS		45	130	61	66	3	13	--	.977	2.82

Division Playoffs Fielding

FIELDING AS SECOND BASEMAN

Year Team	Lg	G	TC	PO	A	E	DP	PB	Pct.	Range
1981 Oakland	AL	3	16	9	6	1	0	--	.938	5.00

League Championship Fielding

FIELDING AS SECOND BASEMAN

Year Team	Lg	G	TC	PO	A	E	DP	PB	Pct.	Range
1981 Oakland	AL	3	14	7	6	1	0	--	.929	4.33

Jim McKeever

James McKeever
Bats: Unknown **Throws:** Unknown

Height: 5'10" **Weight:** 170
Born on April 19, 1861 in St. John, New Brunswick
Died on August 19, 1897 in Boston, Massachusetts

		BATTING																BASERUNNING				PERCENTAGES		
Year Team	Lg	G	AB	H	2B	3B	HR	(Hm	Rd)	TB	R	RBI	TBB	IBB	SO	HBP	SH	SF	SB	CS	SB%	GDP	Avg	OBP	SLG
1884 Boston	UA	16	66	9	0	0	0	--	--	9	13		0											.136	.136	.136

FIELDING AS CATCHER

Year Team	Lg	G	TC	PO	A	E	DP	PB	Pct.	Range
1884 Boston	UA	12	122	94	12	16	1	24	.869	---

FIELDING AS OUTFIELDER

Year Team	Lg	G	TC	PO	A	E	DP	PB	Pct.	Range
1884 Boston	UA	4	2	2	0	0	0	--	1.000	.50

Larry McLean

John Bannerman McLean
Bats: Right **Throws:** Right

Height: 6'5" **Weight:** 228
Born on July 18, 1881 in Fredericton, New Brunswick
Died on March 24, 1921 in Boston, Massachusetts

									BATTING												BASERUNNING				PERCENTAGES		
Year Team	Lg	G	AB	H	2B	3B	HR	(Hm	Rd)	TB	R	RBI	TBB	IBB	SO	HBP	SH	SF	SB	CS	SB%	GDP	Avg	OBP	SLG
1901 Boston	AL	9	19	4	1	0	0	--	--	5	4	2	0			0	0		1				.211	.211	.263
1903 Chicago	NL	1	4	0	0	0	0	--	--	0	0	1	1			0	0		0				.000	.200	.000
1904 St. Louis	NL	27	84	14	2	1	0	--	--	18	5	4	4			0	0		1				.167	.205	.214
1906 Cincinnati	NL	12	35	7	2	0	0	--	--	9	3	2	4			0	2		0				.200	.282	.257
1907 Cincinnati	NL	113	374	108	9	9	0	--	--	135	35	54	13			0	4		4				.289	.313	.361
1908 Cincinnati	NL	99	309	67	9	4	1	--	--	87	24	28	15				2	8		2				.217	.258	.282
1909 Cincinnati	NL	95	324	83	12	2	2	--	--	105	26	36	21				3	10		1				.256	.307	.324
1910 Cincinnati	NL	127	423	126	14	7	2	--	--	160	27	71	26		23	1	5		4				.298	.340	.378
1911 Cincinnati	NL	107	328	94	7	2	0	--	--	105	24	34	20		18	1	5		1				.287	.330	.320
1912 Cincinnati	NL	102	333	81	15	1	1	--	--	101	17	27	18		15	1	6		1				.243	.284	.303
1913 2 ML Teams		78	227	65	13	0	0	--	--	78	10	21	10		13	0	0		1				.286	.316	.344
1914 New York	NL	79	154	40	6	0	0	--	--	46	8	14	4		9	1	2		4				.260	.283	.299
1915 New York	NL	13	33	5	0	0	0	--	--	5	0	4	0		1	0	1		0	0	.00		.152	.152	.152
1913 St. Louis	NL	48	152	41	9	0	0	--	--	50	7	12	6		9	0	0		0				.270	.297	.329
New York	NL	30	75	24	4	0	0	--	--	28	3	9	4		4	0	0		1				.320	.354	.373
13 ML YEARS		862	2647	694	90	26	6	--	--	854	183	298	136			9	43		20				.262	.301	.323

World Series Batting

									BATTING												BASERUNNING				PERCENTAGES		
Year Team	Lg	G	AB	H	2B	3B	HR	(Hm	Rd)	TB	R	RBI	TBB	IBB	SO	HBP	SH	SF	SB	CS	SB%	GDP	Avg	OBP	SLG
1913 New York	NL	5	12	6	0	0	0	(0	0)	6	0	2	0	0	0	0	0		0	0	.00	0	.500	.500	.500

FIELDING AS CATCHER

Year Team	Lg	G	TC	PO	A	E	DP	PB	Pct.	Range
1903 Chicago	NL	1	9	7	1	1	0	0	.889	---
1904 St. Louis	NL	24	153	126	20	7	1	1	.954	---
1906 Cincinnati	NL	12	65	49	13	3	0	4	.954	---
1907 Cincinnati	NL	89	487	365	110	12	12	8	.975	---
1908 Cincinnati	NL	69	376	280	82	14	9	8	.963	---
1909 Cincinnati	NL	95	509	379	119	11	16	14	.978	---
1910 Cincinnati	NL	119	654	485	158	11	18	13	.983	---
1911 Cincinnati	NL	98	570	414	138	18	16	8	.968	---
1912 Cincinnati	NL	98	564	425	124	15	16	2	.973	---
1913 2 ML Teams		70	334	244	80	10	9	5	.970	---
1914 New York	NL	74	260	211	42	7	8	2	.973	---
1915 New York	NL	12	66	47	18	1	0	0	.985	---
1913 St. Louis	NL	42	207	143	60	4	8	3	.981	---
New York	NL	28	127	101	20	6	1	2	.953	---
12 ML YEARS		761	4047	3032	905	110	105	65	.973	---

FIELDING AS FIRST BASEMAN

Year Team	Lg	G	TC	PO	A	E	DP	PB	Pct.	Range
1901 Boston	AL	5	40	38	2	0	2	--	1.000	---
1907 Cincinnati	NL	13	117	111	3	3	10	--	.974	---
1908 Cincinnati	NL	19	178	165	5	8	2	--	.955	---
3 ML YEARS		37	335	314	10	11	14	--	.967	---

World Series Fielding

FIELDING AS CATCHER

Year Team	Lg	G	TC	PO	A	E	DP	PB	Pct.	Range
1913 New York	NL	4	16	13	3	0	0	1	1.000	---

Note: McLean was shot and killed by a bartender.

Charlie Mead

Charles Richard Mead
Bats: Left **Throws:** Right

Height: 6'1" **Weight:** 185
Born on April 9, 1921 in Vermillion, Alberta

									BATTING												BASERUNNING				PERCENTAGES		
Year Team	Lg	G	AB	H	2B	3B	HR	(Hm	Rd)	TB	R	RBI	TBB	IBB	SO	HBP	SH	SF	SB	CS	SB%	GDP	Avg	OBP	SLG
1943 New York	NL	37	146	40	6	1	1	--	--	51	9	13	10		15	0	2		3	0	1.00	3	.274	.321	.349
1944 New York	NL	39	78	14	1	0	1	--	--	18	5	8	5		7	0	3		0	1	.00	2	.179	.229	.231

Year Team	Lg	G	AB	H	2B	3B	HR	(Hm	Rd)	TB	R	RBI	TBB	IBB	SO	HBP	SH	SF	SB	CS	SB%	GDP	Avg	OBP	SLG
1945 New York	NL	11	37	10	1	0	1	--	--	14	4	6	5		2	0	0		0			0	.270	.357	.378
3 ML YEARS		87	261	64	8	1	3	--	--	83	18	27	20		24	0	5		3			5	.245	.299	.318

FIELDING AS OUTFIELDER										
Year Team	Lg	G	TC	PO	A	E	DP	PB	Pct.	Range
1943 New York	NL	37	82	77	3	2	3	--	.976	2.16
1944 New York	NL	23	52	47	4	1	2	--	.981	2.22
1945 New York	NL	11	26	22	3	1	1	--	.962	2.27
3 ML YEARS		71	160	146	10	4	6	--	.975	2.20

Doc Miller

Roy Oscar Miller
Bats: Left   **Throws:** Left

Height: 5'10" **Weight:** 170
Born on February 4, 1883 in Chatham, Ontario
Died on July 31, 1938 in Jersey City, New Jersey

		BATTING																	BASERUNNING			PERCENTAGES			
Year Team	Lg	G	AB	H	2B	3B	HR	(Hm	Rd)	TB	R	RBI	TBB	IBB	SO	HBP	SH	SF	SB	CS	SB%	GDP	Avg	OBP	SLG
1910 2 ML Teams		131	483	138	27	4	3	--	--	182	48	55	33		52	1	18		17				.286	.333	.377
1911 Boston	NL	146	577	192	36	3	7	--	--	255	69	91	43		43	0	12		32				.333	.379	.442
1912 2 ML Teams		118	378	98	20	6	2	--	--	136	50	45	23		30	1	13		9				.259	.303	.360
1913 Philadelphia	NL	69	87	30	6	0	0	--	--	36	9	11	6		6	2	0		2				.345	.400	.414
1914 Cincinnati	NL	93	192	49	7	2	0	--	--	60	8	33	16		18	0	4		4				.255	.313	.313
1910 Chicago	NL	1	1	0	0	0	0	--	--	0	0	0	0		0	0	0		0				.000	.000	.000
Boston	NL	130	482	138	27	4	3	--	--	182	48	55	33		52	1	18		17				.286	.333	.378
1912 Boston	NL	51	201	47	8	1	2	--	--	63	26	24	14		17	1	8		6				.234	.287	.313
Philadelphia	NL	67	177	51	12	5	0	--	--	73	24	21	9		13	0	5		3				.288	.323	.412
5 ML YEARS		557	1717	507	96	15	12	--	--	669	184	235	121		149	4	47		64				.295	.343	.390

FIELDING AS SHORTSTOP										
Year Team	Lg	G	TC	PO	A	E	DP	PB	Pct.	Range
1911 Boston	NL	1	2	2	0	0	0	--	1.000	2.00

FIELDING AS OUTFIELDER										
Year Team	Lg	G	TC	PO	A	E	DP	PB	Pct.	Range
1910 Boston	NL	130	223	203	9	11	3	--	.951	1.63
1911 Boston	NL	146	280	243	26	11	4	--	.961	1.84
1912 2 ML Teams		90	167	140	21	6	5	--	.964	1.79
1913 Philadelphia	NL	12	10	8	0	2	0	--	.800	.67
1914 Cincinnati	NL	47	83	79	2	2	1	--	.976	1.72
1912 Boston	NL	50	96	79	12	5	4	--	.948	1.82
Philadelphia	NL	40	71	61	9	1	1	--	.986	1.75
5 ML YEARS		425	763	673	58	32	13	--	.958	1.72

Jon Morrison

Jonathan W. Morrison
Bats: Left   **Throws:** Unknown

Height: 5'10" **Weight:** 167
Born in 1859 in London, Ontario

		BATTING																	BASERUNNING			PERCENTAGES			
Year Team	Lg	G	AB	H	2B	3B	HR	(Hm	Rd)	TB	R	RBI	TBB	IBB	SO	HBP	SH	SF	SB	CS	SB%	GDP	Avg	OBP	SLG
1884 Indianapolis	AA	44	182	48	6	8	1	--	--	73	26		7			4							.264	.306	.401
1887 New York	AA	9	34	4	0	0	0	--	--	4	7		6			1			0				.118	.268	.118
2 ML YEARS		53	216	52	6	8	1	--	--	77	33		13			5	0						.241	.299	.356

FIELDING AS OUTFIELDER										
Year Team	Lg	G	TC	PO	A	E	DP	PB	Pct.	Range
1884 Indianapolis	AA	44	111	78	9	24	4	--	.784	1.98
1887 New York	AA	9	20	12	0	8	0	--	.600	1.33
2 ML YEARS		53	131	90	9	32	4	--	.756	1.87

Billy Mountjoy

William Henry Mountjoy (Medicine Bill)
Pitches: Right   **Bats:** Left

Height: 5'6" **Weight:** 150
Born on December 11, 1858 in London, Ontario
Died on May 19, 1894 in London, Ontario

		HOW MUCH HE PITCHED						WHAT HE GAVE UP											THE RESULTS					
Year Team	Lg	G	GS	CG	GF	IP	BFP	H	R	ER	HR	SH	SF	HB	TBB	IBB	SO	WP	Bk	W	L	Pct.	ShO	Sv	ERA
1883 Cincinnati	AA	1	1	1	0	8	31	9	4	2	0				2		3	0	0	0	1	.000	0	0	2.25
1884 Cincinnati	AA	33	33	32	0	289	1212	274	148	94	5			16	43		96	18	0	19	12	.613	3	0	2.93
1885 2 ML Teams		23	23	23	0	206.2	907	221	136	86	6			11	65		65	17		12	11	.522	2	0	3.75
1885 Cincinnati	AA	17	17	17	0	153.2	662	149	89	54	5			7	52		50	15		10	7	.588	1	0	3.16
Baltimore	AA	6	6	6	0	53	245	72	47	32	1			4	13		15	2		2	4	.333	1	0	5.43
3 ML YEARS		57	57	56	0	503.2	2150	504	288	182	11			110		164	35			31	24	.564	5	0	3.25

BATTING																			BASERUNNING				PERCENTAGES		
Year Team	Lg	G	AB	H	2B	3B	HR	(Hm Rd)	TB	R	RBI	TBB	IBB	SO	HBP	SH	SF	SB	CS	SB%	GDP	Avg	OBP	SLG
1883 Cincinnati	AA	1	3	0	0	0	0	-- --	0	0	0											.000	.000	.000
1884 Cincinnati	AA	34	119	18	2	1	0	-- --	22	13		9			3							.151	.229	.185
1885 2 ML Teams		24	78	11	0	0	0	-- --	11	12		15			3							.141	.302	.141
1885 Cincinnati	AA	17	60	10	0	0	0	-- --	10	7		8			3							.167	.296	.167
Baltimore	AA	7	18	1	0	0	0	-- --	1	5		7			0							.056	.320	.056
3 ML YEARS		59	200	29	2	1	0	-- --	33	25		24			6	0						.145	.257	.165

FIELDING AS PITCHER										
Year Team	Lg	G	TC	PO	A	E	DP	PB	Pct.	Range
1883 Cincinnati	AA	1	1	0	1	0	0	--	1.000	---
1884 Cincinnati	AA	33	83	13	64	6	2	--	.928	---
1885 2 ML Teams		23	45	3	37	5	1	--	.889	---
1885 Cincinnati	AA	17	30	2	25	3	0	--	.900	---
Baltimore	AA	6	15	1	12	2	1	--	.867	---
3 ML YEARS		57	129	16	102	11	3	--	.915	---

FIELDING AS OUTFIELDER										
Year Team	Lg	G	TC	PO	A	E	DP	PB	Pct.	Range
1884 Cincinnati	AA	2	3	2	1	0	1	--	1.000	1.50
1885 Baltimore	AA	1	1	1	0	0	0	--	1.000	1.00
2 ML YEARS		3	4	3	1	0	1	--	1.000	1.33

Henry Mullin

Henry J. Mullin
Bats: Right   **Throws:** Unknown

Height: 5'9"   **Weight:** 160
Born on November 6, 1862 in St. John, New Brunswick
Died on November 8, 1937 in Beverly, Massachusetts

BATTING																			BASERUNNING				PERCENTAGES		
Year Team	Lg	G	AB	H	2B	3B	HR	(Hm Rd)	TB	R	RBI	TBB	IBB	SO	HBP	SH	SF	SB	CS	SB%	GDP	Avg	OBP	SLG
1884 2 ML Teams		36	128	17	3	1	0	-- --	22	14		8											.133	.184	.172
1884 Washington	AA	34	120	17	3	1	0	-- --	22	13		8				0							.142	.195	.183
Boston	UA	2	8	0	0	0	0	-- --	0	1		0											.000	.000	.000

FIELDING AS THIRD BASEMAN										
Year Team	Lg	G	TC	PO	A	E	DP	PB	Pct.	Range
1884 Washington	AA	1	2	1	1	0	0	--	1.000	2.00

FIELDING AS OUTFIELDER										
Year Team	Lg	G	TC	PO	A	E	DP	PB	Pct.	Range
1884 2 ML Teams		36	68	51	9	8	1	--	.882	1.67
1884 Washington	AA	34	61	47	6	8	0	--	.869	1.56
Boston	UA	2	7	4	3	0	1	--	1.000	3.50

John O'Brien

John J. O'Brien (Chewing Gum)
Bats: Left   **Throws:** Right

Height: Unknown   **Weight:** 175
Born on July 14, 1870 in St. John, New Brunswick
Died on May 13, 1913 in Lewiston, Maine

BATTING																			BASERUNNING				PERCENTAGES		
Year Team	Lg	G	AB	H	2B	3B	HR	(Hm Rd)	TB	R	RBI	TBB	IBB	SO	HBP	SH	SF	SB	CS	SB%	GDP	Avg	OBP	SLG
1891 Brooklyn	NL	43	167	41	4	2	0	-- --	49	22	26	12		17	3			4				.246	.308	.293
1893 Chicago	NL	4	14	5	0	1	0	-- --	7	3	1	2		2	1			0				.357	.471	.500
1895 Louisville	NL	128	539	138	10	4	1	-- --	159	82	50	45	20	10	18			15				.256	.325	.295
1896 2 ML Teams		122	456	135	15	4	6	-- --	176	62	57	40	19	6	8			8				.296	.361	.386
1897 Washington	NL	86	320	78	12	2	3	-- --	103	37	45	19			11	3		6				.244	.309	.322
1899 2 ML Teams		118	414	89	6	4	2	-- --	109	40	50	36			4	13		12				.215	.284	.263
1896 Louisville	NL	49	186	63	9	1	2	-- --	80	24	24	13	7	1	1			4				.339	.385	.430
Washington	NL	73	270	72	6	3	4	-- --	96	38	33	27	12	5	7			4				.267	.344	.356
1899 Baltimore	NL	39	135	26	4	0	1	-- --	33	14	17	15		2	3			4				.193	.283	.244
Pittsburgh	NL	79	279	63	2	4	1	-- --	76	26	33	21		2	10			8				.226	.285	.272
6 ML YEARS		501	1910	486	47	17	12	-- --	603	246	229	154		35	42			45				.254	.322	.316

FIELDING AS FIRST BASEMAN										
Year Team	Lg	G	TC	PO	A	E	DP	PB	Pct.	Range
1895 Louisville	NL	3	37	35	1	1	2	--	.973	---

FIELDING AS SECOND BASEMAN										
Year Team	Lg	G	TC	PO	A	E	DP	PB	Pct.	Range
1891 Brooklyn	NL	43	219	85	102	32	13	--	.854	4.35
1893 Chicago	NL	4	20	10	8	2	1	--	.900	4.50
1895 Louisville	NL	125	746	304	396	46	56	--	.938	5.60
1896 2 ML Teams		122	710	291	375	44	52	--	.938	5.46

Year	Team	Lg	G	AB	H	2B	3B	HR	(Hm	Rd)	TB	R	RBI	TBB	IBB	SO	HBP	SH	SF	SB	CS	SB%	GDP	Avg	OBP	SLG
1897	Washington	NL	86	513	223	260	30	43						--											.942	5.62	
1899	2 ML Teams		118	718	309	375	34	53						--											.953	5.80	
1896	Louisville	NL	49	296	125	147	24	19						--											.919	5.55	
	Washington	NL	73	414	166	228	20	33						--											.952	5.40	
1899	Baltimore	NL	39	238	98	132	8	21						--											.966	5.90	
	Pittsburgh	NL	79	480	211	243	26	32						--											.946	5.75	
	6 ML YEARS		498	2926	1222	1516	188	218						--											.936	5.50	

Dan O'Connor

Daniel Cornelius O'Connor
Bats: Left **Throws:** Right

Height: 6'2" **Weight:** 185
Born in August, 1868 in Guelph, Ontario
Died on March 3, 1942 in Guelph, Ontario

						BATTING														**BASERUNNING**				**PERCENTAGES**		
Year	Team	Lg	G	AB	H	2B	3B	HR	(Hm	Rd)	TB	R	RBI	TBB	IBB	SO	HBP	SH	SF	SB	CS	SB%	GDP	Avg	OBP	SLG
1890	Louisville	AA	6	26	12	1	1	0	--	--	15	3		1			0			5				.462	.481	.577

				FIELDING AS FIRST BASEMAN						
Year	Team	Lg	G	TC	PO	A	E	DP	PB	Pct.	Range
1890	Louisville	AA	6	58	58	0	0	3	--	1.000	---

Greg O'Halloran

Gregory Joseph O'Halloran
Attended Orange Coast (calif.) Jc
Bats: Left **Throws:** Right

Height: 6'2" **Weight:** 205
Born on May 21, 1968 in Toronto, Ontario

						BATTING														**BASERUNNING**				**PERCENTAGES**		
Year	Team	Lg	G	AB	H	2B	3B	HR	(Hm	Rd)	TB	R	RBI	TBB	IBB	SO	HBP	SH	SF	SB	CS	SB%	GDP	Avg	OBP	SLG
1989	St. Cathrns	A	69	265	75	13	2	5	--	--	107	31	27	21	2	33	1	0	1	7	4	.64	4	.283	.338	.404
1990	Dunedin	A	121	465	132	26	4	11	--	--	199	70	75	37	7	70	3	1	3	2	3	.40	4	.284	.339	.428
1991	Dunedin	A	20	74	21	3	1	0	--	--	26	7	4	7	1	8	0	0	0	1	1	.50	1	.284	.346	.351
	Knoxville	AA	110	350	89	13	3	8	--	--	132	37	53	27	3	46	0	2	6	11	6	.65	14	.254	.303	.377
1992	Knoxville	AA	117	409	111	20	5	2	--	--	147	44	34	31	2	64	0	2	5	7	7	.50	10	.271	.319	.359
1993	Syracuse	AAA	109	322	86	14	3	3	--	--	115	32	35	13	3	54	2	0	4	2	1	.67	13	.267	.296	.357
1994	Portland	AA	104	388	102	22	6	7	--	--	157	52	53	37	1	71	3	0	1	2	3	.40	9	.263	.331	.405
1995	Iowa	AAA	7	19	3	1	0	0	--	--	4	1	1	0	0	7	0	0	0	0	0	.00	0	.158	.150	.211
	Duluth-Sup.	IND	23	79	18	1	1	2	--	--	27	10	9	10	2	21	0	1	0	0	2	.00	0	.228	.315	.342
1994	Florida	NL	12	11	2	0	0	0	(0	0)	2	1	1	0	0	1	0	0	1	0	0	.00	0	.182	.167	.182

				FIELDING AS CATCHER						
Year	Team	Lg	G	TC	PO	A	E	DP	PB	Pct.	Range
1994	Florida	NL	1	2	2	0	0	0	0	1.000	---

Bill O'Hara

William Alexander O'Hara
Bats: Left **Throws:** Right

Height: 5'10" **Weight:** Unknown
Born on August 14, 1883 in Toronto, Ontario
Died on June 15, 1931 in Jersey City, New Jersey

						BATTING														**BASERUNNING**				**PERCENTAGES**		
Year	Team	Lg	G	AB	H	2B	3B	HR	(Hm	Rd)	TB	R	RBI	TBB	IBB	SO	HBP	SH	SF	SB	CS	SB%	GDP	Avg	OBP	SLG
1909	New York	NL	115	360	85	9	3	1	--	--	103	48	30	41			2	11		31				.236	.318	.286
1910	St. Louis	NL	9	20	3	0	0	0	--	--	3	1	2	1		3	0	2		0				.150	.190	.150
	2 ML YEARS		124	380	88	9	3	1	--	--	106	49	32	42			2	13		31				.232	.311	.279

				HOW MUCH HE PITCHED				**WHAT HE GAVE UP**									**THE RESULTS**				
Year	Team	Lg	G	GS	CG	GF	IP	BFP	H	R	ER	HR	SH	SF	HB	TBB	IBB	SO	WP	Bk	W	L	Pct.	ShO	Sv	ERA
1910	St. Louis	NL	1	0	0	0	1		0	0	0	0	0	0	0	0	0	0	0	0	0	0	.000	0	0	0.00

				FIELDING AS PITCHER						
Year	Team	Lg	G	TC	PO	A	E	DP	PB	Pct.	Range
1910	St. Louis	NL	1	0	0	0	0	0	--	.000	---

				FIELDING AS FIRST BASEMAN						
Year	Team	Lg	G	TC	PO	A	E	DP	PB	Pct.	Range
1910	St. Louis	NL	1	7	7	0	0	0	--	1.000	---

				FIELDING AS OUTFIELDER						
Year	Team	Lg	G	TC	PO	A	E	DP	PB	Pct.	Range
1909	New York	NL	111	226	202	19	5	4	--	.978	1.99
1910	St. Louis	NL	4	8	7	1	0	0	--	1.000	2.00
	2 ML YEARS		115	234	209	20	5	4	--	.979	1.99

Bill O'Neill

William John O'Neill
Bats: Both **Throws:** Right

Height: 5'11" **Weight:** 175
Born on January 22, 1880 in St. John, New Brunswick
Died on July 20, 1920 in Woodhaven, New York

		BATTING																			BASERUNNING				PERCENTAGES		
Year Team	Lg	G	AB	H	2B	3B	HR	(Hm	Rd)	TB	R	RBI	TBB	IBB	SO	HBP	SH	SF	SB	CS	SB%	GDP	Avg	OBP	SLG
1904 2 ML Teams		112	416	99	11	1	1	--	--	115	40	21	24			4	5		22				.238	.286	.276
1906 Chicago	AL	94	330	82	4	1	1	--	--	91	37	21	22			3	12		19				.248	.301	.276
1904 Boston	AL	17	51	10	1	0	0	--	--	11	7	5	2			0	0		0				.196	.226	.216
Washington	AL	95	365	89	10	1	1	--	--	104	33	16	22			4	5		22				.244	.294	.285
2 ML YEARS		206	746	181	15	2	2	--	--	206	77	42	46			7	17		41				.243	.293	.276

World Series Batting

		BATTING																			BASERUNNING				PERCENTAGES		
Year Team	Lg	G	AB	H	2B	3B	HR	(Hm	Rd)	TB	R	RBI	TBB	IBB	SO	HBP	SH	SF	SB	CS	SB%	GDP	Avg	OBP	SLG
1906 Chicago	AL	1	1	0	0	0	0	(0	0)	0	1	0	0	0	0	0	0		0	0	.00	0	.000	.000	.000

FIELDING AS SECOND BASEMAN

Year Team	Lg	G	TC	PO	A	E	DP	PB	Pct.	Range
1904 Washington	AL	3	14	3	9	2	0	--	.857	4.00

FIELDING AS SHORTSTOP

Year Team	Lg	G	TC	PO	A	E	DP	PB	Pct.	Range
1904 Boston	AL	2	14	2	7	5	0	--	.643	4.50

FIELDING AS OUTFIELDER

Year Team	Lg	G	TC	PO	A	E	DP	PB	Pct.	Range
1904 2 ML Teams		102	183	155	9	19	1	--	.896	1.61
1906 Chicago	AL	93	137	118	12	7	1	--	.949	1.40
1904 Boston	AL	9	15	14	0	1	0	--	.933	1.56
Washington	AL	93	168	141	9	18	1	--	.893	1.61
2 ML YEARS		195	320	273	21	26	2	--	.919	1.51

World Series Fielding

FIELDING AS OUTFIELDER

Year Team	Lg	G	TC	PO	A	E	DP	PB	Pct.	Range
1906 Chicago	AL	1	1	1	0	0	0	--	1.000	1.00

Fred O'Neill

Frederick James O'Neill (Tip)
Bats: Unknown **Throws:** Unknown

Height: 5'7" **Weight:** 142
Born in 1865 in London, Ontario
Died on March 7, 1892 in London, Ontario

		BATTING																			BASERUNNING				PERCENTAGES		
Year Team	Lg	G	AB	H	2B	3B	HR	(Hm	Rd)	TB	R	RBI	TBB	IBB	SO	HBP	SH	SF	SB	CS	SB%	GDP	Avg	OBP	SLG
1887 New York	AA	6	26	8	1	1	0	--	--	11	4		1			1			3				.308	.357	.423

FIELDING AS OUTFIELDER

Year Team	Lg	G	TC	PO	A	E	DP	PB	Pct.	Range
1887 New York	AA	6	5	3	1	1	0	--	.800	.67

Harry O'Neill

Joseph Henry O'Neill
Pitches: Right **Bats:** Right

Height: 6'0" **Weight:** 180
Born on February 20, 1897 in Ridgetown, Ontario
Died on September 5, 1969 in Ridgetown, Ontario

		HOW MUCH HE PITCHED						WHAT HE GAVE UP											THE RESULTS					
Year Team	Lg	G	GS	CG	GF	IP	BFP	H	R	ER	HR	SH	SF	HB	TBB	IBB	SO	WP	Bk	W	L	Pct.	ShO	Sv	ERA
1922 Philadelphia	AL	1	0	0	1	3	12	2	1	1	0	0		1	1		0	0	0	0	0	.000	0	0	3.00
1923 Philadelphia	AL	3	0	0	0	2	9	1	0	0	0	0		0	3		2	0	0	0	0	.000	0	0	0.00
2 ML YEARS		4	0	0	1	5	21	3	1	1	0	0		1	4		2	0	0	0	0	.000	0	0	1.80

		BATTING																			BASERUNNING				PERCENTAGES		
Year Team	Lg	G	AB	H	2B	3B	HR	(Hm	Rd)	TB	R	RBI	TBB	IBB	SO	HBP	SH	SF	SB	CS	SB%	GDP	Avg	OBP	SLG
1922 Philadelphia	AL	1	1	0	0	0	0	--	--	0	0	0	0		0	0	0		0	0	.00		.000	.000	.000
1923 Philadelphia	AL	3	0	0	0	0	0	--	--	0	0	0	0		0	0	0		0	0	.00		.000	.000	.000
2 ML YEARS		4	1	0	0	0	0	--	--	0	0	0	0		0	0	0		0	0	.00		.000	.000	.000

FIELDING AS PITCHER

Year Team	Lg	G	TC	PO	A	E	DP	PB	Pct.	Range
1922 Philadelphia	AL	1	2	0	2	0	0	--	1.000	---
1923 Philadelphia	AL	3	0	0	0	0	0	--	.000	---
2 ML YEARS		4	2	0	2	0	0	--	1.000	---

Tip O'Neill

James Edward O'Neill
Bats: Right **Throws:** Right

Height: 6'1" **Weight:** 167
Born on May 25, 1858 in Woodstock, Ontario
Died on December 31, 1915 in Montreal, Quebec

BATTING / BASERUNNING / PERCENTAGES

Year Team	Lg	G	AB	H	2B	3B	HR	(Hm	Rd)	TB	R	RBI	TBB	IBB	SO	HBP	SH	SF	SB	CS	SB%	GDP	Avg	OBP	SLG
1883 New York	NL	23	76	15	3	0	0	--	--	18	8	5	3		15								.197	.228	.237
1884 St. Louis	AA	78	297	82	13	11	3	--	--	126	49		12			2							.276	.309	.424
1885 St. Louis	AA	52	206	72	7	4	3	--	--	96	44		13			4							.350	.399	.466
1886 St. Louis	AA	138	579	190	28	14	3	--	--	255	106		47			7			9				.328	.385	.440
1887 St. Louis	AA	124	517	225	52	19	14	--	--	357	167	123	50			5			30				.435	.490	.691
1888 St. Louis	AA	130	529	177	24	10	5	--	--	236	96	98	44			4			26				.335	.390	.446
1889 St. Louis	AA	134	534	179	33	8	9	--	--	255	123	110	72	37		5			28				.335	.419	.478
1890 Chicago	PL	137	577	174	20	16	3	--	--	235	112	75	65	36		5			29				.302	.377	.407
1891 St. Louis	AA	129	521	167	28	4	10	--	--	233	112	95	62	33		9			25				.321	.402	.447
1892 Cincinnati	NL	109	419	105	14	6	2	--	--	137	63	52	53	25		3			14				.251	.339	.327
10 ML YEARS		1054	4255	1386	222	92	52	--	--	1948	880		421			44	0						.326	.392	.458

World Series Batting / BASERUNNING / PERCENTAGES

Year Team	Lg	G	AB	H	2B	3B	HR	(Hm	Rd)	TB	R	RBI	TBB	IBB	SO	HBP	SH	SF	SB	CS	SB%	GDP	Avg	OBP	SLG
1885 St. Louis	AA	7	24	5	0	0	0	(0	0)	5	4		0	0					2				.208	.208	.208
1886 St. Louis	AA	6	20	8	0	2	2	--	--	18	4	5	4		5				0				.400	.500	.900
1887 St. Louis	AA	15	65	13	2	1	1	--	--	20	7	5	0	0	2				0				.200	.200	.308
1888 St. Louis	AA	10	37	9	1	0	2	--	--	16	8	11	6		3								.243	.349	.432
4 ML YEARS		38	146	35	3	3	5	--	--	59	23		10										.240	.288	.404

HOW MUCH HE PITCHED / WHAT HE GAVE UP / THE RESULTS

Year Team	Lg	G	GS	CG	GF	IP	BFP	H	R	ER	HR	SH	SF	HB	TBB	IBB	SO	WP	Bk	W	L	Pct.	ShO	Sv	ERA
1883 New York	NL	19	19	15	0	148	694	182	129	67	5				64		55	33	0	5	12	.294	0	0	4.07
1884 St. Louis	AA	17	14	14	3	141	625	125	95	42	3			4	51		36			11	4	.733	0	0	2.68
2 ML YEARS		36	33	29	3	289	1319	307	224	109	8				115		91			16	16	.500	0	0	3.39

FIELDING AS PITCHER

Year Team	Lg	G	TC	PO	A	E	DP	PB	Pct.	Range
1883 New York	NL	19	36	10	23	3	0	--	.917	---
1884 St. Louis	AA	17	42	6	31	5	0	--	.881	---
2 ML YEARS		36	78	16	54	8	0	--	.897	---

FIELDING AS FIRST BASEMAN

Year Team	Lg	G	TC	PO	A	E	DP	PB	Pct.	Range
1884 St. Louis	AA	1	2	2	0	0	0	--	1.000	---

FIELDING AS OUTFIELDER

Year Team	Lg	G	TC	PO	A	E	DP	PB	Pct.	Range
1883 New York	NL	7	10	7	1	2	0	--	.800	1.14
1884 St. Louis	AA	64	90	67	6	17	1	--	.811	1.14
1885 St. Louis	AA	52	101	83	6	12	1	--	.881	1.71
1886 St. Louis	AA	138	316	279	14	23	4	--	.927	2.12
1887 St. Louis	AA	124	285	247	8	30	2	--	.895	2.06
1888 St. Louis	AA	130	255	231	8	16	1	--	.937	1.84
1889 St. Louis	AA	134	295	264	12	19	3	--	.936	2.06
1890 Chicago	PL	137	258	231	8	19	1	--	.926	1.74
1891 St. Louis	AA	129	216	197	5	14	0	--	.935	1.57
1892 Cincinnati	NL	109	218	188	13	17	3	--	.922	1.84
10 ML YEARS		1024	2044	1794	81	169	16	--	.917	1.83

World Series Fielding — FIELDING AS OUTFIELDER

Year Team	Lg	G	TC	PO	A	E	DP	PB	Pct.	Range
1885 St. Louis	AA	7	3	2	0	1	0	--	.667	.29
1886 St. Louis	AA	6	14	13	1	0	0	--	1.000	2.33
1887 St. Louis	AA	15	30	26	2	2	2	--	.933	1.87
1888 St. Louis	AA	10	26	23	0	3	0	--	.885	2.30
4 ML YEARS		38	73	64	3	6	2	--	.918	1.76

Frank O'Rourke

James Francis O'Rourke (Blackie)
Bats: Right **Throws:** Right

Height: 5'10" **Weight:** 165
Born on November 28, 1894 in Hamilton, Ontario
Died on May 14, 1986 in Chatham, New Jersey

BATTING / BASERUNNING / PERCENTAGES

Year Team	Lg	G	AB	H	2B	3B	HR	(Hm	Rd)	TB	R	RBI	TBB	IBB	SO	HBP	SH	SF	SB	CS	SB%	GDP	Avg	OBP	SLG
1912 Boston	NL	61	196	24	3	1	0	--	--	29	11	16	11		50	2	7		1				.122	.177	.148
1917 Brooklyn	NL	64	198	47	7	1	0	--	--	56	18	15	14		25	2	7		11				.237	.294	.283
1918 Brooklyn	NL	4	12	2	0	0	0	--	--	2	0	2	1		3	0	0		0				.167	.231	.167
1920 Washington	AL	14	54	16	1	0	0	--	--	17	8	5	2		5	0	2		2	1	.67		.296	.321	.315
1921 Washington	AL	123	444	104	17	8	3	--	--	146	51	54	26		56	7	9		6	7	.46		.234	.287	.329
1922 Boston	AL	67	216	57	14	3	1	--	--	80	28	17	20		28	3	7		6	6	.50		.264	.335	.370
1924 Detroit	AL	47	181	50	11	2	0	--	--	65	28	19	12		19	3	10		7	4	.64		.276	.332	.359
1925 Detroit	AL	124	482	141	40	7	5	--	--	210	88	57	32		37	11	29		5	8	.38		.293	.350	.436
1926 Detroit	AL	111	363	88	16	1	1	--	--	109	43	41	35		33	7	17		8	6	.57		.242	.321	.300
1927 St. Louis	AL	140	538	144	25	3	1	--	--	178	85	39	64		43	**12**	13		19	8	.70		.268	.358	.331
1928 St. Louis	AL	99	391	103	24	3	1	--	--	136	54	62	21		19	1	25		10	2	.83		.263	.303	.348
1929 St. Louis	AL	154	585	147	23	9	2	--	--	194	81	62	41		28	5	28		14	7	.67		.251	.306	.332
1930 St. Louis	AL	115	400	107	15	4	1	--	--	133	52	41	35		30	0	15		11	9	.55		.268	.326	.333
1931 St. Louis	AL	8	9	2	0	0	0	--	--	2	0	0	0		1	0	1		1	1	.50		.222	.222	.222
14 ML YEARS		1131	4069	1032	196	42	15	--	--	1357	547	430	314		377	53	170		101				.254	.315	.333

FIELDING AS FIRST BASEMAN

Year Team	Lg	G	TC	PO	A	E	DP	PB	Pct.	Range
1927 St. Louis	AL	3	14	10	4	0	2	--	1.000	---
1930 St. Louis	AL	3	15	11	3	1	2	--	.933	---
1931 St. Louis	AL	1	14	14	0	0	0	--	1.000	---
3 ML YEARS		7	43	35	7	1	4	--	.977	---

FIELDING AS SECOND BASEMAN

Year Team	Lg	G	TC	PO	A	E	DP	PB	Pct.	Range
1918 Brooklyn	NL	2	14	2	10	2	1	--	.857	6.00
1924 Detroit	AL	40	257	112	137	8	26	--	.969	6.23
1925 Detroit	AL	118	712	309	382	21	67	--	**.971**	5.86
1926 Detroit	AL	41	241	98	135	8	25	--	.967	5.68
1927 St. Louis	AL	16	107	53	51	3	18	--	.972	6.50
1929 St. Louis	AL	3	10	6	4	0	1	--	1.000	3.33
6 ML YEARS		220	1341	580	719	42	138	--	.969	5.90

FIELDING AS THIRD BASEMAN

Year Team	Lg	G	TC	PO	A	E	DP	PB	Pct.	Range
1912 Boston	NL	1	3	1	1	1	1	--	.667	2.00
1917 Brooklyn	NL	58	216	72	134	10	6	--	.954	3.55
1920 Washington	AL	1	5	3	2	0	0	--	1.000	5.00
1922 Boston	AL	20	50	12	36	2	1	--	.960	2.40
1925 Detroit	AL	6	17	7	9	1	0	--	.941	2.67
1926 Detroit	AL	60	218	83	121	14	18	--	.936	3.40
1927 St. Louis	AL	121	447	183	244	20	27	--	.955	3.53
1928 St. Louis	AL	96	327	150	162	15	13	--	.954	3.25
1929 St. Louis	AL	151	438	171	242	25	30	--	.943	2.74
1930 St. Louis	AL	84	280	116	150	14	16	--	.950	3.17
10 ML YEARS		598	2001	798	1101	102	111	--	.949	3.18

FIELDING AS SHORTSTOP

Year Team	Lg	G	TC	PO	A	E	DP	PB	Pct.	Range
1912 Boston	NL	59	283	92	167	24	16	--	.915	4.39
1920 Washington	AL	13	84	35	45	4	12	--	.952	6.15
1921 Washington	AL	122	705	272	378	55	52	--	.922	5.33
1922 Boston	AL	48	242	86	134	22	17	--	.909	4.58
1924 Detroit	AL	7	40	12	25	3	1	--	.925	5.29
1926 Detroit	AL	10	17	9	7	1	0	--	.941	1.60
1928 St. Louis	AL	2	3	1	2	0	0	--	1.000	1.50
1929 St. Louis	AL	2	16	7	9	0	1	--	1.000	8.00
1930 St. Louis	AL	23	126	40	82	4	13	--	.968	5.30
1931 St. Louis	AL	2	4	1	3	0	0	--	1.000	2.00
10 ML YEARS		288	1520	555	852	113	112	--	.926	4.89

FIELDING AS OUTFIELDER

Year Team	Lg	G	TC	PO	A	E	DP	PB	Pct.	Range
1918 Brooklyn	NL	1	2	1	1	0	0	--	1.000	2.00

Fred Osborne

Frederick W. Osborne
Bats: Unknown **Throws:** Left
Height: Unknown **Weight:** Unknown
Born Unknown in Canada

BATTING / BASERUNNING / PERCENTAGES

Year Team	Lg	G	AB	H	2B	3B	HR	(Hm	Rd)	TB	R	RBI	TBB	IBB	SO	HBP	SH	SF	SB	CS	SB%	GDP	Avg	OBP	SLG
1890 Pittsburgh	NL	41	168	40	8	3	1	--	--	57	24	14	6		18	1			0				.238	.269	.339

HOW MUCH HE PITCHED / WHAT HE GAVE UP / THE RESULTS

Year Team	Lg	G	GS	CG	GF	IP	BFP	H	R	ER	HR	SH	SF	TBB	IBB	SO	WP	Bk	W	L	Pct.	ShO	Sv	ERA
1890 Pittsburgh	NL	8	5	5	3	58	318	82	87	54	6			8		45	14	16	0	5	.000	0	0	8.38

FIELDING AS PITCHER

Year Team	Lg	G	TC	PO	A	E	DP	PB	Pct.	Range
1890 Pittsburgh	NL	8	17	3	11	3	0	--	.824	---

FIELDING AS OUTFIELDER

Year Team	Lg	G	TC	PO	A	E	DP	PB	Pct.	Range
1890 Pittsburgh	NL	35	87	64	8	15	0	--	.828	2.06

Brian Ostrosser

Brian Leonard Ostrosser
Bats: Left **Throws:** Right
Height: 6'0" **Weight:** 175
Born on June 17, 1949 in Hamilton, Ontario

BATTING / BASERUNNING / PERCENTAGES

Year Team	Lg	G	AB	H	2B	3B	HR	(Hm	Rd)	TB	R	RBI	TBB	IBB	SO	HBP	SH	SF	SB	CS	SB%	GDP	Avg	OBP	SLG
1973 New York	NL	4	5	0	0	0	0	(0	0)	0	0	0	0	0	2	0	0	0	0	0	.00	0	.000	.000	.000

FIELDING AS SHORTSTOP

Year Team	Lg	G	TC	PO	A	E	DP	PB	Pct.	Range
1973 New York	NL	4	5	1	4	0	0	--	1.000	1.25

Frank Owens

Frank Walter Owens (Yip)
Bats: Right **Throws:** Right
Height: 6'0" **Weight:** 170
Born on January 26, 1886 in Toronto, Ontario
Died on July 2, 1958 in Minneapolis, Minnesota

BATTING / BASERUNNING / PERCENTAGES

Year Team	Lg	G	AB	H	2B	3B	HR	(Hm	Rd)	TB	R	RBI	TBB	IBB	SO	HBP	SH	SF	SB	CS	SB%	GDP	Avg	OBP	SLG
1905 Boston	AL	1	2	0	0	0	0	--	--	0	0	0	0			0	0		0				.000	.000	.000
1909 Chicago	AL	64	174	35	4	1	0	--	--	41	12	17	8		2	9			3				.201	.245	.236
1914 Brooklyn	FL	58	184	51	7	3	2	--	--	70	15	20	9	16	1	2			2				.277	.314	.380
1915 Baltimore	FL	99	334	84	14	7	3	--	--	121	32	28	17	34	1	8			4				.251	.290	.362
4 ML YEARS		222	694	170	25	11	5	--	--	232	59	65	34		4	19			9				.245	.284	.334

FIELDING AS CATCHER

Year Team	Lg	G	TC	PO	A	E	DP	PB	Pct.	Range
1905 Boston	AL	1	3	2	1	0	0	3	1.000	---
1909 Chicago	AL	57	342	266	62	14	2	10	.959	---
1914 Brooklyn	FL	58	305	228	67	10	10	4	.967	---
1915 Baltimore	FL	99	623	462	146	15	19	5	.976	---
4 ML YEARS		215	1273	958	276	39	31	22	.969	---

Henry Oxley

Henry Havelock Oxley
Bats: Unknown **Throws:** Unknown
Height: 5'11" **Weight:** 163
Born on January 4, 1858 in Covehead, Prince Edward Island
Died on October 12, 1945 in Somerville, Massachusetts

BATTING / BASERUNNING / PERCENTAGES

Year Team	Lg	G	AB	H	2B	3B	HR	(Hm	Rd)	TB	R	RBI	TBB	IBB	SO	HBP	SH	SF	SB	CS	SB%	GDP	Avg	OBP	SLG
1884 2 ML Teams		3	7	0	0	0	0	--	--	0	0		1										.000	.125	.000
1884 New York	NL	2	4	0	0	0	0	--	--	0	0	0	1		2								.000	.200	.000
New York	AA	1	3	0	0	0	0	--	--	0	0		0		0								.000	.000	.000

FIELDING AS CATCHER

Year Team	Lg	G	TC	PO	A	E	DP	PB	Pct.	Range
1884 2 ML Teams		3	19	11	6	2	0	6	.895	---
1884 New York	NL	2	10	4	5	1	0	4	.900	---
New York	AA	1	9	7	1	1	0	2	.889	---

Dave Pagan

David Percy Pagan
Pitches: Right   **Bats:** Right

Height: 6'2"   **Weight:** 175
Born on September 15, 1949 in Nipawin, Saskatchewan

			HOW MUCH HE PITCHED							WHAT HE GAVE UP											THE RESULTS						
Year Team	Lg	G	GS	CG	GF	IP	BFP	H	R	ER	HR	SH	SF	HB	TBB	IBB	SO	WP	Bk	W	L	Pct.	ShO	Sv	ERA
1973 New York	AL	4	1	0	2	12.2	51	16	4	4	1	0	0	0	1	0	9	0	0	0	0	.000	0	0	2.84
1974 New York	AL	16	6	1	2	49.1	214	49	29	28	1	1	0	0	28	0	39	3	0	1	3	.250	0	0	5.11
1975 New York	AL	13	0	0	5	31	135	30	16	14	2	1	2	2	13	5	18	1	0	0	0	.000	0	1	4.06
1976 2 ML Teams		27	7	1	5	70.1	300	72	40	37	2	2	8	1	27	1	47	4	0	2	5	.286	0	1	4.73
1977 2 ML Teams		25	4	1	10	69	310	87	52	45	3	2	4	2	26	2	34	2	0	1	1	.500	1	2	5.87
1976 New York	AL	7	2	1	0	23.2	87	18	7	6	0	0	2	0	4	0	13	0	0	1	1	.500	0	0	2.28
Baltimore	AL	20	5	0	5	46.2	213	54	33	31	2	2	6	1	23	1	34	4	0	1	4	.200	0	1	5.98
1977 Seattle	AL	24	4	1	10	66	300	86	52	45	3	2	4	2	26	2	30	2	0	1	1	.500	1	2	6.14
Pittsburgh	NL	1	0	0	0	3	10	1	0	0	0	0	0	0	0	0	4	0	0	0	0	.000	0	0	0.00
5 ML YEARS		85	18	3	24	232.1	1010	254	141	128	9	6	14	5	95	8	147	10	0	4	9	.308	1	4	4.96

					BATTING														BASERUNNING				PERCENTAGES		
Year Team	Lg	G	AB	H	2B	3B	HR	(Hm	Rd)	TB	R	RBI	TBB	IBB	SO	HBP	SH	SF	SB	CS	SB%	GDP	Avg	OBP	SLG
1977 Pittsburgh	NL	1	0	0	0	0	0	(0	0)	0	0	0	0	0	0	0	0	0	0	0	.00	0	.000	.000	.000

FIELDING AS PITCHER

Year Team	Lg	G	TC	PO	A	E	DP	PB	Pct.	Range
1973 New York	AL	4	3	2	1	0	0	--	1.000	---
1974 New York	AL	16	8	3	5	0	0	--	1.000	---
1975 New York	AL	13	7	5	1	1	0	--	.857	---
1976 2 ML Teams		27	9	6	2	1	0	--	.889	---
1977 2 ML Teams		25	14	3	11	0	0	--	1.000	---
1976 New York	AL	7	3	2	1	0	0	--	1.000	---
Baltimore	AL	20	6	4	1	1	0	--	.833	---
1977 Seattle	AL	24	13	3	10	0	0	--	1.000	---
Pittsburgh	NL	1	1	0	1	0	0	--	1.000	---
5 ML YEARS		85	41	19	20	2	0	--	.951	---

Harley Payne

Harley Fenwick Payne (Lady)
Pitches: Left   **Bats:** Both

Height: 6'0"   **Weight:** 160
Born on January 9, 1868 in Windsor, Ontario
Died on December 29, 1935 in Orwell, Ohio

			HOW MUCH HE PITCHED							WHAT HE GAVE UP											THE RESULTS						
Year Team	Lg	G	GS	CG	GF	IP	BFP	H	R	ER	HR	SH	SF	HB	TBB	IBB	SO	WP	Bk	W	L	Pct.	ShO	Sv	ERA
1896 Brooklyn	NL	34	28	24	6	241.2	1065	284	129	91	4	23		8	58		52	1	0	14	16	.467	2	0	3.39
1897 Brooklyn	NL	40	38	30	2	280	1283	350	215	144	8	16		17	71		86	7	1	14	17	.452	1	0	4.63
1898 Brooklyn	NL	1	1	1	0	9	40	11	8	4	0	0		0	3		2	1	0	1	0	1.000	0	0	4.00
1899 Pittsburgh	NL	5	5	2	0	26.1	117	33	19	11	2	5		2	4		8	0	1	1	3	.250	0	0	3.76
4 ML YEARS		80	72	57	8	557	2505	678	371	250	14	44		27	136		148	9	2	30	36	.455	3	0	4.04

					BATTING														BASERUNNING				PERCENTAGES		
Year Team	Lg	G	AB	H	2B	3B	HR	(Hm	Rd)	TB	R	RBI	TBB	IBB	SO	HBP	SH	SF	SB	CS	SB%	GDP	Avg	OBP	SLG
1896 Brooklyn	NL	38	98	21	4	1	0	--	--	27	5	10	9		3	0	4		0				.214	.280	.276
1897 Brooklyn	NL	41	110	26	0	1	0	--	--	28	13	11	8			0	3		0				.236	.288	.255
1898 Brooklyn	NL	1	4	3	0	0	0	--	--	3	1	3	0			0	0		0				.750	.750	.750
1899 Pittsburgh	NL	5	10	1	0	0	0	--	--	1	1	0	1			0	0		0				.100	.182	.100
4 ML YEARS		85	222	51	4	2	0	--	--	59	20	24	18			0	7		0				.230	.288	.266

FIELDING AS PITCHER

Year Team	Lg	G	TC	PO	A	E	DP	PB	Pct.	Range
1896 Brooklyn	NL	34	95	12	76	7	1	--	.926	---
1897 Brooklyn	NL	40	84	11	68	5	1	--	.940	---
1898 Brooklyn	NL	1	4	0	4	0	0	--	1.000	---
1899 Pittsburgh	NL	5	20	0	18	2	0	--	.900	---
4 ML YEARS		80	203	23	166	14	2	--	.931	---

FIELDING AS OUTFIELDER

Year Team	Lg	G	TC	PO	A	E	DP	PB	Pct.	Range
1896 Brooklyn	NL	1	0	0	0	0	0	--	.000	.00
1897 Brooklyn	NL	1	2	2	0	0	0	--	1.000	2.00
2 ML YEARS		2	2	2	0	0	0	--	1.000	1.00

Bill Pfann

William F. Pfann
Pitches: Unknown **Bats:** Unknown

Height: 6'0" **Weight:** 205
Born in June, 1863 in Hamilton, Ontario
Died on June 3, 1904 in Hamilton, Ontario

		HOW MUCH HE PITCHED						WHAT HE GAVE UP												THE RESULTS					
Year Team	Lg	G	GS	CG	GF	IP	BFP	H	R	ER	HR	SH	SF	HB	TBB	IBB	SO	WP	Bk	W	L	Pct.	ShO	Sv	ERA
1894 Cincinnati	NL	1	1	0	0	3	22	10	10	9	1	0		0	4		0	0	0	0	1	.000	0	0	27.00

		BATTING																	BASERUNNING				PERCENTAGES		
Year Team	Lg	G	AB	H	2B	3B	HR	(Hm	Rd)	TB	R	RBI	TBB	IBB	SO	HBP	SH	SF	SB	CS	SB%	GDP	Avg	OBP	SLG
1894 Cincinnati	NL	1	1	0	0	0	0	--	--	0	0	0	0		0	0	0		0				.000	.000	.000

	FIELDING AS PITCHER									
Year Team	Lg	G	TC	PO	A	E	DP	PB	Pct.	Range
1894 Cincinnati	NL	1	2	0	2	0	0	--	1.000	---

Bill Phillips

William B. Phillips
Bats: Right **Throws:** Right

Height: Unknown **Weight:** 202
Born in 1857 in St. John, New Brunswick
Died on October 7, 1900 in Chicago, Illinois

		BATTING																	BASERUNNING				PERCENTAGES		
Year Team	Lg	G	AB	H	2B	3B	HR	(Hm	Rd)	TB	R	RBI	TBB	IBB	SO	HBP	SH	SF	SB	CS	SB%	GDP	Avg	OBP	SLG
1879 Cleveland	NL	81	365	99	15	4	0	--	--	122	58	29	2		20								.271	.275	.334
1880 Cleveland	NL	85	334	85	14	10	1	--	--	122	41	36	6		29								.254	.268	.365
1881 Cleveland	NL	85	357	97	18	10	1	--	--	138	51	44	5		19								.272	.282	.387
1882 Cleveland	NL	78	335	87	17	7	4	--	--	130	40	47	7		18								.260	.275	.388
1883 Cleveland	NL	97	382	94	29	8	2	--	--	145	42	40	8		49								.246	.262	.380
1884 Cleveland	NL	111	464	128	25	12	3	--	--	186	58	46	18		80								.276	.303	.401
1885 Brooklyn	AA	99	391	118	16	11	3	--	--	165	65		27		13				11				.302	.364	.422
1886 Brooklyn	AA	141	585	160	26	15	0	--	--	216	68		33		13				1				.274	.313	.369
1887 Brooklyn	AA	132	533	142	34	11	2	--	--	204	82		45		16				6				.266	.330	.383
1888 Kansas City	AA	129	509	120	20	10	1	--	--	163	57	56	27		10				7				.236	.284	.320
10 ML YEARS		1038	4255	1130	214	98	17	--		1591	562		178						25	0			.266	.299	.374

	FIELDING AS CATCHER									
Year Team	Lg	G	TC	PO	A	E	DP	PB	Pct.	Range
1879 Cleveland	NL	11	76	48	10	18	2	26	.763	---
1882 Cleveland	NL	1	4	3	1	0	0	0	1.000	---
2 ML YEARS		12	80	51	11	18	2	26	.775	

	FIELDING AS FIRST BASEMAN									
Year Team	Lg	G	TC	PO	A	E	DP	PB	Pct.	Range
1879 Cleveland	NL	75	784	726	22	36	23	--	.954	---
1880 Cleveland	NL	85	900	842	25	33	37	--	.963	---
1881 Cleveland	NL	85	859	806	24	29	51	--	.966	---
1882 Cleveland	NL	78	876	827	24	25	55	--	.971	---
1883 Cleveland	NL	97	1008	953	22	33	53	--	.967	---
1884 Cleveland	NL	111	1185	1107	30	48	59	--	.959	---
1885 Brooklyn	AA	99	1165	1109	24	32	40	--	.973	---
1886 Brooklyn	AA	141	1460	1395	33	32	65	--	.978	---
1887 Brooklyn	AA	132	1369	1299	46	24	62	--	.982	---
1888 Kansas City	AA	129	1563	1476	55	32	66	--	.980	---
10 ML YEARS		1032	11169	10540	305	324	511	--	.971	---

	FIELDING AS OUTFIELDER									
Year Team	Lg	G	TC	PO	A	E	DP	PB	Pct.	Range
1879 Cleveland	NL	2	1	1	0	0	0	--	1.000	.50

Ron Piche

Ronald Jacques Piche
Pitches: Right **Bats:** Right

Height: 5'11" **Weight:** 165
Born on May 22, 1935 in Verdun, Quebec

		HOW MUCH HE PITCHED						WHAT HE GAVE UP												THE RESULTS					
Year Team	Lg	G	GS	CG	GF	IP	BFP	H	R	ER	HR	SH	SF	HB	TBB	IBB	SO	WP	Bk	W	L	Pct.	ShO	Sv	ERA
1960 Milwaukee	NL	37	0	0	27	48	218	48	26	19	3	4	2	3	23	4	38	2	0	3	5	.375	0	9	3.56
1961 Milwaukee	NL	12	1	1	5	23.1	104	20	12	9	1	2	2	0	16	2	16	0	0	2	2	.500	0	1	3.47
1962 Milwaukee	NL	14	8	2	1	52	235	54	32	28	6	2	3	3	29	3	28	0	0	3	2	.600	0	0	4.85
1963 Milwaukee	NL	37	1	0	7	53	236	53	32	20	4	2	2	0	25	6	40	2	1	1	1	.500	0	0	3.40
1965 California	AL	14	1	0	11	19.2	89	20	15	15	5	1	1	0	12	2	14	1	0	0	3	.000	0	0	6.86

Year Team	Lg	G	GS	CG	GF	IP	BFP	H	R	ER	HR	SH	SF	HB	TBB	IBB	SO	WP	Bk	W	L	Pct.	ShO	Sv	ERA
1966 St. Louis	NL	20	0	0	5	25.1	119	21	13	12	4	1	1	1	18	4	21	2	1	1	3	.250	0	2	4.26
6 ML YEARS		134	11	3	56	221.1	1001	216	130	103	23	12	11	7	123	21	157	9	2	10	16	.385	0	12	4.19

BATTING

Year Team	Lg	G	AB	H	2B	3B	HR	(Hm	Rd)	TB	R	RBI	TBB	IBB	SO	HBP	SH	SF	SB	CS	SB%	GDP	Avg	OBP	SLG
1960 Milwaukee	NL	37	7	0	0	0	0	(0	0)	0	0	0	2	0	5	0	0	0	0	0	.00	0	.000	.222	.000
1961 Milwaukee	NL	12	5	0	0	0	0	(0	0)	0	0	0	0	0	2	0	1	0	0	0	.00	0	.000	.000	.000
1962 Milwaukee	NL	16	18	1	0	0	0	(0	0)	1	1	2	1	0	12	0	0	0	0	0	.00	0	.056	.105	.056
1963 Milwaukee	NL	37	7	0	0	0	0	(0	0)	0	0	0	0	0	5	0	0	0	0	0	.00	0	.000	.000	.000
1965 California	AL	14	1	0	0	0	0	(0	0)	0	0	0	0	0	0	0	0	0	0	0	.00	0	.000	.000	.000
1966 St. Louis	NL	20	4	0	0	0	0	(0	0)	0	0	0	0	0	2	0	1	0	0	0	.00	0	.000	.000	.000
6 ML YEARS		136	42	1	0	0	0	(0	0)	1	1	2	3	0	26	0	2	0	0	0	.00	0	.024	.089	.024

FIELDING AS PITCHER

Year Team	Lg	G	TC	PO	A	E	DP	PB	Pct.	Range
1960 Milwaukee	NL	37	9	4	4	1	1	--	.889	---
1961 Milwaukee	NL	12	6	0	6	0	1	--	1.000	---
1962 Milwaukee	NL	14	16	7	9	0	1	--	1.000	---
1963 Milwaukee	NL	37	21	8	13	0	0	--	1.000	---
1965 California	AL	14	5	2	3	0	0	--	1.000	---
1966 St. Louis	NL	20	3	1	2	0	0	--	1.000	---
6 ML YEARS		134	60	22	37	1	3	--	.983	

Ed Pinnance

Edward D. Pinnance
Pitches: Right **Bats:** Left

Height: 6'1" **Weight:** 180
Born on October 22, 1879 in Walpole Island, Ontario
Died on December 12, 1944 in Walpole Island, Ontario

HOW MUCH HE PITCHED / WHAT HE GAVE UP / THE RESULTS

Year Team	Lg	G	GS	CG	GF	IP	BFP	H	R	ER	HR	SH	SF	HB	TBB	IBB	SO	WP	Bk	W	L	Pct.	ShO	Sv	ERA
1903 Philadelphia	AL	2	1	0	1	7	26	5	2	2	0	0	0	0	2		2	0	0	0	0	.000	0	1	2.57

BATTING

Year Team	Lg	G	AB	H	2B	3B	HR	(Hm	Rd)	TB	R	RBI	TBB	IBB	SO	HBP	SH	SF	SB	CS	SB%	GDP	Avg	OBP	SLG
1903 Philadelphia	AL	2	3	0	0	0	0	(--	--)	0	0	0	0	0	0	0	0		0				.000	.000	.000

FIELDING AS PITCHER

Year Team	Lg	G	TC	PO	A	E	DP	PB	Pct.	Range
1903 Philadelphia	AL	2	2	1	1	0	0	--	1.000	---

Dick Pirie

Richard J. Pirie
Bats: Unknown **Throws:** Unknown

Height: 5'8" **Weight:** 169
Born on March 31, 1853 in Ontario
Died on June 2, 1934 in Dundas, Ontario

BATTING

Year Team	Lg	G	AB	H	2B	3B	HR	(Hm	Rd)	TB	R	RBI	TBB	IBB	SO	HBP	SH	SF	SB	CS	SB%	GDP	Avg	OBP	SLG
1883 Philadelphia	NL	5	19	3	0	0	0	(--	--)	3	1	0	0		2								.158	.158	.158

FIELDING AS SHORTSTOP

Year Team	Lg	G	TC	PO	A	E	DP	PB	Pct.	Range
1883 Philadelphia	NL	5	26	6	9	11	1	--	.577	3.00

Gordy Pladson

Gordon Cecil Pladson
Attended Douglas
Pitches: Right **Bats:** Right

Height: 6'4" **Weight:** 210
Born on July 31, 1956 in New Westminster, British Columbia

HOW MUCH HE PITCHED / WHAT HE GAVE UP / THE RESULTS

Year Team	Lg	G	GS	CG	GF	IP	BFP	H	R	ER	HR	SH	SF	HB	TBB	IBB	SO	WP	Bk	W	L	Pct.	ShO	Sv	ERA
1979 Houston	NL	4	0	0	2	4	22	9	2	2	1	0	0	0	2	0	2	0	0	0	0	.000	0	0	4.50
1980 Houston	NL	12	6	0	1	41.1	175	38	23	20	3	2	1	0	16	0	13	0	0	0	4	.000	0	0	4.35
1981 Houston	NL	2	0	0	0	4	24	9	4	4	0	0	0	0	3	0	3	0	1	0	0	.000	0	0	9.00
1982 Houston	NL	2	0	0	1	1.1	16	10	8	8	0	0	0	0	2	0	0	0	0	0	0	.000	0	0	54.00
4 ML YEARS		20	6	0	4	50.2	237	66	37	34	4	2	2	0	23	0	18	0	1	0	4	.000	0	0	6.04

BATTING

Year Team	Lg	G	AB	H	2B	3B	HR	(Hm	Rd)	TB	R	RBI	TBB	IBB	SO	HBP	SH	SF	SB	CS	SB%	GDP	Avg	OBP	SLG
1979 Houston	NL	4	0	0	0	0	0	(0	0)	0	0	0	0	0	0	0	0		0	0	.00	0	.000	.000	.000

1980 Houston	NL	12	10	0	0	0	0	(0	0)	0	1	0	1	0	5	0	0	0	0	0	.00	0	.000	.091	.000
1981 Houston	NL	2	0	0	0	0	0	(0	0)	0	0	0	0	0	0	0	0	0	0	0	.00	0	.000	.000	.000
1982 Houston	NL	2	0	0	0	0	0	(0	0)	0	0	0	0	0	0	0	0	0	0	0	.00	0	.000	.000	.000
4 ML YEARS		20	10	0	0	0	0	(0	0)	0	1	0	1	0	5	0	0	0	0	0	.00	0	.000	.091	.000

FIELDING AS PITCHER

Year Team	Lg	G	TC	PO	A	E	DP	PB	Pct.	Range
1979 Houston	NL	4	0	0	0	0	0	--	.000	---
1980 Houston	NL	12	14	3	9	2	0	--	.857	---
1981 Houston	NL	2	0	0	0	0	0	--	.000	---
1982 Houston	NL	2	0	0	0	0	0	--	.000	---
4 ML YEARS		20	14	3	9	2	0	--	.857	---

Terry Puhl

Terry Stephen Puhl
Bats: Left **Throws:** Right

Height: 6'2" **Weight:** 195
Born on July 8, 1956 in Melville, Saskatchewan

					BATTING														BASERUNNING				PERCENTAGES		
Year Team	Lg	G	AB	H	2B	3B	HR	(Hm	Rd)	TB	R	RBI	TBB	IBB	SO	HBP	SH	SF	SB	CS	SB%	GDP	Avg	OBP	SLG
1974 Covington	R	59	211	60	11	0	0	--	--	71	42	21	24		26	3	2	4	17	2	.89		.284	.360	.336
1975 Dubuque	A	104	346	115	10	2	0	--	--	129	57	28	41		30	1	5	3	30	4	.88		.332	.402	.373
1976 Columbus	AA	28	98	28	5	0	1	--	--	36	13	14	16		12	0	3	0	11	2	.85		.286	.386	.367
Memphis	AAA	105	372	99	17	3	1	--	--	125	50	39	60		57	1	2	1	18	8	.69		.266	.369	.336
1977 Charleston	AAA	78	285	87	12	6	4	--	--	123	53	33	52		27	1	1	3	12	10	.55		.305	.411	.432
1977 Houston	NL	60	229	69	13	5	0	(0	0)	92	40	10	30	0	31	1	5	0	10	1	.91	3	.301	.385	.402
1978 Houston	NL	149	585	169	25	6	3	(1	2)	215	87	35	48	5	46	4	3	7	32	14	.70	11	.289	.343	.368
1979 Houston	NL	157	600	172	22	4	8	(2	6)	226	87	49	58	8	46	4	8	2	30	22	.58	7	.287	.352	.377
1980 Houston	NL	141	535	151	24	5	13	(4	9)	224	75	55	60	3	52	4	6	3	27	11	.71	3	.282	.357	.419
1981 Houston	NL	96	350	88	19	4	3	(1	2)	124	43	28	31	5	49	4	4	5	22	4	.85	3	.251	.315	.354
1982 Houston	NL	145	507	133	17	9	8	(5	3)	192	64	50	51	2	49	2	5	2	17	9	.65	6	.262	.331	.379
1983 Houston	NL	137	465	136	25	7	8	(1	7)	199	66	44	36	2	48	2	5	4	24	11	.69	4	.292	.343	.428
1984 Houston	NL	132	449	135	19	7	9	(2	7)	195	66	55	59	12	45	1	6	4	13	8	.62	5	.301	.380	.434
1985 Houston	NL	57	194	55	14	3	2	(1	1)	81	34	23	18	4	23	1	4	3	6	2	.75	0	.284	.343	.418
1986 Houston	NL	81	172	42	10	0	3	(1	2)	61	17	14	15	1	24	0	4	2	3	2	.60	6	.244	.302	.355
1987 Houston	NL	90	122	28	5	0	2	(1	1)	39	9	15	11	0	16	0	1	0	1	1	.50	3	.230	.293	.320
1988 Houston	NL	113	234	71	7	2	3	(2	1)	91	42	19	35	3	30	1	1	1	22	4	.85	0	.303	.395	.389
1989 Houston	NL	121	354	96	25	4	0	(0	0)	129	41	27	45	3	39	1	4	2	9	8	.53	7	.271	.353	.364
1990 Houston	NL	37	41	12	1	0	0	(0	0)	13	5	8	5	0	7	1	1	1	1	2	.33	0	.293	.375	.317
1991 Kansas City	AL	15	18	4	0	0	0	(0	0)	4	0	3	3	1	2	0	0	0	0	0	.00	1	.222	.333	.222
15 ML YEARS		1531	4855	1361	226	56	62	(21	41)	1885	676	435	505	49	507	26	57	36	217	99	.69	59	.280	.349	.388

Division Playoffs Batting

					BATTING														BASERUNNING				PERCENTAGES		
Year Team	Lg	G	AB	H	2B	3B	HR	(Hm	Rd)	TB	R	RBI	TBB	IBB	SO	HBP	SH	SF	SB	CS	SB%	GDP	Avg	OBP	SLG
1981 Houston	NL	5	21	4	1	0	0	(0	0)	5	2	0	0	0	1	0	0	0	1	0	1.00	0	.190	.190	.238

League Championship Batting

					BATTING														BASERUNNING				PERCENTAGES		
Year Team	Lg	G	AB	H	2B	3B	HR	(Hm	Rd)	TB	R	RBI	TBB	IBB	SO	HBP	SH	SF	SB	CS	SB%	GDP	Avg	OBP	SLG
1980 Houston	NL	5	19	10	2	0	0	(0	0)	12	4	3	3	0	2	0	0	0	2	0	1.00	0	.526	.591	.632
1986 Houston	NL	3	3	2	0	0	0	(0	0)	2	0	0	0	0	0	0	0	0	1	0	1.00	0	.667	.667	.667
2 ML YEARS		8	22	12	2	0	0	(0	0)	14	4	3	3	0	2	0	0	0	3	0	1.00	0	.545	.600	.636

FIELDING AS FIRST BASEMAN

Year Team	Lg	G	TC	PO	A	E	DP	PB	Pct.	Range
1989 Houston	NL	3	8	8	0	0	1	--	1.000	---
1990 Houston	NL	1	1	1	0	0	0	--	1.000	---
2 ML YEARS		4	9	9	0	0	1	--	1.000	---

FIELDING AS OUTFIELDER

Year Team	Lg	G	TC	PO	A	E	DP	PB	Pct.	Range
1977 Houston	NL	59	123	119	3	1	0	--	.992	2.07
1978 Houston	NL	148	395	386	6	3	2	--	.992	2.65
1979 Houston	NL	152	359	352	7	0	3	--	1.000	2.36
1980 Houston	NL	135	328	311	14	3	3	--	.991	2.41
1981 Houston	NL	88	190	185	5	0	1	--	1.000	2.16
1982 Houston	NL	138	264	257	4	3	3	--	.989	1.89
1983 Houston	NL	124	226	220	4	2	1	--	.991	1.81
1984 Houston	NL	126	222	213	6	3	4	--	.986	1.74
1985 Houston	NL	53	95	92	3	0	1	--	1.000	1.79
1986 Houston	NL	47	65	65	0	0	0	--	1.000	1.38

Year	Team	Lg	G	TC	PO	A	E	DP	PB	Pct.	Range
1987	Houston	NL	40	49	48	0	1	0	--	.980	1.20
1988	Houston	NL	78	120	116	2	2	0	--	.983	1.51
1989	Houston	NL	103	207	204	3	0	0	--	1.000	2.01
1990	Houston	NL	8	8	8	0	0	0	--	1.000	1.00
1991	Kansas City	AL	1	0	0	0	0	0	--	.000	.00
15 ML YEARS			1300	2651	2576	57	18	18	--	.993	2.03

Division Playoffs Fielding

FIELDING AS OUTFIELDER

Year	Team	Lg	G	TC	PO	A	E	DP	PB	Pct.	Range
1981	Houston	NL	5	8	7	1	0	0	--	1.000	1.60

League Championship Fielding

FIELDING AS OUTFIELDER

Year	Team	Lg	G	TC	PO	A	E	DP	PB	Pct.	Range
1980	Houston	NL	4	13	13	0	0	0	--	1.000	3.25

Paul Quantrill

Paul John Quantrill
Pitches: Right **Bats:** Left
Height: 6'1" **Weight:** 175
Born on November 3, 1968 in London, Ontario

HOW MUCH HE PITCHED / WHAT HE GAVE UP / THE RESULTS

Year	Team	Lg	G	GS	CG	GF	IP	BFP	H	R	ER	HR	SH	SF	HB	TBB	IBB	SO	WP	Bk	W	L	Pct.	ShO	Sv	ERA
1989	Red Sox	R	2	0	0	2	5	18	2	0	0	0	0	0	0	0	0	5	0	0	0	0	.000	0	0	0.00
	Elmira	A	20	7	5	7	76	326	90	37	29	5	4	3	6	12	2	57	1	2	5	4	.556	0	2	3.43
1990	Winter Havn	A	7	7	1	0	45.2	182	46	24	21	3	0	2	0	6	0	14	3	0	2	5	.286	0	0	4.14
	New Britain	AA	22	22	1	0	132.2	549	149	65	52	3	4	7	4	23	2	53	3	2	7	11	.389	1	0	3.53
1991	New Britain	AA	5	5	1	0	35	142	32	14	8	2	3	1	1	8	0	18	0	0	2	1	.667	0	0	2.06
	Pawtucket	AAA	25	23	6	0	155.2	645	169	81	77	14	9	2	4	30	1	75	2	2	10	7	.588	2	0	4.45
1992	Pawtucket	AAA	19	18	4	1	119	504	143	63	59	16	3	1	4	20	1	56	1	1	6	8	.429	1	0	4.46
1994	Scranton-Wb	AAA	8	8	1	0	57	228	55	25	22	5	2	1	2	6	0	36	1	0	3	3	.500	1	0	3.47
1992	Boston	AL	27	0	0	10	49.1	213	55	18	12	1	4	2	1	15	5	24	1	0	2	3	.400	0	1	2.19
1993	Boston	AL	49	14	1	8	138	594	151	73	60	13	4	2	2	44	14	66	0	1	6	12	.333	1	1	3.91
1994	2 ML Teams		35	1	0	9	53	236	64	31	29	7	5	3	5	15	4	28	0	2	3	3	.500	0	1	4.92
1995	Philadelphia	NL	33	29	0	1	179.1	784	212	102	93	20	9	6	6	44	3	103	0	3	11	12	.478	0	0	4.67
1994	Boston	AL	17	0	0	4	23	101	25	10	9	4	2	2	2	5	1	15	0	0	1	1	.500	0	0	3.52
	Philadelphia	NL	18	1	0	5	30	135	39	21	20	3	3	1	3	10	3	13	0	2	2	2	.500	0	1	6.00
4 ML YEARS			144	44	1	28	419.2	1827	482	224	194	41	22	13	14	118	26	221	1	6	22	30	.423	1	3	4.16

BATTING / BASERUNNING / PERCENTAGES

Year	Team	Lg	G	AB	H	2B	3B	HR	(Hm	Rd)	TB	R	RBI	TBB	IBB	SO	HBP	SH	SF	SB	CS	SB%	GDP	Avg	OBP	SLG
1994	Philadelphia	NL	18	3	0	0	0	0	(0	0)	0	0	0	0	1	0	0	0	0	0	0	.00	0	.000	.000	.000
1995	Philadelphia	NL	33	57	6	0	0	0	(0	0)	6	5	0	3	0	24	0	7	0	0	0	.00	1	.105	.150	.105
2 ML YEARS			51	60	6	0	0	0	(0	0)	6	5	0	3	0	25	0	7	0	0	0	.00	1	.100	.143	.100

FIELDING AS PITCHER

Year	Team	Lg	G	TC	PO	A	E	DP	PB	Pct.	Range
1992	Boston	AL	27	12	4	6	2	0	--	.833	---
1993	Boston	AL	49	23	4	18	1	3	--	.957	---
1994	2 ML Teams		35	11	2	8	1	1	--	.909	---
1995	Philadelphia	NL	33	42	9	32	1	2	--	.976	---
1994	Boston	AL	17	3	1	2	0	0	--	1.000	---
	Philadelphia	NL	18	8	1	6	1	1	--	.875	---
4 ML YEARS			144	88	19	64	5	6	--	.943	---

Newt Randall

Newton J. Randall
Bats: Right **Throws:** Right
Height: 5'10" **Weight:** Unknown
Born on February 3, 1880 in New Lowell, Ontario
Died on May 3, 1955 in Duluth, Minnesota

BATTING / BASERUNNING / PERCENTAGES

Year	Team	Lg	G	AB	H	2B	3B	HR	(Hm	Rd)	TB	R	RBI	TBB	IBB	SO	HBP	SH	SF	SB	CS	SB%	GDP	Avg	OBP	SLG
1907	2 ML Teams		97	336	71	10	5	0	--	--	91	22	19	27				7	8		6				.211	.284	.271
1907	Chicago	NL	22	78	16	4	2	0	--	--	24	6	4	8				0	2		2				.205	.279	.308
	Boston	NL	75	258	55	6	3	0	--	--	67	16	15	19				7	6		4				.213	.285	.260

FIELDING AS OUTFIELDER

Year	Team	Lg	G	TC	PO	A	E	DP	PB	Pct.	Range
1907	2 ML Teams		94	177	150	12	15	2	--	.915	1.72
1907	Chicago	NL	21	52	44	3	5	1	--	.904	2.24
	Boston	NL	73	125	106	9	10	1	--	.920	1.58

Claude Raymond

Jean Claude Marc Raymond (Frenchy)
Pitches: Right **Bats:** Right

Height: 5'10" **Weight:** 175
Born on May 7, 1937 in St. Jean, Quebec

			HOW MUCH HE PITCHED					WHAT HE GAVE UP												THE RESULTS					
Year	Team	Lg	G	GS	CG	GF	IP	BFP	H	R	ER	HR	SH	SF	HB	TBB	IBB	SO	WP	Bk	W	L	Pct.	ShO	Sv	ERA
1959	Chicago	AL	3	0	0	1	4	19	5	4	4	2	1	1	0	2	0	1	1	0	0	0	.000	0	0	9.00
1961	Milwaukee	NL	13	0	0	8	20.1	91	22	9	9	2	1	0	1	9	1	13	0	0	1	0	1.000	0	2	3.98
1962	Milwaukee	NL	26	0	0	23	42.2	176	37	15	13	5	1	1	2	15	2	40	1	0	5	5	.500	0	10	2.74
1963	Milwaukee	NL	45	0	0	23	53.1	246	57	36	32	12	2	0	4	27	4	44	2	3	4	6	.400	0	5	5.40
1964	Houston	NL	38	0	0	11	79.2	314	64	28	25	3	6	3	3	22	1	56	3	0	5	5	.500	0	0	2.82
1965	Houston	NL	33	7	2	16	96.1	387	87	35	31	6	8	2	5	16	2	79	4	0	7	4	.636	0	5	2.90
1966	Houston	NL	62	0	0	42	92	386	85	39	32	10	3	3	4	25	6	73	7	0	7	5	.583	0	16	3.13
1967	2 ML Teams		49	0	0	33	65.1	274	64	23	21	7	3	3	2	18	9	31	1	0	4	5	.444	0	10	2.89
1968	Atlanta	NL	36	0	0	24	60.1	247	56	21	19	4	7	2	1	18	9	37	2	0	3	5	.375	0	10	2.83
1969	2 ML Teams		48	0	0	26	70	305	77	46	38	6	7	3	4	21	5	26	5	1	3	4	.429	0	2	4.89
1970	Montreal	NL	59	0	0	43	83.1	354	76	48	41	13	4	4	2	27	7	68	4	0	6	7	.462	0	23	4.43
1971	Montreal	NL	37	0	0	20	53.2	249	81	34	28	5	4	3	0	25	8	29	2	0	1	7	.125	0	0	4.70
1967	Houston	NL	21	0	0	13	31	131	31	12	11	5	0	1	2	7	4	17	1	0	0	4	.000	0	5	3.19
	Atlanta	NL	28	0	0	20	34.1	143	33	11	10	2	3	2	0	11	5	14	0	0	4	1	.800	0	5	2.62
1969	Atlanta	NL	33	0	0	18	48	209	56	34	28	4	4	2	2	13	2	15	3	1	2	2	.500	0	1	5.25
	Montreal	NL	15	0	0	8	22	96	21	12	10	2	3	1	2	8	3	11	2	0	1	2	.333	0	1	4.09
	12 ML YEARS		449	7	2	270	721	3048	711	338	293	75	47	25	28	225	54	497	32	4	46	53	.465	0	83	3.66

			BATTING																	BASERUNNING				PERCENTAGES		
Year	Team	Lg	G	AB	H	2B	3B	HR	(Hm	Rd)	TB	R	RBI	TBB	IBB	SO	HBP	SH	SF	SB	CS	SB%	GDP	Avg	OBP	SLG
1959	Chicago	AL	3	0	0	0	0	0	(0	0)	0	0	0	0	0	0	0	0	0	0	0	.00	0	.000	.000	.000
1961	Milwaukee	NL	13	3	0	0	0	0	(0	0)	0	1	0	0	0	1	0	0	0	0	0	.00	0	.000	.000	.000
1962	Milwaukee	NL	26	8	0	0	0	0	(0	0)	0	0	0	0	0	4	0	1	0	0	0	.00	0	.000	.000	.000
1963	Milwaukee	NL	45	4	2	2	0	0	(0	0)	4	0	1	1	0	1	1	0	0	0	0	.00	0	.500	.667	1.000
1964	Houston	NL	41	14	1	1	0	0	(0	0)	2	1	2	0	0	7	0	2	1	0	0	.00	0	.071	.067	.143
1965	Houston	NL	34	26	3	0	0	0	(0	0)	3	2	1	1	0	12	0	0	0	0	0	.00	0	.115	.148	.115
1966	Houston	NL	62	9	1	0	0	0	(0	0)	1	1	0	0	0	5	0	1	0	0	0	.00	0	.111	.111	.111
1967	2 ML Teams		49	7	1	1	0	0	(0	0)	2	0	1	0	0	2	0	0	0	0	0	.00	1	.143	.143	.286
1968	Atlanta	NL	36	7	1	0	0	0	(0	0)	1	1	0	0	0	2	0	0	0	0	0	.00	0	.143	.143	.143
1969	2 ML Teams		48	11	2	0	0	0	(0	0)	2	0	2	0	0	3	0	1	0	0	0	.00	0	.182	.182	.182
1970	Montreal	NL	59	11	0	0	0	0	(0	0)	0	0	1	1	0	7	0	2	0	0	0	.00	0	.000	.083	.000
1971	Montreal	NL	37	1	0	0	0	0	(0	0)	0	0	0	0	0	0	0	1	0	0	0	.00	0	.000	.000	.000
1967	Houston	NL	21	5	1	1	0	0	(0	0)	2	0	1	0	0	1	0	0	0	0	0	.00	0	.200	.200	.400
	Atlanta	NL	28	2	0	0	0	0	(0	0)	0	0	0	0	0	1	0	0	0	0	0	.00	1	.000	.000	.000
1969	Atlanta	NL	33	7	2	0	0	0	(0	0)	2	0	2	0	0	2	0	1	0	0	0	.00	0	.286	.286	.286
	Montreal	NL	15	4	0	0	0	0	(0	0)	0	0	0	0	0	1	0	0	0	0	0	.00	0	.000	.000	.000
	12 ML YEARS		453	101	11	4	0	0	(0	0)	15	6	8	3	0	44	1	8	1	0	0	.00	1	.109	.142	.149

			FIELDING AS PITCHER							
Year	Team	Lg	G	TC	PO	A	E	DP	PB	Pct.	Range
1959	Chicago	AL	3	1	0	1	0	0	--	1.000	---
1961	Milwaukee	NL	13	7	2	5	0	0	--	1.000	---
1962	Milwaukee	NL	26	5	2	3	0	0	--	1.000	---
1963	Milwaukee	NL	45	16	4	12	0	1	--	1.000	---
1964	Houston	NL	38	25	4	20	1	3	--	.960	---
1965	Houston	NL	33	23	5	15	3	1	--	.870	---
1966	Houston	NL	62	12	7	4	1	0	--	.917	---
1967	2 ML Teams		49	14	4	10	0	0	--	1.000	---
1968	Atlanta	NL	36	18	4	12	2	0	--	.889	---
1969	2 ML Teams		48	21	7	11	3	2	--	.857	---
1970	Montreal	NL	59	17	6	7	4	0	--	.765	---
1971	Montreal	NL	37	17	4	13	0	0	--	1.000	---
1967	Houston	NL	21	5	2	3	0	0	--	1.000	---
	Atlanta	NL	28	9	2	7	0	0	--	1.000	---
1969	Atlanta	NL	33	10	2	6	2	1	--	.800	---
	Montreal	NL	15	11	5	5	1	1	--	.909	---
	12 ML YEARS		449	176	49	113	14	7	--	.920	---

Billy Reid

William Alexander Reid
Bats: Left **Throws:** Right

Height: 6'0" **Weight:** 170
Born on May 17, 1857 in London, Ontario
Died on June 26, 1940 in London, Ontario

BATTING | | BASERUNNING | PERCENTAGES

Year	Team	Lg	G	AB	H	2B	3B	HR	(Hm	Rd)	TB	R	RBI	TBB	IBB	SO	HBP	SH	SF	SB	CS	SB%	GDP	Avg	OBP	SLG
1883	Baltimore	AA	24	97	27	3	0	0	--	--	30	14		4										.278	.307	.309
1884	Pittsburgh	AA	19	70	17	2	0	0	--	--	19	11		4			1							.243	.293	.271
	2 ML YEARS		43	167	44	5	0	0	--	--	49	25		8			1	0						.263	.301	.293

FIELDING AS SECOND BASEMAN

Year	Team	Lg	G	TC	PO	A	E	DP	PB	Pct.	Range
1883	Baltimore	AA	23	146	61	62	23	7	--	.842	5.35
1884	Pittsburgh	AA	1	3	1	1	1	0	--	.667	2.00
	2 ML YEARS		24	149	62	63	24	7	--	.839	5.21

FIELDING AS THIRD BASEMAN

Year	Team	Lg	G	TC	PO	A	E	DP	PB	Pct.	Range
1884	Pittsburgh	AA	1	2	0	1	1	0	--	.500	1.00

FIELDING AS SHORTSTOP

Year	Team	Lg	G	TC	PO	A	E	DP	PB	Pct.	Range
1883	Baltimore	AA	1	4	0	3	1	0	--	.750	3.00

FIELDING AS OUTFIELDER

Year	Team	Lg	G	TC	PO	A	E	DP	PB	Pct.	Range
1884	Pittsburgh	AA	17	29	21	0	8	0	--	.724	1.24

Kevin Reimer

Kevin Michael Reimer
Attended Cal St. Fullerton
Bats: Left **Throws:** Right

Height: 6'2" **Weight:** 215
Born on June 28, 1964 in Macon, Georgia

BATTING | | BASERUNNING | PERCENTAGES

Year	Team	Lg	G	AB	H	2B	3B	HR	(Hm	Rd)	TB	R	RBI	TBB	IBB	SO	HBP	SH	SF	SB	CS	SB%	GDP	Avg	OBP	SLG
1985	Burlington	A	80	292	67	12	0	8	--	--	103	25	33	22	0	43	8	0	1	0	4	.00	10	.229	.300	.353
1986	Salem	A	133	453	111	21	2	16	--	--	184	57	76	61	6	71	7	2	2	4	5	.44	15	.245	.342	.406
1987	Charlotte	A	74	271	66	13	7	6	--	--	111	36	34	29	2	48	2	0	2	2	1	.67	6	.244	.319	.410
1988	Tulsa	AA	133	486	147	30	11	21	--	--	262	74	76	38	9	95	5	0	5	4	4	.50	9	.302	.356	.539
1989	Okla. City	AAA	133	514	137	37	7	10	--	--	218	59	73	33	3	91	2	1	4	4	1	.80	13	.267	.311	.424
1990	Okla. City	AAA	51	198	56	18	2	4	--	--	90	24	33	18	3	25	0	0	1	2	0	1.00	7	.283	.341	.455
1988	Texas	AL	12	25	3	0	0	1	(0	1)	6	2	2	0	0	6	0	0	1	0	0	.00	0	.120	.115	.240
1989	Texas	AL	3	5	0	0	0	0	(0	0)	0	0	0	0	0	1	0	0	0	0	0	.00	1	.000	.000	.000
1990	Texas	AL	64	100	26	9	1	2	(0	2)	43	5	15	10	0	22	1	0	0	0	1	.00	3	.260	.333	.430
1991	Texas	AL	136	394	106	22	0	20	(13	7)	188	46	69	33	6	93	7	0	6	0	3	.00	10	.269	.332	.477
1992	Texas	AL	148	494	132	32	2	16	(10	6)	216	56	58	42	5	103	10	0	1	2	4	.33	10	.267	.336	.437
1993	Milwaukee	AL	125	437	109	22	1	13	(8	5)	172	53	60	30	4	72	5	1	4	5	4	.56	12	.249	.303	.394
	6 ML YEARS		488	1455	376	85	4	52	(31	21)	625	162	204	115	15	297	23	1	12	7	12	.37	36	.258	.320	.430

FIELDING AS OUTFIELDER

Year	Team	Lg	G	TC	PO	A	E	DP	PB	Pct.	Range
1988	Texas	AL	1	0	0	0	0	0	--	.000	.00
1990	Texas	AL	9	14	12	0	2	0	--	.857	1.33
1991	Texas	AL	66	116	110	0	6	0	--	.948	1.67
1992	Texas	AL	110	216	198	7	11	1	--	.949	1.86
1993	Milwaukee	AL	37	79	75	1	3	0	--	.962	2.05
	5 ML YEARS		223	425	395	8	22	1	--	.948	1.81

Jim Riley

James Norman Riley
Bats: Left **Throws:** Right

Height: 5'10" **Weight:** 185
Born on May 25, 1895 in Bayfield, New Brunswick
Died on May 25, 1969 in Seguin, Texas

BATTING | | BASERUNNING | PERCENTAGES

Year	Team	Lg	G	AB	H	2B	3B	HR	(Hm	Rd)	TB	R	RBI	TBB	IBB	SO	HBP	SH	SF	SB	CS	SB%	GDP	Avg	OBP	SLG
1921	St. Louis	AL	4	11	0	0	0	0	--	--	0	0	0	1		3	0	0		0	0	.00		.000	.083	.000
1923	Washington	AL	2	3	0	0	0	0	--	--	0	1	0	2		0	0	0		0	0	.00		.000	.400	.000
	2 ML YEARS		6	14	0	0	0	0	--	--	0	1	0	3		3	0	0		0	0	.00		.000	.176	.000

Year	Team	Lg	G	TC	PO	A	E	DP	PB	Pct.	Range
1923	Washington	AL	2	17	15	0	2	2	--	.882	---

FIELDING AS SECOND BASEMAN

Year	Team	Lg	G	TC	PO	A	E	DP	PB	Pct.	Range
1921	St. Louis	AL	4	11	4	5	2	0	--	.818	2.25

Sherry Robertson

Sherrard Alexander Robertson

Bats: Left   **Throws:** Right

Height: 6'0"   **Weight:** 180

Born on January 1, 1919 in Montreal, Quebec

Died on October 23, 1970 in Houghton, South Dakota

BATTING / BASERUNNING / PERCENTAGES

Year	Team	Lg	G	AB	H	2B	3B	HR	(Hm	Rd)	TB	R	RBI	TBB	IBB	SO	HBP	SH	SF	SB	CS	SB%	GDP	Avg	OBP	SLG
1940	Washington	AL	10	33	7	0	1	0	--	--	9	4	0	5		6	0	0		0	0	.00	0	.212	.316	.273
1941	Washington	AL	1	3	0	0	0	0	--	--	0	0	0	0		3	0	0		0	0	.00	0	.000	.000	.000
1943	Washington	AL	59	120	26	4	1	3	--	--	41	22	14	17		19	1	0		0	2	.00	1	.217	.319	.342
1946	Washington	AL	74	230	46	6	3	6	--	--	76	30	19	30		42	0	2		6	2	.75	0	.200	.292	.330
1947	Washington	AL	95	266	62	9	3	1	--	--	80	25	23	32		52	1	5		4	5	.44	3	.233	.318	.301
1948	Washington	AL	71	187	46	11	3	2	--	--	69	19	22	24		26	1	3		8	0	1.00	2	.246	.335	.369
1949	Washington	AL	110	374	94	17	3	11	--	--	150	59	42	42		35	1	3		10	3	.77	6	.251	.329	.401
1950	Washington	AL	71	123	32	3	3	2	(0	2)	47	19	16	22		18	0	0		1	1	.50	2	.260	.372	.382
1951	Washington	AL	62	111	21	2	1	1	(0	1)	28	14	10	9		22	1	1		2	1	.67	1	.189	.256	.252
1952	2 ML Teams		44	60	12	3	0	0	(0	0)	15	8	5	21		15	0	0		1	2	.33	1	.200	.407	.250
1952	Washington	AL	1	0	0	0	0	0	(0	0)	0	0	0	0		0	0	0		0	0	.00	0	.000	.000	.000
	Philadelphia	AL	43	60	12	3	0	0	(0	0)	15	8	5	21		15	0	0		1	2	.33	1	.200	.407	.250
10	ML YEARS		597	1507	346	55	18	26	--	--	515	200	151	202		238	5	14		32	16	.67	16	.230	.323	.342

FIELDING AS SECOND BASEMAN

Year	Team	Lg	G	TC	PO	A	E	DP	PB	Pct.	Range
1946	Washington	AL	14	95	43	48	4	10	--	.958	6.50
1947	Washington	AL	4	14	7	7	0	1	--	1.000	3.50
1949	Washington	AL	71	380	149	211	20	41	--	.947	5.07
1950	Washington	AL	12	60	30	27	3	5	--	.950	4.75
1952	Philadelphia	AL	8	24	11	12	1	2	--	.958	2.88
5	ML YEARS		109	573	240	305	28	59	--	.951	5.00

FIELDING AS THIRD BASEMAN

Year	Team	Lg	G	TC	PO	A	E	DP	PB	Pct.	Range
1941	Washington	AL	1	4	1	2	1	0	--	.750	3.00
1943	Washington	AL	27	78	27	43	8	1	--	.897	2.59
1946	Washington	AL	38	102	29	63	10	8	--	.902	2.42
1947	Washington	AL	10	27	11	15	1	0	--	.963	2.60
1949	Washington	AL	19	64	19	41	4	2	--	.938	3.16
1950	Washington	AL	1	0	0	0	0	0	--	.000	.00
1952	Philadelphia	AL	2	0	0	0	0	0	--	.000	.00
7	ML YEARS		98	275	87	164	24	11	--	.913	2.56

FIELDING AS SHORTSTOP

Year	Team	Lg	G	TC	PO	A	E	DP	PB	Pct.	Range
1940	Washington	AL	10	50	17	30	3	9	--	.940	4.70
1943	Washington	AL	1	2	0	2	0	0	--	1.000	2.00
1946	Washington	AL	12	39	13	21	5	4	--	.872	2.83
3	ML YEARS		23	91	30	53	8	13	--	.912	3.61

FIELDING AS OUTFIELDER

Year	Team	Lg	G	TC	PO	A	E	DP	PB	Pct.	Range
1946	Washington	AL	1	3	3	0	0	0	--	1.000	3.00
1947	Washington	AL	55	138	126	5	7	1	--	.949	2.38
1948	Washington	AL	51	115	105	3	7	0	--	.939	2.12
1949	Washington	AL	13	19	17	1	1	0	--	.947	1.38
1950	Washington	AL	14	21	19	1	1	0	--	.952	1.43
1951	Washington	AL	22	59	54	2	3	1	--	.949	2.55
1952	Philadelphia	AL	7	16	15	0	1	0	--	.938	2.14
7	ML YEARS		163	371	339	12	20	2	--	.946	2.15

Goody Rosen

Goodwin George Rosen (Goody)
Bats: Left   **Throws:** Left

Height: 5'9"   **Weight:** 160
Born on August 28, 1912 in Toronto, Ontario
Died on April 6, 1994 in Toronto, Ontario

							BATTING											BASERUNNING				PERCENTAGES		
Year Team	Lg	G	AB	H	2B	3B	HR	(Hm | Rd)	TB	R	RBI	TBB	IBB	SO	HBP	SH	SF	SB	CS	SB%	GDP	Avg	OBP	SLG
1937 Brooklyn	NL	22	77	24	5	1	0	--	--	31	10	6	6		6	0	0		2			0	.312	.361	.403
1938 Brooklyn	NL	138	473	133	17	11	4	--	--	184	75	51	65		43	0	3		0			5	.281	.368	.389
1939 Brooklyn	NL	54	183	46	6	4	1	--	--	63	22	12	23		21	0	2		4			1	.251	.335	.344
1944 Brooklyn	NL	89	264	69	8	3	0	--	--	83	38	23	26		27	1	2		0	0	.00		.261	.330	.314
1945 Brooklyn	NL	145	606	197	24	11	12	--	--	279	126	75	50		36	3	14		4			4	.325	.379	.460
1946 2 ML Teams		103	313	88	11	4	5	--	--	122	39	30	48		33	0	4		2	3	.40	10	.281	.377	.390
1946 Brooklyn	NL	3	3	1	0	0	0	--	--	1	0	0	0		1	0	0		0	0	.00	0	.333	.333	.333
New York	NL	100	310	87	11	4	5	--	--	121	39	30	48		32	0	4		2	3	.40	10	.281	.377	.390
6 ML YEARS		551	1916	557	71	34	22	--	--	762	310	197	218		166	4	25		12			22	.291	.364	.398

				FIELDING AS OUTFIELDER							
Year Team	Lg	G	TC	PO	A	E	DP	PB	Pct.	Range
1937 Brooklyn	NL	21	52	50	1	1	1	--	.981	2.43
1938 Brooklyn	NL	113	285	263	19	3	4	--	.989	2.50
1939 Brooklyn	NL	47	106	106	0	0	0	--	1.000	2.26
1944 Brooklyn	NL	65	213	199	12	2	0	--	.991	3.25
1945 Brooklyn	NL	141	402	392	7	3	1	--	.993	2.83
1946 2 ML Teams		85	208	200	3	5	0	--	.976	2.39
1946 Brooklyn	NL	1	0	0	0	0	0	--	.000	.00
New York	NL	84	208	200	3	5	0	--	.976	2.42
6 ML YEARS		472	1266	1210	42	14	6	--	.989	2.65

Ernie Ross

Ernest Bertram Ross (Curly)
Pitches: Left   **Bats:** Left

Height: 5'8"   **Weight:** 150
Born on March 31, 1880 in Toronto, Ontario
Died on March 28, 1950 in Toronto, Ontario

		HOW MUCH HE PITCHED						WHAT HE GAVE UP										THE RESULTS					
Year Team	Lg	G	GS	CG	GF	IP	BFP	H	R	ER	HR	SH	SF	HB	TBB	IBB	SO	WP	Bk	W	L	Pct.	ShO	Sv	ERA
1902 Baltimore	AL	2	2	2	0	17	84	20	18	14	0	3		1	12		2	0	0	1	1	.500	0	0	7.41

							BATTING											BASERUNNING				PERCENTAGES		
Year Team	Lg	G	AB	H	2B	3B	HR	(Hm | Rd)	TB	R	RBI	TBB	IBB	SO	HBP	SH	SF	SB	CS	SB%	GDP	Avg	OBP	SLG
1902 Baltimore	AL	2	8	0	0	0	0	--	--	0	1	0	0			1	0						.000	.111	.000

				FIELDING AS PITCHER							
Year Team	Lg	G	TC	PO	A	E	DP	PB	Pct.	Range
1902 Baltimore	AL	2	4	1	1	2	0	--	.500	----

Dave Rowan

David Rowan
Bats: Left   **Throws:** Left

Height: 5'11"   **Weight:** 175
Born on December 6, 1882 in Elora, Ontario
Died on July 30, 1955 in Toronto, Ontario

							BATTING											BASERUNNING				PERCENTAGES		
Year Team	Lg	G	AB	H	2B	3B	HR	(Hm | Rd)	TB	R	RBI	TBB	IBB	SO	HBP	SH	SF	SB	CS	SB%	GDP	Avg	OBP	SLG
1911 St. Louis	AL	18	65	25	1	1	0	--	--	28	7	11	4			0	1		0				.385	.420	.431

				FIELDING AS FIRST BASEMAN							
Year Team	Lg	G	TC	PO	A	E	DP	PB	Pct.	Range
1911 St. Louis	AL	18	182	161	11	10	5	--	.945	----

Jean-Pierre Roy

Jean-Pierre Roy
Pitches: Right   **Bats:** Both

Height: 5'10"   **Weight:** 160
Born on June 26, 1920 in Montreal, Quebec

		HOW MUCH HE PITCHED						WHAT HE GAVE UP										THE RESULTS					
Year Team	Lg	G	GS	CG	GF	IP	BFP	H	R	ER	HR	SH	SF	HB	TBB	IBB	SO	WP	Bk	W	L	Pct.	ShO	Sv	ERA
1946 Brooklyn	NL	3	1	0	0	6.1	30	5	7	7	1	0		0	5		6	1	0	0	0	.000	0	0	9.95

							BATTING											BASERUNNING				PERCENTAGES		
Year Team	Lg	G	AB	H	2B	3B	HR	(Hm | Rd)	TB	R	RBI	TBB	IBB	SO	HBP	SH	SF	SB	CS	SB%	GDP	Avg	OBP	SLG
1946 Brooklyn	NL	3	2	0	0	0	0	--	--	0	0	0	0		0	0	0		0	0	.00		.000	.000	.000

					FIELDING AS PITCHER							
Year Team	Lg	G	TC	PO	A	E	DP	PB	Pct.	Range		
1946 Brooklyn	NL	3	0	0	0	0	0	--	.000	---		

Johnny Rutherford

John William Rutherford (Doc)
Pitches: Right **Bats:** Left

Height: 5'10" **Weight:** 170
Born on May 5, 1925 in Belleville, Ontario

		HOW MUCH HE PITCHED						WHAT HE GAVE UP									THE RESULTS					
Year Team	Lg	G	GS	CG	GF	IP	BFP	H	R	ER	HR	SH	SF	HB	TBB	IBB	SO	WP	Bk	W	L	Pct.	ShO	Sv	ERA
1952 Brooklyn	NL	22	11	4	8	97.1	408	97	51	46	9	7		2	29		29	2	1	7	7	.500	0	2	4.25

World Series Pitching

		HOW MUCH HE PITCHED						WHAT HE GAVE UP									THE RESULTS					
Year Team	Lg	G	GS	CG	GF	IP	BFP	H	R	ER	HR	SH	SF	HB	TBB	IBB	SO	WP	Bk	W	L	Pct.	ShO	Sv	ERA
1952 Brooklyn	NL	1	0	0	1	1	5	1	1	1	0	0	0	0	1	0	1	0	0	0	0	.000	0	0	9.00

		BATTING																	BASERUNNING				PERCENTAGES		
Year Team	Lg	G	AB	H	2B	3B	HR	(Hm	Rd)	TB	R	RBI	TBB	IBB	SO	HBP	SH	SF	SB	CS	SB%	GDP	Avg	OBP	SLG
1952 Brooklyn	NL	22	31	9	1	0	0	(0	0)	10	3	3	1		11	0	1		0	0	.00	0	.290	.313	.323

World Series Batting

		BATTING																	BASERUNNING				PERCENTAGES		
Year Team	Lg	G	AB	H	2B	3B	HR	(Hm	Rd)	TB	R	RBI	TBB	IBB	SO	HBP	SH	SF	SB	CS	SB%	GDP	Avg	OBP	SLG
1952 Brooklyn	NL	1	0	0	0	0	0	(0	0)	0	0	0	0	0	0	0	0	0	0	0	.00	0	.000	.000	.000

					FIELDING AS PITCHER							
Year Team	Lg	G	TC	PO	A	E	DP	PB	Pct.	Range		
1952 Brooklyn	NL	22	27	3	24	0	1	--	1.000	---		

World Series Fielding

					FIELDING AS PITCHER							
Year Team	Lg	G	TC	PO	A	E	DP	PB	Pct.	Range		
1952 Brooklyn	NL	1	0	0	0	0	0	--	.000	---		

Patrick Scannell

Patrick J. Scannell
Bats: Unknown **Throws:** Unknown

Height: Unknown **Weight:** Unknown
Born on March 25, 1861 in Nova Scotia
Died on July 17, 1913 in Springfield, Massachusetts

		BATTING																	BASERUNNING				PERCENTAGES		
Year Team	Lg	G	AB	H	2B	3B	HR	(Hm	Rd)	TB	R	RBI	TBB	IBB	SO	HBP	SH	SF	SB	CS	SB%	GDP	Avg	OBP	SLG
1884 Boston	UA	6	24	7	1	0	0	--	--	8	2		0										.292	.292	.333

					FIELDING AS OUTFIELDER							
Year Team	Lg	G	TC	PO	A	E	DP	PB	Pct.	Range		
1884 Boston	UA	6	10	6	2	2	0	--	.800	1.33		

George Selkirk

George Alexander Selkirk (Twinkletoes)
Bats: Left **Throws:** Right

Height: 6'1" **Weight:** 182
Born on January 4, 1908 in Huntsville, Ontario
Died on January 19, 1987 in Ft. Lauderdale, Florida

		BATTING																	BASERUNNING				PERCENTAGES		
Year Team	Lg	G	AB	H	2B	3B	HR	(Hm	Rd)	TB	R	RBI	TBB	IBB	SO	HBP	SH	SF	SB	CS	SB%	GDP	Avg	OBP	SLG
1934 New York	AL	46	176	55	7	1	5	--	--	79	23	38	15		17	1	0		1	1	.50		.313	.370	.449
1935 New York	AL	128	491	153	29	12	11	--	--	239	64	94	44		36	3	3		2	7	.22		.312	.372	.487
1936 New York	AL	137	493	152	28	9	18	--	--	252	93	107	94		60	1	4		13	7	.65		.308	.420	.511
1937 New York	AL	78	256	84	13	5	18	--	--	161	49	68	34		24	2	1		8	2	.80		.328	.411	.629
1938 New York	AL	99	335	85	12	5	10	--	--	137	58	62	68		52	3	1		9	4	.69		.254	.384	.409
1939 New York	AL	128	418	128	17	4	21	--	--	216	103	101	103		49	8	8		12	5	.71	3	.306	.452	.517
1940 New York	AL	118	379	102	17	5	19	--	--	186	68	71	84		43	3	4		3	6	.33	3	.269	.406	.491
1941 New York	AL	70	164	36	5	0	6	--	--	59	30	25	28		30	2	1		1	0	1.00	3	.220	.340	.360
1942 New York	AL	42	78	15	3	0	0	--	--	18	15	10	16		8	0	1		0	0	.00	1	.192	.330	.231
9 ML YEARS		846	2790	810	131	41	108	--	--	1347	503	576	486		319	23	23		49	32	.60		.290	.400	.483

All-Star Game Batting

Year Team	Lg	G	AB	H	2B	3B	HR	(Hm	Rd)	TB	R	RBI	TBB	IBB	SO	HBP	SH	SF	SB	CS	SB%	GDP	Avg	OBP	SLG
1936 New York	AL	1	0	0	0	0	0	(0	0)	0	0	0	1	0	0	0	0	0	0	0	.00	0	.000	1.000	.000
1939 New York	AL	1	2	1	0	0	0	(0	0)	1	0	1	2	1	0	0	0	0	0	0	.00	0	.500	.750	.500
2 ML YEARS		2	2	1	0	0	0	(0	0)	1	0	1	3	1	0	0	0	0	0	0	.00	0	.500	.800	.500

World Series Batting

Year Team	Lg	G	AB	H	2B	3B	HR	(Hm	Rd)	TB	R	RBI	TBB	IBB	SO	HBP	SH	SF	SB	CS	SB%	GDP	Avg	OBP	SLG
1936 New York	AL	6	24	8	0	1	2	--	--	16	6	3	4	0	4	0	0		0	0	.00	0	.333	.429	.667
1937 New York	AL	5	19	5	1	0	0	(0	0)	6	5	6	2	0	0	0	0		0	0	.00	0	.263	.333	.316
1938 New York	AL	3	10	2	0	0	0	(0	0)	2	0	1	2	0	1	0	0		0	0	.00	0	.200	.333	.200
1939 New York	AL	4	12	2	1	0	0	(0	0)	3	0	0	3	0	2	0	0		0	0	.00	0	.167	.333	.250
1941 New York	AL	2	2	1	0	0	0	(0	0)	1	0	0	0	0	0	0	0		0	0	.00	0	.500	.500	.500
1942 New York	AL	1	1	0	0	0	0	(0	0)	0	0	0	0	0	0	0	0		0	0	.00	0	.000	.000	.000
6 ML YEARS		21	68	18	2	1	2	--	--	28	11	10	11	0	7	0	0		0	0	.00	0	.265	.367	.412

Fielding as Outfielder

Year Team	Lg	G	TC	PO	A	E	DP	PB	Pct.	Range
1934 New York	AL	46	94	90	3	1	1	--	.989	2.02
1935 New York	AL	127	285	269	9	7	1	--	.975	2.19
1936 New York	AL	135	308	290	10	8	3	--	.974	2.22
1937 New York	AL	69	151	140	9	2	1	--	.987	2.16
1938 New York	AL	95	188	176	7	5	3	--	.973	1.93
1939 New York	AL	124	261	254	4	3	1	--	.989	2.08
1940 New York	AL	111	238	220	9	9	6	--	.962	2.06
1941 New York	AL	47	91	84	4	3	2	--	.967	1.87
1942 New York	AL	19	36	36	0	0	0	--	1.000	1.89
9 ML YEARS		773	1652	1559	55	38	18	--	.977	2.09

All-Star Game Fielding

Fielding as Outfielder

Year Team	Lg	G	TC	PO	A	E	DP	PB	Pct.	Range
1939 New York	AL	1	0	0	0	0	0	--	.000	.00

World Series Fielding

Fielding as Outfielder

Year Team	Lg	G	TC	PO	A	E	DP	PB	Pct.	Range
1936 New York	AL	6	10	9	0	1	0	--	.900	1.50
1937 New York	AL	5	7	7	0	0	0	--	1.000	1.40
1938 New York	AL	3	3	3	0	0	0	--	1.000	1.00
1939 New York	AL	4	9	9	0	0	0	--	1.000	2.25
4 ML YEARS		18	29	28	0	1	0	--	.966	1.56

Harvey Shank

Harvey Tillman Shank
Pitches: Right **Bats:** Right

Height: 6'4" **Weight:** 220
Born on July 29, 1946 in Toronto, Ontario

How Much He Pitched / What He Gave Up / The Results

Year Team	Lg	G	GS	CG	GF	IP	BFP	H	R	ER	HR	SH	SF	HB	TBB	IBB	SO	WP	Bk	W	L	Pct.	ShO	Sv	ERA
1970 California	AL	1	0	0	0	3	13	2	0	0	0	0	0	0	2	0	1	0	0	0	0	.000	0	0	0.00

Batting

Year Team	Lg	G	AB	H	2B	3B	HR	(Hm	Rd)	TB	R	RBI	TBB	IBB	SO	HBP	SH	SF	SB	CS	SB%	GDP	Avg	OBP	SLG
1970 California	AL	1	0	0	0	0	0	(0	0)	0	0	0	0	0	0	0	0	0	0	0	.00	0	.000	.000	.000

Fielding as Pitcher

Year Team	Lg	G	TC	PO	A	E	DP	PB	Pct.	Range
1970 California	AL	1	0	0	0	0	0	--	.000	---

Vince Shields

Vincent William Shields
Pitches: Right **Bats:** Left

Height: 5'11" **Weight:** 185
Born on November 18, 1900 in Fredericton, New Brunswick
Died on October 17, 1952 in Plaster Rock, New Brunswick

How Much He Pitched / What He Gave Up / The Results

Year Team	Lg	G	GS	CG	GF	IP	BFP	H	R	ER	HR	SH	SF	HB	TBB	IBB	SO	WP	Bk	W	L	Pct.	ShO	Sv	ERA
1924 St. Louis	NL	2	1	0	1	12	51	10	5	4	1	1		3	3		4	0	0	1	1	.500	0	0	3.00

		BATTING																			BASERUNNING				PERCENTAGES		
Year Team	Lg	G	AB	H	2B	3B	HR	(Hm	Rd)	TB	R	RBI	TBB	IBB	SO	HBP	SH	SF		SB	CS	SB%	GDP	Avg	OBP	SLG
1924 St. Louis	NL	3	5	2	0	0	0	--	--	2	0	1	0	0	0	0	0	0		0	0	.00		.400	.400	.400

		FIELDING AS PITCHER								
Year Team	Lg	G	TC	PO	A	E	DP	PB	Pct.	Range
1924 St. Louis	NL	2	2	0	1	1	0	--	.500	---

Dave Shipanoff

David Noel Shipanoff **Height:** 6'2" **Weight:** 185
Pitches: Right **Bats:** Right **Born** on November 13, 1959 in Edmonton, Alberta

		HOW MUCH HE PITCHED						WHAT HE GAVE UP											THE RESULTS					
Year Team	Lg	G	GS	CG	GF	IP	BFP	H	R	ER	HR	SH	SF	HB	TBB	IBB	SO	WP	Bk	W	L	Pct.	ShO	Sv	ERA
1985 Philadelphia	NL	26	0	0	12	36.1	162	33	15	13	3	0	2	1	16	3	26	0	1	1	2	.333	0	3	3.22

		BATTING																			BASERUNNING				PERCENTAGES		
Year Team	Lg	G	AB	H	2B	3B	HR	(Hm	Rd)	TB	R	RBI	TBB	IBB	SO	HBP	SH	SF		SB	CS	SB%	GDP	Avg	OBP	SLG
1985 Philadelphia	NL	26	3	0	0	0	0	(0	0)	0	0	0	0	0	3	0	0	0		0	0	.00	0	.000	.000	.000

		FIELDING AS PITCHER								
Year Team	Lg	G	TC	PO	A	E	DP	PB	Pct.	Range
1985 Philadelphia	NL	26	5	2	2	1	0	--	.800	---

Joe Siddall

Joseph Todd Siddall **Height:** 6'1" **Weight:** 197
Bats: Left   **Throws:** Right **Born** on October 25, 1967 in Windson, Ontario

		BATTING																			BASERUNNING				PERCENTAGES		
Year Team	Lg	G	AB	H	2B	3B	HR	(Hm	Rd)	TB	R	RBI	TBB	IBB	SO	HBP	SH	SF		SB	CS	SB%	GDP	Avg	OBP	SLG
1988 Jamestown	A	53	178	38	5	3	1	--	--	52	18	16	14	1	29	1	4	2		5	4	.56	3	.213	.272	.292
1989 Rockford	A	98	313	74	15	2	4	--	--	105	36	38	26	2	56	6	5	4		8	5	.62	3	.236	.304	.335
1990 W. Palm Bch	A	106	348	78	12	1	0	--	--	92	29	32	20	0	55	1	10	2		6	7	.46	7	.224	.267	.264
1991 Harrisburg	AA	76	235	54	6	1	1	--	--	65	28	23	23	2	53	1	2	3		8	3	.73	7	.230	.298	.277
1992 Harrisburg	AA	95	288	68	12	0	2	--	--	86	26	27	29	1	55	3	1	3		4	4	.50	7	.236	.310	.299
1993 Ottawa	AAA	48	136	29	6	0	1	--	--	38	14	16	19	5	33	0	3	2		2	2	.50	6	.213	.306	.279
1994 Ottawa	AAA	38	110	19	2	1	3	--	--	32	9	13	10	2	21	2	7	2		1	1	.50	3	.173	.250	.291
1995 Ottawa	AAA	83	248	53	14	2	1	--	--	74	26	23	23	0	42	4	2	0		3	3	.50	6	.214	.291	.298
1993 Montreal	NL	19	20	2	1	0	0	(0	0)	3	0	1	1	1	5	0	0	0		0	0	.00	0	.100	.143	.150
1995 Montreal	NL	7	10	3	0	0	0	(0	0)	3	4	1	3	0	3	1	0	0		0	0	.00	0	.300	.500	.300
2 ML YEARS		26	30	5	1	0	0	(0	0)	6	4	2	4	1	8	1	0	0		0	0	.00	0	.167	.286	.200

		FIELDING AS CATCHER								
Year Team	Lg	G	TC	PO	A	E	DP	PB	Pct.	Range
1993 Montreal	NL	15	38	33	5	0	0	1	1.000	---
1995 Montreal	NL	7	17	14	1	2	0	2	.882	---
2 ML YEARS		22	55	47	6	2	0	3	.964	---

		FIELDING AS FIRST BASEMAN								
Year Team	Lg	G	TC	PO	A	E	DP	PB	Pct.	Range
1993 Montreal	NL	1	0	0	0	0	0	--	.000	---

		FIELDING AS OUTFIELDER								
Year Team	Lg	G	TC	PO	A	E	DP	PB	Pct.	Range
1993 Montreal	NL	1	0	0	0	0	0	--	.000	.00

Bert Sincock

Herbert Sylvester Sincock **Height:** 5'10" **Weight:** 165
Pitches: Left **Bats:** Left **Born** on September 8, 1887 in Barkerville, British Columbia
Died on August 1, 1946 in Houghton, Michigan

		HOW MUCH HE PITCHED						WHAT HE GAVE UP											THE RESULTS					
Year Team	Lg	G	GS	CG	GF	IP	BFP	H	R	ER	HR	SH	SF	HB	TBB	IBB	SO	WP	Bk	W	L	Pct.	ShO	Sv	ERA
1908 Cincinnati	NL	1	0	0	1	4.2	19	3	2	2	0	2		0	1		0	1	0	0	0	.000	0	0	3.86

		BATTING																			BASERUNNING				PERCENTAGES		
Year Team	Lg	G	AB	H	2B	3B	HR	(Hm	Rd)	TB	R	RBI	TBB	IBB	SO	HBP	SH	SF		SB	CS	SB%	GDP	Avg	OBP	SLG
1908 Cincinnati	NL	1	2	0	0	0	0	--	--	0	0	0	0		0	0				0				.000	.000	.000

		FIELDING AS PITCHER								
Year Team	Lg	G	TC	PO	A	E	DP	PB	Pct.	Range
1908 Cincinnati	NL	1	1	0	1	0	0	--	1.000	---

221

Bud Sketchley

Harry Clement Sketchley
Bats: Left   **Throws:** Left

Height: 5'10" **Weight:** 180
Born on March 30, 1919 in Virden, Manitoba
Died on December 19, 1979 in Los Angeles, California

| | | | | | | | | BATTING | | | | | | | | | | | | BASERUNNING | | | | PERCENTAGES | | |
Year Team	Lg	G	AB	H	2B	3B	HR	(Hm	Rd)	TB	R	RBI	TBB	IBB	SO	HBP	SH	SF	SB	CS	SB%	GDP	Avg	OBP	SLG
1942 Chicago	AL	13	36	7	1	0	0	--	--	8	1	3	7		4	0	2		0	1	.00	0	.194	.326	.222

| | | | FIELDING AS OUTFIELDER | | | | | | | |
Year Team	Lg	G	TC	PO	A	E	DP	PB	Pct.	Range
1942 Chicago	AL	12	21	19	1	1	0	--	.952	1.67

Frank Smith

Frank L. Smith
Bats: Unknown **Throws:** Unknown

Height: Unknown **Weight:** Unknown
Born on November 24, 1857 in Canada
Died on October 11, 1928 in Canandaigua, New York

| | | | | | | | | BATTING | | | | | | | | | | | | BASERUNNING | | | | PERCENTAGES | | |
Year Team	Lg	G	AB	H	2B	3B	HR	(Hm	Rd)	TB	R	RBI	TBB	IBB	SO	HBP	SH	SF	SB	CS	SB%	GDP	Avg	OBP	SLG
1884 Pittsburgh	AA	10	36	9	0	1	0	--	--	11	3		0		0								.250	.250	.306

| | | | FIELDING AS CATCHER | | | | | | | |
Year Team	Lg	G	TC	PO	A	E	DP	PB	Pct.	Range
1884 Pittsburgh	AA	7	43	34	6	3	1	15	.930	---

| | | | FIELDING AS OUTFIELDER | | | | | | | |
Year Team	Lg	G	TC	PO	A	E	DP	PB	Pct.	Range
1884 Pittsburgh	AA	3	7	5	1	1	0	--	.857	2.00

Pop Smith

Charles Marvin Smith
Bats: Right   **Throws:** Right

Height: 5'11" **Weight:** 170
Born on October 12, 1856 in Digby, Nova Scotia
Died on April 18, 1927 in Boston, Massachusetts

| | | | | | | | | BATTING | | | | | | | | | | | | BASERUNNING | | | | PERCENTAGES | | |
Year Team	Lg	G	AB	H	2B	3B	HR	(Hm	Rd)	TB	R	RBI	TBB	IBB	SO	HBP	SH	SF	SB	CS	SB%	GDP	Avg	OBP	SLG
1880 Cincinnati	NL	83	334	69	10	9	0	--	--	97	35	27	6		36								.207	.221	.290
1881 3 ML Teams		24	86	7	0	0	0	--	--	7	5	6	6		18								.081	.141	.081
1882 2 ML Teams		4	14	2	0	0	0	--	--	2	1		0										.143	.143	.143
1883 Columbus	AA	97	405	106	14	**17**	4	--	--	166	82		22										.262	.300	.410
1884 Columbus	AA	108	445	106	18	10	6	--	--	162	78		20			12							.238	.289	.364
1885 Pittsburgh	AA	106	453	113	11	13	0	--	--	150	85		25			3							.249	.293	.331
1886 Pittsburgh	AA	126	483	105	20	9	2	--	--	149	75		42			6			38				.217	.288	.308
1887 Pittsburgh	NL	122	456	98	12	7	2	--	--	130	69	54	30		**48**	**13**			30				.215	.283	.285
1888 Pittsburgh	NL	131	481	99	15	2	4	--	--	130	61	52	22		**78**	5			37				.206	.248	.270
1889 2 ML Teams		131	466	108	23	6	5	--	--	158	47	59	47		**68**	10			23				.232	.315	.339
1890 Boston	NL	134	463	106	16	12	1	--	--	149	82	53	80		**81**	9			39				.229	.353	.322
1891 Washington	AA	27	90	16	2	2	0	--	--	22	13	13	13		**16**	2			2				.178	.295	.244
1881 Cleveland	NL	10	34	4	0	0	0	--	--	4	1	3	0		8								.118	.118	.118
Worcester	NL	11	41	3	0	0	0	--	--	3	1	2	3		5								.073	.136	.073
Buffalo	NL	3	11	0	0	0	0	--	--	0	3	1	3		5								.000	.214	.000
1882 Baltimore	AA	1	3	0	0	0	0	--	--	0	0		0										.000	.000	.000
Louisville	AA	3	11	2	0	0	0	--	--	2	1		0										.182	.182	.182
1889 Pittsburgh	NL	72	258	54	10	2	5	--	--	83	26	27	24		38	6			12				.209	.292	.322
Boston	NL	59	208	54	13	4	0	--	--	75	21	32	23		30	4			11				.260	.345	.361
12 ML YEARS		1093	4176	935	141	87	24	--	--	1322	633		313			60	0						.224	.288	.317

| | | | | HOW MUCH HE PITCHED | | | | WHAT HE GAVE UP | | | | | | | | | | | | THE RESULTS | | | | | |
Year Team	Lg	G	GS	CG	GF	IP	BFP	H	R	ER	HR	SH	SF	HB	TBB	IBB	SO	WP	Bk	W	L	Pct.	ShO	Sv	ERA
1883 Columbus	AA	3	0	0	3	5.2	30	10	7	4	0				0		0	0	0	0	0	.000	0	0	6.35

| | | | FIELDING AS PITCHER | | | | | | | |
Year Team	Lg	G	TC	PO	A	E	DP	PB	Pct.	Range
1883 Columbus	AA	3	1	1	0	0	0	--	1.000	---

| | | | FIELDING AS CATCHER | | | | | | | |
Year Team	Lg	G	TC	PO	A	E	DP	PB	Pct.	Range
1886 Pittsburgh	AA	1	3	1	2	0	0	0	1.000	---

FIELDING AS SECOND BASEMAN

Year	Team	Lg	G	TC	PO	A	E	DP	PB	Pct.	Range
1880	Cincinnati	NL	83	614	282	243	89	32	--	.855	6.33
1881	2 ML Teams		6	42	22	15	5	4	--	.881	6.17
1883	Columbus	AA	73	559	250	247	62	38	--	.889	6.81
1884	Columbus	AA	108	793	324	394	75	55	--	.905	6.65
1885	Pittsburgh	AA	106	820	372	384	64	53	--	.922	7.13
1886	Pittsburgh	AA	28	204	88	98	18	8	--	.912	6.64
1887	Pittsburgh	NL	89	572	225	298	49	32	--	.914	5.88
1888	Pittsburgh	NL	56	348	131	184	33	24	--	.905	5.63
1889	Pittsburgh	NL	9	64	31	29	4	5	--	.938	6.67
1890	Boston	NL	134	692	234	401	57	41	--	.918	4.74
1891	Washington	AA	19	124	53	61	10	11	--	.919	6.00
1881	Worcester	NL	3	17	8	8	1	0	--	.941	5.33
	Buffalo	NL	3	25	14	7	4	4	--	.840	7.00
	11 ML YEARS		711	4832	2012	2354	466	303	--	.904	6.14

FIELDING AS THIRD BASEMAN

Year	Team	Lg	G	TC	PO	A	E	DP	PB	Pct.	Range
1881	Cleveland	NL	10	37	16	15	6	0	--	.838	3.10
1883	Columbus	AA	24	96	35	49	12	2	--	.875	3.50
1889	Pittsburgh	NL	3	12	6	6	0	2	--	1.000	4.00
1891	Washington	AA	4	14	4	7	3	0	--	.786	2.75
	4 ML YEARS		41	159	61	77	21	4	--	.868	3.37

FIELDING AS SHORTSTOP

Year	Team	Lg	G	TC	PO	A	E	DP	PB	Pct.	Range
1882	Louisville	AA	3	18	4	10	4	0	--	.778	4.67
1886	Pittsburgh	AA	98	545	132	356	57	28	--	.895	4.98
1887	Pittsburgh	NL	33	206	71	119	16	7	--	.922	5.76
1888	Pittsburgh	NL	75	375	91	247	37	18	--	.901	4.51
1889	2 ML Teams		117	639	214	357	68	44	--	.894	4.88
1890	Boston	NL	1	5	2	2	1	0	--	.800	4.00
1891	Washington	AA	5	30	6	19	5	1	--	.833	5.00
1889	Pittsburgh	NL	58	312	93	187	32	21	--	.897	4.83
	Boston	NL	59	327	121	170	36	23	--	.890	4.93
	7 ML YEARS		332	1818	520	1110	188	98	--	.897	4.91

FIELDING AS OUTFIELDER

Year	Team	Lg	G	TC	PO	A	E	DP	PB	Pct.	Range
1881	Worcester	NL	8	22	17	4	1	1	--	.955	2.63
1882	Baltimore	AA	1	2	1	0	1	0	--	.500	1.00
1889	Pittsburgh	NL	3	2	2	0	0	0	--	1.000	.67
	3 ML YEARS		12	26	20	4	2	1	--	.923	2.00

Tom Smith

Thomas N. Smith
Bats: Unknown **Throws:** Unknown

Height: Unknown **Weight:** Unknown
Born in 1851 in Guelph, Ontario
Died on March 28, 1889 in Detroit, Michigan

BATTING / BASERUNNING / PERCENTAGES

Year	Team	Lg	G	AB	H	2B	3B	HR	(Hm	Rd)	TB	R	RBI	TBB	IBB	SO	HBP	SH	SF	SB	CS	SB%	GDP	Avg	OBP	SLG
1882	Philadelphia	AA	20	65	6	0	0	0	--	--	6	10		12										.092	.234	.092

FIELDING AS SECOND BASEMAN

Year	Team	Lg	G	TC	PO	A	E	DP	PB	Pct.	Range
1882	Philadelphia	AA	2	16	4	9	3	0	--	.813	6.50

FIELDING AS THIRD BASEMAN

Year	Team	Lg	G	TC	PO	A	E	DP	PB	Pct.	Range
1882	Philadelphia	AA	11	56	15	26	15	0	--	.732	3.73

FIELDING AS SHORTSTOP

Year	Team	Lg	G	TC	PO	A	E	DP	PB	Pct.	Range
1882	Philadelphia	AA	4	31	5	21	5	0	--	.839	6.50

FIELDING AS OUTFIELDER

Year	Team	Lg	G	TC	PO	A	E	DP	PB	Pct.	Range
1882	Philadelphia	AA	3	5	4	1	0	0	--	1.000	1.67

Cooney Snyder

Frank C. Snyder
Bats: Unknown **Throws:** Unknown

Height: 6'3" **Weight:** 180
Born Unknown in Toronto, Ontario
Died on March 9, 1917 in Toronto, Ontario

							BATTING												BASERUNNING				PERCENTAGES		
Year Team	Lg	G	AB	H	2B	3B	HR	(Hm	Rd)	TB	R	RBI	TBB	IBB	SO	HBP	SH	SF	SB	CS	SB%	GDP	Avg	OBP	SLG
1898 Louisville	NL	17	61	10	0	0	0	--	--	10	4	6	3			1	3		0				.164	.215	.164

			FIELDING AS CATCHER							
Year Team	Lg	G	TC	PO	A	E	DP	PB	Pct.	Range
1898 Louisville	NL	17	62	43	15	4	1	5	.935	---

Paul Spoljaric

Paul Nikola Spoljaric
Attended Douglas College
Pitches: Left **Bats:** Right

Height: 6'3" **Weight:** 205
Born on September 24, 1970 in Kelowna, British Columbia

		HOW MUCH HE PITCHED						WHAT HE GAVE UP										THE RESULTS					
Year Team	Lg	G	GS	CG	GF	IP	BFP	H	R	ER	HR	SH	SF	HB	TBB	IBB	SO	WP	Bk	W	L	Pct.	ShO	Sv	ERA
1990 Medicne Hat	R	15	13	0	2	66.1	291	57	43	32	6	0	3	0	35	0	62	3	3	3	7	.300	0	1	4.34
1991 St. Cathrns	A	4	4	0	0	18.2	85	21	14	10	1	0	0	1	9	0	21	0	0	0	2	.000	0	0	4.82
1992 Myrtle Bch	A	26	26	1	0	162.2	647	111	68	51	7	4	4	5	58	0	161	7	1	10	8	.556	0	0	2.82
1993 Dunedin	A	4	4	0	0	26	99	16	5	4	1	0	0	2	12	0	29	2	0	3	0	1.000	0	0	1.38
Knoxville	AA	7	7	0	0	43.1	175	30	12	11	3	1	0	1	22	0	51	2	1	4	1	.800	0	0	2.28
Syracuse	AAA	18	18	1	0	95.1	424	97	63	56	14	1	6	2	52	0	88	8	1	8	7	.533	1	0	5.29
1994 Syracuse	AAA	8	8	0	0	47.1	224	47	37	30	7	1	3	0	28	1	38	4	0	1	5	.167	0	0	5.70
Knoxville	AA	17	16	0	0	102	446	88	50	41	12	2	5	7	48	0	79	4	1	6	5	.545	0	0	3.62
1995 Syracuse	AAA	43	9	0	27	87.2	382	69	51	48	13	3	1	2	54	3	108	8	0	2	10	.167	0	10	4.93
1994 Toronto	AL	2	1	0	0	2.1	21	5	10	10	3	0	0	0	9	1	2	2	0	0	1	.000	0	0	38.57

				FIELDING AS PITCHER						
Year Team	Lg	G	TC	PO	A	E	DP	PB	Pct.	Range
1994 Toronto	AL	2	3	0	2	1	0	--	.667	---

Matt Stairs

Matthew Wade Stairs
Bats: Left **Throws:** Right

Height: 5'9" **Weight:** 175
Born on February 27, 1969 in Fredericton, New Brunswick

							BATTING												BASERUNNING				PERCENTAGES		
Year Team	Lg	G	AB	H	2B	3B	HR	(Hm	Rd)	TB	R	RBI	TBB	IBB	SO	HBP	SH	SF	SB	CS	SB%	GDP	Avg	OBP	SLG
1989 Jamestown	A	14	43	11	1	0	1	--	--	15	8	5	3	0	5	0	0	0	1	2	.33	0	.256	.304	.349
W. Palm Bch	A	36	111	21	3	1	1	--	--	29	12	9	9	0	18	0	1	1	0	0	.00	3	.189	.248	.261
Rockford	A	44	141	40	9	2	2	--	--	59	20	14	15	3	29	2	2	1	5	4	.56	4	.284	.358	.418
1990 W. Palm Bch	A	55	184	62	9	3	3	--	--	86	30	30	40	4	19	5	0	2	15	2	.88	5	.337	.463	.467
Jacksonville	AA	79	280	71	17	0	3	--	--	97	26	34	22	1	42	3	0	5	5	3	.63	6	.254	.310	.346
1991 Harrisburg	AA	129	505	168	30	10	13	--	--	257	87	78	66	8	47	3	2	3	23	11	.68	14	.333	.411	.509
1992 Indianaplls	AAA	110	401	107	23	4	11	--	--	171	57	56	49	3	61	4	4	2	11	11	.50	10	.267	.351	.426
1993 Ottawa	AAA	34	125	35	4	2	3	--	--	52	18	20	11	1	15	2	1	0	4	1	.80	3	.280	.348	.416
1994 New Britain	AA	93	317	98	25	2	9	--	--	154	44	61	53	7	38	3	0	5	10	7	.59	10	.309	.407	.486
1995 Pawtucket	AAA	75	271	77	17	0	13	--	--	133	40	56	29	3	41	1	1	3	3	3	.50	10	.284	.352	.491
1992 Montreal	NL	13	30	5	2	0	0	(0	0)	7	2	5	7	0	7	0	0	1	0	0	.00	0	.167	.316	.233
1993 Montreal	NL	6	8	3	1	0	0	(0	0)	4	1	2	0	0	1	0	0	0	0	0	.00	1	.375	.375	.500
1995 Boston	AL	39	88	23	7	1	1	(0	1)	35	8	17	4	0	14	1	1	1	0	1	.00	4	.261	.298	.398
3 ML YEARS		58	126	31	10	1	1	(0	1)	46	11	24	11	0	22	1	1	2	0	1	.00	5	.246	.307	.365

Division Playoffs Batting

							BATTING												BASERUNNING				PERCENTAGES		
Year Team	Lg	G	AB	H	2B	3B	HR	(Hm	Rd)	TB	R	RBI	TBB	IBB	SO	HBP	SH	SF	SB	CS	SB%	GDP	Avg	OBP	SLG
1995 Boston	AL	1	1	0	0	0	0	(0	0)	0	0	0	0	0	1	0	0	0	0	0	.00	0	.000	.000	.000

				FIELDING AS OUTFIELDER						
Year Team	Lg	G	TC	PO	A	E	DP	PB	Pct.	Range
1992 Montreal	NL	10	15	14	0	1	0	--	.933	1.40
1993 Montreal	NL	1	1	1	0	0	0	--	1.000	1.00
1995 Boston	AL	23	23	19	2	2	0	--	.913	.91
3 ML YEARS		34	39	34	2	3	0	--	.923	1.06

Bob Steele

Robert Wesley Steele
Pitches: Left **Bats:** Both

Height: 5'10" **Weight:** 175
Born on January 5, 1894 in Cassburn, Ontario
Died on January 27, 1962 in Ocala, Florida

		HOW MUCH HE PITCHED						WHAT HE GAVE UP									THE RESULTS					
Year Team	Lg	G	GS	CG	GF	IP	BFP	H	R	ER	HR	SH	SF	HB	TBB	IBB	SO	WP	Bk	W	L	Pct.	ShO	Sv	ERA
1916 St. Louis	NL	29	22	7	4	148	619	156	74	56	6	27		3	42		67	2	1	5	15	.250	1	0	3.41
1917 2 ML Teams		39	25	14	11	221.2	920	191	88	70	1	29		5	72		105	8	2	6	14	.300	1	1	2.84
1918 2 ML Teams		22	11	7	6	115	479	100	54	37	3	15		5	28		45	3	0	5	8	.385	2	2	2.90
1919 New York	NL	1	0	0	1	3	15	3	3	2	0	1		0	2		0	0	0	0	1	.000	0	0	6.00
1917 St. Louis	NL	12	6	1	3	42	173	33	18	15	1	6		0	19		23	2	0	1	3	.250	0	0	3.21
Pittsburgh	NL	27	19	13	8	179.2	747	158	70	55	0	23		5	53		82	6	2	5	11	.313	1	1	2.76
1918 Pittsburgh	NL	10	4	2	3	49	209	44	25	18	2	7		2	17		21	0	0	2	3	.400	1	1	3.31
New York	NL	12	7	5	3	66	270	56	29	19	1	8		3	11		24	3	0	3	5	.375	1	1	2.59
4 ML YEARS		91	58	28	22	487.2	2033	450	219	165	10	72		13	144		217	13	3	16	38	.296	4	3	3.05

		BATTING															BASERUNNING				PERCENTAGES		
Year Team	Lg	G	AB	H	2B	3B	HR	(Hm	Rd)	TB	R	RBI	TBB	IBB	SO	HBP	SH	SF	SB	CS	SB% GDP	Avg	OBP	SLG
1916 St. Louis	NL	29	51	10	0	0	0	--	--	10	0	0	0		11	0	0		0			.196	.196	.196
1917 2 ML Teams		45	89	22	2	1	0	--	--	26	8	5	0		14	0	1		1			.247	.247	.292
1918 2 ML Teams		22	37	8	0	2	0	--	--	12	4	2	3		5	0	0		3			.216	.275	.324
1919 New York	NL	1	1	0	0	0	0	--	--	0	0	0	0		1	0	0		0			.000	.000	.000
1917 St. Louis	NL	12	13	5	1	0	0	--	--	6	2	0	0		0	0	0		0			.385	.385	.462
Pittsburgh	NL	33	76	17	1	1	0	--	--	20	6	5	0		14	0	1		1			.224	.224	.263
1918 Pittsburgh	NL	10	16	2	0	1	0	--	--	4	1	0	1		3	0	0		1			.125	.176	.250
New York	NL	12	21	6	0	1	0	--	--	8	3	2	2		2	0	0		2			.286	.348	.381
4 ML YEARS		97	178	40	2	3	0	--	--	48	12	7	3		31	0	1		4			.225	.238	.270

		FIELDING AS PITCHER								
Year Team	Lg	G	TC	PO	A	E	DP	PB	Pct.	Range
1916 St. Louis	NL	29	32	3	26	3	0	--	.906	---
1917 2 ML Teams		39	64	5	52	7	3	--	.891	---
1918 2 ML Teams		22	25	2	21	2	0	--	.920	---
1919 New York	NL	1	0	0	0	0	0	--	.000	---
1917 St. Louis	NL	12	11	1	9	1	0	--	.909	---
Pittsburgh	NL	27	53	4	43	6	3	--	.887	---
1918 Pittsburgh	NL	10	13	1	12	0	0	--	1.000	---
New York	NL	12	12	1	9	2	0	--	.833	---
4 ML YEARS		91	121	10	99	12	3	--	.901	---

Kid Summers

William Summers
Bats: Unknown **Throws:** Right

Height: Unknown **Weight:** Unknown
Born Unknown in Toronto, Ontario
Died on October 16, 1895 in Toronto, Ontario

		BATTING															BASERUNNING				PERCENTAGES		
Year Team	Lg	G	AB	H	2B	3B	HR	(Hm	Rd)	TB	R	RBI	TBB	IBB	SO	HBP	SH	SF	SB	CS	SB% GDP	Avg	OBP	SLG
1893 St. Louis	NL	2	1	0	0	0	0	--	--	0	1	0	0		0	1			0			.000	.500	.000

		FIELDING AS CATCHER								
Year Team	Lg	G	TC	PO	A	E	DP	PB	Pct.	Range
1893 St. Louis	NL	1	2	0	1	1	0	0	.500	---

		FIELDING AS OUTFIELDER								
Year Team	Lg	G	TC	PO	A	E	DP	PB	Pct.	Range
1893 St. Louis	NL	1	2	1	0	1	0	--	.500	1.00

Ron Taylor

Ronald Wesley Taylor
Attended University of Toronto
Pitches: Right **Bats:** Right

Height: 6'1" **Weight:** 195
Born on December 13, 1937 in Toronto, Ontario

		HOW MUCH HE PITCHED						WHAT HE GAVE UP									THE RESULTS					
Year Team	Lg	G	GS	CG	GF	IP	BFP	H	R	ER	HR	SH	SF	HB	TBB	IBB	SO	WP	Bk	W	L	Pct.	ShO	Sv	ERA
1962 Cleveland	AL	8	4	1	3	33.1	144	36	23	22	6	0	2	1	13	4	15	1	1	2	2	.500	0	0	5.94
1963 St. Louis	NL	54	9	2	22	133.1	540	119	44	42	10	11	6	4	30	6	91	3	1	9	7	.563	0	11	2.84
1964 St. Louis	NL	63	2	0	31	101.1	441	109	56	52	15	7	2	1	33	7	69	1	1	8	4	.667	0	7	4.62
1965 2 ML Teams		57	1	0	29	101.1	439	111	66	63	11	7	7	6	31	10	63	3	0	3	6	.333	0	5	5.60
1966 Houston	NL	36	1	0	11	64.2	291	89	47	41	5	5	4	5	10	4	29	1	0	2	3	.400	0	0	5.71
1967 New York	NL	50	0	0	31	73	297	60	21	19	1	7	5	1	23	14	46	1	2	4	6	.400	0	8	2.34

Year Team	Lg	G	GS	CG	GF	IP	BFP	H	R	ER	HR	SH	SF	HB	TBB	IBB	SO	WP	Bk	W	L	Pct.	ShO	Sv	ERA
1968 New York	NL	58	0	0	44	76.2	307	64	24	23	4	5	2	1	18	9	49	0	0	1	5	.167	0	13	2.70
1969 New York	NL	59	0	0	44	76	300	61	23	23	7	5	2	1	24	6	42	1	0	9	4	.692	0	13	2.72
1970 New York	NL	57	0	0	40	66.1	275	65	31	29	5	9	5	0	16	10	28	1	0	5	4	.556	0	13	3.93
1971 New York	NL	45	0	0	25	69	281	71	28	28	7	4	1	1	11	6	32	0	0	2	2	.500	0	2	3.65
1972 San Diego	NL	4	0	0	2	5	24	9	7	7	5	0	0	0	0	0	0	0	0	0	0	.000	0	0	12.60
1965 St. Louis	NL	25	0	0	9	43.2	185	43	24	22	6	1	3	1	15	4	26	1	0	2	1	.667	0	1	4.53
Houston		32	1	0	20	57.2	254	68	42	41	5	6	4	5	16	6	37	2	0	1	5	.167	0	4	6.40
11 ML YEARS		491	17	3	282	800	3339	794	370	349	76	60	36	21	209	76	464	12	5	45	43	.511	0	72	3.93

League Championship Pitching

	HOW MUCH HE PITCHED						WHAT HE GAVE UP										THE RESULTS						
Year Team	Lg	G	GS	CG	GF	IP	BFP	H	R	ER	HR	SH	SF	HB	TBB	IBB	SO	WP	Bk	W	L	Pct.	ShO	Sv	ERA
1969 New York	NL	2	0	0	1	3.1	13	3	0	0	0	0	0	0	0	0	4	0	0	1	0	1.000	0	1	0.00

World Series Pitching

	HOW MUCH HE PITCHED						WHAT HE GAVE UP										THE RESULTS						
Year Team	Lg	G	GS	CG	GF	IP	BFP	H	R	ER	HR	SH	SF	HB	TBB	IBB	SO	WP	Bk	W	L	Pct.	ShO	Sv	ERA
1964 St. Louis	NL	2	0	0	1	4.2	14	0	0	0	0	0	0	0	1	0	2	0	0	0	0	.000	0	1	0.00
1969 New York	NL	2	0	0	2	2.1	7	0	0	0	0	0	0	0	1	0	3	0	0	0	0	.000	0	1	0.00
2 ML YEARS		4	0	0	3	7	21	0	0	0	0	0	0	0	2	0	5	0	0	0	0	.000	0	2	0.00

	BATTING																	BASERUNNING			PERCENTAGES		
Year Team	Lg	G	AB	H	2B	3B	HR	(Hm | Rd)	TB	R	RBI	TBB	IBB	SO	HBP	SH	SF	SB	CS	SB%	GDP	Avg	OBP	SLG
1962 Cleveland	AL	8	11	3	0	0	0	(0 | 0)	3	1	0	0	0	3	0	0	0	0	0	.00	0	.273	.273	.273
1963 St. Louis	NL	54	32	1	0	0	0	(0 | 0)	1	0	1	0	0	22	0	2	0	0	0	.00	0	.031	.031	.031
1964 St. Louis	NL	63	15	2	0	0	0	(0 | 0)	2	0	0	0	0	9	0	0	0	0	0	.00	0	.133	.133	.133
1965 2 ML Teams		57	18	2	1	0	0	(0 | 0)	3	0	0	0	0	9	0	0	0	0	0	.00	0	.111	.111	.167
1966 Houston	NL	36	12	2	1	0	0	(0 | 0)	3	0	0	0	0	5	0	0	0	0	0	.00	1	.167	.167	.250
1967 New York	NL	50	7	0	0	0	0	(0 | 0)	0	0	0	0	0	5	0	1	0	0	0	.00	0	.000	.000	.000
1968 New York	NL	58	9	0	0	0	0	(0 | 0)	0	0	0	0	0	6	0	0	0	0	0	.00	0	.000	.000	.000
1969 New York	NL	59	4	1	0	0	0	(0 | 0)	1	0	0	0	0	2	0	0	0	0	0	.00	0	.250	.250	.250
1970 New York	NL	57	4	0	0	0	0	(0 | 0)	0	0	0	1	0	4	0	1	0	0	0	.00	0	.000	.200	.000
1971 New York	NL	45	4	1	0	0	0	(0 | 0)	1	1	0	0	0	3	0	0	0	0	0	.00	0	.250	.250	.250
1972 San Diego	NL	4	0	0	0	0	0	(0 | 0)	0	0	0	0	0	0	0	0	0	0	0	.00	0	.000	.000	.000
1965 St. Louis	NL	25	5	2	1	0	0	(0 | 0)	3	0	0	0	0	2	0	0	0	0	0	.00	0	.400	.400	.600
Houston	NL	32	13	0	0	0	0	(0 | 0)	0	0	0	0	0	7	0	0	0	0	0	.00	0	.000	.000	.000
11 ML YEARS		491	116	12	2	0	0	(0 | 0)	14	2	1	1	0	68	0	4	0	0	0	.00	1	.103	.111	.121

World Series Batting

	BATTING																	BASERUNNING			PERCENTAGES		
Year Team	Lg	G	AB	H	2B	3B	HR	(Hm | Rd)	TB	R	RBI	TBB	IBB	SO	HBP	SH	SF	SB	CS	SB%	GDP	Avg	OBP	SLG
1964 St. Louis	NL	2	1	0	0	0	0	(0 | 0)	0	0	0	0	0	1	0	0	0	0	0	.00	0	.000	.000	.000
1969 New York	NL	2	0	0	0	0	0	(0 | 0)	0	0	0	0	0	0	0	0	0	0	0	.00	0	.000	.000	.000
2 ML YEARS		4	1	0	0	0	0	(0 | 0)	0	0	0	0	0	1	0	0	0	0	0	.00	0	.000	.000	.000

FIELDING AS PITCHER									
Year Team	Lg	G	TC	PO	A	E	DP	PB	Pct.	Range
1962 Cleveland	AL	8	5	0	5	0	0	--	1.000	---
1963 St. Louis	NL	54	15	2	13	0	0	--	1.000	---
1964 St. Louis	NL	63	30	2	27	1	3	--	.967	---
1965 2 ML Teams		57	20	5	15	0	0	--	1.000	---
1966 Houston	NL	36	7	0	7	0	0	--	1.000	---
1967 New York	NL	50	19	7	11	1	1	--	.947	---
1968 New York	NL	58	24	9	14	1	1	--	.958	---
1969 New York	NL	59	19	6	13	0	1	--	1.000	---
1970 New York	NL	57	17	5	12	0	0	--	1.000	---
1971 New York	NL	45	12	1	11	0	0	--	1.000	---
1972 San Diego	NL	4	1	0	1	0	0	--	1.000	---
1965 St. Louis	NL	25	10	2	8	0	0	--	1.000	---
Houston	NL	32	10	3	7	0	0	--	1.000	---
11 ML YEARS		491	169	37	129	3	6	--	.982	---

League Championship Fielding

FIELDING AS PITCHER									
Year Team	Lg	G	TC	PO	A	E	DP	PB	Pct.	Range
1969 New York	NL	2	1	1	0	0	0	--	1.000	---

World Series Fielding

FIELDING AS PITCHER										
Year Team	Lg	G	TC	PO	A	E	DP	PB	Pct.	Range
1964 St. Louis	NL	2	2	0	2	0	0	--	1.000	---
1969 New York	NL	2	1	0	1	0	0	--	1.000	---
2 ML YEARS		4	3	0	3	0	0	--	1.000	---

Tug Thompson

John P. Thompson
Bats: Unknown **Throws:** Right

Height: 5'8" **Weight:** 160
Born Unknown in London, Ontario

BATTING																			BASERUNNING				PERCENTAGES		
Year Team	Lg	G	AB	H	2B	3B	HR	(Hm	Rd)	TB	R	RBI	TBB	IBB	SO	HBP	SH	SF	SB	CS	SB%	GDP	Avg	OBP	SLG
1882 Cincinnati	AA	1	5	1	0	0	0	--	--	1	0		0										.200	.200	.200
1884 Indianapolis	AA	24	97	20	3	0	0	--	--	23	10		2			0							.206	.222	.237
2 ML YEARS		25	102	21	3	0	0	--	--	24	10		2			0	0						.206	.221	.235

FIELDING AS CATCHER										
Year Team	Lg	G	TC	PO	A	E	DP	PB	Pct.	Range
1884 Indianapolis	AA	12	84	58	14	12	0	17	.857	---

FIELDING AS OUTFIELDER										
Year Team	Lg	G	TC	PO	A	E	DP	PB	Pct.	Range
1882 Cincinnati	AA	1	1	0	0	1	0	--	.000	.00
1884 Indianapolis	AA	12	21	7	2	12	0	--	.429	.75
2 ML YEARS		13	22	7	2	13	0	--	.409	.69

John Upham

John Leslie Upham
Bats: Left **Throws:** Left

Height: 6'0" **Weight:** 180
Born on December 29, 1941 in Windsor, Ontario

BATTING																			BASERUNNING				PERCENTAGES		
Year Team	Lg	G	AB	H	2B	3B	HR	(Hm	Rd)	TB	R	RBI	TBB	IBB	SO	HBP	SH	SF	SB	CS	SB%	GDP	Avg	OBP	SLG
1967 Chicago	NL	8	3	2	0	0	0	(0	0)	2	1	0	0	0	0	0	0	0	0	0	.00	0	.667	.667	.667
1968 Chicago	NL	13	10	2	0	0	0	(0	0)	2	0	0	0	0	3	0	0	0	0	0	.00	0	.200	.200	.200
2 ML YEARS		21	13	4	0	0	0	(0	0)	4	1	0	0	0	3	0	0	0	0	0	.00	0	.308	.308	.308

HOW MUCH HE PITCHED								WHAT HE GAVE UP												THE RESULTS					
Year Team	Lg	G	GS	CG	GF	IP	BFP	H	R	ER	HR	SH	SF	HB	TBB	IBB	SO	WP	Bk	W	L	Pct.	ShO	Sv	ERA
1967 Chicago	NL	5	0	0	2	1.1	10	4	5	5	1	0	1	0	2	1	2	1	0	0	1	.000	0	0	33.75
1968 Chicago	NL	2	0	0	1	7	27	2	0	0	0	0	0	1	3	0	2	1	0	0	0	.000	0	0	0.00
2 ML YEARS		7	0	0	3	8.1	37	6	5	5	1	0	1	1	5	1	4	2	0	0	1	.000	0	0	5.40

HOW MUCH HE PITCHED								WHAT HE GAVE UP												THE RESULTS					
Year Team	Lg	G	GS	CG	GF	IP	BFP	H	R	ER	HR	SH	SF	HB	TBB	IBB	SO	WP	Bk	W	L	Pct.	ShO	Sv	ERA
1967 Chicago	NL	5	0	0	2	1.1	10	4	5	5	1	0	1	0	2	1	2	1	0	0	1	.000	0	0	33.75
1968 Chicago	NL	2	0	0	1	7	27	2	0	0	0	0	0	1	3	0	2	1	0	0	0	.000	0	0	0.00
2 ML YEARS		7	0	0	3	8.1	37	6	5	5	1	0	1	1	5	1	4	2	0	0	1	.000	0	0	5.40

BATTING																			BASERUNNING				PERCENTAGES		
Year Team	Lg	G	AB	H	2B	3B	HR	(Hm	Rd)	TB	R	RBI	TBB	IBB	SO	HBP	SH	SF	SB	CS	SB%	GDP	Avg	OBP	SLG
1967 Chicago	NL	8	3	2	0	0	0	(0	0)	2	1	0	0	0	0	0	0	0	0	0	.00	0	.667	.667	.667
1968 Chicago	NL	13	10	2	0	0	0	(0	0)	2	0	0	0	0	3	0	0	0	0	0	.00	0	.200	.200	.200
2 ML YEARS		21	13	4	0	0	0	(0	0)	4	1	0	0	0	3	0	0	0	0	0	.00	0	.308	.308	.308

FIELDING AS PITCHER										
Year Team	Lg	G	TC	PO	A	E	DP	PB	Pct.	Range
1967 Chicago	NL	5	0	0	0	0	0	--	.000	---
1968 Chicago	NL	2	3	0	3	0	0	--	1.000	---
2 ML YEARS		7	3	0	3	0	0	--	1.000	---

FIELDING AS OUTFIELDER										
Year Team	Lg	G	TC	PO	A	E	DP	PB	Pct.	Range
1968 Chicago	NL	2	0	0	0	0	0	--	.000	.00

Gene Vadeboncoeur

Eugene F. Vadeboncoeur
Bats: Unknown **Throws:** Unknown

Height: 5'6" **Weight:** 150
Born on July 15, 1858 in Louiseville, Quebec
Died on October 16, 1935 in Haverhill, Massachusetts

							BATTING												BASERUNNING				PERCENTAGES		
Year Team	Lg	G	AB	H	2B	3B	HR	(Hm	Rd)	TB	R	RBI	TBB	IBB	SO	HBP	SH	SF	SB	CS	SB%	GDP	Avg	OBP	SLG
1884 Philadelphia	NL	4	14	3	0	0	0	--	--	3	1	3	1		2								.214	.267	.214

				FIELDING AS CATCHER							
Year Team	Lg	G	TC	PO	A	E	DP	PB	Pct.	Range	
1884 Philadelphia	NL	4	26	13	9	4	0	9	.846	---	

Ozzie Van Brabant

Camille Oscar Van Brabant
Pitches: Right **Bats:** Right

Height: 6'1" **Weight:** 165
Born on September 28, 1926 in Kingsville, Ontario

		HOW MUCH HE PITCHED						WHAT HE GAVE UP											THE RESULTS					
Year Team	Lg	G	GS	CG	GF	IP	BFP	H	R	ER	HR	SH	SF	HB	TBB	IBB	SO	WP	Bk	W	L	Pct.	ShO	Sv	ERA
1954 Philadelphia	AL	9	2	0	2	26.2	124	35	23	21	3	3	1	1	18		10	2	1	0	2	.000	0	0	7.09
1955 Kansas City	AL	2	0	0	1	2	13	4	4	4	1	0	1	0	2	1	1	0	0	0	0	.000	0	0	18.00
2 ML YEARS		11	2	0	3	28.2	137	39	27	25	4	3	2	1	20		11	2	1	0	2	.000	0	0	7.85

							BATTING												BASERUNNING				PERCENTAGES		
Year Team	Lg	G	AB	H	2B	3B	HR	(Hm	Rd)	TB	R	RBI	TBB	IBB	SO	HBP	SH	SF	SB	CS	SB%	GDP	Avg	OBP	SLG
1954 Philadelphia	AL	9	5	1	0	0	0	(0	0)	1	1	0	2		2	0	0	0	0	0	.00	0	.200	.429	.200
1955 Kansas City	AL	2	0	0	0	0	0	(0	0)	0	0	0	0		0	0	0	0	0	0	.00	0	.000	.000	.000
2 ML YEARS		11	5	1	0	0	0	(0	0)	1	1	0	2		2	0	0	0	0	0	.00	0	.200	.429	.200

				FIELDING AS PITCHER							
Year Team	Lg	G	TC	PO	A	E	DP	PB	Pct.	Range	
1954 Philadelphia	AL	9	9	1	8	0	0	--	1.000	---	
1955 Kansas City	AL	2	0	0	0	0	0	--	.000	---	
2 ML YEARS		11	9	1	8	0	0	--	1.000		

Rube Vickers

Harry Porter Vickers
Pitches: Right **Bats:** Left

Height: 6'2" **Weight:** 225
Born on May 17, 1878 in St. Mary's, Ontario
Died on December 9, 1958 in Belleville, Michigan

		HOW MUCH HE PITCHED						WHAT HE GAVE UP											THE RESULTS					
Year Team	Lg	G	GS	CG	GF	IP	BFP	H	R	ER	HR	SH	SF	HB	TBB	IBB	SO	WP	Bk	W	L	Pct.	ShO	Sv	ERA
1902 Cincinnati	NL	3	3	3	0	21	102	31	20	14	0	1		1	8		6	0	0	0	3	.000	0	0	6.00
1903 Brooklyn	NL	4	1	1	3	14	77	27	23	17	0	2		1	9		5	2	0	0	1	.000	0	0	10.93
1907 Philadelphia	AL	10	4	3	5	50.1	208	44	27	19	1	4		1	12		21	1	0	2	2	.500	1	0	3.40
1908 Philadelphia	AL	53	34	21	17	317	1276	264	114	78	0	50		11	71		156	12	0	18	19	.486	6	2	2.21
1909 Philadelphia	AL	18	3	1	9	55.2	246	60	32	21	0	6		2	19		25	3	0	3	2	.600	0	1	3.40
5 ML YEARS		88	45	29	34	458	1909	426	216	149	1	63		16	119		213	18	0	23	27	.460	7	3	2.93

							BATTING												BASERUNNING				PERCENTAGES		
Year Team	Lg	G	AB	H	2B	3B	HR	(Hm	Rd)	TB	R	RBI	TBB	IBB	SO	HBP	SH	SF	SB	CS	SB%	GDP	Avg	OBP	SLG
1902 Cincinnati	NL	4	11	4	1	0	0	--	--	5	0	3	0			0	0		0				.364	.364	.455
1903 Brooklyn	NL	5	10	1	0	0	0	--	--	1	0	3	0			0	0		0				.100	.100	.100
1907 Philadelphia	AL	10	20	3	0	0	0	--	--	3	0	0	0			0	1		0				.150	.150	.150
1908 Philadelphia	AL	53	106	17	3	0	0	--	--	20	4	4	10			0	4		0				.160	.233	.189
1909 Philadelphia	AL	18	16	1	0	0	0	--	--	1	0	3	0			0	1		0				.063	.063	.063
5 ML YEARS		90	163	26	4	0	0			30	4	13	10			0	6		0				.160	.208	.184

				FIELDING AS PITCHER							
Year Team	Lg	G	TC	PO	A	E	DP	PB	Pct.	Range	
1902 Cincinnati	NL	3	3	0	3	0	0	--	1.000	---	
1903 Brooklyn	NL	4	11	0	10	1	0	--	.909	---	
1907 Philadelphia	AL	10	20	2	17	1	1	--	.950	---	
1908 Philadelphia	AL	53	100	10	83	7	0	--	.930	---	
1909 Philadelphia	AL	18	15	3	11	1	0	--	.933	---	
5 ML YEARS		88	149	15	124	10	1	--	.933		

				FIELDING AS CATCHER							
Year Team	Lg	G	TC	PO	A	E	DP	PB	Pct.	Range	
1902 Cincinnati	NL	1	1	0	1	0	0	6	1.000	---	

				FIELDING AS OUTFIELDER							
Year Team	Lg	G	TC	PO	A	E	DP	PB	Pct.	Range	
1903 Brooklyn	NL	1	1	1	0	0	0	--	1.000	1.00	

David Wainhouse

David Paul Wainhouse
Attended Washington St.
Pitches: Right **Bats:** Left

Height: 6'2" **Weight:** 190
Born on November 7, 1967 in Toronto, Ontario

			HOW MUCH HE PITCHED						WHAT HE GAVE UP										THE RESULTS					
Year	Team	Lg	G	GS	CG	GF	IP	BFP	H	R	ER	HR	SH	SF	HB	TBB	IBB	SO	WP	Bk	W	L	Pct.	ShO	Sv	ERA
1989	W. Palm Bch	A	13	13	0	0	66.1	286	75	35	30	4	3	2	8	19	0	26	6	3	1	5	.167	0	0	4.07
1990	W. Palm Bch	A	12	12	2	0	76.2	327	68	28	18	1	0	3	5	34	0	58	2	3	6	3	.667	1	0	2.11
	Jacksonvlle	AA	17	16	2	0	95.2	428	97	59	46	8	2	3	7	47	2	59	2	0	7	7	.500	0	0	4.33
1991	Harrisburg	AA	33	0	0	27	52	224	49	17	15	1	2	0	4	17	2	46	3	0	2	2	.500	0	11	2.60
	Indianapols	AAA	14	0	0	8	28.2	127	28	14	13	1	2	1	3	15	1	13	3	0	2	0	1.000	0	1	4.08
1992	Indianapols	AAA	44	0	0	41	46	208	48	22	21	4	2	2	2	24	6	37	4	0	5	4	.556	0	21	4.11
1993	Calgary	AAA	13	0	0	10	15.2	62	10	7	7	2	2	2	1	7	1	7	2	0	0	1	.000	0	5	4.02
1995	Syracuse	AAA	26	0	0	21	24.1	111	29	13	10	1	1	2	1	11	3	18	4	0	3	2	.600	0	5	3.70
	Portland	AA	17	0	0	5	25	122	39	22	20	3	0	1	1	8	1	16	1	0	2	1	.667	0	0	7.20
	Charlotte	AAA	4	0	0	1	3.2	21	6	6	4	1	0	1	0	4	0	2	2	0	0	0	.000	0	0	9.82
1991	Montreal	NL	2	0	0	1	2.2	14	2	2	2	0	0	1	0	4	0	1	2	0	0	1	.000	0	0	6.75
1993	Seattle	AL	3	0	0	0	2.1	20	7	7	7	1	0	0	1	5	0	2	0	0	0	0	.000	0	0	27.00
	2 ML YEARS		5	0	0	1	5	34	9	9	9	1	0	1	1	9	0	3	2	0	0	1	.000	0	0	16.20

			BATTING															BASERUNNING				PERCENTAGES		
Year	Team	Lg	G	AB	H	2B	3B	HR	(Hm | Rd)	TB	R	RBI	TBB	IBB	SO	HBP	SH	SF	SB	CS	SB%	GDP	Avg	OBP	SLG
1991	Montreal	NL	2	0	0	0	0	0	(0 | 0)	0	0	0	0	0	0	0	0	0	0	0	.00	0	.000	.000	.000

		FIELDING AS PITCHER								
Year	Team	Lg	G	TC	PO	A	E	DP	PB	Pct.	Range
1991	Montreal	NL	2	0	0	0	0	0	--	.000	---
1993	Seattle	AL	3	0	0	0	0	0	--	.000	---
	2 ML YEARS		5	0	0	0	0	0	--	.000	---

George Walker

George A. Walker
Pitches: Unknown **Bats:** Unknown

Height: 5'9" **Weight:** 184
Born in 1863 in Hamilton, Ontario

			HOW MUCH HE PITCHED						WHAT HE GAVE UP										THE RESULTS					
Year	Team	Lg	G	GS	CG	GF	IP	BFP	H	R	ER	HR	SH	SF	HB	TBB	IBB	SO	WP	Bk	W	L	Pct.	ShO	Sv	ERA
1888	Baltimore	AA	4	4	4	0	35	155	36	31	23	2		0		14		18	5	0	1	3	.250	1	0	5.91

			BATTING															BASERUNNING				PERCENTAGES		
Year	Team	Lg	G	AB	H	2B	3B	HR	(Hm	Rd)	TB	R	RBI	TBB	IBB	SO	HBP	SH	SF	SB	CS	SB%	GDP	Avg	OBP	SLG
1888	Baltimore	AA	4	13	1	0	0	0	--	--	1	1	1	0		0				0				.077	.077	.077

		FIELDING AS PITCHER								
Year	Team	Lg	G	TC	PO	A	E	DP	PB	Pct.	Range
1888	Baltimore	AA	4	8	0	7	1	0	--	.875	---

Larry Walker

Larry Kenneth Robert Walker
Bats: Left **Throws:** Right

Height: 6'2" **Weight:** 185
Born on December 1, 1966 in Maple Ridge, British Columbia

			BATTING															BASERUNNING				PERCENTAGES		
Year	Team	Lg	G	AB	H	2B	3B	HR	(Hm	Rd)	TB	R	RBI	TBB	IBB	SO	HBP	SH	SF	SB	CS	SB%	GDP	Avg	OBP	SLG
1985	Utica	A	62	215	48	8	2	2	--	--	66	24	26	18	4	57	5	2	1	12	6	.67	1	.223	.297	.307
1986	Burlington	A	95	332	96	12	6	29	--	--	207	67	74	46	1	112	9	0	3	16	8	.67	4	.289	.387	.623
	W. Palm Bch	A	38	113	32	7	5	4	--	--	61	20	16	26	2	32	2	0	1	2	2	.50	2	.283	.423	.540
1987	Jacksonville	AA	128	474	136	25	7	26	--	--	253	91	83	67	5	120	9	0	3	24	3	.89	6	.287	.383	.534
1989	Indianapols	AAA	114	385	104	18	2	12	--	--	162	68	59	50	8	87	9	5	7	36	6	.86	8	.270	.361	.421
1989	Montreal	NL	20	47	8	0	0	0	(0	0)	8	4	4	5	0	13	1	3	0	1	1	.50	0	.170	.264	.170
1990	Montreal	NL	133	419	101	18	3	19	(9	10)	182	59	51	49	5	112	5	3	2	21	7	.75	8	.241	.326	.434
1991	Montreal	NL	137	487	141	30	2	16	(5	11)	223	59	64	42	2	102	5	5	4	14	9	.61	7	.290	.349	.458
1992	Montreal	NL	143	528	159	31	4	23	(13	10)	267	85	93	41	10	97	6	0	8	18	6	.75	9	.301	.353	.506
1993	Montreal	NL	138	490	130	24	5	22	(13	9)	230	85	86	80	20	76	6	0	6	29	7	.81	8	.265	.371	.469
1994	Montreal	NL	103	395	127	44	2	19	(7	12)	232	76	86	47	5	74	4	0	6	15	5	.75	8	.322	.394	.587
1995	Colorado	NL	131	494	151	31	5	36	(24	12)	300	96	101	49	13	72	14	0	5	16	3	.84	13	.306	.381	.607
	7 ML YEARS		805	2860	817	178	21	135	(71	64)	1442	464	485	313	55	546	41	7	31	114	38	.75	53	.286	.361	.504

All-Star Game Batting

			BATTING															BASERUNNING				PERCENTAGES		
Year	Team	Lg	G	AB	H	2B	3B	HR	(Hm | Rd)	TB	R	RBI	TBB	IBB	SO	HBP	SH	SF	SB	CS	SB%	GDP	Avg	OBP	SLG
1992	Montreal	NL	1	1	1	0	0	0	(0 | 0)	1	0	0	0	0	0	0	0	0	0	0	.00	0	1.000	1.000	1.000

Division Playoffs Batting

									BATTING											BASERUNNING				PERCENTAGES		
Year Team	Lg	G	AB	H	2B	3B	HR	(Hm	Rd)	TB	R	RBI	TBB	IBB	SO	HBP	SH	SF		SB	CS	SB%	GDP	Avg	OBP	SLG
1995 Colorado	NL	4	14	3	0	0	1	(1	0)	6	3	3	3	1	4	1	0	0		1	0	1.00	1	.214	.389	.429

FIELDING AS FIRST BASEMAN

Year Team	Lg	G	TC	PO	A	E	DP	PB	Pct.	Range
1991 Montreal	NL	39	347	313	30	4	28	--	.988	---
1993 Montreal	NL	4	46	43	3	0	2	--	1.000	---
1994 Montreal	NL	35	312	283	24	5	20	--	.984	---
3 ML YEARS		78	705	639	57	9	50	--	.987	---

FIELDING AS OUTFIELDER

Year Team	Lg	G	TC	PO	A	E	DP	PB	Pct.	Range
1989 Montreal	NL	15	21	19	2	0	1	--	1.000	1.40
1990 Montreal	NL	124	265	249	12	4	5	--	.985	2.10
1991 Montreal	NL	102	231	223	6	2	2	--	.991	2.25
1992 Montreal	NL	139	287	269	16	2	2	--	.993	2.05
1993 Montreal	NL	132	292	273	13	6	2	--	.979	2.17
1994 Montreal	NL	68	149	140	5	4	1	--	.973	2.13
1995 Colorado	NL	129	241	225	13	3	1	--	.988	1.84
7 ML YEARS		709	1486	1398	67	21	14	--	.986	2.07

Division Playoffs Fielding

FIELDING AS OUTFIELDER

Year Team	Lg	G	TC	PO	A	E	DP	PB	Pct.	Range
1995 Colorado	NL	4	3	3	0	0	0	--	1.000	.75

Gold Glove in 1992, 1993.

Pete Ward

Peter Thomas Ward

Bats: Left **Throws:** Right

Height: 6'1" **Weight:** 185

Born on July 26, 1939 in Montreal, Quebec

									BATTING											BASERUNNING				PERCENTAGES		
Year Team	Lg	G	AB	H	2B	3B	HR	(Hm	Rd)	TB	R	RBI	TBB	IBB	SO	HBP	SH	SF		SB	CS	SB%	GDP	Avg	OBP	SLG
1962 Baltimore	AL	8	21	3	2	0	0	(0	0)	5	1	2	4	0	5	0	0	0		0	0	.00	0	.143	.280	.238
1963 Chicago	AL	157	600	177	34	6	22	(13	9)	289	80	84	52	1	77	5	4	6		7	6	.54	6	.295	.353	.482
1964 Chicago	AL	144	539	152	28	3	23	(9	14)	255	61	94	56	11	76	2	3	7		1	1	.50	7	.282	.348	.473
1965 Chicago	AL	138	507	125	25	3	10	(3	7)	186	62	57	56	11	83	6	2	3		2	4	.33	10	.247	.327	.367
1966 Chicago	AL	84	251	55	7	1	3	(2	1)	73	22	28	24	0	49	3	1	5		3	1	.75	5	.219	.290	.291
1967 Chicago	AL	146	467	109	16	2	18	(9	9)	183	49	62	61	9	109	11	0	3		3	2	.60	5	.233	.334	.392
1968 Chicago	AL	125	399	86	15	0	15	(7	8)	146	43	50	76	8	85	10	1	1		4	3	.57	3	.216	.354	.366
1969 Chicago	AL	105	199	49	7	0	6	(4	2)	74	22	32	33	1	38	3	1	2		0	0	.00	2	.246	.359	.372
1970 New York	AL	66	77	20	2	2	1	(0	1)	29	5	18	9	0	17	0	0	1		0	0	.00	1	.260	.333	.377
9 ML YEARS		973	3060	776	136	17	98	(47	51)	1240	345	427	371	41	539	40	12	28		20	17	.54	39	.254	.339	.405

FIELDING AS FIRST BASEMAN

Year Team	Lg	G	TC	PO	A	E	DP	PB	Pct.	Range
1966 Chicago	AL	5	25	19	5	1	2	--	.960	---
1967 Chicago	AL	39	316	295	19	2	23	--	.994	---
1968 Chicago	AL	31	256	238	18	0	17	--	1.000	---
1969 Chicago	AL	25	180	167	12	1	12	--	.994	---
1970 New York	AL	13	86	83	3	0	7	--	1.000	---
5 ML YEARS		113	863	802	57	4	61	--	.995	---

FIELDING AS SECOND BASEMAN

Year Team	Lg	G	TC	PO	A	E	DP	PB	Pct.	Range
1963 Chicago	AL	1	1	1	0	0	0	--	1.000	1.00
1965 Chicago	AL	1	1	0	1	0	0	--	1.000	1.00
2 ML YEARS		2	2	1	1	0	0	--	1.000	1.00

FIELDING AS THIRD BASEMAN

Year Team	Lg	G	TC	PO	A	E	DP	PB	Pct.	Range
1963 Chicago	AL	154	496	156	302	38	27	--	.923	2.97
1964 Chicago	AL	138	454	126	309	19	24	--	.958	3.15
1965 Chicago	AL	134	437	97	319	21	22	--	.952	3.10
1966 Chicago	AL	16	45	10	34	1	3	--	.978	2.75
1967 Chicago	AL	22	44	7	33	4	3	--	.909	1.82
1968 Chicago	AL	77	222	59	151	12	7	--	.946	2.73
1969 Chicago	AL	21	51	15	34	2	1	--	.961	2.33
7 ML YEARS		562	1749	470	1182	97	87	--	.945	2.94

FIELDING AS SHORTSTOP

Year Team	Lg	G	TC	PO	A	E	DP	PB	Pct.	Range
1963 Chicago	AL	1	2	1	1	0	1	--	1.000	2.00

FIELDING AS OUTFIELDER

Year Team	Lg	G	TC	PO	A	E	DP	PB	Pct.	Range
1962 Baltimore	AL	6	10	10	0	0	0	--	1.000	1.67
1966 Chicago	AL	59	87	83	3	1	1	--	.989	1.46
1967 Chicago	AL	89	111	107	3	1	0	--	.991	1.24
1968 Chicago	AL	22	29	28	1	0	1	--	1.000	1.32
1969 Chicago	AL	9	13	11	2	0	0	--	1.000	1.44
5 ML YEARS		185	250	239	9	2	2	--	.992	1.34

Bill Watkins

William Henry Watkins

Bats: Unknown **Throws:** Unknown

Height: 5'10" **Weight:** 156
Born on May 5, 1858 in Brantford, Ontario
Died on June 9, 1937 in Port Huron, Michigan

BATTING / BASERUNNING / PERCENTAGES

Year Team	Lg	G	AB	H	2B	3B	HR	(Hm	Rd)	TB	R	RBI	TBB	IBB	SO	HBP	SH	SF	SB	CS	SB%	GDP	Avg	OBP	SLG
1884 Indianapolis	AA	34	127	26	4	0	0	--	--	30	16	5				1							.205	.241	.236

FIELDING AS SECOND BASEMAN

Year Team	Lg	G	TC	PO	A	E	DP	PB	Pct.	Range
1884 Indianapolis	AA	9	57	23	29	5	3	--	.912	5.78

FIELDING AS THIRD BASEMAN

Year Team	Lg	G	TC	PO	A	E	DP	PB	Pct.	Range
1884 Indianapolis	AA	23	58	21	28	9	1	--	.845	2.13

FIELDING AS SHORTSTOP

Year Team	Lg	G	TC	PO	A	E	DP	PB	Pct.	Range
1884 Indianapolis	AA	2	8	1	6	1	0	--	.875	3.50

Joe Weber

Harry Weber

Bats: Unknown **Throws:** Unknown

Height: Unknown **Weight:** Unknown
Born Unknown in Indianapolis, Indiana

BATTING / BASERUNNING / PERCENTAGES

Year Team	Lg	G	AB	H	2B	3B	HR	(Hm	Rd)	TB	R	RBI	TBB	IBB	SO	HBP	SH	SF	SB	CS	SB%	GDP	Avg	OBP	SLG
1884 Detroit	NL	2	8	0	0	0	0	--	--	0	0	0	0		2								.000	.000	.000

FIELDING AS OUTFIELDER

Year Team	Lg	G	TC	PO	A	E	DP	PB	Pct.	Range
1884 Detroit	NL	2	4	2	1	1	0	--	.750	1.50

Milt Whitehead

Milton P. Whitehead

Bats: Both **Throws:** Unknown

Height: Unknown **Weight:** Unknown
Born in 1862 in Canada
Died on August 15, 1901 in Highland, California

BATTING / BASERUNNING / PERCENTAGES

Year Team	Lg	G	AB	H	2B	3B	HR	(Hm	Rd)	TB	R	RBI	TBB	IBB	SO	HBP	SH	SF	SB	CS	SB%	GDP	Avg	OBP	SLG
1884 2 ML Teams		104	415	86	15	1	1	--	--	106	63		8										.207	.222	.255
1884 St. Louis	UA	99	393	83	15	1	1	--	--	103	61		8										.211	.227	.262
Kansas City	UA	5	22	3	0	0	0	--	--	3	2		0										.136	.136	.136

HOW MUCH HE PITCHED / WHAT HE GAVE UP / THE RESULTS

Year Team	Lg	G	GS	CG	GF	IP	BFP	H	R	ER	HR	SH	SF	HB	TBB	IBB	SO	WP	Bk	W	L	Pct.	ShO	Sv	ERA
1884 St. Louis	UA	1	1	1	0	8	35	14	9	8	0				2		2	3	0	0	1	.000	0	0	9.00

FIELDING AS PITCHER

Year Team	Lg	G	TC	PO	A	E	DP	PB	Pct.	Range
1884 St. Louis	UA	1	2	0	2	0	0	--	1.000	---

FIELDING AS CATCHER

Year Team	Lg	G	TC	PO	A	E	DP	PB	Pct.	Range
1884 Kansas City	UA	1	4	4	0	0	0	0	1.000	---

FIELDING AS SECOND BASEMAN

Year Team	Lg	G	TC	PO	A	E	DP	PB	Pct.	Range
1884 2 ML Teams		4	22	5	13	4	0	--	.818	4.50
1884 St. Louis	UA	1	8	3	3	2	0	--	.750	6.00
Kansas City	UA	3	14	2	10	2	0	--	.857	4.00

FIELDING AS THIRD BASEMAN										
Year Team	Lg	G	TC	PO	A	E	DP	PB	Pct.	Range
1884 2 ML Teams		2	6	1	3	2	0	--	.667	2.00
1884 St. Louis	UA	1	4	1	1	2	0	--	.500	2.00
Kansas City	UA	1	2	0	2	0	0	--	1.000	2.00

FIELDING AS SHORTSTOP										
Year Team	Lg	G	TC	PO	A	E	DP	PB	Pct.	Range
1884 2 ML Teams		95	444	85	272	87	19	--	.804	3.76
1884 St. Louis	UA	94	441	85	269	87	19	--	.803	3.77
Kansas City	UA	1	3	0	3	0	0	--	1.000	3.00

FIELDING AS OUTFIELDER										
Year Team	Lg	G	TC	PO	A	E	DP	PB	Pct.	Range
1884 St. Louis	UA	2	7	6	1	0	0	--	1.000	3.50

Lefty Wilkie

Aldon Jay Wilkie
Pitches: Left   **Bats:** Left

Height: 5'11"   **Weight:** 175
Born on October 30, 1914 in Zealandia, Saskatchewan
Died on August 5, 1992 in Tualatin, Oregon

		HOW MUCH HE PITCHED						WHAT HE GAVE UP											THE RESULTS					
Year Team	Lg	G	GS	CG	GF	IP	BFP	H	R	ER	HR	SH	SF	HB	TBB	IBB	SO	WP	Bk	W	L	Pct.	ShO	Sv	ERA
1941 Pittsburgh	NL	26	6	2	12	79	362	90	42	40	1	10		1	40		16	4	1	2	4	.333	1	2	4.56
1942 Pittsburgh	NL	35	6	3	19	107.1	468	112	53	50	4	14		1	37		18	1	1	6	7	.462	0	1	4.19
1946 Pittsburgh	NL	7	0	0	4	7.2	37	13	9	9	0	0		0	3		3	0	0	0	0	.000	0	0	10.57
3 ML YEARS		68	12	5	35	194	867	215	104	99	5	24		2	80		37	5	2	8	11	.421	1	3	4.59

		BATTING																		BASERUNNING				PERCENTAGES		
Year Team	Lg	G	AB	H	2B	3B	HR	(Hm	Rd)	TB	R	RBI	TBB	IBB	SO	HBP	SH	SF		SB	CS	SB%	GDP	Avg	OBP	SLG
1941 Pittsburgh	NL	26	24	7	0	0	0	--	--	7	2	2	0		5	0	0			0			0	.292	.292	.292
1942 Pittsburgh	NL	36	38	10	0	1	0	--	--	12	5	4	1		2	0	0			0			0	.263	.282	.316
1946 Pittsburgh	NL	7	0	0	0	0	0	--	--	0	0	0	0		0	0	0			0			0	.000	.000	.000
3 ML YEARS		69	62	17	0	1	0	--	--	19	7	6	1		7	0	0			0			0	.274	.286	.306

FIELDING AS PITCHER										
Year Team	Lg	G	TC	PO	A	E	DP	PB	Pct.	Range
1941 Pittsburgh	NL	26	24	2	22	0	1	--	1.000	---
1942 Pittsburgh	NL	35	40	3	36	1	0	--	.975	---
1946 Pittsburgh	NL	7	1	0	1	0	0	--	1.000	---
3 ML YEARS		68	65	5	59	1	1	--	.985	---

Nigel Wilson

Nigel Edward Wilson
Bats: Left   **Throws:** Left

Height: 6'1"   **Weight:** 185
Born on January 12, 1970 in Oshawa, Ontario

		BATTING																		BASERUNNING				PERCENTAGES		
Year Team	Lg	G	AB	H	2B	3B	HR	(Hm	Rd)	TB	R	RBI	TBB	IBB	SO	HBP	SH	SF		SB	CS	SB%	GDP	Avg	OBP	SLG
1988 St. Cathrns	A	40	103	21	1	2	2	--	--	32	12	11	12	0	32	4	1	1		8	4	.67	0	.204	.308	.311
1989 St. Cathrns	A	42	161	35	5	2	4	--	--	56	17	18	11	0	50	4	1	0		8	2	.80	0	.217	.284	.348
1990 Myrtle Bch	A	110	440	120	23	9	16	--	--	209	77	62	30	3	71	6	2	2		22	12	.65	4	.273	.326	.475
1991 Dunedin	A	119	455	137	18	13	12	--	--	217	64	55	29	4	99	9	4	7		26	11	.70	4	.301	.350	.477
1992 Knoxville	AA	137	521	143	34	7	26	--	--	269	85	69	33	5	137	7	2	2		13	8	.62	2	.274	.325	.516
1993 Edmonton	AAA	96	370	108	26	7	17	--	--	199	66	68	25	7	108	10	1	2		8	3	.73	6	.292	.351	.538
1994 Edmonton	AAA	87	314	97	24	1	12	--	--	159	50	62	22	3	79	10	0	4		2	3	.40	3	.309	.369	.506
1995 Indianapols	AAA	82	304	95	27	3	17	--	--	179	53	51	13	4	95	8	0	1		5	3	.63	2	.313	.356	.589
1993 Florida	NL	7	16	0	0	0	0	(0	0)	0	0	0	0	0	11	0	0	0		0	0	.00	0	.000	.000	.000
1995 Cincinnati	NL	5	7	0	0	0	0	(0	0)	0	0	0	0	0	4	0	0	0		0	0	.00	0	.000	.000	.000
2 ML YEARS		12	23	0	0	0	0	(0	0)	0	0	0	0	0	15	0	0	0		0	0	.00	0	.000	.000	.000

FIELDING AS OUTFIELDER										
Year Team	Lg	G	TC	PO	A	E	DP	PB	Pct.	Range
1993 Florida	NL	3	4	4	0	0	0	--	1.000	1.33
1995 Cincinnati	NL	2	2	2	0	0	0	--	1.000	1.00
2 ML YEARS		5	6	6	0	0	0	--	1.000	1.20

Steve Wilson

Stephen Douglas Wilson
Attended Portland
Pitches: Left **Bats:** Left

Height: 6'4" **Weight:** 205
Born on December 13, 1964 in Victoria, British Columbia

			HOW MUCH HE PITCHED					WHAT HE GAVE UP											THE RESULTS					
Year	Team	Lg	G	GS	CG	GF	IP	BFP	H	R	ER	HR	SH	SF	HB	TBB	IBB	SO	WP	Bk	W	L	Pct.	ShO	Sv	ERA
1985	Burlington	A	21	10	0	4	72.2	317	71	44	37	11	1	4	2	27	1	76	1	3	3	5	.375	0	0	4.58
1986	Tulsa	AA	24	24	2	0	136.2	617	117	83	74	10	5	8	7	103	0	95	12	6	7	13	.350	0	0	4.87
1987	Charlotte	A	20	17	1	1	107	442	81	41	29	5	0	2	3	44	0	80	5	2	9	5	.643	1	0	2.44
1988	Tulsa	AA	25	25	5	0	165.1	698	147	72	58	14	6	4	8	53	1	132	3	1	15	7	.682	3	0	3.16
1991	Iowa	AAA	25	16	1	4	114	482	102	55	49	11	0	1	7	45	2	83	7	0	3	8	.273	0	0	3.87
1993	Albuquerque	AAA	13	12	0	0	51.1	220	57	29	25	5	4	1	2	14	0	44	4	2	0	3	.000	0	0	4.38
1994	New Orleans	AAA	51	3	0	15	76.2	332	78	39	37	5	1	2	4	33	5	67	5	1	8	6	.571	0	1	4.34
1995	Nashville	AAA	20	7	0	4	51.1	234	60	32	26	7	3	4	3	17	1	26	1	1	2	2	.500	0	1	4.56
1988	Texas	AL	3	0	0	1	7.2	31	7	5	5	1	0	0	0	4	1	1	0	0	0	0	.000	0	0	5.87
1989	Chicago	NL	53	8	0	9	85.2	364	83	43	40	6	5	4	1	31	5	65	0	1	6	4	.600	0	2	4.20
1990	Chicago	NL	45	15	1	5	139	597	140	77	74	17	9	3	2	43	6	95	2	1	4	9	.308	0	1	4.79
1991	2 ML Teams		19	0	0	5	20.2	81	14	7	6	1	0	1	0	9	1	14	0	0	0	0	.000	0	2	2.61
1992	Los Angeles	NL	60	0	0	18	66.2	301	74	37	31	6	5	4	1	29	7	54	7	0	2	5	.286	0	0	4.19
1993	Los Angeles	NL	25	0	0	4	25.2	120	30	13	13	2	1	0	1	14	4	23	3	0	1	0	1.000	0	1	4.56
1991	Chicago	NL	8	0	0	2	12.1	53	13	7	6	1	0	1	0	5	1	9	0	0	0	0	.000	0	0	4.38
	Los Angeles	NL	11	0	0	3	8.1	28	1	0	0	0	0	0	0	4	0	5	0	0	0	0	.000	0	2	0.00
	6 ML YEARS		205	23	1	42	345.1	1494	348	182	169	33	20	12	5	130	24	252	12	2	13	18	.419	0	6	4.40

League Championship Pitching

			HOW MUCH HE PITCHED					WHAT HE GAVE UP											THE RESULTS					
Year	Team	Lg	G	GS	CG	GF	IP	BFP	H	R	ER	HR	SH	SF	HB	TBB	IBB	SO	WP	Bk	W	L	Pct.	ShO	Sv	ERA
1989	Chicago	NL	2	0	0	1	3.1	16	7	5	2	2	0	0	0	1	0	4	1	0	0	1	.000	0	0	5.40

			BATTING															BASERUNNING				PERCENTAGES		
Year	Team	Lg	G	AB	H	2B	3B	HR	(Hm | Rd)	TB	R	RBI	TBB	IBB	SO	HBP	SH	SF	SB	CS	SB%	GDP	Avg	OBP	SLG
1989	Chicago	NL	53	16	1	0	0	0	(0 | 0)	1	1	0	1	0	3	0	1	0	0	0	.00	0	.063	.118	.063
1990	Chicago	NL	45	37	6	1	0	0	(0 | 0)	7	3	3	3	0	11	0	5	0	0	0	.00	0	.162	.225	.189
1991	2 ML Teams		20	2	0	0	0	0	(0 | 0)	0	0	0	0	0	0	0	0	0	0	0	.00	0	.000	.000	.000
1992	Los Angeles	NL	60	3	1	0	0	0	(0 | 0)	1	0	0	0	0	2	0	0	0	0	0	.00	0	.333	.333	.333
1993	Los Angeles	NL	25	2	0	0	0	0	(0 | 0)	0	0	0	0	0	0	0	0	0	0	0	.00	0	.000	.000	.000
1991	Chicago	NL	9	1	0	0	0	0	(0 | 0)	0	0	0	0	0	0	0	0	0	0	0	.00	0	.000	.000	.000
	Los Angeles	NL	11	1	0	0	0	0	(0 | 0)	0	0	0	0	0	0	0	0	0	0	0	.00	0	.000	.000	.000
	5 ML YEARS		203	60	8	1	0	0	(0 | 0)	9	4	3	4	0	17	0	6	0	0	0	.00	0	.133	.188	.150

League Championship Batting

			BATTING															BASERUNNING				PERCENTAGES		
Year	Team	Lg	G	AB	H	2B	3B	HR	(Hm | Rd)	TB	R	RBI	TBB	IBB	SO	HBP	SH	SF	SB	CS	SB%	GDP	Avg	OBP	SLG
1989	Chicago	NL	2	0	0	0	0	0	(0 | 0)	0	0	0	0	0	0	0	0	0	0	0	.00	0	.000	.000	.000

		FIELDING AS PITCHER								
Year	Team	Lg	G	TC	PO	A	E	DP	PB	Pct.	Range
1988	Texas	AL	3	0	0	0	0	0	--	.000	---
1989	Chicago	NL	53	22	6	14	2	0	--	.909	---
1990	Chicago	NL	45	22	4	16	2	0	--	.909	---
1991	2 ML Teams		19	0	0	0	0	0	--	.000	---
1992	Los Angeles	NL	60	12	2	9	1	1	--	.917	---
1993	Los Angeles	NL	25	7	2	4	1	0	--	.857	---
1991	Chicago	NL	8	0	0	0	0	0	--	.000	---
	Los Angeles	NL	11	0	0	0	0	0	--	.000	---
	6 ML YEARS		205	63	14	43	6	1	--	.905	---

League Championship Fielding

		FIELDING AS PITCHER								
Year	Team	Lg	G	TC	PO	A	E	DP	PB	Pct.	Range
1989	Chicago	NL	2	1	0	1	0	0	--	1.000	---

Ed Wingo

Edmund Armand Wingo
Bats: Right **Throws:** Right

Height: 5'6" **Weight:** 145
Born on October 8, 1895 in Ste. Anne de Bellevue, Quebec
Died on December 5, 1964 in Lachine, Quebec

									BATTING									BASERUNNING				PERCENTAGES		
Year Team	Lg	G	AB	H	2B	3B	HR	(Hm | Rd)	TB	R	RBI	TBB	IBB	SO	HBP	SH	SF	SB	CS	SB%	GDP	Avg	OBP	SLG
1920 Philadelphia	AL	1	4	1	0	0	0	--	--	1	0	1	0		0	0	0	0	0	0	.00		.250	.250	.250

				FIELDING AS CATCHER							
Year Team	Lg	G	TC	PO	A	E	DP	PB	Pct.	Range
1920 Philadelphia	AL	1	9	8	1	0	0	0	1.000	---

Fred Wood

Fred S. Wood
Bats: Unknown **Throws:** Unknown

Height: 5'5" **Weight:** 150
Born in 1863 in Hamilton, Ontario
Died on August 23, 1933 in New York, New York

									BATTING									BASERUNNING				PERCENTAGES		
Year Team	Lg	G	AB	H	2B	3B	HR	(Hm | Rd)	TB	R	RBI	TBB	IBB	SO	HBP	SH	SF	SB	CS	SB%	GDP	Avg	OBP	SLG
1884 Detroit	NL	12	42	2	0	0	0	--	--	2	4	1	3		18								.048	.111	.048
1885 Buffalo	NL	1	4	1	0	0	0	--	--	1	0	0	0		0								.250	.250	.250
2 ML YEARS		13	46	3	0	0	0	--	--	3	4	1	3		18	0	0						.065	.122	.065

				FIELDING AS CATCHER							
Year Team	Lg	G	TC	PO	A	E	DP	PB	Pct.	Range
1884 Detroit	NL	7	54	36	12	6	1	19	.889	---
1885 Buffalo	NL	1	6	4	1	1	1	0	.833	---
2 ML YEARS		8	60	40	13	7	2	19	.883	---

				FIELDING AS SHORTSTOP							
Year Team	Lg	G	TC	PO	A	E	DP	PB	Pct.	Range
1884 Detroit	NL	1	1	0	0	1	0	--	.000	.00

				FIELDING AS OUTFIELDER							
Year Team	Lg	G	TC	PO	A	E	DP	PB	Pct.	Range
1884 Detroit	NL	6	13	5	2	6	0	--	.538	1.17

Pete Wood

Peter Burke Wood
Pitches: Right **Bats:** Unknown

Height: 5'7" **Weight:** 185
Born on February 1, 1857 in Hamilton, Ontario
Died on March 15, 1923 in Chicago, Illinois

		HOW MUCH HE PITCHED						WHAT HE GAVE UP									THE RESULTS					
Year Team	Lg	G	GS	CG	GF	IP	BFP	H	R	ER	HR	SH	SF	HB	TBB	IBB	SO	WP	Bk	W	L	Pct.	ShO	Sv	ERA
1885 Buffalo	NL	24	22	21	2	198.2	906	235	170	98	8					66		38	21	0	8	15	.348	0	0	4.44
1889 Philadelphia	NL	3	2	2	1	19	70	28	15	11	0			0		3		8	0	0	1	1	.500	0	0	5.21
2 ML YEARS		27	24	23	3	217.2	976	263	185	109	8					69		46	21	0	9	16	.360	0	0	4.51

									BATTING									BASERUNNING				PERCENTAGES		
Year Team	Lg	G	AB	H	2B	3B	HR	(Hm | Rd)	TB	R	RBI	TBB	IBB	SO	HBP	SH	SF	SB	CS	SB%	GDP	Avg	OBP	SLG
1885 Buffalo	NL	28	104	23	3	1	0	--	--	28	10	5	0		18								.221	.221	.269
1889 Philadelphia	NL	3	8	0	0	0	0	--	--	0	0	2	0		1	0			0				.000	.000	.000
2 ML YEARS		31	112	23	3	1	0	--	--	28	10	7	0		19	0	0						.205	.205	.250

				FIELDING AS PITCHER							
Year Team	Lg	G	TC	PO	A	E	DP	PB	Pct.	Range
1885 Buffalo	NL	24	60	8	43	9	0	--	.850	---
1889 Philadelphia	NL	3	6	0	4	2	1	--	.667	---
2 ML YEARS		27	66	8	47	11	1	--	.833	---

				FIELDING AS FIRST BASEMAN							
Year Team	Lg	G	TC	PO	A	E	DP	PB	Pct.	Range
1885 Buffalo	NL	2	20	17	0	3	0	--	.850	---

				FIELDING AS OUTFIELDER							
Year Team	Lg	G	TC	PO	A	E	DP	PB	Pct.	Range
1885 Buffalo	NL	4	3	3	0	0	0	--	1.000	.75

Gus Yost

August Yost

Height: 6'5" **Weight:** Unknown
Pitches: Unknown **Bats:** Unknown
Born Unknown

			HOW	MUCH	HE	PITCHED					WHAT	HE	GAVE	UP									THE	RESULTS			
Year Team	Lg	G	GS	CG	GF	IP	BFP	H	R	ER	HR	SH	SF	HB	TBB	IBB	SO	WP	Bk	W	L	Pct.	ShO	Sv	ERA
1893 Chicago	NL	1	1	0	0	2.2	17	3	4	4	0			0	8		1	1	0	0	1	.000	0	0	13.50

					BATTING													BASERUNNING				PERCENTAGES		
Year Team	Lg	G	AB	H	2B	3B	HR	(Hm | Rd)	TB	R	RBI	TBB	IBB	SO	HBP	SH	SF	SB	CS	SB%	GDP	Avg	OBP	SLG
1893 Chicago	NL	1	1	0	0	0	0	--	--	0	0	0	0	0	0	0			0				.000	.000	.000

			FIELDING	AS	PITCHER					
Year Team	Lg	G	TC	PO	A	E	DP	PB	Pct.	Range
1893 Chicago	NL	1	2	1	1	0	1	--	1.000	---

Manager Register

Name: George "Moon" Gibson, **Born**: 07/22/1880 in London, Ontario, **Died**: 01/25/1967 in London, Ontario

Year	Team	League	Games	Won	Lost	Pct	Finish	GBL
1920	Pittsburgh	N.L.	155	79	75	.513	4th	14.0
1921	Pittsburgh	N.L.	154	90	63	.588	2nd	4.0
1922	Pittsburgh	N.L.	65	32	33	.492	5th	--
1925	Chicago	N.L.	26	12	14	.462	7th	--
1932	Pittsburgh	N.L.	154	86	68	.558	2nd	4.0
1933	Pittsburgh	N.L.	154	87	67	.565	2nd	5.0
1934	Pittsburgh	N.L.	51	27	24	.529	4th	--
	M.L. Totals		759	413	344	.546		

Name: Arthur "Doc" Irwin, **Born**: 02/14/1858 in Toronto, Ontario, **Died**: 07/16/1921 in Atlantic Ocean

Year	Team	League	Games	Won	Lost	Pct	Finish	GBL
1889	Washington	N.L.	76	28	45	.384	8th	--
1891	Boston	A.A.	139	93	42	.689	1st	0.0
1892	Washington	N.L.	108	46	60	.426	11th	--
1894	Philadelphia	N.L.	132	71	57	.555	4th	18.0
1895	Philadelphia	N.L.	133	78	53	.595	3rd	9.5
1896	New York	N.L.	90	36	53	.404	7th	--
1898	Washington	N.L.	30	10	19	.345	11th	--
1899	Washington	N.L.	155	54	98	.355	11th	49.0
	M.L. Totals		863	416	427	.493		

Name: Fred Lake, **Born**: 10/16/1866 in Nova Scotia, **Died**: 11/24/193 in Boston, Massachusetts

Year	Team	League	Games	Won	Lost	Pct	Finish	GBL
1908	Boston	A.L.	40	22	17	.564	5th	--
1909	Boston	A.L.	152	88	63	.583	3rd	9.5
1910	Boston	N.L.	157	53	100	.346	8th	50.5
	M.L. Totals		349	163	180	.475		

Name: William Henry Watkins, **Born**: 05/05/1858 in Brantford, Ontario, **Died**: 06/09/1937 in Port Huron, Michigan

Year	Team	League	Games	Won	Lost	Pct	Finish	GBL
1884	Indianapolis	A.A	23	4	18	.182	10th	--
1885	Detroit	N.L.	70	34	36	.486	8th	--
1886	Detroit	N.L.	126	87	36	.707	2nd	3.5
1887	Detroit	N.L.	127	79	45	.637	1st	0.0
1888	Detroit	N.L.	94	49	44	.527	3rd	--
1888	Kansas City	A.A.	25	8	17	.320	8th	--
1889	Kansas City	A.A.	139	55	82	.401	7th	38.0
1893	St. Louis	N.L.	135	57	75	.432	10th	30.5
1898	Pittsburgh	N.L.	151	72	76	.486	8th	29.5
1899	Pittsburgh	N.L.	24	7	15	.318	10th	--
	M.L. Totals		914	452	444	.504		

Postseason Record

Year	Team	League	Games	Won	Lost	Pct	Finish
1887	Detroit	N.L.	15	10	5	.667	Won World Series

Note: Finish includes only the time spent under that manager for partial seasons. GBL (games behind leader) is given only for full seasons managed.

About Neil Munro

Neil Munro has served as research consultant for STATS, Inc. in compiling baseball statistical data for the last 10 years, and he is also listed by the National Baseball Library as a referral source for inquiries on baseball statistics.

Munro wrote a regular column for three years, "The Munro Doctrine," for *Innings*, a Canadian baseball newspaper, and has also authored numerous baseball articles appearing in such publications as the *Grandstand Baseball Annual*, *Blue Jay Chatter*, and the *SABR Baseball Research Journal*.

Munro currently teaches high school mathematics in North Bay, Ontario.

About STATS, Inc.

STATS, Inc. is the nation's leading independent sports information and statistical analysis company, providing detailed sports services for a wide array of clients.

STATS provides the most up-to-the-minute sports information to professional teams, print and broadcast media, software developers and interactive srevice providers around the country. Some of our major clients are ESPN, Turner Sports, the Associated Press and Motorola.

STATS Publishing, a division of STATS, Inc., produces 11 annual books, including the *STATS Major League Handbook*, the *Pro Football Handbook*, the *Pro Basketball Handbook* and, new for 1996, the first *STATS Hockey Handbook*. These publications deliver STATS expertise to fans, scouts, general managers and media around the country.

In addition, STATS offers the most innovative—and fun—fantasy sports games around, from *Bill James Fantasy Baseball* and *Bill James Classic Baseball* to *STATS Fantasy Football* and *STATS Fantasy Hoops*.

For more information on our products, or on joining our reporter network, write us at:

STATS, Inc.
8131 Monticello Ave.
Skokie, IL 60076-3300

...or call us at 1-800-63-STATS (1-800-637-8287). Outside the U.S., dial 1-708-676-3383.

The Ultimate Hockey Resource

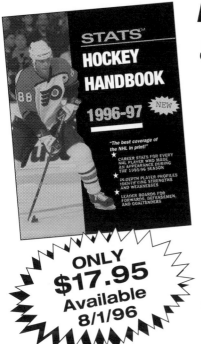

"The best coverage of the NHL in print!"

★ CAREER STATS FOR EVERY NHL PLAYER WHO MADE AN APPEARANCE DURING THE 1995-96 SEASON

★ IN-DEPTH PLAYER PROFILES IDENTIFYING STRENGTHS AND WEAKNESSES

★ LEADER BOARDS FOR FORWARDS, DEFENSEMEN, AND GOALTENDERS

ONLY $17.95 Available 8/1/96

Presenting... STATS Hockey Handbook 1996

Introducing the most complete statistics in print on today's NHL players! STATS has spent the last three years building its vast hockey database, and now proudly presents the *Hockey Handbook*.

STATS Hockey Handbook debuts the one-of-a-kind player breakdowns that only STATS can provide, available immediately following the 1995-96 NHL season.

Unique Features:

☆ Complete career register for every active NHL player

☆ Exclusive player and goalie breakdowns identifying strengths and weaknesses

☆ In-depth team and league profiles

☆ Standard and exclusive leader boards

"STATS Hockey Handbook *shoots and scores*."
— Adam Fell, *St. Louis Blues*

Order from STATS INC. Today!

Use Order Form in This Book, or Call 1-800-63-STATS or 847-676-3383 or e-mail: info@stats.com

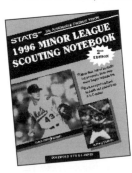

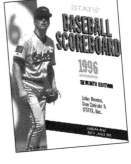

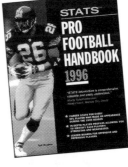
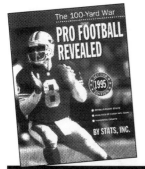

Bill James Fantasy Baseball

Bill James Fantasy Baseball enters its eighth season of offering baseball fans the most unique, realistic and exciting game fantasy sports has to offer.

You draft a 25-player roster and can expand to as many as 28. Players aren't ranked like in rotisserie leagues—you'll get credit for everything a player does, like hitting homers, driving in runs, turning double plays, pitching quality outings and more!

Also, the team which scores the most points among all leagues, plus wins the World Series, will receive the John McGraw Award, which includes a one-week trip to the Grapefruit League in spring training, a day at the ballpark with Bill James, and a new fantasy league named in his/her honor!

Unique Features Include:

• **Live fantasy experts** — available seven days a week

• **The best weekly reports in the business** — detailing who is in the lead, win-loss records, MVPs, and team strengths and weaknesses

• **On-Line computer system** — a world of information, including daily updates of fantasy standings and stats

• **Over twice as many statistics as rotisserie**

• **Transactions that are effective the very next day!**

"My goal was to develop a fantasy league based on the simplest yet most realistic principle possible. A league in which the values are as nearly as possible what they ought to be, without being distorted by artificial category values or rankings...."

- **Bill James**

All this, all summer long...for less than $5 per week!

Order from *STATS* INC. Today!

Use Order Form in This Book, or Call 1-800-63-STATS or 847-676-3383 or e-mail: info@stats.com!

Bill James Classic Baseball

Joe Jackson, Walter Johnson, and Roberto Clemente are back on the field of your dreams!

If you're not ready to give up baseball in the fall, or if you're looking to relive its glorious past, then Bill James Classic Baseball is the game for you!

The Classic Game features players from all eras of Major League Baseball at all performance levels - not just the stars. You could see Honus Wagner, Josh Gibson, Carl Yastrzemski, Bob Uecker, Billy Grabarkewitz, and Dick Fowler...on the SAME team!

As owner, GM and manager all in one, you'll be able to...

- "Buy" your team of up to 25 players from our catalog of over 2,000 historical players (You'll receive $1 million to buy your favorite players)
- Choose the park your team will call home—current or historical, 63 in all!
- Rotate batting lineups for a right- or left-handed starting pitcher
- Change your pitching rotation for each series. Determine your set-up man, closer, and long reliever
- Alter in-game strategies, including stealing frequency, holding runners on base, hit-and-run, and much more!
- Select your best pinch hitter and late-inning defensive replacements (For example, Curt Flood will get to more balls than Hack Wilson!)

How to Play The Classic Game:

1. Sign up to be a team owner TODAY! Leagues forming year-round
2. STATS, Inc. will supply you with a catalog of eligible players and a rule book
3. You'll receive $1 million to buy your favorite major leaguers
4. Take part in a player and ballpark draft with 11 other owners
5. Set your pitching rotation, batting lineup, and managerial strategies
6. STATS runs the game simulation...a 154-game schedule, 14 weeks!
7. You'll receive customized in-depth weekly reports, featuring game summaries, stats, and boxscores

Order from *STATS* INC. Today!

Use Order Form in This Book, or Call 1-800-63-STATS or 847-676-3383 or e-mail: info@stats.com!

STATS Fantasy Hoops

Soar into the 1995-96 season with STATS Fantasy Hoops! SFH puts YOU in charge. Don't just sit back and watch Grant Hill, Shawn Kemp, and Alonzo Mourning - get in the game and coach your team to the top!

How to Play SFH:
1. Sign up to coach a team.
2. You'll receive a full set of rules and a draft form with SFH point values for all eligible players - anyone who played in the NBA in 1994-95, plus all 1995 NBA draft picks.
3. Complete the draft form and return it to STATS.
4. You will take part in the draft with nine other owners, and we will send you league rosters.
5. You make unlimited weekly transactions including trades, free agent signings, activations, and benchings.
6. Six of the 10 teams in your league advance to postseason play, with two teams ultimately advancing to the Finals.

SFH points values are tested against actual NBA results, mirroring the real thing. Weekly reports will tell you everything you need to know to lead your team to the SFH Championship!

STATS Fantasy Football

STATS Fantasy Football puts YOU in charge! You draft, trade, cut, bench, activate players and even sign free agents each week. SFF pits you head-to-head against 11 other owners.

STATS' scoring system applies realistic values, tested against actual NFL results. Each week, you'll receive a superb in-depth report telling you all about both team and league performances.

How to Play SFF:
1. Sign up today!
2. STATS sends you a draft form listing all eligible NFL players.
3. Fill out the draft form and return it to STATS, and you will take part in the draft along with 11 other team owners.
4. Go head-to-head against the other owners in your league. You'll make week-by-week roster moves and transactions through STATS' Fantasy Football experts, via phone, fax, or on-line!

Order from *STATS* INC. Today!

Use Order Form in This Book, or Call 1-800-63-STATS or 847-676-3383 or e-mail: info@stats.com!

STATS On-Line

Now you can have a direct line to a world of sports information just like the pros use with STATS On-Line. If you love to keep up with your favorite teams and players, STATS On-Line is for you. From Shaquille O'Neal's fast-breaking dunks to Ken Griffey's tape-measure blasts — if you want baseball, basketball, football and   hockey stats, we put them at your fingertips!

STATS On-Line

- **Player Profiles and Team Profiles** — The #1 resource for scouting your favorite professional teams and players with information you simply can't find anywhere else! The most detailed info you've ever seen, including real-time stats. Follow baseball pitch-by-pitch, foot ball snap-by-snap, and basketball and hockey shot-by-shot, with scores and player stats updated continually!

- **NO monthly or annual fees**

- **Local access numbers** — avoid costly long-distance charges!

- **Unlimited access** — 24 hours a day, seven days a week

- **Downloadable files** — get year-to-date stats in an ASCII format for baseball, football, basketball, and hockey

- **In-progress box scores** — You'll have access to the most up-to-the-second scoring stats for every team and player. When you log into STATS On-Line, you'll get detailed updates, including player stats and scoring plays while the games are in progress!

- **Other exclusive features** — transactions and injury information, team and player profiles and updates, standings, leader and trailer boards, game-by-game logs, fantasy game features, and much more!

Sign-up fee of $30 (applied towards future use), 24-hour access with usage charges of $.75/min. Mon.-Fri., 8am-6pm CST; $.25/min. all other hours and weekends.

Order from *STATS* INC. Today!

Use Order Form in This Book, or Call 1-800-63-STATS or 847-676-3383 or e-mail: info@stats.com!

STATS INC. Order Form

Name_____ Phone_____
Address_____ Fax_____
City_____ State_____ Zip_____

Method of Payment (U.S. Funds Only):

❑ Check/Money Order ❑ Visa ❑ MasterCard

Cardholder Name_____
Credit Card Number_____ Exp. _____
Signature_____

BOOKS

Qty	Product Name	Item #	Price	Total
	STATS 1996 Major League Handbook	HB96	$17.95	
	STATS Hockey Handbook 1996-97	HH97	$17.95	
	STATS Projections Update 1996	PJUP	$9.95	
	The Scouting Notebook: 1996	SN96	$16.95	
	STATS Player Profiles 1996	PP96	$17.95	
	Player Profiles 1996 (Comb-bound)	PC96	$19.95	
	STATS Minor Lg. Scouting Ntbk. 1996	MN96	$16.95	
	STATS Minor League Handbook 1996	MH96	$17.95	
	Minor League Hndbk. 1996 (Comb-bnd)	MC96	$19.95	
	STATS 1996 BVSP Match-Ups!	BP96	$12.95	
	STATS Baseball Scoreboard 1996	SB96	$16.95	
	STATS 1995-96 Pro Basketball Hndbk.	BH96	$17.95	
	Pro Football Revealed (1995 Edition)	PF96	$16.95	
	STATS Pro Football Handbook 1996	FH96	$17.95	
	For previous editions, circle appropriate years:			
	Major League Handbook 91 92 93 94 95		$9.95	
	Scouting Report/Notebook 92 94 95		$9.95	
	Player Profiles 93 94 95		$9.95	
	Minor League Handbook 92 93 94 95		$9.95	
	Baseball Scoreboard 92 93 94 95		$9.95	
	Basketball Scoreboard 94 95		$9.95	
	Pro Football Handbook 95		$9.95	
	Pro Football Revealed 94		$9.95	

FANTASY GAMES & STATSfax

Qty	Product Name	Item #	Price	Total
	Bill James Classic Baseball	BJCG	$129.00	
	How to Win The Classic Game (book)	CGBK	$16.95	
	The Classic Game STATSfax	CGX5	$20.00	
	Bill James Fantasy Baseball	BJFB	$89.00	
	BJFB STATSfax/5-day	SFX5	$20.00	
	BJFB STATSfax/7-day	SFX7	$25.00	
	STATS Fantasy Hoops	SFH	$85.00	
	SFH STATSfax/5-day	SFH5	$20.00	
	SFH STATSfax/7-day	SFH7	$25.00	
	STATS Fantasy Football	SFF	$69.00	
	SFF STATSfax/3-day	SFF3	$15.00	

STATS ON-LINE

Qty	Product Name	Item #	Price	Total
	STATS On-Line	ONLE	$30.00	

**For faster service, call
1-800-63-STATS or 847-676-3383, fax
this form to STATS at 847-676-0821, or
send e-mail to info@stats.com**

1st Fantasy Team Name (ex. Colt 45's):_____ _____
   What Fantasy Game is this team for?_____
2nd Fantasy Team Name (ex. Colt 45's):_____ _____
   What Fantasy Game is this team for?_____

NOTE: $1.00/player is charged for all roster moves and transactions.

For Bill James Fantasy Baseball
Would you like to play in a league drafted by Bill James?   ❑ Yes   ❑ No

TOTALS

	Price	Total
Product Total (excl. Fantasy Games and On-Line)		
For first class mailing in U.S. add:	+$2.50/book	
Canada—all orders—add:	+$3.50/book	
Order 2 or more books—subtract:	-$1.00/book	
IL residents add 8.5% sales tax		
Subtotal		
Fantasy Games & On-Line Total		
GRAND TOTAL		

FREE Information Kits:

❑ STATS Reporter Networks
❑ Bill James Classic Baseball
❑ Bill James Fantasy Baseball
❑ STATS On-Line
❑ STATS Fantasy Hoops
❑ STATS Fantasy Football
❑ STATS Year-end Reports
❑ STATSfax

BOOK

Mail to: STATS, Inc., 8131 Monticello Ave., Skokie, IL 60076-3300